W9-BGJ-958

# Budgeting in the States

# Budgeting in the States

## INSTITUTIONS, PROCESSES, AND POLITICS

Edited by
Edward J. Clynch and Thomas P. Lauth

Westport, Connecticut
London

**Library of Congress Cataloging-in-Publication Data**

Budgeting in the states : institutions, processes, and politics / edited by Edward J. Clynch and Thomas P. Lauth.

p. cm.

Includes bibliographical references and index.

ISBN 0–275–98013–8 (alk. paper)

1. Budget—United States—States. 2. Budget—United States—States—Case studies. I. Clynch, Edward J. II. Lauth, Thomas P. III. Title.

HJ2053.A1B74 2006

352.4′ 82130973–dc22          2006018358

British Library Cataloguing in Publication Data is available.

Library of Congress Catalog Card Number: 2006018358

ISBN: 0–275–98013–8

First published in 2006

Praeger Publishers, 88 Post Road West, Westport, CT 06881

An imprint of Greenwood Publishing Group, Inc.

www.praeger.com

Printed in the United States of America

The paper used in this book complies with the Permanent Paper Standard issued by the National Information Standards Organization (Z39.48–1984).

10  9  8  7  6  5  4  3  2  1

# Contents

# Acknowledgments

We could not have completed this book without the contributions of our colleagues who wrote state chapters, and without the cooperation of state budget officials who shared information and insights.

We thank Bob Bland, Don Boyd, Robert Bradley, Wes Clarke, Jim Conant, Dall Forsythe, Blease Graham, Jim Gosling, Merl Hackbart, Carol Lewis, Jerry McCaffrey, Barbara Patrick, Jim Ramsey, Irene Rubin, Bill Simonsen, Doug Snow, and Paula Yeary for writing their respective chapters. Their budgeting expertise and sound professional judgments are the *sine qua non* of this volume. We also wish to thank Tracy Britt for her valuable help in assembling and editing this book.

On behalf of all the authors, we thank the many state budget officials who granted interviews, participated in informal conservations, and provided requested data. They contributed substantially to our efforts.

# CHAPTER 1

# Budgeting in the States: Institutions, Processes, and Policies

*Edward J. Clynch and Thomas P. Lauth*

## INTRODUCTION

Budgeting is a central activity in state governments, and annual or biennial appropriations are the most important recurring decisions made by state legislatures. Gubernatorial recommendations reflect state agency program needs and portray the policy priorities of the chief executive. Legislative appropriations determine that agency programs, gubernatorial policy initiatives, and legislative constituencies receive financial support. Budget execution decisions by state agencies determine how the policy decisions of the governor and legislature are actually implemented. In short, state budgeting determines how much money will be available for state spending, which policies will be initiated and implemented, and whose social and political values will prevail in state governance.

Aggregate data studies incorporating all fifty states provide numerous insights about the influence of selected demographic, economic, and institutional factors on the patterns of state spending.[1] However, the strength of such studies, and the generalizations across states, is also a weakness. Aggregate data studies tend to mask the important institutional and contextual differences among states in the ways they allocate available resources among competing agencies, programs, and constituencies. Sometimes, aggregate data conclusions bear little resemblance to individual state conditions or practices.[2]

There have been a few single-state studies that address institutions, processes, patterns of behavior, and fiscal environment.[3] However, those studies were conducted at different points in time, without the benefit of a common organizing framework that would permit other scholars to compare and contrast findings, and frequently focused on only one facet of state budgeting.[4]

This volume overcomes both aggregate and single-state study deficiencies by presenting a set of in-depth, individual state studies developed at a common point in time and following a common organizing framework. It employs the framework first presented in *Governors, Legislatures and Budgets: Diversity Across the American States* (1991),[5] but is more than an update of that work. It examines a wide array of changes occurring in state budgeting during the past 15 years, a period of robust revenue growth followed by the biggest revenue crisis in more than 20 years. In addition to characterizing formal executive-legislative relationships across the states, it also examines several informal factors that help governors and legislators overcome institutional weaknesses and increase their leverage over budget decisions.

## Executive-Legislative Institutional Powers

The executive budget was the centerpiece of efforts in the twentieth century to strengthen the powers of governors. Executive budget documents reflect agency program needs and the policy priorities of governors, and governors use budget reviews and resource allocations to control and direct agencies within the executive branch. In most states, legislatures exercise fiscal control over the executive branch by concentrating responsibility for budget preparation and execution in the office of the governor. However, within this context, states vary in the institutional influence of governors and legislatures over the preparation, approval, and execution phases of the budgetary process.

In some states, the governor dominates the process by developing budget instructions, receiving and reviewing agency budget requests, and preparing and submitting a unified budget recommendation to the legislature. Legislatures in those states do not have access to original agency requests and use the governor's recommendation as the basis for their deliberations during the approval phase of the budget process. In other states, the governor holds a central position in the budgetary process, but legislatures with the aid of professional staff have the ability to make independent judgments and challenge executive budget assumptions and initiatives. In yet other states, legislatures exert substantial influence over budget formulation; they receive budget recommendations from both the governor and the legislative leadership, and the legislature works with the governor to develop consensus revenue estimates.[6] Previous research suggests that a positive relationship exists between the amount of budget information available to the legislature and this body's influence over budget decisions.[7]

Independently elected governors and legislatures are likely to have conflict over budget decisions. Governors are elected from statewide constituencies and legislators are elected from district constituencies. Differing constituency preferences are likely to exacerbate differing institutional perspectives. In this separation of powers system budget outcomes are influenced by who has power and how it is used to influence spending priorities.[8]

## Court Decisions

Courts serve as reluctant referees when governors and legislators disagree about the division of institutional budget authority, such as the scope of the line item veto.[9] Courts also exercise infrequent impact on state spending decisions, but their influence is profound when they intervene in such policy areas as spending for prisons and public schools.[10]

## *Rational Budget Reform*

For over a century budget change advocates have proposed an array of budget reforms to give governors more control over budget decisions. Recent budget reforms attempt to incorporate data about program performance into the resource allocation process. Many states initiated such high-profile reform efforts as the planning, programming, and budgeting system (PPBS), and the zero-base budgeting (ZBB) in the 1960s and 1970s. Recent reforms aim at linking program and performance data with resource allocation decisions, e.g., strategic planning, bench marking, results-based budgeting (RBB), and the "new" performance budgeting.[11] The essential features of these new directions in program budgeting are agency identification of outcomes to be produced by programs, and the development of performance measures to gauge progress toward achieving those outcomes. A 1997 survey of state budget offices found that forty-seven states have some form of performance-based budgeting requirements.[12]

## Political Parties

Political party divisions affect the influence of governors and legislators. If the governor's party controls both chambers of the legislature, the chief executive uses party loyalty to affect budget decisions. Divided legislatures give the governor some leverage because the branch controlled by the executive party often pushes executive positions in conference committees. When the other political party controls both legislative chambers, governors often face confrontation over spending decisions.[13]

## Voter Initiatives

Ballot initiatives in some states have constrained the influence of governors and legislators over budget decisions by imposing limits on revenue collections and mandating expenditures. In twenty-four states voters have taken matters into their own hands when governors and legislators ignore their concerns.[14]

**Table 1.1**
**State Characteristics**

| State | Population, 2000 (in Thousands) | Population, Percent Change, 1990 to 2000 | Population Percent Caucasian, 2000 | Median Household Income, 1999 | Personal Income Per Capita 2000 | Population Per Sq. Mile of Land Area, 2002 | Percent Urban |
|---|---|---|---|---|---|---|---|
| California | 33,871 | 13.6 | 59.5 | $47,493 | $32,363 | 225.2 | 94.4 |
| Connecticut | 3,405 | 3.6 | 81.6 | $53,935 | $41,446 | 714.3 | 87.7 |
| Florida | 15,982 | 23.5 | 78.0 | $38,819 | $28,366 | 309.9 | 89.3 |
| Georgia | 8,186 | 26.4 | 65.1 | $42,433 | $28,103 | 147.8 | 71.6 |
| Illinois | 12,419 | 8.6 | 73.5 | $46,590 | $32,297 | 226.7 | 87.8 |
| Kentucky | 4,041 | 9.6 | 90.1 | $33,672 | $24,258 | 103 | 55.8 |
| Mississippi | 2,844 | 10.5 | 61.4 | $31,330 | $20,920 | 61.2 | 48.8 |
| Nevada | 1,998 | 66.3 | 75.2 | $44,581 | $29,794 | 19.8 | 91.5 |
| New York | 18,976 | 5.5 | 67.9 | $43,393 | $35,041 | 405.8 | 87.5 |
| Oregon | 3,421 | 20.4 | 86.6 | $40,916 | $27,836 | 36.7 | 78.7 |
| South Carolina | 4,012 | 15.1 | 67.2 | $37,082 | $24,209 | 136.4 | 60.5 |
| Texas | 20,851 | 22.8 | 71.0 | $39,927 | $27,290 | 83.2 | 82.5 |
| Utah | 2,233 | 29.6 | 89.2 | $45,726 | $23,410 | 28.2 | 88.2 |
| Virginia | 7,078 | 14.4 | 72.3 | $46,677 | $31,210 | 184.2 | 73 |
| Wisconsin | 5,363 | 9.6 | 88.9 | $43,791 | $28,389 | 100.2 | 68.3 |
| USA | 281,421 | 13.1 | 75.1 | $41,994 | $29,760 | 81.5 | 79 |

## Revenue

State generated revenues fund a substantial portion of state spending each year. Many states utilize "voluntary taxes" such as lotteries and taxes on casinos in addition to revenue from traditional sources such as income and sales taxes.[15] The adequacy of revenue, largely influenced by state economic conditions, is an important determinant of budget behavior. States experienced substantial revenue increases in the 1990s followed by revenue contractions after 2000. An explosion of new dollars followed by a severe revenue downturn can disrupt ongoing budget relationships and the distribution of the budget shares among competing state government claimants.

State budgets are also formulated within the context of fiscal federalism. Grants from the federal government, along with state tax collections and bond proceeds, provide an important additional source of state revenue. Federal transfers grew from 22 percent of state budgets in 1993 to 31 percent in 2002.[16] Federal grants supplement state generated resources and also serve as inducements for states to participate in federal government programs, e.g., the medicaid program, interstate highway program, and the welfare reform program Temporary Assistance To Needy Families. Despite the growth of federal money flowing to the states, unfunded mandates and fiscal devolution have significant cost implications for state budgets.[17] States also provide funding for their local governments, funding for education being the most prominent example.

### Profiled States

The fifteen states profiled in this book differ from each other with regard to the strength of their chief executive, fiscal condition, intergovernmental finance, experience with rational budgeting reforms, and the impact of court decisions. They come from each of the major regions of the nation. Table 1.1 shows the diversity of states covered in the following chapters.

Demographically, they range from very rural to heavily urban, from resource rich to resource poor, from high-population growth to static population, and from high-tech economies to workforces dominated by unskilled and semiskilled labor. Collectively, they depict differences amid similarities in budgeting in the American states.

## NOTES

1. Abrams A. Burton and William R. Dougan, "The Effects of Constitutional Restraints on Governmental Spending," *Public Choice*, 49 (1986), 101–116; Philip G. Joyce, "What's So Magical about Five Percent? A Nationwide Look at Factors that Influence the Optimal Size of State Rainy Day Funds," *Public Budgeting & Finance*, 21 (Summer 2001), 62–87; Ira Sharkansky, "Agency Requests, Gubernatorial Support, and Budget Success in State Legislature," *The American Political Science Review*, 62 (December 1968), 1220–1231; and Joel A. Thompson, "Agency Requests, Gubernatorial Support,

and Budget Success in State Legislatures Revisited," *Journal of Politics*, 49 (August 1987), 756–779.

2. Jeffrey M. Stonecash, "Observations from New York: The Limits of 50-State Studies and the Case for Case Studies," *Comparative State Politics*, 12 (December 1991), 1–9.

3. Thomas J. Anton, *The Politics of Expenditures in Illinois*. Urbana, IL: University of Illinois Press, 1966; and Joseph C. Pilegge, Jr., *Taxing and Spending: Alabama's Budget in Transition*. University, AL: University of Alabama Press, 1978.

4. James G. Gosling, "Wisconsin Item-Veto Lessons," *Public Administration Review*, 46 (July/August 1986), 292–300; and Thomas P. Lauth, "Zero-Base Budgeting in Georgia State Government: Myth and Reality," *Public Administration Review*, 38 (September/October 1978), 420–430.

5. Edward J. Clynch and Thomas P. Lauth, eds., *Governors, Legislatures and Budgets: Diversity across the American States*. Westport, CT: Greenwood Press, 1991.

6. Edward J. Clynch and Thomas P. Lauth, eds., *Governors, Legislatures, and Budgets: Diversity across the American States*. New York: Greenwood Press, 1991, pp. 152–155.

7. Roderick D. Kiewiet and Mathew D. McCubbins, *The Logic of Delegation: Congressional Parties and the Appropriations Process*. Chicago: University of Chicago Press, 1991.

8. Aaron Wildavsky, *Budgeting: A Comparative Theory of Budgetary Processes*. New Brunswick, NJ: Transaction, Inc., 1986, p. 220.

9. Robert D. Lee, "State Item Veto Legal Issues in the 1990s," *Public Budgeting & Finance*, 20 (Summer 2000), 49–73.

10. Jeffrey D. Straussman, "Courts and Purse Strings: Have Portraits of Budgeting Missed Something?" *Public Administration Review*, 46 (1986), 345–351.

11. Meagan M. Jordan and Merl M. Hackbart, "Performance Budgeting and Performance Funding in the States: A Status Assessment," *Public Budgeting & and Finance*, 19 (Spring 1999), 68–88; and Katherine G. Willoughby and Julia E. Melkers, "Implementing PBB: Conflicting Views of Success," *Public Budgeting & Finance*, 20 (Spring 2000), 105–120.

12. Julia E. Melkers and Katherine G. Willoughby, "The State of the States: Performance Based Budgeting Requirements in 47 out of 50," *Public Administration Review*, 58 (January/February 1998), 66–73.

13. Alan Rosenthal, *Governors and Legislators: Contending Powers*. Washington, DC: Congressional Quarterly, 1990, pp. 67–94; Laura A. Van Assendelft, *Governors, Agenda Setting, and Divided Government*. Landam, MD: University Press of America, 1997, pp. 1–37; and Wes Clarke, "Divided Government and Budget Conflict in the U.S. States," *Legislative Studies Quarterly*, XXIII(1) (February 1998), 5–21.

14. Bill Piper, *A Brief Analysis of Voter Behavior Regarding Tax Initiatives*. Los Angeles: Initiative and Referendum Institute at the University of Southern California, 1994 (http://www.iandrinstitute.org); John Matsusaka, *Fiscal Effects of the Voter Initiative: Evidence from the Last 30 Years*. Los Angeles: Initiative and Referendum Institute at the University of Southern California, 1994 (http://www.iandrinstitute.org).

15. Edward J. Clynch and William C. Rivenbark, "Need Money? Roll the Dice," *International Journal of Public Administration*, 22 (1999), 1681–1703; John Mikesell and C. Kurt Zorn, "State Lotteries as a Fiscal Savior or Fiscal Fraud: A Look at the Evidence," *Public Administration Review*, 46 (July/August 1986), 311–320; and Charles

J. Spindler, "The Lottery and Education: Robbing Peter to Pay Paul?" *Public Budgeting & Finance*, 15 (Fall 1995).

16. http://www.census.gov/govs/www/state.html.

17. Theresa A. Gullo and Janet M. Kelly, "Federal Unfunded Mandate Reform: A First-Year Retrospective," *Public Administration Review*, 57 (September/October 1998), 379–387.

# CHAPTER 2

# California: Revenue Scarcity, Incremental Solutions, the Rise of Citizen Initiatives, and the Decline of Trust

*Jerry L. McCaffrey*

California is a study in myth and reality. Its statutes require an annual budget, but from 1987 through 2002, its budget was on time only three times. For the other 13 years, it averaged 29.5 days late. In 2002, the budget was 67 days late. The Constitution requires that the Governor submit a balanced budget and, if it is not balanced, recommend revenue sources or program cuts to make it so.[1] However, the state has run operating deficits in 13 of the last 24 years.[2] In May of 2000, California had a surplus of $12.3 billion; in November of 2002 forecasts indicated a deficit of $35 billion over the following 18 months. Thanks to the lure of the golden state myth, California's massive population growth continues. However, growth has brought public policy problems in land use, zoning, infrastructure, transportation and traffic management, education, health, welfare, and indeed, in almost every policy area. California's poverty rate is above the U. S. average; its working poor have increased over the last decade and the gap between high-income and low-income taxpayers continues to widen. Housing is very expensive. Studies showed that California has the fourth lowest rate of home ownership in the nation and that about 25 percent of renters in metropolitan areas (1 million of 4.1 million) paid more than 51 percent of their income in rent.[3] Many critics feel that California, once a leader among the states in almost all policy areas, has now fallen behind.

The volatility in state income tax revenues complicated these issues. In the last decade, California twice has had to cope with deficits of more than 30 percent of its general fund revenues. Considering all this, there would seem to be much for state policymakers to do, but the fact is that much of California's policymaking machinery is on automatic pilot. It seems that Californians' trust in their elected representatives is limited; hence, citizens have used the initiative mechanism to limit the actions that state and local policymakers may take. Sometimes this limits the process (two-third vote of legislature for new taxes), sometimes the players (term limits) and sometimes the policy (repeal of the sales tax on snacks and the prohibition of any future sales tax on food items, including candy and bottled water). Politicians thus have limited time and limited options for crafting solutions. The general fund budget itself reflects this situation, because about two-thirds of it is required by mandatory expenditures.[4] On the revenue side, California's policymakers have increasingly relied upon a very progressive income tax with the result that the budget is linked to a highly volatile revenue source, which may overproduce revenue in some years, but lead to substantial deficits in others. As if this were not enough, the people do not trust them to make good decisions. This chapter describes how this came to be and how it works.

## HISTORICAL PERSPECTIVE

In 2001, California's gross state product exceeded $1.3 trillion, making it the fifth largest economy in the world. It accounted for 13 percent of the United States' output, trailing only the United States itself, Japan, Germany, and the United Kingdom. The economy of New York, the next largest state, was about 60 percent the size of California. This powerful economy is highly diversified. The largest industry sector is services, which accounts for nearly one-fourth of all the output in the state and includes computer and software design, motion picture production, health care, and hotels. Services accounted for half of the new jobs created in the state in the decade of the 1990s. California is the nation's leading agricultural producer: receipts from farming in California in 2001 were $27 billion; this represented about one-eighth of the national total and was greater than that of Texas and Iowa combined, the next two largest agricultural producers.[5] California's population continues to increase dramatically: it is home to 35 million people and increases by about 550,000 persons annually. The 2000 census confirmed that no ethnic group has a majority in California, but Californians do not see ethnic conflict as a problem. Most seem to subscribe to the idea that "diversity is always better," and eight of ten Californians thought that racial and ethnic groups were getting along very well or somewhat well.[6] While Californians were aware that the state's immigrant population was increasing (in 2000, 20% of its population was foreign-born), only one in twelve said that legal and illegal immigration was the most important issue facing the state.[7]

While the mix of programs in the state budget has shifted a bit over the last 40 years, with transportation down and health, social services, and K-12 education up, the budget of 2002 would be recognizable to the informed citizen of 1962. The state still bears a heavy responsibility for education, both K-12 and higher education, and for health and social services. Together, education, health, and social services accounted for 71 percent of total state spending in 2002–2003. The share of total spending on education is about 43 percent

($41.4 billion). Health and social services represent the next largest share of total spending at 28 percent ($26.4 billion).[8] From 1979 to 1999, California's state revenues increased from $17.7 billion to $71.4 billion, and spending increased from $18.5 billion to $73.2 billion, while its population increased from 22.8 million to 33.5 million. The number of school children increased from 4.0 million to 5.8 million, and the state's share of families living below the poverty line increased from 11 percent to 16.8 percent. Notwithstanding these strains, measured as a percentage of personal income, California spent less in 1999 (7.8%) than it did in 1979 (8.6%).[9]

California's recent history is one of fiscal crisis. General fund spending declined in 1991–1992, in 1992–1993, and in 1993–1994 due to recession. It grew modestly during the midyears of the decade, then accelerated in 1998, 1999, and 2000; from 1993–1994 when the economic recovery began, state general fund spending more than doubled, from $39 to $79 billion, with about half of this increase occurring in 1999–2000 and 2000–2001.[10] Of this $40 billion increase, about $15 billion (39%) was due to workload (increased caseloads and school enrollments) and inflation-related costs. About $17 billion (43%) was related to new or expanded programs, mostly in education, but also in resources and health-related areas. About 6 percent was related to tax relief programs funded through the budget, primarily for vehicle license fee reductions averaging 67 percent and expanded senior citizen tax relief. Finally, about $4.6 billion (12%) was due to other factors, such as expanded trial court funding and other forms of local fiscal relief as well as spending related to court cases, federal mandates, and additional funding to offset student and park fee reductions.

When controlled for inflation, real per capita general fund spending increased for seven straight years, from 1993 to 1994 until 2000–2001.[11] It then decreased under the impact of the revenue crisis in 2001 and marginally decreased again in 2002. The single biggest beneficiary of this growth was K-12 education, where about two-thirds of the growth was for new and expanded programs. Proposition 98 required that California increase educational expenditures annually to meet inflation and student growth. During the last few years, policymakers have chosen to provide more funding for education than required by Proposition 98, and much of this overburden amount has gone into the budget base and is included in budget needs for subsequent years. In 2002, the California state budget funded 169 different departments and agencies and included 1,106 separate line items. The largest single line item was $10 billion for the federal government's share of "Medi-cal," the state version of "Medicaid." The state government employed 284,500 persons and spent $21 billion on state operations.[12]

California appears to be a two-party state, but this is somewhat misleading. Democrats held the Governor's office and majority control of both houses in 1982. Republicans controlled the Governor's office from then through 1998, but the Democrats continued to hold the Assembly. In 1998, California swung to the Democrats; they won the Governor's office and every statewide race except two, as well as control of the legislature. In 2000, the Democrats extended their control of both houses of the state legislature, holding twenty-six of forty state senate seats and fifty of the eighty state assembly seats, almost enough to organize the two-thirds majority necessary to pass the budget bill— almost, but not quite. Mark Baldassare asserts that California is emerging as an "un-party" state, where voters are distrustful of parties, and growing political clout has come to rest outside the mainstream political parties, in the form of the initiative process and in the independent voter. Thus, the state's voters hold a weak party loyalty and an issue-oriented focus. As a result, both parties must appeal to the independent voter. In 2000, almost 20 percent of the electorate registered as either independent or belonging to the minor parties, while Democrats held 45.4 percent and Republicans 34.9 percent of the registrations. It appears that whichever party wins depends on the extent to which that party can take over issues that the independent voters feel strongly about. For example, the Democrats swept the California state elections in 2000 because they were able to connect with issues important to independents. Nonetheless, even at floodtide, the Democrats did not possess enough power to mobilize the two-thirds vote requirement for the budget bill in the legislature. Democrats again dominated the 2002 elections, but Republican votes were still needed to get the necessary two-thirds majority to pass a budget. The result of this is that parties must accommodate each other as well as surface solutions important to independent voters.

In addition to these factors, decisions in California are further constrained by a watchful public's distrust of the political process. Consequently, Californians have used the initiative process to limit the choices their policymakers may consider. Initiatives have been used to shape how the state policy apparatus functions as well as directing what policy choices will be made. They have given the citizen of one era a role in the governmental process of all eras. For example, Proposition 13 in 1978 limited property tax increases and in so doing has limited what could be spent on local education by local government for the last 25 years. While protecting the elderly from being driven out of their homes by rapidly increasing property taxes, Proposition 13 has also had some unintended consequences. For example, it has shifted the burden of property tax toward the young and mobile homeowner group, and between classes of property, it favors commercial properties because they do not turn over as frequently as residential properties. Whatever its drawbacks, Proposition 13 retains great political support, particularly among homeowners who are able to compare their property tax bill with that of someone who has moved into the neighborhood in the last 2 or 3 years.

Initiatives have set boundaries for the political process, floors for inflation and workload growth, ceilings for spending tax windfalls, and fences for bounding spending for earmarked programs. Moreover, they have set voting requirements for the legislature and for localities when they pass budgets and change tax rates. As a result, politicians must play within a carefully bounded fiscal field. This situation exists because the people of California like it that way. Mark Baldassare says, "Californians have been telling us for years in our statewide surveys that they could do a better job than the paid professionals in Sacramento and they would thus prefer to make all of the important decisions at the ballot box through the initiative process."[13] In a statewide survey in 2000, 69 percent (66% Democrats, 69% Republicans, and 73% other voters) of all adults felt it was a good thing that voters could make changes through the initiative process. Only 23 percent said it was probably worse. Fifty-six percent (50% democrats, 56% Republicans, and 69% other voters) felt that the policy decisions made through the initiative process were probably better than the decisions made by the Governor and the legislature. Only 24 percent said those decisions were probably worse.[14] In some ways, the initiative system and the supermajority vote favor a lowest common denominator choice system, barring solutions that are highly partisan and/or highly innovative.

The initiative process was part of the progressive reform movement; it began in California in 1911 when voters passed a series of reforms "aimed at reducing political corruption and the power of the railroads and big business over state government."[15] Proposition 13 in 1978, which limited the local property tax assessment increase, is generally given credit with setting off the modern boom in government-limiting initiatives. Some of these are decisions the legislature wants the public to make, some the legislature is forced to go to the public with, and some are generated by the public itself. Since 1980, 626 statewide initiatives have been circulated for signatures: "123 qualified for elections and 52 passed."[16] While recent initiatives have focused on taking growth issues away from local politicians,[17] the usual focus of initiatives has been taxation, government regulations, and fiscal and governance issues. In Table 2.1, Propositions 4, 13, 62, and 162 limit process, while the rest primarily limit or direct policy.

Baldassare notes that there are problems with the initiative process resulting from such things as confusing language, dubious legality, and hidden special interest sponsorship and observes that his surveys found wide support for improving the initiative process. However, four in ten believed that minor changes would be sufficient, and only three in ten felt major changes were necessary.[18]

Successful initiatives may be challenged in the courts, and not all initiatives survive these challenges. For example, in March 2000, the 1996 initiative for an open primary was overruled by the U.S. Supreme Court. The major political parties joined together in a court challenge to the 1996 campaign finance initiative.[19] Still, voters are protective of the initiative process and generally give it rave reviews,[20] and voters are confronted by initiatives at every statewide election. In 2000, voters were faced with twenty state propositions in March and eight in November; about half were placed on the ballot by the legislature and the rest came through a voter petition process where the proposal is

**Table 2.1**
**Initiatives with Major State-Local Fiscal Implications**

| Measure/Election | Major Provisions |
|---|---|
| Proposition 13/June 1978 | Limit local property tax rate; limit increase in assessment after property is bought; require two-thirds vote for legislature to increase taxes |
| Proposition 4/November 1979 | Limit spending by state and local governments to prior year amount adjusted for population growth and inflation; requires states to reimburse local governments for mandates |
| Proposition 6/June 1982 | Prohibits state gift and inheritance taxes |
| Proposition 7/June 1982 | Requires indexing of state personal income tax brackets for inflation |
| Proposition 37/November 1984 | Establishes state lottery and dedicates revenue to education; places prohibition for casino gambling in constitution |
| Proposition 62/November 1986 | Requires two-thirds approval of new local general taxes by the governing body and a majority of local voters |
| Proposition 98/November 1988 | Establishes minimum state funding guarantee for K-12 schools and community colleges |
| Proposition 99/November 1988 | Imposes 25-cent surtax on cigarettes and other tobacco products and limits surtax revenues to augmenting health-related programs |
| Proposition 162/November 1992 | Limits legislature's authority over California public retirement systems, including their administrative costs and actuarial assumptions |
| Proposition 163/November 1992 | Repeals "snack tax" and prohibits any future sales tax on food items, including candy, snacks, and bottled water |
| Proposition 172/November 1992 | Imposes half-cent sales tax and dedicates the revenue to local public safety programs |
| Proposition 218/November 1996 | Limits authority of local governments to impose taxes and property-related assessments, fees, and charges |
| Proposition 10/November 1998 | Imposes 50-cent surtax on cigarettes and other tobacco products; earmarks revenues for early childhood development programs |
| Proposition 42/March 2002 | Directs to transportation purposes sales taxes on gasoline previously deposited in the general fund |
| Proposition 49/November 2002 | Requires state to provide funds for after-school programs, beginning in 2004–2005 |

*Source: Cal FACTS*, LAO, p. 15.

reviewed by the Attorney General and then must be supported by a minimum number of valid voter signatures.[21]

In 2001, the legislature approved a measure that dedicated the sales tax paid on fuel sales to transportation. This was approved by the voters as Proposition 42 in March 2002, and it is forecast to reduce general fund revenues by $1.4 billion when fully implemented.

In 2002, the legislature approved a measure that appeared on the 2004 statewide primary ballot and allocated increasing shares of the general fund, up to a ceiling of 3 percent, to state and local infrastructure. Estimates are that this will redirect approximately $950 million from the general fund in 2006–2007. This measure also includes various triggers that reduce the infrastructure set aside under various conditions. Because these are Constitutional Amendments, they must not only be passed by the legislature, but they also must be ratified by popular vote.[22]

The initiative process exists because Californians "have barely budged from their long-held perspective that their elected officials [are] incompetent when it [comes] to managing money and solving problems."[23] Term limits are another manifestation of this syndrome. Proposition 140 in 1990 limited terms for the Governor (two 4-year terms) and all other Constitutional officials and set the limit for the State Senate at two 4-year terms and the Assembly at three 2-year terms. It is generally held that limits have significantly impacted California's Legislature the few years they have been in place: "Term limits have already dramatically impacted California politics. Since the adoption of term limits in 1990, almost thirty new members have been elected to the State Assembly every 2 years, and several new legislators have joined the Senate as well. Numerous special elections have been held, as incumbents leave their current positions to pursue openings in the other House, in Congress, or in local government."[24] Some critics have argued that term limits are bad because they decrease expertise and lead to late budgets and poor decisions, but California voters like them and in 2002 rejected an initiative that would have slightly modified the limits for legislators.

Not only is California politics shaped by weak party loyalties and a strong initiative system, but also, as Baldassare says, "Californians seemed to hold on as stubbornly as ever to the view that state and local governments should give them something for nothing."[25] When asked about the state budget deficit after September 11, 2001, Californians wanted the state to give high priority to such things as education, health, and welfare, but they preferred that state government reduce spending and avoid tax increases.[26] Evidently, they saw no inconsistency in these desires.

## THE EXECUTIVE BUDGET PROCESS

California is an annual budget state where the fiscal year begins on July 1. The State Constitution requires that the Governor present the budget to the legislature by January 10. It also provides that this budget be balanced. If the proposed expenditures for the budget year exceed available resources, the Governor is required to recommend the sources for additional funding. In effect, the Governor is required to propose a balanced budget, but whether or not it is balanced relies upon what the legislature does with that recommendation. In some years, California has run deficits and has borrowed from private capital sources to fund those deficits.

The Director of Finance is appointed by the Governor and serves as his chief financial advisor. As director of the Department of Finance, he supervises efforts to prepare and execute the budget. The Department of Finance is also responsible for issuing the guidelines and instructions for budget preparation to the agencies and departments. Finance also maintains the critical indices that control estimates for population growth and inflation, and it issues instructions to departments and agencies indicating how much they are allowed to adjust their budgets for these factors. It is directly comparable to the U.S. Office of Management and Budget.

Budget construction and passage is a 2-year process. In the first year the budget is constructed in the executive branch. In the second year the budget is submitted to the legislature for review and approval. The Constitution requires the legislature to pass the budget bill by June 15. The Governor has until June 30 to sign it. Agencies in this system in the spring of any particular year are beginning to build one budget while they are testifying on, answering questions about, or suggesting modifications of the budget, which will begin the new fiscal year on July 1. While spring and early summer are the peak seasons, some budget work occurs throughout the year.

Budget construction begins in mid-April (15 months ahead of its fiscal year) when the Department of Finance issues technical budget instructions. In mid-July the Department issues the budget policy letter, followed in early August by the annual price letter. Departments follow these instructions and policy guidance to build their budgets. California has long had an automated budget system administered by the Department of Finance. This provides departments and agencies with their current budget base and includes any subsequent legislative changes to it. It automatically includes mandated price increases and budget changes driven by demographic changes.

In September, departments submit their baseline budgets to the Department of Finance; as might be expected, these are usually routine. In the second week of September, Departments submit their Budget Change Proposals (BCPs). These are the central mechanism in the budget process. They capture and explain the change from one year to the next in an agency budget and are composed of fiscal data and explanatory prose to explain and justify any budget changes. BCPs are submitted for all kinds of reasons. Common ones include changes in workload or prices, the need for new technology, the impact of court decisions, changes in federal law, or new policy directions.[27] They are the focus of discussion later with the Department of Finance and with the legislature.

In the 1980s the Department of Finance authored a directive on how to write a good BCP and has updated it periodically. The guidance is provided to departments with the technical budget instructions that start the budget process. To write a good BCP, departments are first urged to know their audience, have a succinct title, provide a concise summary, document the needs or problem, quantify the workload, identify the benefits to be achieved with quantitative information if possible, present and evaluate viable alternatives, address the history, risks, and uncertainties, document the resources needed, and have an independent "skeptical person" review the proposal before submission. Departments are warned against common pitfalls such as a lack of detail relating to actual needs, little or no quantification of needs or benefits, unachievable objectives, no discussion of alternatives, insufficient documentation of workload or cost justification, and unsupportable and unreasonable assumptions. Departments are also warned that no matter how well the case is presented, it not only must address a compelling public policy problem, but it must also agree with the Administration's goals and policies. Realistically, it must also rank as a high priority among these to get funding.

The Department of Finance provides several model BCPs on its budget analyst Web page. Their length and substance differ. One to improve an aging overhead utility power line asks $257,000, and in addition to the line item detail includes one page of single-spaced justification, while another adding a full-time social worker is supported by ten single-spaced narrative pages. As usual, personnel are harder to justify than obvious and dangerous utility situations.[28] For the agencies in a department responsible to a Department Secretary appointed by the Governor, agency-level hearings are held; these are attended by Department of Finance staff. This step would mark the end of the internal agency-department budget process. The process then turns to a dialogue between the Department of Finance budgeters and the agencies and departments. Nonagency departments, (those under boards and commissions, like the University of California or Superintendent of Public Instruction) submit their budgets directly to the Department of Finance. From September on, discussions and hearings are held between Department of Finance staff and the budgeting agencies and departments, first with budget analysts, then with Program Budget Managers (budget team supervisors), then with the Director of Finance.

Each October, state forecasters put together a preliminary estimate of what revenues they think will be available during the budget year that begins the next July. In mid-November the Department of Finance meets privately with outside experts and discusses the economic outlook for the budget year that will begin in July. This group includes economists from universities and certain key industries such as agriculture, telecommunications, and technology. In addition, in November the Legislative Analyst releases revenue estimates for the coming budget year. The differences between these two sets of estimates can be striking. In 2002, the Legislative Analyst estimated a deficit of $21.1 billion, while the Governor announced a deficit of $34.8 billion. Revenue estimates are a moving target, thus the Governor's estimate in May of 2002 was for income tax revenues of $40.5 billion in the coming year; in December the Governor revised that estimate downward to $33.6 billion, a decrease of $6.9 billion in 6 months. The Department of Finance announced that a weaker outlook for the economy, combined with lower income tax receipts and higher income tax refunds led to the revision.[29] Revenues (and spending) were again estimated in May by both the Department of Finance and the Legislative Analyst's Office. Re-estimates can be issued at any time, as is appropriate.

In December, the Director of Finance briefs the Governor on updated General Fund revenues and expenditures and the preliminary status of the budget for the current and budget year. In mid-December, the Governor holds budget meetings and makes decisions. From mid to late December, the Department of Finance finalizes the Governor's budget, the Budget Summary, the Budget Highlights, and the Budget Bill. On January 10, these are submitted to the legislature by the Department of Finance. The simplified general budget timetable lists twelve steps in the budget calendar; the Department of Finance is involved with eleven of them, either in directing the action or in reviewing actions taken by others. The only step where it is not included is when the Governor holds budget meetings and makes decisions in mid-December. This is a typographical oversight, for the Director of the Department of Finance is heavily involved in these meetings.

The Department of Finance has been called the Governor's budget-maker, responsible for budget formulation and analysis, budget implementation, revenue estimating, population growth estimates for caseload-driven functions, and price inflation factors, ranging from price growth on periodicals to a pound of laundry. Seventy to eighty budget analysts comprise the core of the Department. In addition to their normal hours, they tend to work 7 days a week for two periods: in December when they prepare the budget submission, and in April through June to do the May revision for the legislature and work the budget through the legislature, while at the same time starting the budget for the following year. The demands placed on this unit are high, as are expectations of its performance. Most observers believe the Department meets these expectations. As a result, the Governor has a powerful impact on the State budget process.

California's history was similar to that of the rest of the country at the turn of the twentieth century (before 1910). There was no executive budget process. Although the Governor had an item veto, he did not initiate a plan of expenditures or defend it as bills were being considered. Each department head was required to be present in Sacramento every day of the 4 months that the legislature was in session. Each state institution was treated as a separate department, and the heads of these institutions (prisons and hospitals) were frequently asked "to buy coal or supplies from a certain individual, or to make certain hires, and they cooperated in order to keep their appropriation bills alive and moving through the process." Governor Young described the situation in a speech in 1926:

When I first entered the legislature in 1909, there was little short of chaos as far as any orderly provisions for State expenditures were concerned. There had been no audit of State finances for over twenty years. The finance committees of the two houses were scenes of a blind scramble on the part of the various institutions and departments of the State in an endeavor to secure as large a portion as possible of whatever money might happen to be in the treasury. Heads of institutions encamped night after night in committee rooms, each alert for his own interest regardless of the interests of other institutions. Logrolling and trading of votes on appropriations bills was the common practice among members of the legislature.[30]

In 1910, Hiram Johnson was elected Governor. He was an advocate of progressive governmental reforms and started California off on the path to a reformed budget process by asking for justification with the first appropriation bills presented to him in 1911. He also created a Board of Control to advise him on the justification for appropriation bills before he would sign them, but there was still no process for a consolidated budget submission. In 1922, California passed a Constitutional amendment to provide what was missing, a consolidated administration proposal over all state revenues and expenditures in the form of a Governor's budget. From this start, the budget has developed into a comprehensive, annual budget, with itemized accounts and explanatory statements. The California process requires that the budget be introduced as a bill in each house so that changes to the budget may be tracked through the legislative process. If changes in the budget necessitate other legislative changes, then the Governor must send such trailer bills to the legislature by February 1. If the budget is not balanced, the governor must recommend the revenue sources to establish the balance.

In a 1996 survey, budget analyst staff in the Department of Finance listed what they perceived to be the essential strengths of the Department. These included such items as high quality staff; making better use of technology and having access to better information than it did a few years earlier; having a positive reputation historically; being relied upon by the governor's office and playing a strong central budget office role in the state.[31] Weaknesses focused on personnel turnover, increasing competition for quality personnel, and technological changes that led to analysts reviewing a greater level of detail.

This picture of executive dominance must be modified by the understanding that some parts of the budget are less well controlled by the Governor than others, either because they are administered through separately elected heads or because they report to independent boards or commissions whose tenure may exceed that of the Governor. Education is a good case in point. It makes up about 43 percent of the state budget and is not directly under the control of the Governor. Thus, the Governor is powerful, but some portions of the state budget are somewhat outside his direct control. They are still included in the Governor's budget, but their route of appeal to the legislature is less complicated than those Departments where the Governor appoints the chief administrative officer.

## THE BUDGET IN THE LEGISLATURE

The legislative session begins with a State of the State Address by the Governor in January and the presentation of his budget. In 2003, the State of the State speech occurred on January 8, and was unusually short. It hinted at draconian budget measures to come. Two days later, on January 10, the budget was unveiled. In addition to the budget documents, the budget is introduced as two bills, one in the Assembly and one in the Senate where it is referred to the Assembly Budget Committee and the Senate Budget and Fiscal Review Committee. Changes to the Governor's budget appear as amendments to these bills, thus providing a more transparent tracking mechanism. Both the Assembly and Senate committees are divided into subcommittees. They hold hearings and take testimony from the Department of Finance, the departments and agencies, lobbyists and the public in general. These committees are assisted by legislative staff, both on the majority and on the minority side. In addition, California profits from the expertise of the Legislative Analyst's Office, a nonpartisan staff agency that is involved in all aspects of budget review, from revenue estimates to analysis of vacant positions. The Office of Legislative Analyst was established in 1942 and has long been a model of a professionalized legislative staff agency based on nonpartisan neutral expertise. Californians like to point out that it is like the Congressional Budget Office, only older and better. While the official estimates used in the budget process are from the Department of Finance, the Legislative Analyst Office is a powerful source of confirming and contrasting information. It has about the same number of budget analysts as the Department of Finance, and they too compute everything from workload adjustments to impending deficits. Recently, their efforts have focused on urging both the Governor and the Legislature to think strategically about how to meet deficits facing the state.

In committee hearings, both the Department of Finance and the Legislative Analyst Office analysts are usually present. This has certain consequences:

In some cases the hearing becomes a subtle joust between the Department of Finance analysts and the analyst from the Office of the Legislative Analyst. In this way issues are exposed, mistakes aired and viewpoints expressed. Because it serves everyone, the Legislative Analyst Office is able to raise questions about everything, from the "most routine to the most powerful." Legislative analysts were observed supporting an EDP position request, recommending six vacant positions be dropped, and chiding an agency for "not doing what we said last year." Good analysis at this level of detail is rare for a legislative staff agency and if it were not accompanied by equally good analysis at the macrolevel, on, for example, strategies for closing the deficit, some might think the agency too detail oriented. However, the Legislative Analyst Office has a good reputation for being able to do both micro and macro budgetary analysis.[32]

In May, as hearings are still proceeding, the Department of Finance provides the annual May revision to general fund revenues and expenditures. This usually leads to changes in the focus of the budget debate as the revenues either exceed or fall short of predictions. In addition, Departments are given a chance to change their budget submissions in view of fiscal conditions or demographic changes. In general, these changes serve as minor course corrections to the budget already under discussion. In times of great change, the May revision is an important event. In 2001, the Legislature delayed much of its action on the budget to wait for a crucial May revision of revenues and the budget. Normally, in late May the subcommittees report and the full committees meet, vote, and send their bill to the floor.

As soon as one house has passed its budget bill, it is sent to conference with the other house. The budget conference committee tries to work out the differences between Assembly and Senate versions of the budget bill and discusses amendments that will enable the bill to get a two-thirds majority in each house. If the conference committee cannot work out a solution, then the Big Five meet and conference to get a compromise that will be accepted in each chamber. The Big Five include the Governor, the Speaker of the Assembly, the Speaker Pro Tempore (Senate), and the Minority Leaders of both houses.

The Conference Committees usually are able to work out a solution. These committees are usually small, perhaps six members, two from the majority and one from the minority from each chamber. Time pressure is intense; the committee meets "six days a week from 8 a.m. to midnight." Rigid rules govern who attends; there is one staff member allowed for each participant. Conference committees do not take public testimony, nor is access open to nonconference committee members. The conference committee does hold a Members Day where legislators may appear and argue for items that did not make it into final versions of the budget bill.[33] Secrecy provisions are invoked. Hundreds of issues are aired, decisions made, and a formal record created and sent back with the revised and amended bill for consideration in each chamber. The conferees also work directly with the Governor in some years to get a package that is acceptable to both the legislature and to the Governor. This was especially true in the fiscal crisis years of 2001 and 2002.

The Constitution calls for the legislature to pass the budget bill by June 15. From mid to late June, the Governor would sign the budget bill, any trailer bills needed to execute the budget, and implement his item veto[34] prerogatives. Sometimes the legislature indicates a maximum amount that they think the Governor should item veto to close a revenue-spending gap. The Governor need not follow these recommendations. The two-thirds majority vote requirement means that that there must be a high degree of agreement on the budget in the legislature.

California is one of only three states that require a supermajority, rather than a simple majority, vote of the legislature to pass a spending plan. The legislature must approve the budget by a two-thirds majority. Rhode Island and Arkansas also require a supermajority vote. Only eleven states, including California, require more than a simple majority of lawmakers to increase any state tax. California is the largest and most diverse of these states; Washington, the largest of the other ten, has one-sixth the population of California. Bounding the process with supermajorities may help explain why the budget in California is often late.[35] From 1986 to 2003, the Governor signed the budget on time three times, in 1993, 1999, and 2000; the latter 2 years were both years of surplus. In 13 of the 18 years, the budget was late, averaging 29.5 days late if the 3 years it was on time are excluded.[36] These dry figures hardly do justice to the impact of the steady drumbeat of news stories detailing the annual summer budget stalemates and the failure of the state policymaking apparatus.

Once the budget is passed, Departments are supposed to operate within budgeted levels and respect legislative intent. The legislature has included provisions in the budget act that allow agencies some flexibility to meet changed circumstances. In general, the Department of Finance must agree to these changes and may require a formal notice to the Legislature and a waiting period to allow for legislative review and response before final approval and action. Changes are allowed for such things as deficits, changed federal funding levels, and reimbursement changes. The Department of Finance approves the changes using Budget Revisions, Executive Orders, and letters. Once approved the changes are sent to the State Controller's Office where the statewide appropriation control accounts are kept.[37]

## THE ADVENT OF THE CURRENT FISCAL CRISIS

In November 2002, Governor Davis was reelected for his second 4-year term. In late November, the Legislative Analyst's Office predicted a new deficit of $21 billion, in part blaming the governor and the legislature for the poor job they did in closing the last deficit hole. In December 2002, the Governor proposed $10.2 billion in midyear budget reductions, mostly cuts, including an immediate reduction of $1.7 billion in spending on public schools, saying his new spending plan would be out early and take drastic measures. By the end of December, newspapers began to talk about a $35 billion deficit, about how everything was now on the table and that there were no more sacred cows, including taxing lobbyists and making rural counties pay for their wildfires.

In addition, nonviolent crime prisoners were set free early, a step already taken by Kentucky to help cope with its deficit and contemplated by Montana, Arkansas, Virginia, Texas, and Oklahoma.[38] This latter step would be a new direction for Governor Davis who "has made a political career lavishing money on prison uniforms and punishing criminals."[39] The budget shortfall number remained in the mid $30 billion range during the spring and summer of 2003.

Springtime is budget time in most states. While the process does not enter into the endgame until summer, it is the spring season that sees most of the budget argument unveiled in the legislature and when most hearings are taken and testimony conducted in an atmosphere of due deliberation. Summer is often given up to heated arguments on the floor or to closed-door deliberations by conference committees. The fiscal condition of the late 1990s was such that states often received a pleasant April surprise when the final settlements were made with the tax returns filed in April and a final reckoning was made on income earned on capital gains and stock options and the like. (Whatever their budget year, most states' income tax filing deadlines are April 15; those that do not collect their final settlement in April do so in May.) In the latter half of the 1990s, the final settlement was a pleasant surprise to the upside. In California this surprise accelerated each year from 1996, with the capital gains/options category averaging an increase of 48 percent a year over the previous year through 2001. In 2000 and 2001, this meant an increase on these sources alone of $5 billion in revenue. In 2002, the spring surprise was negative, down an average of 26.3 percent from the year before in the income tax states, with a median decline of 19.3 percent. In California, payments were off by over 40 percent and "helped stall enactment of a fiscal 2003 budget."[40] If the bright side of this picture was that the market downturn affected relatively few wage earners, it turned gains into losses for investors and sharply contracted a rich source of revenue for state coffers almost overnight.[41] California hardly had time to get used to this revenue windfall before it collapsed and vanished.

California was not alone in its revenue situation. Other states also suffered. For the quarter ending in June 2002, state tax revenue declined 10.4 percent compared to the same quarter in 2001. This was the sharpest decline in 11 years. Personal income tax revenue declined 22.3 percent, declining for the fourth straight quarter. State corporate income taxes continued their decline (11.7%), a seven-quarter long collapse. State sales tax revenues were up slightly (1.7%), largely due to legislated tax increases.[42] The sharpest drop occurred in the far west, but thirty-nine of the forty-one states with a personal income tax experienced declines. Twenty-nine states recorded double-digit declines. California was hit the hardest, "with an astonishing 39.4 percent decline" in income tax revenue. Connecticut, Massachusetts, and Idaho suffered declines of about 30 percent, and New York, New Jersey, and Arizona declined 26.8 percent. While California was not alone, it was in the worst shape, and by a substantial margin.

California's roller coaster ride was accentuated by the structure of California's tax system. California's personal income tax is highly progressive. A progressive rate structure means that taxable income is subject to increasingly higher rates as income increases. A primer on California's tax system explains it thus: "For example, a married couple filing jointly with two dependents and taking the standard deduction would have an effective tax rate of 1.4 percent on an income of $50,000 versus an effective rate of 4.8 % based on a $100,000 income."[43] While income doubles, tax paid increases almost seven times, from $700 to $4,800. In 1998 taxpayers earning annual incomes of $200,000 or more accounted for less than 3 percent of returns, but almost 50 percent of tax liabilities, while taxpayers with incomes of less than $50,000 accounted for over 70 percent of the returns, but less than 10 percent of tax liabilities.[44] Moreover, taxpayers with incomes over $500,000 accounted for 1 percent of the tax returns, but 40 percent of the tax liability.[45] At the other end of the scale, a family of four with an income of $42,358 owed no state income taxes at all in 2002.[46] The Budget explains that $1 of income on a high-income tax return can generate nine times the revenue compared to $1 on a low-income tax return.[47] However, high-income taxpayers usually have considerable discretion over the timing of income and deductions and thus substantial changes in the portfolios or tax planning of "relatively few high-income taxpayers can have a dramatic impact on state revenues."[48]

In 1998–1999, California's personal income tax burden was above the average of all other states and all industrial states at $3.74 per $100 of personal income. Its highest marginal rate of 9.3 percent was above that of most states. California's overall tax burden ($11.35 per $100 of personal income) was slightly over the national average ($11.04), higher than most other western states, but not as high as many of the industrial states.[49] California's overall tax burden was about average because the income tax burden was offset by a lower combined burden in other taxes.[50] In 1991, the sales tax and the income tax both held about a 40 percent share of the general fund revenues. Thanks to the windfall of the late 1990s, the personal income tax rose to 56 percent of state general fund revenues in 2001, while the sales tax share fell to 29 percent.[51] In 2002, the income tax share of the general fund fell to 46 percent but remained the largest general fund contributor.[52]

The dramatic growth in stock options and capital gains in the late 1990s was the single most important factor in recent increases in revenue volatility. Total income from stock options and capital gains increased from "$25 billion in 1994 to a peak of about $200 billion in 2000 an eight-fold rise—before falling an estimated 62 percent to $77 billion in 2001. At their peak, combined personal income tax revenues from these sources totaled about $17 billion in 2000–2001, or roughly 22 percent of total General Fund revenues during the year."[53] The report noted that this decrease of 62 percent was equivalent to about 13 percent of general fund revenues, about $10.5 billion. This had the same percentage decrease that occurred a decade earlier, when capital gains and stock options accounted for just 5 percent of total revenues, "the impact on the General Fund would have been just $1.3 billion, or only about 3 percent of total revenues during 1990–91."[54]

## COPING STRATEGIES

In December of 2001, the Legislative Analyst presented a strategy for coping with fiscal crisis. This was divided into three parts, consisting of key principals, basic strategies, and individual tools. The key principals included considering a wide range of budget solutions, assessing out-year repercussions, ensuring that budget solutions "made sense" (eliminate low priority, ineffective programs, and avoid excessively costly disruptions) and adopting current-year solutions (solutions adopted quickly in the current year would accrue more savings). The basic strategies included determining the relative roles of spending and revenue options, identifying the appropriate contributions of different program areas, establishing the desired mix of one-time versus ongoing solutions and assessing whether a multiyear solution was appropriate. Individual tools ranged from spending options like modifying or eliminating programs, suspending COLAs, and deferring spending, to revenue options like raising tax rates, broadening tax bases, and eliminating or modifying tax expenditures.[55] The Legislative Analyst observed that California had substantial budget shortfalls in the early 1990s amounting to nearly one-third of General Fund expenditures.[56] Solutions adopted to address the $14 billion shortfall in 1991–1992 included $7.7 billion in tax increases (including the imposition of 10 and 11 percent marginal income brackets and a 1.25 cent sales tax increase), an increase in the sales tax base, and an increase in vehicle license fees. The state also adopted about $3.4 billion in expenditure reductions, including $1.9 billion from education. The rest of the gap was made up from $1.6 billion in retirement contribution cost shifts and $1.4 billion from special fund transfers.

To meet the lesser shortfalls in 1993 through 1995, California policymakers relied increasingly on spending cuts and cost shifts. These included large shifts of property tax from local governments to schools, special fund transfers, grant reductions in social service programs, various fee increases, assumptions about increases in federal revenues related to immigration (only a small portion appeared), and off-the-book loans to K-12 education. Both the 1993–1994 and 1994–1995 budgets were based on 2-year budget plans and relied on borrowing substantial amounts from private credit markets. The Legislative Analyst report observes that a significant number of these solutions were reversed by the courts and resulted in additional fund costs in the latter half of the decade; these included the invalidation of the off-the-book school loans, smog impact fees, deferred state contributions to retirement funds, and various special transfers.[57]

## CONCLUSION

Thus California faced a revenue crunch in 2003, estimated at more than 30 percent (about $38 billion) of its general fund spending accounts. California, however, has been here before. It faced and defeated a revenue crisis amounting to one-third of its general fund budget in 1991–1992, and it left a set of tools both on the revenue and expenditure side for guidance. It also left a pattern that included using 2-year plans in an annual-budget state and relying on borrowing in the capital market to close the tax revenue deficit in a state that has a requirement that the budget as presented be balanced. It took 4 years for California to work its way out of the 1991–1992 crisis. To some extent, as the economy improved, so too did California, but the state's policymakers also found effective solutions to the crisis, with the mix each year being a little different than what had gone before.

While the surplus budgets of 1999 and 2000 were focused on one-time spending, the Governor and the legislature also committed money to new programs that were then included in the base for future years. This may have been as much as 60 percent in the windfall revenue years. The Governor emphasized education and was able to increase the amount of money for K-14 education over the amount required by the Proposition 98 guarantee. Much of this additional "overburden" money went to teacher salaries and thus became part of the budget base in future years. This priority was supported by the legislature, and, in fact, California's supermajority requirement meant that both parties had to support these policies.

It may be said that recognition of the windfall revenue and careful strategizing about options did not help California get out of the way of the collapse of the Internet bubble. From 2001 to 2003 California faced deficits that grew steadily worse. However, it must also be said that California did spend about 40 percent of the money on one-time expenditures and while its array of solutions was also skewed toward one-time gimmicks, implausible revenue recognitions, and borrowings, it did avoid raising the major taxes at a time when both the economy and the consumer were clearly troubled.

In respect to the windfall money itself: what were California policymakers to do, return the money? These revenue gains on capital gains and stock options were the state's share of events that made some high-income taxpayers very well-off. Some money went back to all taxpayers in the form of a substantial reduction of vehicle license fees. As for the rest, California policymakers took that money and put it to use. They were suspicious that the good times would not last, and they used some of the windfall for one-time solutions, but there were only so many one-time problems with a higher priority than needs related to continuing programs. It would not have been wise to put the money all in one-time expenditures and ignore higher priority programs just because they were of a continuing nature. Some critics believe California has not kept pace with the demands created by its fast-growing population, and that California lags well behind other states in the nation in spending on such amenities as schools, highways, prisons, and infrastructure.[58]

In the world of budgeting, much is made of incremental change. California's budget system, with its emphasis on demographic and inflationary adjustments and its system of budget change proposals, its supermajority vote requirements, and the initiatives that limit what politicians can do, would seem to be uniquely incremental. However, this system has twice now faced periods of nonincremental deficits, 33 percent of general fund revenues in the early 1990s, and 30 percent in 2002 and 2003. These are not incremental numbers, yet California has found ways to close those gaps by relying on complicated mixtures of spending reductions, tax and fee increases, fund transfers, revenue recognitions, and loans. It has used one-time and continuing measures on both the spending and revenue sides. As an annual budget state, it has adopted multiyear solutions. Some of the solutions used in the early 1990s were later held illegal by the courts and led to larger expenditures toward the end of the decade. However, even the illegal solutions helped California get by the deficits it was facing at the time. It paid for these in years when it could afford to pay for them, that is, later.

In the early 1990s, California adopted significant but temporary income and sales tax increases; through 2002 it had avoided such tax increases. California's policymakers thought strategically about spending windfall funds in 1999 and 2000 and in reacting to the fiscal crises that followed. Some behavior has been incremental; some has not. In the 2002–2003 budget, some programs were reduced 60 percent or more. Budgets have been presented on time and passed late. Major adjustments have been made in May and in various times during the year, both to the budget year proposal and to current year expenditures.

Persistence over time is also part of budgetary incrementalism. Just as the budget base persists and is projected into the future, so too, do problems. They persist and are eroded away, rather than being solved once and for all by some masterstroke of budgetary policymaking. Californians, then, ought not to have expected that the fiscal crisis of 2003 would be vanquished overnight; after all, it already was in existence since May 2001. In the summer of 2003 policymakers avoided raising taxes significantly, but college and university fees were raised an average of 30 percent, park fees increased 20 percent, and layoffs began to occur in health care systems and public protection programs. The ad valorem portion of vehicle license fees tripled. As loans were negotiated, the state's bond rating fell to the lowest among the states and into the lowest possible category, and a recall campaign succeeded in forcing a recall election on a Governor elected by a substantial margin in the previous year. On July 23, the recall petition was ordered and on July 24, 2003, Standard and Poor's debt rating service dropped California's rating by three notches to BBB, the worst in the nation and the lowest rating states have ever been given. This is two notches above junk-bond levels, where big investors cannot buy. The rating change has been estimated to cost California up to an additional $1 billion on a $24 billion bond issue.[59]

In 2002, the final budget California passed in September closed a deficit that was double the size estimated in January. Although not universally loved, it *was* a solution. Thus, policymakers were seen to cope. In these years, the budget story was not the big story. September 11, 2001, the war on terrorism, homeland security, the invasion of Afghanistan, air travel security, and the war in Iraq: these were the big stories. Knitting together acceptable plans to meet a fiscal crisis was just a subtext to that story, but it was one in which California's policymakers did rather well in 2002. Politics in 2003 tell a different story, one where politicians chose to avoid major tax increases, but cut agency spending, raised fees and charges, decreased funding to local governments, and borrowed the rest. In a sense, this constituted a downsizing of general government and a move toward provision of government services on a contractual basis for those who could afford them via charges and fees. Voters did not embrace this solution. Governor Gray Davis was subjected to a recall election and lost, and the outcome was clear weeks before the votes were counted as it became clear that voters were tired of the usual solutions applied by the usual cast of characters. Thus, they overwhelmingly turned to Republican Arnold Schwarzenegger, actor and businessman, who generated a sense of caring and involvement and promised to bridge the gap between Republicans and Democrats. However, this was not to be; the new governor found the state's political structures and environment just as intractable as his predecessors had. While he maintained his personal popularity, he was able to do little to change the policies and procedures that had put California at risk. From 2003 to 2006, California survived on a regimen of short-term borrowings, fee increases, and program decrements. In the spring of 2006, revenues suddenly exceeded the estimates made in the winter of 2005, but political leaders could not decide where to put the new money because they could not decide whether this was the end of the lean times or the calm before another fiscal storm. The continuing deficit closure efforts and the extraordinary recall election of 2003 left most California voters with new knowledge about the perverse impacts on the policy process of such items as the supermajorities required to move budgets, the role of initiatives in handcuffing state policymakers, the effect of term limits on depriving the state legislative process of seniority and leadership, and the impact of redistricting, which guarantees the reelection of legislators from a certain party, but not leadership or vision. In the best California tradition, Californians appear to want to hold on to their protections against the excesses of politics, but they also want their politicians to overcome these obstacles and step up and lead and, being Californians, they see no conflict in desiring these contradictory outcomes.

## NOTES

1. Twenty-nine states require that the budget adopted by the legislature be strictly in balance between revenues equal expenditures. California's Constitution does not require that the legislature pass a balanced budget, but limitations on state borrowing power provide a stimulus to balance the budget as passed.

2. California Budget Project, *Betting on a Brighter Future: The Social and Economic Context of the Governor's Proposed 2002–3 Budget* (January 2002), 14.

3. California Budget Project, *BudgetWatch* 8(3) (October 2002).

4. For FY 1999 it was estimated that 65 percent of the general fund budget was mandated, including expenses for K-14 education (42% of the general fund budget), low income health care ("Medi-cal" 12%), public assistance related to federal block grants (5%), child welfare state matching for federal funds (1.7%), local government tax relief (0.7%), state contributions for public employees pensions (0.7%), and general obligation debt interest (3%). California Budget Project, *Dollars and Democracy: An Advocate's Guide to the California State Budget Process*. Sacramento, CA: 1999, p. 11.

5. Elisabeth G. Hill, Legislative Analyst, *Cal FACTS, California's Economy and Budget in Perspective*. Sacramento, CA: Office of the Legislative Analyst, December 2002, p. 12.

6. Mark Baldassare, *A California State of Mind: The Conflicted Voter in a Changing World*. Berkeley, CA: University of California Press, p. 149. Baldassare conducted eleven statewide telephone opinion surveys of over 22,000 Californians from September 1999 to May 2001. These were supplemented with focus groups.

7. Baldassare, 149.

8. *Cal FACTS*, 35.

9. *Dollars and Democracy*, 5.

10. Elisabeth G. Hill, Legislative Analyst, *Addressing the State's Fiscal Problems*. Sacramento, CA: Office of the Legislative Analyst, December 19, 2001, p. 4.

11. *Addressing the State's Fiscal Problems*, 5.

12. *Dollars and Democracy*, 14.

13. Baldassare, 249.

14. Baldassare, 213.

15. Baldassare, 213. For more on California and initiatives, see Fred Silva, *The California Initiative Process: Background Material*. San Francisco, CA: Public Policy Institute of California, 2000.

16. Baldassare, 214.

17. Baldassare, 13.

18. Baldassare, 216.

19. Baldassare, 216.

20. Baldassare, 215.

21. For a simple initiative, 5 percent of the total votes cast for governor in the last election (419,260 signatures in 2002); for a Constitutional amendment, 8 percent is required (670,816). *Initiative Watch*, http://www.calvoter.org/Iwatch.

22. *Budget Watch*, 3.

23. Baldassare, 245.

24. California's Legislature, Office of the Assembly Clerk. Sacramento, CA: 2000, p. 88. This 304-page volume is made available to the public by the California Legislature.

25. Baldassare, 256.

26. Ibid.

27. *Dollars and Democracy*, 16.

28. The budget change proposal instructions and the model budget change proposals may be viewed from the budget analyst Web page of the California Department of Finance Web site.

29. Jeffrey L. Rabin, "California's Economists Frequently are Wrong," *Los Angeles Times Online* (January 14, 2003), http://www.latimes.com.

30. *Executive Summary, History of Budgeting in California*, California Department of Finance Web page, http://www.dof.ca.gov/. Quoted material is from A.E. Buck, *Public Budgeting*, 1929.

31. *Strategic Plan, 1997–98*, California Department of Finance, p. 12.

32. McCaffery, 12.

33. *Dollars and Democracy*, 30.

34. The Governor may reduce or eliminate any item in the budget; this can be overridden if a two-thirds majority in both houses agree to do so. He may not increase items or add new items. In the FY 2003 budget, Governor Davis made eighty-eight line item vetoes worth $247 million ($2.8 million on average). In 1983–1984, Governor Deukmejian made the greatest number of item vetoes, 367, for $1.659 billion. Item vetoes are sometimes challenged by the legislature, but since 1966 only in FY 1980 have some item vetoes been overturned. *Chart P Historical Data, Budget Act Dates and Veto Information*, Department of Finance, 2003.

35. *Budget Watch*, California Budget Project, 8(3) (October 2002).

36. Author's computation from calendar on *Chart P Historical Data, Dates for May Revision and Budget Enactment*, Department of Finance, September 2002.

37. This description relies on various sources including interviews, the description of California's Budget Process from the Department of Finance Web site, (http://www.dof.ca.gov), from various publications available on the Web site of the Legislative Analyst Office (http://www.lao.ca.gov), and from the Governor's Budget for 2002–2003.

38. Robert Salladay, "Huge Fiscal Gap Topples Taboos," *San Francisco Chronicle* (December 26, 2002), A1 and A23.

39. Salladay, A23.

40. Jenny, 7.

41. Jenny, 10.

42. Nicholas W. Jenny, "State Tax Revenue Decline Accelerates," *State Revenue Report*, Fiscal Studies Program, Nelson A. Rockefeller Institute of Government, 49 (September 2003), 1.

43. *California's Tax System, A Primer*, Legislative Analyst Office, January 2001, chapter 2, Personal Income Tax, p. 4.

44. Ibid.

45. *Cal FACTS*, 29.

46. Scott Thurm and Rhonda L. Rundle, "Behind California Budget Mess is Pattern of Political Paralysis," *Wall Street Journal* (January 10, 2003), 1.

47. "Revenue Estimates," *Governor's Budget Summary, 2002–3: State of California*, p. 102.

48. Ibid.

49. *Cal FACTS*, 17.

50. *California's Tax System: A Primer*, Legislative Analyst Office, January 2001, chapter 2, Personal Income Tax, pp. 6–7.

51. Department of Finance Chart, "Personal Income Tax Provides the Largest Share of State General Fund Revenues."

52. *California's Fiscal Outlook: 2002-2003—2007-2008*, Legislative Analyst Office, November 2002, p. 18.

53. *Governor's Budget Summary, 2002-2003*, p. 5.

54. Ibid.

55. *Addressing the State's Fiscal Problems*, 7.

56. *Addressing the State's Fiscal Problems*, 10.

57. *Addressing the State's Fiscal Problems*, 11.

58. Baldassare, 9; Also see Peter Schrag, *Paradise Lost: California's Experience, America's Future*. New York: The New Press, 1998.

59. Rick Jurgens, "State Bond Rating Lowest Ever," *Contra Costa Times* (July 25, 2003).

# CHAPTER 3

# Georgia: Shared Power and Fiscal Conservatism

*Thomas P. Lauth*

The executive budget has been the centerpiece of efforts to strengthen the powers of state governors. The budget reflects gubernatorial policy priorities as well as agency needs, and governors use funding decisions to direct and control executive branch agencies. Compared with other states, the budget powers of the governor of Georgia are relatively strong. However, the General Assembly has the ability to make independent judgments and challenge executive initiatives. Power in the Georgia budget and appropriation process is shared.

For 125 years following the end of Reconstruction, the Georgia state government was controlled by the Democratic Party. In 2002, the Republican Party gained control of the governor's office and state Senate and for a brief period Georgia experienced divided party government. In 2004, Republicans also gained control of the House of Representatives, returning state government to unified party control. For most of the twentieth century, Democratic Party control was so dominant that competition in the budgetary process was largely between the executive and legislative branches rather than between political parties. Early in the twenty-first century, competition in the budgetary process remains primarily interbranch competition but with a somewhat stronger interparty flavor than in the past.

## FISCAL CONSERVATISM

In fiscal matters, Georgia is a conservative state where policymakers favor balanced budgets, low taxes, limited debt, and limited government spending. On the revenue side, policymakers resist tax increases and usually prefer cash over bond revenue to pay for government spending. On the expenditure side, policymakers prefer private spending over public spending and within public sector spending prefer infrastructure projects and economic development over transfer payments. Fiscal conservatism in Georgia state government is manifest in several ways.[1]

First, the state has a constitutional balanced budget requirement. This means that the state cannot incur a deficit or borrow to obtain operating funds. The General Assembly is prohibited from appropriating funds in excess of an amount equal to the sum of anticipated revenue collections and any surplus remaining in the state treasury at the beginning of the fiscal year.[2] Second, the state has low debt limits and low use of debt. State debt is limited to 10 percent of the net revenue receipts in the fiscal year immediately preceding the year in which debt is incurred.[3] In most recent years, the state's debt has been 5–6 percent, well below the constitutional limit. Third, the state requires reserves. The Revenue Shortfall Reserve, established in 1976 in response to a severe revenue shortfall in the previous year, is Georgia's "rainy day" fund. On June 30 of each year, the state auditor is required to transfer to the Revenue Shortfall Reserve an amount equal to but not less than 3 percent and not more than 5 percent, as directed by the director of the budget (governor), of the new revenue collections for the fiscal year, provided funds for such purposes are available. The purpose of the rainy day fund is to enable the state to absorb decreases in revenue collections due to an economic recession without having to reduce the adopted budget. Fourth, the state has low taxes, a graduated income tax with a top rate of 6 percent and a sales tax of 4 percent (with food purchased for at-home consumption and prescription drugs exempted). Fifth, the governor has the sole authority to set the state's revenue estimate. The state economist[4] calculates a range of likely revenue yields under various assumptions, but the selection of a specific figure that becomes the official state revenue estimate is a policy decision of the governor. This revenue-setting prerogative is the keystone of the governor's budget power. Revenue estimates traditionally have been conservative leading in most years to an underestimation of actual revenue collections.[5] An advantage of conservative revenue estimates is that they reduce the risk of revenue shortfalls. An "incorrect" estimate that underestimates the actual revenue yield is also politically preferable to one that overestimates collections. Of course, if revenue estimates are too conservative, there is insufficient new revenue projected to permit the funding of gubernatorial and legislative initiatives. Nevertheless, the practice in Georgia of underestimating revenue collections has contributed to the presence of a surplus in most years.[6] Sixth, conservative financial management practices in combination with a relatively robust economy, have earned for the state AAA bond ratings. A long-time chairman of the Senate Appropriations Committee frequently spoke of the connection between conservative financial practices and the state's ability to achieve AAA bond ratings.[7] The balanced budget requirement, reserve requirement, low debt limit and low use of debt, low tax rates, conservative revenue estimating practices, and financial management practices that earn AAA bond ratings, taken as a whole, are manifestations of the culture of fiscal conservatism in Georgia government.

## FORMAL BUDGET POWERS IN GEORGIA

Strong executive budget powers exist whenever a governor has direct responsibility for budget preparation and execution, the central budget office is located in the office of the governor, and the governor has authority to line-item veto legislative appropriations. Unrestricted tenure in office and the ability to appoint all or most heads of executive branch agencies are formal powers that may indirectly have ramifications for budget making.

By these standards, the formal budget powers of the Georgia governor are relatively strong. Responsibility for budget preparation rests with the governor rather than with a budget commission or board. The Georgia Office of Planning and Budget (OPB) is a staff agency located within the governor's office, rather than within a department of finance or administration, as is the case in many other states. Georgia's governor is one of forty-four governors who possess the line-item veto, a tool to discourage pork barrel appropriations. To the extent that tenure in office is related to budgetary power, the governor's office in Georgia was strengthened in 1976 when a constitutional amendment made it possible for a sitting governor to seek reelection.[8] Executive branch agencies and legislators now have fewer opportunities to attempt to take budgetary advantage of a lame duck governor. The governor's formal appointment power is relatively weak. Seven executive branch agency heads (a total of eleven officials), plus the lieutenant governor are directly elected.[9] Although shared power within the executive branch is usually regarded as a weakness in the formal powers of chief executives, previous research has demonstrated that the method of agency selection is not systematically related to agency budget success in Georgia.[10] On balance, Georgia's governor has relatively strong formal budget powers.

### Development of the Executive Budget in Georgia

The Georgia budget process was dominated by the legislative branch until 1931. In that year, the General Assembly established the state's first executive budget system. A Budget Bureau was created consisting of the governor as ex officio director of the budget and the state auditor as associate director of the budget and chief operating head. The three decades between 1931 and 1961 were characterized by a shift of budgetary control away from the legislature to the executive.[11]

A major struggle between the governor and the General Assembly over appropriations in 1961 resulted in actions to limit the governor's nearly total power in budgetary matters.[12] Ironically, the 1962 Budget Act and 1962 constitutional amendments, which were designed to curtail the governor's power, also established the foundation for the current strong executive budget system in Georgia.[13] The 1962 Act reconstituted the Budget Bureau in the governor's office, established the position of state budget officer, and authorized professional support staff for the new agency.[14] Since the Executive Reorganization Act of 1972, the central budget office has been known as the Office of Planning and Budget.

### Strengthening the General Assembly

In addition to the 1962 limitations placed on the governor's discretionary budget authority, several subsequent actions have helped strengthen legislative influence in the budgetary process. In 1966 the Speaker of the House of Representatives became more independent of the governor. Prior to that time, the governor hand-picked the speaker and committee chairpersons, and was able to have his budget approved by the legislature without much difficulty.[15] A new era of legislative independence began when the House elected its officers without suggestions from the executive branch of government.[16]

In 1969, the General Assembly established the Legislative Budget Office (LBO) consisting of the legislative budget analyst and approximately ten other professional budget analysts. This agency provides the legislature with alternative expertise to the governor's Office of Planning and Budget. The Legislative Budget Office was intended to serve as a staff agency for both the House and Senate appropriations committees, but in practice has had a closer association with the House committee. The Senate appropriations committee, until recently, relied more extensively on the governor's Office of Planning and Budget for staff assistance. When Republicans won the governorship and gained control of the state Senate in November 2002, divided party control of the House (Democrats) and Senate (Republicans) exacerbated decades of dissatisfaction with the relationship between the Senate and the Legislative Budget Office. In July 2003, a Senate Budget Office (SBO) was established to provide staff support for the Senate appropriations committee. The Legislative Budget Office continues to provide staff support for the House appropriations committee. However, it is very likely in a future session of the General Assembly to become the House Budget Office (HBO).

Prior to 1975, the General Assembly appropriated in four major object classifications: personal services, operating expenses, lease rental, and capital outlays. Since 1975, the appropriations act has contained approximately a dozen standard object-of-expenditure classifications and several other sub-object classifications. This development was largely an effort to increase legislative control of spending. However, as will be seen later in the chapter, Georgia is in the process of moving from a line item, object of expenditure budget system to a program budget system. It is very likely that in a future session of the General Assembly the terminology "object class" will be changed to "program" to reflect this innovation.[17]

During budget execution, legislative control is manifest in the requirement that agency funds cannot be transferred from one object of expenditure classification to another without approval of the legislature's Fiscal Affairs Subcommittee.[18] (Reprogramming of funds within the same object class requires only the approval of the governor's Office of Planning and Budget). The Fiscal Affairs Subcommittee is composed of four members appointed by the Speaker of the House of Representatives, four members appointed by the president of the Senate (the lieutenant governor), five members of each house selected by the governor, as well as the speaker of the House and the lieutenant governor. State law requires this subcommittee to meet at least once each quarter, or at the call of the governor, for the purpose of reviewing and approving budget unit object class transfers recommended by the governor. However, in recent years it has met only once a year, usually in June, just before the end of one and the beginning of the next fiscal year. Although Fiscal Affairs is an instrument of legislative control over the transfer of funds, its agenda is set by gubernatorial recommendations. It is, therefore, a reactive rather than a proactive form of legislative influence. It is very likely that in a future session of the General Assembly the role of the Fiscal Affairs Subcommittee will be modified to approve program transfers rather than budget unit object class transfers recommended by the governor.[19]

## THE STATE ECONOMY AND REVENUE COLLECTIONS

The adequacy of revenue substantially influences the behavior of participants in state budgeting.[20] Approximately 55 percent of the Georgia budget comes from state appropriations, with the remainder coming from the federal government and state agency earnings. Georgia own-source revenue is derived from a general sales tax (33%), special sales taxes on such products as motor fuel, alcoholic beverages and tobacco (13%), individual and corporate income taxes (49%), and earmarked lottery proceeds (5%).[21] Georgia revenues increased in current dollars between 1990 and 2001 by 105.2 percent, or an average annual increase of 6.8 percent. Controlling for the effects of inflation, revenues in constant dollars increased by 52.1 percent, or an average annual increase of 3.9 percent. Further controlling for population growth, state revenues in constant per capita dollars increased by 18 percent, or an average annual rate of 1.5 percent.[22]

The Georgia economy was robust compared with many other states during the 1990s, and that strength was reflected in stable revenue collections for state government.[23] Between 1990 and 1999, Georgia employment grew at the rate of 3.0 percent per year, compared to the national rate of 1.3 percent per year. Georgia employment grew more rapidly than U.S. employment in every year of this period, and Georgia employment, as a share of U.S. employment, increased steadily from 2.6 percent in 1990 to 3.1 percent in 1999.[24] The Georgia unemployment rate was also below the national rate each year between 1990 and 1999.[25] During the same period, Georgia per capita personal income grew at a rate of 4.9 percent per year, while U.S. per capita personal income grew at the rate of 4.3 percent per year. Georgia per capita personal income as a percent of U.S. per capita personal income grew steadily from 90.6 percent in 1990 to 95.7 percent in 1999.[26] In short, a robust state economy contributed to the state's revenue growth during the 1990s.[27]

### Coping with Recession—Threat to Structural Balance

The state's strong economy and conservative revenue estimating practices historically provided a hedge against revenue shortfalls during a recession phase of the business cycle. However, the nationwide recession at the beginning of this century also led to revenue shortfalls in Georgia. Revenue collections for the 2002 fiscal year were 5 percent less than revenue collections for the previous fiscal year, the worst revenue decline in 50 years. Several gap-closing measures became necessary, including state agency spending reductions, the substitution of bond proceeds for tax revenues, and the reallocation of funds freed up by the substitution of bond proceeds. Spending reductions imposed on state agencies permitted funding of the governor's policy initiatives, while maintaining a balanced budget.[28] Despite the state's worst revenue decline in 50 years, the Georgia budget remained in better shape than the budgets of many other states. Elsewhere, it has been argued that budget decisions in the 1990s positioned Georgia to successfully handle a cyclical downturn in the 2002 and 2003 fiscal years. By not overcommitting to program spending or tax cuts during the expansion phase of the business cycle, it was possible to achieve budget balance in the recession phase of the business cycle.[29]

However, when Georgia was slow in coming out of the recession, the structural balance of its budget was compromised. Spending reductions imposed on state agencies in fiscal years 2002 and 2003 amounted to a 10 percent reduction for most state agency budgets. Revenue collections for the 2003 fiscal year were less than revenue collections for the previous fiscal year. During the 2003 session of the General Assembly, the new Republican governor ordered an additional state agency budget reduction of 1 percent. This action was well received by those in the General Assembly who believe that agencies can easily absorb funding reductions by improving their operational efficiency, as well as by those who believe it is desirable to reduce the size and scope of state government. However, on the heels of the 10 percent budget reductions ordered by the previous governor in fiscal years 2002 and 2003, state agencies probably had less capacity to absorb additional reductions than some legislators believed.

Despite the general aversion in Georgia to new taxes, the governor proposed to the 2003 General Assembly tobacco and alcoholic beverage tax increases. Legislative leaders from both sides of the aisle concluded that no other revenue options or additional budget reductions were available to them and approved a modest tax increase (less than the governor's recommendation) on tobacco

products. Increasing this "sin" tax was more acceptable to the governor, legislators, and their constituents than increasing a higher yield tax such as the
sales or income tax. (It actually was proposed as a contribution to good health.)
When power is divided, difficult taxing and spending decisions, especially taxing decisions, become even more difficult. In the 2003 session of the General
Assembly, Democrats (in control in the House of Representatives) were reluctant to support tax increases unless Republicans (in control of the governor's
office and the Senate) shared the political exposure. Some Republicans had
pledged not to increase taxes, and some believed holding fast on no new taxes
provided an opportunity to reduce the size of government. The governor announced that there would be no new taxes in 2004 and ordered state agencies
to reduce their fiscal year 2004 budgets by an additional 2.5 percent and to
plan for an additional 5 percent reduction in fiscal year 2005. State agencies
had reduced their budgets by a total of 11 percent in fiscal years 2002 and
2003.

Until 2003, Georgia had been able to maintain structural balance in its
budget, even when cyclical fluctuations required periodic budget reductions.
However, the budgets that emerged from the 2003 and 2004 sessions of the
General Assembly for the 2004 and 2005 fiscal years lacked structural balance,
that is, the mismatch between recurring expenditures and anticipated revenues
was covered by gimmicks and temporary solutions. During the same period,
funds from the state's rainy day fund (Revenue Shortfall Reserve) were largely
depleted.

Throughout the period of Recession, the General Assembly developed a
pattern of under-funding Medicaid in one legislative session with the hope
that revenue collections would be stronger during the next session. When
the hoped for collections did not appear, the legislature became ensnared in
a cycle of recurring catch up for Medicaid funding. Similarly, in an effort to
fund public education and health care within the constraint of no new taxes,
2 percent pay raises for teachers and other state employees were delayed until
January, in effect making them 1 percent raises in the first year even though
they would have to be annualized at 2 percent in future years. Further, the
governor proposed but later withdrew a plan to shift the final fiscal year payday from June 30 to July 1, thereby shifting the cost from one fiscal year to
the next. The General Assembly approved this accounting gimmick when it
adopted the 2005 fiscal year budget and used it to balance the budget. When
the governor, motivated by concern for the state's credit rating, decided to
shift the June 30 payday back into its rightful fiscal year, a $197.4 million
hole in that year's budget was created that had to be offset by spending reductions. These three gimmicks are illustrations of structural imbalance creeping
into Georgia's budget process. Until recently, that process had carefully ad-
hered to structural balance, even during periods of cyclical imbalance. However, economic downturns and strong opposition to tax increases within both
political parties undermined the long-standing practice of structural balance
in the budget process. This situation represents a significant departure from

past practice and now poses a threat to the state's standing in financial markets as well as a threat to programmatic achievements of the previous two decades.

Unlike some states, Georgia has not used tobacco settlement funds to off-set budget shortfalls. Funds received from the Master Settlement Agreement (MSA) have been used for health care, economic development in tobacco growing areas, and a small amount for use prevention programs.

Revenue collection for the 2004 fiscal year increased 7.1 percent over the 2003 fiscal year and collections for the 2005 fiscal year increased 8 percent over the 2004 fiscal year. It remains to be seen if sustained economic recovery will permit a return to structural balance in the state budget. The persistently rising costs of Medicaid will continue to make budget balancing a challenge for decision makers, especially if new revenues are expected to come from economic growth, not new taxes.

## Lottery as a Funding Source for Education

The Georgia lottery earmarks proceeds for education.[30] It has been highly successful, achieving 10 consecutive years of revenue growth and transfer-ring $7.4 billion to the state's Lottery for Education account.[31] State law[32] provides that proceeds from the lottery be appropriated for programs in five areas: voluntary prekindergarten for 4-year-olds; HOPE scholarships[33] and student loans; capital improvements for education; costs of providing training to teachers; and repairing and maintaining instructional technology. The act also states that, "net proceeds of lottery games ... shall be used to support improvements and enhancements for educational purposes and that such net proceeds shall be used to supplement, not supplant, existing resources for ed-ucational purposes and programs." However, fungibility is difficult to detect unless budget and appropriations processes are transparent. In an effort to ensure that state general funds for education will not be cut and replaced by lottery proceeds, the Georgia Constitution was amended and the following language was added:

Net proceeds after payment of ... operating expenses shall be separately accounted for and shall be specifically identified by the Governor in his annual budget presented to the General Assembly as a separate budget category entitled "Lottery Proceeds" and the Governor shall make specific recommendations as to educational programs and educational purposes to which said net proceeds shall be appropriated. In the General Appropriations Act adopted by the General Assembly, the General Assembly shall appropriate all net proceeds of the lottery or lotteries by such separate budget category to educational programs and educational purposes as specified by the General Assembly.[34]

A study in 2002 by Lauth and Robins concluded that while there was some evidence of substitution, lottery funds produced a net increase in spending for education in Georgia.[35]

Why has Georgia, for the most part, resisted the temptation to replace general purpose funding for education with lottery proceeds and shift general purpose funds to other state government functions? The transparency of the budget and appropriations process is surely an important factor. When fungibility is detectible, it is rendered more difficult. The policy architecture of the lottery-for-education program also made fungibility unlikely because proceeds were pledged for the initiation of specific new programs such as prekindergarten, HOPE scholarships and student loans, and instructional technology improvements, not simply for more spending on education in general. The commitment of Governor Zell Miller, the chief advocate of the lottery-for-education initiative, to ensure that lottery proceeds "be used to supplement, not supplant, existing resources for educational purposes and programs," also was an important factor. Finally, the overall strength of state revenues enabled Georgia decision makers, for the most part, to resist the temptation of fungibility and to appropriate lottery funds as additions to, rather than substitutions for, state general education funds.[36]

## THE BUDGET PROCESS

The Georgia budget process is typical of most executive budget systems.[37] Agencies submit spending requests to the governor's Office of Planning and Budget (OPB) in accord with OPB instructions and based upon program needs. The Office of Planning and Budget reviews agency request for accuracy, necessity, and past performance. It evaluates agency requests for compatibility with the governor's policy priorities and recommends a coordinated spending plan to the governor. The governor sets the official state revenue estimate, establishes his policy priorities, decides among competing agency requests, and recommends appropriations bills to the General Assembly. The General Assembly modifies the governor's recommendations, in accord with policy preferences of the legislative leadership and constituency interests of individual members, and passes the appropriations acts.

One of the major responsibilities of the Director of the Office of Planning and Budget is to find enough money each year to fund the governor's policy initiatives. If, in the aggregate, agency requests for funding new programs and maintaining existing ones absorb too large a share of the revenues projected in the governor's official revenue estimate, agency priorities have the potential to crowd out gubernatorial initiatives. It is a responsibility of the Office of Planning and Budget to prevent that from happening. Similarly, the Legislative Budget Office (House) and the Senate Budget Office attempt to find funds under the cap of the governor's revenue estimate to fund the policy preferences of legislative leaders and the constituency interests of individual members. Inevitably, this means substituting the policy priorities of legislative leaders for those of the governor, resulting in some interbranch conflict over the final budget.

After the appropriations acts have been passed by the General Assembly and signed into law by the governor, the Office of Planning and Budget is responsible for ensuring that agency funds are spent legally and for the purposes for which they were authorized. The following illustrates the phases and timetable of the budget cycle using fiscal year 2005 as an example.

### Fiscal Year 2005 Budget Cycle

Spring 2003

- Preliminary Planning by Departments.
- Agency Heads and Governing Boards develop Policy Positions.
- Agency Personnel develop Cost Estimates.

June 1, 2003

- "Budget Call" issued by Office of Planning and Budget to Agencies and *Budget Preparation Procedures Manual* distributed.

June–August, 2003

- Agencies review Preliminary Policy Positions and Cost Estimates.

September 1, 2003

- Agencies submit Budget Requests to Office of Planning and Budget.

September–December

- Office of Planning and Budget reviews Agency Budget Requests updated information, or additional justifications may be requested.
- Office of Planning and Budget makes Funding Level Recommendations to the Governor.
- Agency Heads meet with Office of Planning and Budget and the Governor to negotiate differences between Requests and Recommendations.
- Office of Planning and Budget Director and Professional Staff Economist develop the Revenue Estimate; Governor specifies the Official Revenue Estimate.
- Concurrent with Office of Planning and Budget Review of Agency Requests, Legislative Budget Office and Senate Budget Office review Agency Requests to develop an Estimate of "Continuation."
- Appropriations Committees meet with Agency Heads prior to the Session.

## January 2004

- The General Assembly convenes on the second Monday in January each year and may meet for not more than 40 days each year, excluding days in recess.
- Within 5 days of the convening of the General Assembly, Governor delivers Budget Message to the General Assembly.
- Governor Presents *Budget Report(s)* to the General Assembly (Fiscal Year 2004 Amended Budget and Fiscal Year 2005 Budget).
- Governor announces Revenue Estimate.
- Appropriations Bills introduced in House of Representatives.

## January–March

- House and Senate Appropriations Committees hold Joint Budget Hearings.
- Appropriations Committees "mark up" Bills and Report to House and Senate.
- Legislative Budget Office and Senate Budget Office provide Analysis to Appropriations Committees.
- House Adopts Appropriations Bill and transmits it to the Senate; Senate Adopts Substitute to House Bill and returns it to the House; House rejects Senate Substitute; Conference Committee is appointed; Conference Committee Report adopted by House and Senate with No Amendments Permitted.

## February 2004

- House and Senate Adopt amended FY 2004 Appropriations Act.

## March 2004

- House and Senate Adopt FY 2005 Appropriations Act.

## April 2004

- Governor signs Appropriations Acts within 40 days after Adjournment.
- Governor may line item veto selected amounts of money or narrative passages in the Appropriations Bill.

## June 30, 2004

- 2004 Fiscal Year ends (FY 2004 begins July 1, 2003 and ends June 30, 2004).

## July 1, 2004

- 2005 Fiscal Year begins (FY 2005 begins July 1, 2004 and ends June 30, 2005).

July 1 to June 30

• Agencies prepare and submit to the Office of Planning and Budget an Annual Operating Budget in conformity with the Appropriations Act.
• Agencies Receive a Quarterly Allotment of Funds based upon a Proposed Work Plan.
• Agencies submit a Quarterly Report of Expenditures.

End of Fiscal Year

• As of June 30 of each fiscal year, the State Auditor is required to transfer from the state surplus to the Mid-Year Adjustment Reserve an amount equal to 1 percent of the fiscal year's net revenue collection, provided funds for such purpose are available. Such funds may be appropriated and usually are at the next session in the Amended Budget.
• As of June 30 of each fiscal year, the State Auditor is required to transfer from the state surplus to the Revenue Shortfall Reserve an amount equal to not less than 3 percent nor more than 5 percent, as directed by the Director of the Budget, of the fiscal year's net revenue collection, provided funds for such purpose are available after transfer made to Mid-Year Adjustment Reserve. Such funds may not be appropriated, but may be drawn when expenditures exceed revenues collected.
• State Auditor issues on or before December 31, 2004, a Final Report on state agency spending of FY 2004 Appropriated Funds.

### Midyear Appropriation Amendment

One of the more unique features of the Georgia budget process is the midyear amendment.[38] The General Assembly enacts two budget laws each session, a general appropriations act for the fiscal year that will begin on the ensuing July 1, and an amendment to the appropriations act passed in the previous legislative session. The midyear amendment to the general appropriations act internally redirects previously appropriated funds and adjusts the state's spending plan to conditions of revenue shortfall or surplus. A single omnibus appropriations act sets the annual budget. The governor has unlimited authority to transfer appropriations between programs within a department. However, fund transfers between departments, fund transfers between object classes within a department, or increases in the appropriations act total require legislative amendment to the appropriations, accomplished through an omnibus midyear appropriations amendment.[39]

Funding for the midyear appropriation amendment comes from surplus funds. Surplus funds come from revenue collections that exceed revenue estimates and unspent appropriations that lapse back to the state treasury and are available for reappropriation. Lapses are appropriations that were never allotted by the Office of Planning and Budget to agencies for expenditure or that were allotted for expenditure but were unspent at the end of the year.[40]

Two reserves are established at the end of the state fiscal year: the midyear adjustment reserve and the revenue shortfall reserve (see budget cycle example above). The former is in play each year as part of the midyear appropriation amendment. The midyear adjustment reserve provides additional spending for state agencies in the amended appropriation at the next session of the General Assembly. The midyear adjustment reserve was established in 1982 to be the primary fund source for the state Board of Education's midterm adjustment. Georgia continues to experience annual population growth that makes it difficult for the state Board of Education to fully and accurately project local school district enrollment. In a typical year, additional funds are required in midcourse to provide the state's share of the education funding formula.[41]

The midyear adjustment reserve is funded prior to the revenue shortfall reserve. When surplus funds are available at the end of a fiscal year, the midyear adjustment reserve fills up first and overflows into the revenue shortfall reserve, which in turn overflows into the general surplus. The presence of the midyear adjustment reserve ensures fund availability for meeting the state's share of the cost of funding the Quality Basic Education (QBE) program.[42]

Legislators also view the midyear appropriation amendment as an opportunity to fund local projects that do not compete very well with statewide projects when the original appropriation act is being considered and adopted. Local projects funded through the midyear appropriation amendment are also appealing because they tend to be one-time expenditures without recurring costs.[43]

Like legislators, executive branch agencies have come to regard the midyear appropriations amendment as a regular part of the state's budget process. Because annual agency budget requests are submitted approximately 10 months prior to the beginning of the fiscal year and at least 16 months prior to consideration of the midyear amendment by the General Assembly, agency program costs and clientele needs are likely to have changed (often increased) between the date of initial estimate and the time of midyear adjustment. The midyear adjustment is an opportunity for funding adjustments. Further, items not recommended for funding in the original appropriation may be deferred for partial-year funding in the midyear amendment. In addition, some projects may be initiated through partial-year funding in the midyear amendment with full funding to following in the next year's general appropriation act. In short, agency behavior is influenced by the expectation that two appropriations will be enacted in each legislative session.[44] During most recent years, the midyear appropriation amendment increased the state budget even in years of fiscal stress. In 2005, Governor Sonny Perdue instructed state agencies to restrict the midyear appropriation for low estimates of student enrollment and true emergencies, not for legislative pork-barrel projects. It remains to be seen whether or not this instruction will have an impact on longstanding state practices.

## Line-Item Veto

Georgia was the first state to adopt the line-item veto (1865) and has had the longest experience with it of any government in the nation. From 1973 to 2002, Georgia governors exercised the line-item veto 228 times, or an average of approximately seven times each legislative session. Between 1973 and 2002, the line-item veto was more likely to be used by Georgia governors to eliminate objectionable policy provisions from appropriations bills than to remove specific appropriations of money.[45] Georgia governors hold the budget initiative vis-à-vis the legislature and do not need to use the item veto to restrain excessive legislative spending. The governor sets the budget agenda through the review and coordination of executive agency requests, preparation of the *Budget Report*, and preparation of a draft appropriations bill. The General Assembly meets for only 40 legislative days each year and is largely dependent on the budget agenda presented by the governor. The governor's official revenue estimate establishes a constitutionally protected ceiling on the total amount that can be appropriated. Legislative changes to the governor's budget recommendation do not increase the budget total; they occur within the ceiling established by the official revenue estimate. Therefore, gubernatorial item vetoes are about restoring executive spending priorities, not about controlling the size of the state budget. In such an environment, interbranch conflict usually is about a small number of legislative initiatives, which, in order to be accommodated, require slight modifications of the governor's priorities.

Once cast, Georgia line-item vetoes are not overridden. There is, of course, a constitutional provision for overriding vetoes by extraordinary legislative majorities. However, item vetoes always occur after the General Assembly has adjourned its 40-day annual session, and legislative leaders have not been inclined to revisit vetoed items when the body meets again 10 months later. There have been no overrides of line-item vetoes in the state's history.

In the modern era, Georgia governors have used the line-item veto sparingly. When used, it frequently was to eliminate legislative language even though that language did not include specific appropriations of money. Some vetoes eliminated items that had only symbolic importance to the legislature, some eliminated pork-barrel projects that had tangible importance to legislators, and some vetoes enforced gubernatorial policy preferences even though they did not achieve spending reductions. Compared with other states, the line-item veto is not frequently used in Georgia.[46] However, that does not mean it is an ineffective instrument for defending the governor's budget proposals against legislative additions or changes that the governor regards as unnecessary or unwise. The threat of the item veto may be as important as its actual use.

# GEORGIA BUDGET INNOVATIONS: ZBB, "REDIRECTION," RBB, AND PPB

## Zero-Base Budgeting

In 1973, Georgia was the first state in the United States to adopt zero-base budgeting (ZBB) as its official budgeting system.[47] Zero-base budgeting is a management-oriented system for budget development and review. Agencies develop requests at different funding and service levels for each activity or program, and requests are presented in order of decreasing benefit to the agency. It is intended to improve efficiency in allocating available resources. The core techniques are decision packages and a ranking process. Agencies begin the zero-base process by identifying cost-centers (agency subunits or programs) for which it is feasible and appropriate to assign costs for activities or services. Decision packages are prepared for each cost center. They include a statement of goals, a description of the work program by which goals are to be achieved, a statement of benefits expected from activities or services in relationship to costs, an assessment of alternative methods of achieving goals, alternative levels of funding for the decision packages, and a statement of the consequences of not funding a decision package.

Decision packages typically contain at least three funding levels: minimum, below the current level of operations; continuation, maintenance of current operations; and improvement, activities or services not funded in the previous budget. Each decision package is ranked in order of decreasing benefit. Minimum level requests are placed higher than current level requests; and current level requests for most cost centers tend to be ranked ahead of improvement level requests. Each funding level for a decision package may be identified by a priority number for that package, such as 1 of 3, 2 of 3, and 3 of 3 (for a decision package containing three funding levels). Consolidation of rankings usually stops at the department level and is not attempted governmentwide. The Georgia version of ZBB depicted on a summary schedule a cumulative total for each decision package entered into the rank order, expressed as a percentage of the previous year. Before the first decision package is entered into the ranking, the cumulative total is zero, hence the designation—zero-base budgeting. Decision makers are able to observe the consequences of each additional package entered into the ranking. Rankings depict incremental levels of funding effort.

Zero-base budgeting was promoted as a rational decision-making alternative to incrementalism; in practice it was a refined form of incrementalism. Agencies pursued strategies to protect, increase, and expand the base. Managers tended to use the minimum package as an opportunity to argue against reductions in the base, citing negative consequences of operating with only minimal level funding. Managers tended to use the current level package to argue for protection of the base and use improvement level funding requests to argue for increases in program funding. When decision packages are arrayed in rank order, incremental decision-making was facilitated, not discouraged.

It was not realistic to expect from zero-base budgeting major cost savings or even major reallocations within budgets. Budget decisions are the products of political pressures and constraints exerted by actors and events outside of agencies. The ability of zero-base budgeting to achieve cost savings or fund reallocations is constrained by several factors: constitutional or statutory requirements for programs; public expectations that service levels will not be reduced from one year to the next; interest group demands for the funding of new programs and the protection of existing ones; legislative support for programs that benefit the districts and constituencies of individual members; requirements of intergovernmental grant-in-aid programs, especially unfunded mandates; and relatively uncontrollable spending, particularly entitlement programs.

ZBB had a much publicized beginning in Georgia, but on balance was only moderately successful. The formal documents and procedures including decision packages, multiple funding levels, and ranking processes were in place during the 1970s. However, the budgetary process was not able to assimilate the program focus or decision package techniques of ZBB into existing budget practices and procedures. Rational comprehensive techniques failed to penetrate incremental decision strategies at the microlevel and were never perceived as useful at the macroresource allocation level.[48]

### Budget "Redirection"

Budget "Redirection" emerged in Georgia in the late 1990s as an innovation designed to achieve both managerial and policy objectives within a constricted fiscal environment. Lessons learned from previous state experience with ZBB were used to design a reform that was compatible with both the administrative system and the political system.[49]

Budget Redirection is an approach to budgeting that seeks to: (1) fund ongoing agency services and enhancements using the current level of resources; (2) fund formula and entitlement-related services in a way that minimizes the need for additional resources; and (3) increase fund availability for priority areas within state government as a whole.

Agencies are encouraged to identify activities or programs that no longer are necessary or of high priority and eliminate or downsize them. Funds realized through this process become available for redirection to activities or programs that have a high priority for the agency or to other sectors of state government that have a high priority for the governor. Specifically, agencies were required to identify a minimum of 5 percent of their current year's budget that then became the primary means for funding new programs and services in the coming fiscal year. A limit, based upon revenue projections, was set by the Office of Planning and Budget on the amount an agency was permitted to request above the current year's budget. This feature was intended to force agencies to recognize that revenues are limited and the governor's priorities in addition to those of agencies must be accommodated within revenue limitations.

What were the results of "redirection"? In fiscal year 1997, 66 percent of funds made available for redirection stayed in agencies (including funds shifted from lower to higher agency priorities). In fiscal year 1998, 88 percent stayed in agencies. In fiscal year 1999, 88 percent stayed in agencies. The State Board of Education and Board of Regents of the University System of Georgia were winners in the first years of redirection because of the governor's priority to fund teacher salary increases. Even agencies that sustained a net reduction benefited from having greater flexibility to internally redirect funds. They were able to redirect funds away from activities or programs that otherwise might have been politically difficult, and able to redirect funds to activities or programs that otherwise might not have been able to compete successfully outside the agency for new funding.

There were three motivations for "redirection." The first was a managerial objective of strategic planning. The second was the policy priorities of the governor, including increasing teachers' salaries, removing the sales tax from food purchased for at-home consumption, the operating cost of new prisons, obligations to fund the education formula (kindergarten through high school), and obligations of Medicaid entitlements. The third was prevailing fiscal conditions, including revenue loss from the removal of sales tax on food, revenue collections that were increasing at a decreasing rate, federal government deficit reduction plans likely to result in reduced federal funds for state government, and the belief that new taxes or increased tax rates were politically out of the question.

### Results-Based Budgeting

Results Based Budgeting (RBB) was implemented in Georgia in the 1998 fiscal year, as required by the state's Budget Accountability and Planning Act of 1993. RBB requires that a purpose, goal, and desired result be developed for each program. The desired result for each program is to be measured at the completion of each funding period and progress toward achieving the result will be measured. This initiative is designed to relate program results with program expenditures. The 1998 fiscal year was set as the benchmark year for most programs. The governor stated that the focus is not simply on how resources are spent, but on what is accomplished. RBB is a method to achieve accountability for tax dollars, with documentation of whether or not expenditures are achieving their intended results.

The objectives of RBB were to enable the governor and legislature, agency managers, and program customers to identify successful and unsuccessful programs, to aid policymakers in determining if expended funds are worth it in terms of achieving intended results, and to make government more accountable to Georgia citizens.

Some programs had difficulty in identifying measurable program outcomes. Program managers have been encouraged to improve their data collection systems and to identify more valid and reliable measures for program results. Following years of implementation, RBB trend data are expected to enable program managers to identify effective and ineffective program strategies, resulting from poor planning, faulty program design, ineffective management, inadequate resources, missing or inaccurate data, or conditions outside the program's control. Trend data can be used as a "report card" on government performance.

The objective of RBB was to change budget conversations by shifting the focus from inputs to outcomes. However, the General Assembly resisted; they wanted to use what they knew best, that is, inputs and to control the budget by controlling line items. It was easier to obtain executive agency participation than to obtain legislative participation. Initially RBB and Budget Redirection coexisted, but because the governor became more interested in the ability of redirection to generate funds for his program priorities, RBB as a good management approach was of less interest to him. In the absence of either legislative support or strong gubernatorial support, RBB rapidly diminished in importance as either a management or a budget tool in Georgia. This development again illustrates the importance of support from top policymakers if budget innovation techniques are to be successful.

### Prioritized Program Budgeting

Following the election of Georgia's first Republican governor in more than 130 years, Prioritized Program Budgeting (PPB) was introduced in 2004 as the state's new budgeting system. PPB is predicated on each agency having developed a strategic business plan. It emphasizes programs rather than agencies as the primary budgetary units, and requires that measures of demand for the program, program efficiency, program output, and program results be delineated and utilized. According to the Director of the Office of Planning and Budget, if agencies receive lump sum appropriations for programs and greater flexibility in the use of those funds, some mechanism must be put in place to achieve accountability.[50] Performance measures are intended to be mechanisms for accountability assuring citizens that public managers and political decision makers are attempting to provide services efficiently and effectively. Also, agencies are required to propose program budgets at three levels: a 5 percent reduction of the base budget; redistribution of an amount equal to 3 percent of the base budget; and enhancement limited to 2 percent of the base budget. Redistribution is a way to shift existing funds from low priority programs or subprograms to higher priority programs or subprograms. Redistribution seems conceptually indistinguishable from Budget Redirection used in the 1990s, and the requirement that program results be measured is very similar to Results Based Budgeting (RBB) of the 1990s. Nevertheless, a new governor and new administration now seek to promote their own brand of program budgeting.

## CONCLUSION

The governor of Georgia has relatively strong executive budget powers. Yet, the General Assembly is not without significant influence. For more than a century following the end of Reconstruction, Georgia state government was controlled by the Democratic Party. Now, it is controlled by the Republican Party, a pattern that is likely to continue into the foreseeable future. Thus, competition in the budgetary process remains primarily interbranch rather than interparty competition.

Throughout the 1990s, a robust state economy fueled by population increases supported budgetary growth without significant tax increases. In 2002–2003, Georgia experienced the effects of the national recession and is only slowly recovering in 2004–2005. In fiscal matters, Georgia is a conservative state where policymakers favor balanced budgets, low taxes, limited debt, and limited government spending. In the 1990s, the robust economy and a culture of fiscal conservatism enabled the state to achieve a structural balance in its budget even during periods of cyclical imbalance. Several decisions in 2003 and 2004 aimed at closing the gap between expenditures and revenues threatened the structural balance of the state's budget. However, as the state's economy recovers it is quite possible that the culture of fiscal conservatism will restore structural balance in the state's budget.

## NOTES

1. Thanks to Henry M. Huckaby for helping me frame this topic.
2. Constitution of the State of Georgia 1983, art. III, sec. IX, par. IV[b].
3. Constitution of the State of Georgia, 1983, art. VII, sec. IV, par. II[b].
4. The state economist is a contract employee of the Office of Planning and Budget.
5. The recession years of 1991, 1992, 2003, and 2004 are notable exceptions.
6. Thomas P. Lauth, "Budgeting During a Recession Phase of the Business Cycle: The Georgia Experience," *Public Budgeting & Finance*, 23 (Summer 2003), 31.
7. George Hooks, *Biennial Institute for Georgia Legislators*. Athens, GA: University of Georgia, December 1994, 1996, 1998, 2000, and 2002.
8. Prior to that amendment, sitting governors could not seek consecutive terms in office, but former governors were eligible then, as they are now, to run for reelection 4 years after the end of their terms.
9. Secretary of State, Attorney General, State School Superintendent, Commissioner of Insurance, Commissioner of Agriculture, Commissioner of Labor, and five members of the Public Service Commission.
10. Thomas P. Lauth, "Impact of Agency Head Selection on Gubernatorial Influence over State Agency Appropriations," *Public Administration Quarterly*, 7 (Winter 1984), 396–409.

11. Augustus B. Turnbull, III, "Politics in the Budgetary Process: The Case of Georgia," Ph.D. Dissertation, University of Virginia, 1967, chapters II and III.

12. Ibid., 81–118.

13. Ibid., 121–122; and Ronald B. Hoskins, "Within-Year Appropriation Changes in Georgia State Government: The Implications for Budget Theory," DPA Dissertation, University of Georgia, 1983, p. 79.

14. Augustus B. Turnbull, III, "Georgia Budgeting: Development of Executive Budget," *Georgia Government Review*, 1 (Fall 1968).

15. Thomas B. Murphy, *Atlanta Journal Constitution* (December 15, 1985), 1-C.

16. *Atlanta Journal Constitution* (January 11, 1967), 1 and (January 13, 1967), 1.

17. Conversation with Kevin Fillion, Director, Senate Budget Office, June 6, 2005.

18. *Georgia Laws 1967 Session 722–725*; *Official Code of Georgia Annotated*, May 21, 1925.

19. Conversation with Kevin Fillion, Director, Senate Budget Office, June 6, 2005.

20. Aaron Wildavsky, *Budgeting: A Comparative Theory of Budgetary Processes*. New Brunswick, NJ: Transaction, Inc., 1986, p. 240.

21. Percentages are an average over fiscal years 2001–2006.

22. Thomas P. Lauth, "Budgeting during a Recession Phase of the Business Cycle: The Georgia Experience," *Public Budgeting & Finance*, 23 (Summer 2003), 28–29.

23. Ibid.

24. U.S. Census Bureau, *Statistical Abstract of the United States*, Employment Status of Civilian Population; and U.S. Department of Labor, Bureau of Labor Statistics, Employment-Georgia.

25. U.S. Department of Labor, Bureau of Labor Statistics, Local Area Unemployment Statistics.

26. U.S. Department of Commerce, Bureau of Economic Analysis, Regional Accounts Data, Local Area Personal Income.

27. Thomas P. Lauth, "Budgeting during a Recession Phase of the Business Cycle: The Georgia Experience," *Public Budgeting & Finance*, 23 (Summer 2003), 28.

28. Ibid., 27.

29. Ibid., 35.

30. The lottery was part of Zell B. Miller's platform in the 1990 gubernatorial campaign. It was proposed in the 1991 and 1992 Sessions of the General Assembly, voters approved a constitutional amendment in November 1992 to permit the lottery, the Georgia Lottery Corporation was established in 1993, and the lottery proceeds were part of the state budget in the 1994 fiscal year.

31. http://www.galottery.com.

32. Sec. 50-27-1 et seq. O.C.G.A.

33. HOPE is the acronym for Help Outstanding Pupils Educationally.

34. Constitution of the State of Georgia 1983, art. I, sec. II, par. VIII(c).

35. Thomas P. Lauth and Mark D. Robbins, "The Georgia Lottery and State Appropriations for Education: Substitution or Additional Funding," *Public Budgeting & Finance*, 22 (Fall 2002), 89–100.

36. Ibid., 99.

37. Glenn Abney and Thomas P. Lauth, "The Executive Budget in the States: Normative Idea and Empirical Observation," *Policy Studies Journal* 17 (Summer 1989), 829–840.

38. The next several paragraphs draw extensively on Thomas P. Lauth, "The Midyear Appropriation in Georgia; A Threat to Comprehensiveness?" *State and Local Government Review*, 34 (Fall 2002), 198–202.

39. The state constitution provides that in addition to the General Appropriations Act and its amendments, the General Assembly may pass a "supplementary" Appropriation Act to change the appropriation for a particular agency. Relatively few supplementary Appropriations Acts have been passed in recent years, in part because of increased reliance on the "supplemental" appropriation to amend the General Appropriation Act. See, Constitution of the State of Georgia 1983, art. III, sec. IX, par. V.

40. Ibid., 199.

41. Ibid., 200.

42. Ibid.

43. Ibid.

44. Ibid., 201.

45. Thomas P. Lauth and Catherine C. Reese, "The Line-Item Veto in Georgia: Fiscal Restraint or Inter-Branch Politics?" *Public Budgeting & Finance*, 25 (Summer 2006), 1–19.

46. James J. Gosling, "Wisconsin Item-Veto Lessons," *Public Administration Review*, 46 (July/August 1986), 292–300, and Catherine C. Reese, "The Line Item Veto in Practice in Ten Southern States," *Public Administration Review*, 57 (November/December 1997), 510–516.

47. Thomas P. Lauth, "Zero-Base Budgeting in Georgia State Government: Myth and Reality," *Public Administration Review*, 38 (September/October 1978), 420–430.

48. Thomas P. Lauth, "Zero-Base Budgeting in Georgia: Myth and Reality," *Public Administration Review*, 38 (September/October 1978), 420–230, and Thomas P. Lauth and Stephen C. Reick, "Modifications in Georgia Zero-Base Budgeting Procedures: 1973–1980," *Midwest Review of Public Administration*, 13 (December 1979), 225–238.

49. Henry M. Huckaby and Thomas P. Lauth, "Budget Redirection in Georgia," *Public Budgeting & Finance*, 18 (Winter 1998), 36–44.

50. Conversations with Timothy A. Connell, Director, Office of Planning and Budget, June 17, 2004 and May 9, 2005.

# CHAPTER 4

# New York: The Growth, Waning, and Resurgence of Executive Power

*Dall W. Forsythe and Donald J. Boyd*

New York is often criticized in the press and by watchdog groups, rating agencies, and elected officials for its contentious budgets. Over the last 20 years, the budget process has been characterized by frequent gridlock on important budget issues, disagreement over revenue estimates, secretive budget deliberations, and habitual and increasingly late budgets. This chapter examines how the budget process has evolved in New York, and the role that decades of divided government has played in institutionalizing this process.

## THE INSTITUTIONAL FRAMEWORK IN NEW YORK

Within the executive branch, the New York State Division of the Budget (DOB) plays the central role in budgeting in New York. Formally, it is part of the Executive Department of the state government. As a practical matter, DOB is a powerful separate agency that reports directly to the governor's office, with a director who is a cabinet-level gubernatorial appointee requiring no legislative confirmation. From time to time, governors have delegated substantial budget decision-making responsibility to the chief of staff (known in New York as the secretary to the governor), but more frequently the governor is directly engaged with the budget director in budget decision-making.

The budget division, with more than 300 employees, reviews agency budget requests, makes many of the policy decisions embedded in the budget proposed by the governor, and plays a major advisory role in those decisions made directly by the governor.[1] The DOB also plays the lead role in most budget negotiations with the legislature, although the governor's direct program staff and agency staff also play important roles. After the budget is adopted, the budget division monitors and manages it as the year progresses, controlling the release of funds, deciding whether or when positions may be filled, and influencing many important policy decisions.

The budget process is continuous, but the starting point for each upcoming fiscal year is the budget director's "call letter" to state agencies, requesting proposed budgets and establishing guidelines to use in developing these budgets. Guidelines can range from high-level decisions such as whether proposed agency budgets must reduce spending by a given percentage, to detailed instructions on assumptions to make about employee turnover. The call letter usually is issued in August, with agencies required to submit responses by mid-fall. The budget division reviews these requests, consults with agency officials and the governor's direct staff, conducts its own analysis, and makes recommendations to the governor by mid-December about the structure and contents of the executive budget, which ordinarily is released in mid-January. During the same period, the DOB prepares the official revenue estimates included in the executive budget, in consultation with the tax department, other revenue-collecting agencies, and outside economic advisors.

The legislature's role also is continuous, but most activity is concentrated in the months between the release of the executive budget and final budget passage. (A timely budget would be adopted by New York's April 1, fiscal year start, but, as we discuss below, the budget has been adopted as late as August in recent years.) The legislature reviews the executive budget and agency budget requests, conducts public hearings, and does its own analysis to develop its policy and negotiating positions. The legislature may increase or decrease any appropriation, but the governor may veto any increases in funding. The state constitution also requires that any legislative addition to the budget must be contained in a separate item of appropriation, making it vulnerable to the governor's line-item veto power. The state's highest court recently ruled that this constitutional provision protects both the governor's proposed appropriations *and* proposed changes in law relating to the budget from legislative alteration, significantly strengthening the governor's budgetary power. The legislature is not required to accept the governor's revenue estimates, and the majority and minority in each house all prepare their own revenue estimates, which sometimes differ substantially from the governor's. These differences can lead to major budget disagreements. There is no constitutional or statutory requirement for the legislature to adopt a balanced budget, but many other factors impose constraints, including professionalism, financial markets, and the political implications of budget shortfalls. In most years, the governor negotiates the substance of the final budget deal with the legislature, creating an additional constraint on the legislature as it makes budgetary decisions.

## SHIFTING BUDGET POWER

New York State was a latecomer to the executive budget movement, creating its budget office and process in 1927. However, that new budget system, championed by Governor Al Smith, gave New York's chief executives unusually strong budgetary powers. These include a line-item veto and a budget officer reporting directly to the governor with constitutional standing. One New York budget director, Howard Miller, commented on this system in a volume celebrating the fiftieth anniversary of the creation of the executive budget:

The term "strong governor" has special application to New York State. During the middle fifty years of the twentieth century New Yorkers elected Governors such as Franklin Delano Roosevelt, Herbert H. Lehman, Thomas E. Dewey, Averell Harriman, Nelson A. Rockefeller and Hugh L. Carey—all of national prominence. They attained prominence because of their intellects and leadership, because opportunity presented itself to them in the form of important problems to be solved, and because, as Governors, they had strong executive powers and thus were in a unique position to get things done.[2]

Seventeen years later, Peter Goldmark, another former budget director, chaired a gubernatorial panel on constitutional change. Goldmark pointed out that "there has been an ongoing, deep concern in New York about our budget process and about the borrowing and financing practices of the state."[3] The in-house historian of the Budget Division expanded on these issues:

Considerable attention has been given in recent years to changing the state constitutional provisions concerning budgeting and finance ... The causes for this are numerous: the legacy of the mid-1970s fiscal crises; the difficulties recently encountered by the legislature and governor in producing a timely budget.[4]

What changed in the intervening years to undermine the "strong governor" and destabilize the budget process? What are the choices and forces that contributed to the "recurrent stalemates"[5] that are the most visible manifestations of what is now widely seen as a dysfunctional budget process?

In Washington, a brutal battle between Richard Nixon and Congress over budget powers resulted in the passage of the Congressional Budget and Impoundment Control Act in 1974. This landmark statute shifted power from the executive to Congress. That action in Washington served as a backdrop to the decline of executive power in New York and in other states. Legislatures around the country emulated Congress by building up professional staff expertise and extending the length of their working sessions. In the last four decades, gubernatorial power over the budget in the typical state declined considerably, while legislative capacity increased.[6] New York's legislature participated in this trend. The state Senate and Assembly both built up professional staff and expertise, more than tripling the inflation-adjusted legislative budget between 1970 and 1990, and strengthening the legislative leaders' ability to weigh-in on budget debates.[7]

Because New York is a large state and a national media center, its elected officials do look to Washington, sometimes for guidance about organizational and policy issues, and sometimes for bigger and better jobs. What may in fact be most surprising about New York is that the power shift from the executive to the legislature came later than in other states and has been informal, not accompanied by constitutional or even significant statutory change. The executive budget system in New York frayed and then unraveled, but has not been replaced with a redesigned budget process.

## THE POLITICAL BACKDROP FOR BUDGETING IN NEW YORK

Nelson Rockefeller, a Republican from Westchester, served as governor of New York from 1959 to 1973, when he resigned to become Vice President of the United States. His lieutenant governor, Malcolm Wilson, served out the remainder of Rockefeller's term, but lost his bid for reelection in 1974. Republicans controlled both houses of the state legislature from 1959 to 1964, and from 1969 to 1974. Rockefeller was a strong governor, using his political skills, his popularity, and his great personal fortune as resources in dealing with the legislature even when Republicans did not control both houses.

Since 1975, Republicans have held the majority in the State Senate, and Democrats have been in control of the Assembly. Democrats held the governor's office for 20 years, with Hugh Carey serving from 1975 to 1982, and Mario Cuomo holding office from 1983 to 1994. Since 1995, Republican George Pataki has been governor. In short, divided government has been a fact of political life in New York for more than a quarter of a century. The last year when a single party held all three leadership posts was in 1974.

One important variable determining state budget outcomes is the degree of cooperation possible between governors and legislative leaders.[8] While partisan control of both the executive and the legislature does not guarantee cooperation, divided government creates opportunities and incentives for legislative resistance to gubernatorial initiatives. Robert Kurtter, vice president for state ratings at Moody's Investors Service has made a similar point:

In most states, you'll see divided control when a dominant party temporarily loses one house, or because there's a gradual transition from one party dominating to another. Only in New York is this a permanent condition. That has allowed them to become more and more entrenched in their positions.[9]

Not only is power divided in Albany, but within each house the majority's power is also nearly absolute. The majority party in each house is at little risk of losing the majority. The leaders also exercise almost complete control over the votes of their own legislators, by careful allocation of committee assignments, chairmanships, additional stipends for legislators, staffing, and other instruments and symbols of power.[10] As a result, the leader in each house can establish a position for that house, and defy the governor and the other house.

Political incentives also make cooperation difficult. The high national profile of New York governors encourages national party leaders to seek assistance from state legislative leaders to "rough up" governors of opposing parties, especially as presidential elections approach. New York, then, may be imitating Washington, where partisan conflict has spread from electoral arenas into institutional conflict.[11] The budget process creates a highly visible arena for such conflict.

While they are anxious to elect Republican presidents, New York Republicans otherwise do not always sound like national Republicans. Rockefeller was a free-spending governor. In a retrospective look at his tenure in office, aides commented that "Nelson was never one for technicalities," and "sometimes he never stopped to think where we were going to get the money."[12] New York got the money from higher taxes and new mechanisms for borrowing. The result was an extraordinary capital building program and reduced bond ratings. Many of his supporters spoke up in support for the tradeoff, including one who made the case with unusual candor:

We don't have a "triple A" rating, but what we do have is the heritage of Nelson Rockefeller, an incredible set of facilities and services that were meant to meet genuine public needs and have done so in a remarkable fashion. It doesn't come cheap—God knows—with all the taxes. But you don't get something for nothing. And I've seen too many states in this country where nothing is being given and they have a "triple A" rating. I'd rather have what Nelson Rockefeller left behind.[13]

From the Rockefeller years to the present, the Republican majority in the Senate also has a taste for spending and borrowing, and a tolerance for low credit ratings. These predilections have made it easier for the Senate Republicans to create alliances with the Democrats in the Assembly. The power of these alliances was especially evident during the adoptions of budgets between 1989 and 1991, when Ralph Marino served as Senate Majority leader and Mel Miller was Speaker of the Assembly.

In many crises, executives are temporarily strengthened in their relations with the legislature,[14] and that is another factor influencing budgetary power. New York City's mid-1970s fiscal collapse followed this pattern. Hugh Carey, who was governor during the fiscal crisis, played a highly visible role as crisis manager and was hailed as the savior of the City. Because of this power shift, the fiscal crisis probably helped to postpone the decline in executive power described in this chapter. Under threat of default by New York City in 1975, Governor Carey got grudging consent from the Republican majority in the Senate for most of his fiscal initiatives. When the fiscal crisis was resolved, however, cooperation between Carey and Warren Anderson, the Senate Majority leader, broke down. During Carey's last 2 years in office, budgets were not adopted by the beginning of the fiscal year on April 1, and the legislature overrode Carey's vetoes in 1982.

## LATE BUDGETS IN NEW YORK

The two late budgets under Governor Carey were the first hints that New York might follow the federal government's lead and develop a chronic disregard for budget adoption deadlines.

Governor Cuomo's first two budgets were adopted shortly before the April 1 start of the fiscal year, but between then and 2004, New York's budget has been late for 20 consecutive years. Most states do not even contemplate late budgets. In those jurisdictions, state officials take seriously the idea that the state government would have to shut down some or all of its services, if no budget is in place.[15] Some states have late budgets from time to time, especially California, Massachusetts, North Carolina, and Wisconsin, particularly in periods of fiscal stress. At least six states were late in 2003 as they grappled with unusually large budget gaps. Usually late states return to on time budgets afterward. Only California competes with New York in the frequency of late budgets. California has missed its deadline in 21 of the last 25 years,[16] but usually its budget is late for relatively short periods of time. New York, in contrast, has often operated without a budget for months into the fiscal year, as Table 4.1 shows.

New York is the only state in the nation with a fiscal year commencing on April 1. Two states begin their fiscal year on October 1, mirroring the federal fiscal year, and one starts on September 1.[17] The other forty-six states begin their fiscal year on July 1.

This unique budget calendar creates several problems for New York:

- First, legislators complain, with some justification, that they have less time than other states to review the budget that the governor submits in mid-January.
- Second, an April 1 deadline for budget passage means that the governor and the legislature must act before receiving complete information about mid-April payments on the personal income tax (PIT), which makes up more than half of New York's general fund receipts. As legislative staff grew, revenue forecasters on the finance committee staffs grew more sophisticated, and by the mid-1980s both houses were employing their own econometricians as well as outside econometric firms to help them provide credible tax forecasts. When their PIT forecasts were higher than the Division of the Budget, legislative staff and leaders agreed that it made sense to wait a few weeks for data about final returns. (Interestingly, an important rationale for New York's 1943 move to an April 1 fiscal year from a July 1 start was that it would put PIT uncertainty at the start of a fiscal year rather than the end, allowing more time to respond.)[18]

**Table 4.1**
**When Did the Budget Pass?**

| Year of Passage | Date of Passage | Days Late |
|---|---|---|
| 1975 | April 1 | 0 |
| 1976 | March 30 | −2 |
| 1977 | April 12 | 11 |
| 1978 | April 14 | 13 |
| 1979 | April 9 | 8 |
| 1980 | March 31 | −1 |
| 1981 | May 12 | 41 |
| 1982 | May 4 | 33 |
| 1983 | March 28 | −4 |
| 1984 | March 31 | −1 |
| 1985 | April 5 | 4 |
| 1986 | April 5 | 4 |
| 1987 | April 11 | 10 |
| 1988 | April 20 | 19 |
| 1989 | April 19 | 18 |
| 1990 | May 19 | 48 |
| 1991 | June 4 | 64 |
| 1992 | April 2 | 1 |
| 1993 | April 5 | 4 |
| 1994 | June 8 | 68 |
| 1995 | June 7 | 67 |
| 1996 | July 13 | 103 |
| 1997 | August 4 | 125 |
| 1998 | April 14 | 13 |
| 1999 | August 4 | 125 |
| 2000 | May 5 | 34 |
| 2001 | August 3 | 124 |
| 2002 | May 16 | 45 |
| 2003 | May 15 | 44 |

*Sources: Associated Press*, NYS Division of the Budget.

- Third, the legislature is typically in session until the middle or end of June, and the leaders find it difficult to complete their most important business—passage of the budget—before reaching agreement on other key legislative agenda items. While members might be reluctant to stay in session beyond the end of June, they can delay budget passage until then without affecting their personal or political schedules.

While New York's unique fiscal year may play a role in late budgets, clearly there is more to it than that—after all, a July 1 fiscal year does not prevent California's chronically late budgets.

Late passage can serve other legislative ends. As suggested earlier, leaders of the party that does not hold the governor's office look for opportunities to make the governor look weak or ineffective. Failure to achieve timely passage of the budget is a highly visible sign that leadership in Albany has failed. Since most New Yorkers cannot identify the legislative leaders, the governor, who is much more visible, ends up with most of the blame. This scenario is especially attractive to party leaders as presidential elections approach.

Finally, a legislative leader can use delay to prove to his members and constituents that he has worked as hard as possible to achieve their goals. Indeed, after years of delay, timely passage might look like a cave in to the governor and the leader of the other house. This can be especially important for the leader of the party that does not hold the governor's office. In New York's landscape of divided government, that leader is the weakest of the three, and needs to prove his independence and resolve.

Delayed passage can have political impact. In late 1991, for example, Mario Cuomo tried to reach early agreement on the budget to clear the way for a run for national office, and failure to do so may have contributed to his decision not to run. However, late passage has not affected the functioning of government itself in significant ways. Technicians in the Division of the Budget and the fiscal committees of the legislature developed procedures that minimized the substantive impact on state government. Every 2 weeks, the governor proposed and the legislature agreed to emergency appropriations, so paychecks for prison guards, mental health attendants, state police, and less-critical workers were not interrupted. More recently, the duration of emergency appropriations has lengthened, giving elected officials even more freedom. In some early years emergency appropriations were set at the prior year's level even if workload and prices had increased, meaning that savings would accrue while the budget was unpassed (a consolation to DOB and a fiscally conservative governor). In most later years emergency appropriations were high enough to fund continuing services without cuts.

Whatever the political impact, late passage does create problems in the real world. Nonprofit organizations providing services under state contracts (such as care for the disabled, day care, and job training) cannot be paid without an appropriation from the state. Absent a budget, they typically take the risk of paying rent, providing services, and operating as if they will be paid eventually. This does create cash flow problems, but most of them have arranged lines of credit or other mechanisms to keep operations funded until the budget passes.

The state's 700-plus school districts depend on the budget for more than $14 billion in aid. If there is no state budget when they levy taxes in August or September, they do not know how much aid they will receive. Without information about that key revenue source, the school districts cannot accurately determine the amount of taxes they will need to levy. In short, logistical difficulties, consternation, and dysfunction result.

Even the legislature has trouble functioning, and usually cannot deal with nonfinancial policy issues, which are held hostage to budget passage. Finally, the most important stakeholders of state government—citizens and voters— grow cynical and lose faith in their government's ability to do its job. Most of these costs are hard to track and measure, but they are real and widespread, even if not headline-grabbing.

## BUDGET DELAY AND THE SPRING BORROWING

Before 1991, delays did not extend beyond mid-June because the state did not have cash for aid payments to local governments and school districts and needed to borrow in the capital markets to fund those payments. But without an enacted budget, investors would not buy state notes, and what came to be known as the Spring Borrowing could not proceed.

For years, the state had used the overlap between the state fiscal year, which began on April 1, and the fiscal year used by schools and many localities, which ended on June 30. During that quarter, which came to be known as the "magic window," the state was able to accelerate aid from its upcoming fiscal year for schools and local governments. Those front-loaded aid payments created huge cash needs in the state's first quarter, far beyond what could be funded with tax receipts. The state had also accelerated sales tax collections from their normal payment dates in early April to late March, to increase cash for budgeted needs. This "spin-up" of tax collections further exacerbated cash flow in the first quarter of the state fiscal year. So the state went to the capital markets to sell revenue and tax anticipation notes every spring in what became the largest regular state and local government borrowing in the nation. The proceeds of the Spring Borrowing were used to fund these payments to school districts and local governments. The state opened the magic window wider and wider during the 1980s, and the Spring Borrowing eventually reached a peak of $4.3 billion.

In anticipation of state aid payments in their final quarter, some school districts and localities—including New York City—issued billions of dollars of their own cash flow notes, which typically matured in June. If state aid payments were delayed, those school districts and local governments would default on their cash flow borrowings, or would be forced to issue deficit notes under conditions of confusion and uncertainty. Thus, budget delay apparently had a natural limit so long as the state needed to access the capital markets in June.

## BACK ON TRACK AGAIN?

The early signs of damage to the system at the end of the Carey years were followed by a period when the budget system seemed to be working successfully again. After New York's relatively mild recession in 1981, the economy rebounded and revenue growth was sufficient to pay the new obligations incurred by the state to bail out New York City. Specifically, the state picked up the costs of the court system and the City University, and sweetened the state-local formula for Medicaid cost sharing.

For the first 2 years of the Cuomo administration, budgets passed on time. Insiders joked that Cuomo, who had a reputation as a capable negotiator, had resorted to "pre-emptive capitulation," giving the legislative leaders everything they wanted to achieve timely passage. However, the increase in the general fund from executive to adopted budget was relatively modest during those years, averaging less than 1 percent. (In contrast, during much of the 1990s the adopted budget was 2 to 4 percent higher than the proposed budget.) Partly as a result, budget negotiations with Senate Majority Leader Warren Anderson and Assembly Speaker Stanley Fink seemed orderly. Indeed, some important fiscal improvements were legislated, most notably the introduction of Generally Accepted Accounting Principles (or GAAP) in 1981 as the state's standard for financial statements. GAAP was also a required supplementary presentation for budgets, and steps were taken to close the "magic window" and avoid further growth of the Spring Borrowing. However, the cash-basis budget continued as the focus of decision-making in the executive and legislative branches, as it is today.

In 1985, the legislature once again began to miss budget deadlines. However, the delays were relatively modest, and budget harmony seemed to survive until 1987, swept along by a strong economy. As Cuomo said frequently, that period was a politician's paradise, when it was possible to spend more, cut taxes, and balance the budget all at the same time. Standard and Poor's agreed and upgraded the state credit rating to AA in 1987.

Earlier that year, the Democrats in the Assembly, led by Mel Miller, a new speaker, joined with the Senate Republicans to pass a large, multiyear cut in the personal income tax. Cuomo complained about the fiscal impact, but did not veto the tax bill. Indeed, Cuomo rarely used his veto powers on legislative changes to the budget. As Hugh Carey's lieutenant governor, Cuomo had watched with dismay as the legislature overrode Carey's vetoes in 1982. He believed that this emboldened the legislature and weakened the governor, and vowed to avoid an override in the future. He also was keenly aware of the constituencies supporting each legislative "add," and wanted to avoid antagonizing those interest groups. Although Cuomo always reserved his right to veto during budget negotiations, legislative leaders were more and more certain that he would not use that power and planned accordingly during their negotiations.

While the budget system seemed to be functioning well on the surface, close observers could detect more subtle signs of stress. One indication of instability in the budget system was increasing turnover in the leadership of DOB. Dr. T. Norman Hurd had served as budget director under Governor Dewey from 1950 to 1954, and again under Rockefeller from 1959 to 1970, until becoming Rockefeller's director of operations. After Hurd, tenure in that critical office became much shorter. Cuomo tried to compensate by selecting directors who had previously served as first deputies in DOB, a practice eventually abandoned by Governor Pataki, who went outside the state for a budget director for the first time since Carey recruited Peter Goldmark from Massachusetts state government. While this may have reflected the natural inclination when the party of the governor changes, nonetheless it contributed to continued turnover in this key position.

In contrast, current top legislative fiscal staff have had long experience working for their houses on the state budget. Dean Fuleihan, the top fiscal staffer in the state Assembly in 2004, has worked in one capacity or another on the budget for the Assembly for approximately 25 years. His Senate counterpart, Mary Louise Mallick, has worked on the state budget for the Senate for approximately 20 years.

## THE BUDGET SYSTEM UNRAVELS

Mel Miller, a Democrat from Brooklyn, became Speaker of the Assembly in 1988. Ralph Marino, a Long Island Republican, succeeded Warren Anderson as Senate Majority Leader in 1989. Miller and Marino had worked closely together on criminal justice legislation as chairs of the Codes Committees in each house. Marino had also hired as staff to his committee an investigator who had tried to dig up dirt about Cuomo's family, so there was personal animus between the governor and the new Majority Leader. Miller's temporary alliance with Anderson to pass a cut in the personal income tax extended into a 3-year alliance between Miller and Marino.

In the spring of 1988, the "politician's paradise" turned into a budget hell. After the federal tax reform, New York was one of several states that missed its PIT estimates by large amounts. By mid-May, only 6 weeks after the passage of the budget, actual receipts were $900 million short of estimates, or about 3 percent lower than expected.

Worse news was soon to follow. After the stock market crash in the fall of 1987, New York's economy began to cool off. By 1988, New York was joining its neighbors in the northeast at the forward edge of what would become the national recession of 1990–1991. Fiscal year 1988–1989 ended with a shortfall of $2 billion, about 6 percent of the general fund budget.

To fill what New York officials hoped was a largely transitory budget gap, the Budget Division refinanced debt, undertook sales and leasebacks of state assets, and searched out other nonrecurring actions, called "gimmicks" by the state comptroller and fiscal watchdogs like the Citizens Budget Commission.

By 1989, as the economy slowed, it became clearer that the impact on the budget would be serious and protracted. Cuomo decided to send up a budget that maintained the scheduled tax cut, but used budget cuts and other tax increases to close the budget gap, together with a new helping of one-timers. The credit rating agencies began to express concern, and Standard and Poor's dropped the state's rating two notches in spring of 1989. By 1990, budget delays were extending into May. Both the budget-making process internal to the executive branch and the legislative adoption process were struggling through repeated budget adjustments, and principals and staff alike were showing signs of stress.

In 1989, the governor and the legislature pushed hard to reduce the costs of annual contributions to the state's pension system. In response to that pressure, the state comptroller, who serves as the sole trustee of the pension system, increased the earnings assumption, a step that reduced the required contribution from the state and from local participants in the system. By agreeing to this action, the comptroller hoped to ward off more far-reaching raids. The next year, however, the legislature proposed and the governor agreed to change the actuarial underpinnings of the system. This statute reduced state and local contributions to zero, as the plan sponsors enjoyed the multiyear amortization of the surplus that appeared under the new actuarial system.

At the same time, the governor was battling with the chief judge of the Court of Appeals over the costs of the state court systems. As confused onlookers wondered where this dispute could be settled (in the Vermont courts, perhaps?), the news media watched the unusual spectacle of a verbal brawl between the chief executive and the chief judge. When the state comptroller sued to overturn the change in the pension system, the judges may have felt more sympathy than usual. In any event, the court held against the executive and legislature, and the state began to pay back those savings in 1993.

In 1991, Governor Cuomo also dusted off his veto pen. As budget passage dragged on into early June, fiscal staffs began to worry about getting the Spring Borrowing done in time to repay notes issued by schools and localities. In the absence of a negotiated agreement on the financial plan, the legislature passed a budget nearly a billion dollars larger than the governor thought wise. Cuomo vetoed more than $900 million in added spending, the Spring Borrowing took place, and the governor and the legislative leaders immediately began negotiating changes in the budget. More than $700 million was restored in a supplemental budget, which did not pass until July 4. The Spring Borrowing deadline had forced the passage of a formal budget, but no longer marked the end of budget negotiations.

Meanwhile, a 1990 fiscal reform allowed the state to replace the Spring Borrowing notes with long-term bonds over 3 years. By 1995, the Spring Borrowing was no more, replaced by nearly $5 billion in bonds issued by a public authority created for this purpose called the Local Government Assistance Corporation (LGAC). Whatever pressure the Spring Borrowing lent to budget passage was gone as well. In the 10 years since the borrowing was eliminated, the budget has been late by more than 30 days nine times, including four times by more than 100 days.

As the budget was completed in 1991, Speaker Miller left office and was replaced by Saul Weprin, a Democrat from Cuomo's home borough of Queens. With a gubernatorial ally in the legislative leadership, budgets were passed in the first week of April in 1992 and 1993. Then Weprin died. Sheldon Silver, a Democrat from the Lower East Side, replaced him and the battle was rejoined.

As the economy improved, so did fiscal performance, but budget passage dates slipped back into June. The legislature, which had developed the technical capability in each house to develop a full-fledged revenue estimate, now passed a new statute designed to force itself to reach agreement on a joint revenue estimate. The process was simply ignored.

In 1993, the state's highest court addressed the first of several cases raising constitutional questions about the legislature and the governor's power to include programmatic language in budget bills. These debates, while technical, affect the balance of budgetary and policymaking power between the governor and the legislature. In this case, in a blow to the legislature, the court held that lawmakers could change numbers in the governor's bills, but not the language.[19]

## PATAKI'S BUDGETS, 1995–2003

George Pataki was elected in 1994 and took office in January 1995, determined to fulfill his pledge to fix the budget process. As he took office, he helped Joseph Bruno, a senator from Rensselaer County, overthrow Ralph Marino. He also appointed a hard-nosed and fiscally conservative budget officer named Patricia Woodworth. She had served as a budget director of the states of Florida and Michigan, but had no experience in New York.

Pataki threatened to withhold his consent for emergency appropriations that allow the state to operate if no budget is in place at the start of the fiscal year, but withdrew the threat in the face of legislative pressure. Eventually, he did succeed in having legislation adopted to withhold the pay of legislators while the budget is late, a step that did little to improve the sense of comity between the executive and the legislature. He also succeeded in reducing emergency appropriations below the continuation level, in the hope that modest budget cuts would build pressure for early passage. Pataki did get much of his substantive legislative agenda passed, including some large tax cuts. His initial budgets cut the rate of increase in nominal state spending significantly below the levels of growth in Cuomo's budgets, and actually decreased general fund spending in inflation-adjusted dollars as Table 4.2 shows. However, budget delays grew, stretching from June 7 in 1995 to July 13 in 1996, and August 4 in 1997. The budget adoption process was now overlapping with the racing season in Saratoga, a late-summer tradition in Albany.

In response to this unprecedented delay, both branches of government began to experiment with changes in the budgeting system. In 1998, the legislature did reach quick agreement on revenue estimates. The two houses also

Table 4.2
General Fund Spending and Growth (in
Millions of 2002 Dollars)

| | | |
|---|---|---|
| Cuomo Budgets | | |
| 1983–1984 | 32,889 | 2.6% |
| 1984–1985 | 35,280 | 7.3% |
| 1985–1986 | 37,044 | 5.0% |
| 1986–1987 | 38,985 | 5.2% |
| 1987–1988 | 40,640 | 4.2% |
| 1988–1989 | 41,277 | 1.6% |
| 1989–1990 | 41,260 | 0.0% |
| 1990–1991 | 39,018 | −5.4% |
| 1991–1992 | 39,163 | 0.4% |
| 1992–1993 | 39,725 | 1.4% |
| 1993–1994 | 40,075 | 0.9% |
| 1994–1995 | 40,881 | 2.0% |
| | | |
| Pataki Budgets | | |
| 1995–1996 | 38,883 | −4.9% |
| 1996–1997 | 38,269 | −1.6% |
| 1997–1998 | 39,087 | 2.1% |
| 1998–1999 | 40,767 | 4.3% |
| 1999–2000 | 40,287 | −1.2% |
| 2000–2001 | 41,244 | 2.4% |
| 2001–2002 | 41,695 | 1.1% |
| 2002–2003 | 37,613 | −9.8% |

*Sources:* New York State Division of the Budget, U.S.
Bureau of Economic Analysis.

convened conference committees to settle disputes between the Senate and
Assembly without the governor's participation, and succeeded in passing a
budget in mid-April with spending totaling about $2 billion more than the
governor's recommendations. Pataki shocked the legislative leaders by vetoing 1,300 items of spending, amounting to $1.9 billion in total. The governor
vetoed not only spending amounts, but also over seventy pages of programmatic language inserted by the legislature, triggering a new lawsuit over budgetary language by the speaker of the Assembly, which was resolved 6 years
later.[20] The governor avoided an override by targeting his vetoes to hit Democratic spending items harder than Republican items.[21] This strategy persuaded
Majority Leader Bruno not to join Speaker Silver in overrides and returned
substantial power over the budget process to the governor for 1 year.

In 1999, Speaker Silver refused to pass a budget without an agreement
from Pataki not to use his veto, and budget passage was again delayed until
August 4. Meanwhile, the governor initially refused to negotiate but ultimately

relented.[22] The long delay dampened but did not extinguish Pataki's hopes of getting a place on the Republican national ticket in 2000. In the fall of 1999, budget leaders also began to exchange press releases with proposals to reform the budget process, but no action was taken.The budget passed in 2000 with relatively little animosity in early May, only 34 days late.

The budget debate in 2001 was again contentious. After presenting his executive budget, Governor Pataki refused to join negotiations, arguing that it was the legislature's responsibility to pass a budget. Meanwhile, in a break with past practice, the governor included far more extensive legislative language in the appropriation bills than had been included before. For example, the bill appropriating more than $8 billion in aid to public schools included seventeen pages of language that determined by formula how much aid would go to each school district. This action, if constitutional, would protect substantive law and policy as well as gubernatorial appropriations from legislative alteration, drastically reducing the legislature's power over the budget. The legislature argued that this sort of policymaking did not belong in appropriation bills, and this disagreement contributed to the contentious nature of the budget. Finally, in August the legislature passed what it called a bare bones budget, cutting many of the governor's favorite spending items.[23] The legislature also deleted the governor's proposed language in appropriation bills and introduced and passed thirty-seven separate bills implementing budget-related policies. Most parties presumed at the time that the bare bones budget was a ploy designed to drive the governor to the negotiating table, which would in turn lead to further budget negotiations and restoration of spending that both the governor and legislature would find attractive. However, the September 11 terrorist attacks intervened, strengthening the governor and instilling fears related to the economic and financial fallout of the attacks. On September 13, the legislature passed some modest amendments to the budget and the debate ended for the year.[24] The governor signed the thirty-seven separate bills, but contended they were unconstitutional and filed litigation against the Senate and Assembly.

The budget debate for the 2002–2003 fiscal year took place at the beginning of a period of sharp and protracted fiscal crisis in New York. The national economy entered a recession in March 2001, budget officials were wrestling with the economic fallout of the September 11 attacks, and forecasters were braced for a sharp decline in income tax collections when tax returns for 2001 were filed in April 2002. The Governor and legislators had to run for reelection in November, creating a difficult environment in which to cut the budget. Governor Pataki's executive budget closed a projected a fiscal gap of $6.8 billion, but miraculously involved relatively little true cutting. On an "all funds" basis, the proposed budget actually increased by $4 billion from 2001–2002. Nonetheless, the legislature added money to the all-funds budget, especially for school aid, and the governor signed the bills when they arrived on his desk in mid-May.

Mid-May 2002 was also the time when states around the country learned that the stock market decline was finally catching up to their budgets, causing a precipitous decline in payments with tax returns for 2001, due in April. Although a budget had been passed, New York was hit especially hard by this decline in tax receipts, and concerns arose that the budget would be out of balance. In September, the Republican Senate majority leader opined that the state's finances were deteriorating and it would face a $10 billion budget gap in 2003–2004, but the governor dismissed this.[25] In fact, the situation was worse than Senator Bruno's estimate. When the governor submitted his 2003–2004 budget in January, it closed a projected $12 billion gap.

The 2003–2004 budget debate, while once again contentious, was remarkable for its differences from other debates. Although the state faced a budget gap of nearly unprecedented size, for the first time in memory there was no disagreement over revenue estimates. The disagreement was over policy. The governor sent up a budget with large cuts in school aid and health programs, and moderate tax and fee increases, and refused to assent to additional increases in "job killing taxes." Most observers thought that meant that he was opposed to increases in the personal income tax, and many speculated that he was playing to a national audience.

The legislature did not want the spending cuts and local tax increases that they thought would be required by a "no job-killing taxes" policy. As a result, Senate Republicans and Assembly Democrats teamed up to pass a budget that restored most of the governor's school aid and health cuts and increased the state sales tax and the income tax on high-income taxpayers. As he had threatened, the governor vetoed 119 spending items totaling at least $1.3 billion. In a resounding demonstration of the gap between the governor and the legislature, two-thirds of the legislators in each house promptly voted 119 times to override each and every one of Governor Pataki's vetoes. This was the first time the legislature had overridden a governor's budget veto since Carey's budget of 1982. The legislature handed the governor a major defeat and reasserted their power, at least for the moment, over the budget process.[26]

## THE RESURGENCE OF GUBERNATORIAL POWER

In December 2004, New York's highest court, the Court of Appeals, acted decisively to interpret the balance of budgetary power between the governor and the legislature. In a 5–2 decision (the chief judge dissenting),[27] the court dived into the messy controversy between the executive and legislative branches, and the decision dramatically reaffirmed the governor's constitutional power. At issue were provisions in the constitution that stated:

The legislature may not alter an appropriation bill submitted by the governor except to strike out or reduce items therein . . . separate items added to the governor's bills by the legislature shall be subject to [the governor's line-item veto].

And

No provision shall be embraced in any appropriation bill submitted by the governor ... unless it relates specifically to some specific appropriation in the bill, and any such provision shall be limited in its operation to such appropriation.

Wrapped in this arcane language are issues at the heart of budgetary power. The first provision limits the right of the legislature to amend language in the governor's appropriation bills directing how money will be spent, as it attempted in 1998. The second provision addresses whether the governor has the power to use appropriation bills to propose significant policy changes in a manner that shields these proposals from legislative amendment, effectively giving the legislature a take-it-or-leave-it choice.

The court ruled resoundingly, albeit not unanimously, in favor of gubernatorial power. On the first question, it said, "If the Legislature disagrees with the Governor's spending proposals, it is free ... to reduce or eliminate them; it is also free to refuse to act on the Governor's proposed legislation at all, thus forcing him to negotiate. But it cannot adopt a budget that substitutes its spending proposals for the Governor's." On the second it ruled that the governor's substantive proposals in 2001 relating to school aid, Medicaid, and agency organization all were budgetary in nature and could be included in appropriation bills, preventing the legislature from amending them. In his opinion, Judge Smith pointed to the original intent of the executive budget process in New York, as stated by Henry Stimson, a key player in New York's 1915 Constitutional Convention:

... when the Governor introduces his budget that budget must be disposed of without addition. The Legislature can cut down, the Legislature can strike out but they must approach it from the standpoint of a critic and not from the standpoint of a rival constructor. The budget must be protected against its being wholly superseded by a new legislative budget ...

The court noted that the legislature does have some power to change the governor's budget: It can reduce or delete the governor's appropriations. While it cannot change appropriations or substitute its own for the governor's, it can enact new ones, subject to the governor's line-item veto. It can override vetoes. Finally, as the *New York Law Journal* put it, the ruling "left the Legislature with only one trump card in its budget dealings with the executive, the power to do nothing and create chaos."[28]

Legislative leaders were frustrated by the decision. Republican Senate Majority Leader Joe Bruno said, "The judges essentially ruled that 212 legislators can either rubber stamp an executive budget or take no action and attempt to force a governor to negotiate a budget once it is late ..." Democratic Assembly Speaker Sheldon Silver said the decision appeared "to have reduced New York's budget process to a one-sided charade."[29]

One month later, Governor Pataki submitted his 2005–2006 executive budget, taking advantage of the power that the court affirmed governors have. For example, his appropriation for tuition assistance to college students proposed holding back half of a student's assistance, to be distributed only if the student graduates within 4 years. Other appropriation language would have cut Medicaid benefits for some poor people.[30]

Many knowledgeable observers predicted that the combination of the shift in power to the governor and the governor's use of that power would lead to the latest budget in state history, or to no budget at all.[31] However, many press reports also highlighted public concerns about the budget process, stating that the voters were fed up with late budgets and disillusioned with Albany's closely held budget process. As evidence, press reports pointed to the loss of three Republican seats in the Senate and the reelection of a fourth long-time incumbent by a margin of only eighteen votes. Another wild card was a report from the Brennan Center for Justice at New York University Law School that rated New York's legislature as the most dysfunctional in the nation. Whatever the cause, budget players adopted the appearance of more open debate, holding several public "leaders' meetings" and conference committee meetings to negotiate the budget.[32]

Confounding predictions, the legislature and the governor passed an on time budget—or nearly so—for the first time in more than two decades. The process was smoothed by increases in revenue estimates during the course of budget debates. The governor agreed to resubmit several budget proposals with language reworked to an agreed-upon liking. Where the parties could not agree, they agreed to leave about $1.5 billion in health care, welfare, and environmental spending out of the budget, to be negotiated later—a nuance that did not prevent legislative claims of a timely budget, although the governor noted that the budget as adopted was not "final."[33]

Twelve days after the budget deadline, the legislature and the governor reopened the budget to put finishing touches on it and resolve issues that had not quite been closed. According to one report, "Tuesday's deal was a reversion to form: it was struck after private deliberations, and lawmakers had to wait into the night for bills to be printed so they could vote. Even as they prepared for the votes, the state's leaders were hazy about how much money the revised plan called for spending . . ." Legislators said the last-minute private deal making was necessary to hammer out final details and stave off potential gubernatorial vetoes.[34]

## BUDGET REFORM

Major players in the budget process and observers of the process have proposed many reforms in recent years, including:

- Changing the fiscal year, but with a wide range of possible new dates, including May 1, June 1, and July 1.

- Earlier submission of the governor's executive budget (e.g., by December 15 rather than mid-January).
- Consensus forecasting of some kind when the legislative leaders are unable to reach an agreement. Candidates for this tiebreaking role included the state comptroller or a new independent budget office.
- An automatic continuation budget, a proposal that sharply undercuts executive power.
- Further modifications and institutionalization of the new conference committee structure, intended to iron out differences between the two houses through an orderly and open process. This would necessarily shift some of the power in each house from leadership to committee chairs and rank and file members.
- Additional steps toward multiyear planning.

Cynics were not surprised to see no agreement on a reform package while Pataki was under consideration for federal jobs in a new Bush administration. Under similar logic, it was not surprising to see that the Democratic Assembly and governor did not agree to budget reform while Governor Pataki was preparing to run for reelection in 2002.

However, legislative interest in budget reform picked up considerably in late 2004 and 2005. Some of the reforms under active discussion require amendments to the state constitution. The normal procedure for doing this, absent a constitutional convention, requires passage of a resolution by two successive legislatures, which must then be approved by the voters. In 2004, before the Court of Appeals decision that strengthened the executive's budget hand, the legislature achieved "first passage" of a resolution that would have increased their power substantially. In early 2005, both newly elected houses achieved second passage, meaning that the resolution will be before the voters in November 2005. Read in conjunction with its implementing legislation, the amendment would, among other things:

- Change the state fiscal year from April 1 to May 1, on the argument that revenue will be more predictable if the fiscal year is extended to allow for analysis of data from final and estimated income tax payments due in April 15.
- Put a contingency budget in place if the budget is not adopted by that May 1 deadline. The contingency budget would be based on the prior year's spending, except that welfare spending, debt service, and certain other spending could be above the prior year's amount. Once the contingency budget was put into effect, the legislature would have freedom to dispense with the governor's proposed budget bills and enact their own, a radical departure from their sharply limited power defined by the state Court of Appeals.
- Require the governor's budget to include 2-year funding for education, to provide more certainty to school districts.
- Lengthen the legislative budget consideration period and institutionalize a "fast start" process designed to start budget negotiations earlier.

- Establish a legislative budget office.
- Increase state reserve funds.

The governor cannot veto proposed constitutional amendments, but Governor Pataki could and did veto the implementing legislation associated with this proposal in 2004 and again in 2005. His strongest objection was to the contingency budget provisions, which could create incentives for late budgets. Once the new fiscal year ended and a contingency budget went into effect, the legislature would have far greater control over the budget process.[35] The legislature overrode the governor's veto in May 2005.

Voters will decide whether to adopt the proposed constitutional amendment in November 2005. The amendment has many opponents, including Governor Pataki; Attorney General Eliot Spitzer, a possible Democratic candidate for governor in 2006; the Business Council, New York's largest business trade organization; the Citizens Budget Commission, a fiscal watchdog organization; the Manhattan Institute, a conservative think tank; and several of the state's newspapers. Most opponents have argued that the amendment is likely to shift too much power from the governor to the legislature, will create incentives for higher spending, and will create incentives for late budgets. The League of Women Voters and the New York Public Interest Research Group have come out in favor of the amendment.

## CONCLUSION

Before the Court of Appeals affirmed and clarified the extraordinary executive budget powers granted by the New York constitution, the governor had been slowly ceding budgetary power to a legislature growing in strength. Without that court decision, dysfunction seemed sure to continue and worsen as the legislature challenged the governor more frequently and successfully, with no constitutional mechanisms in place to force agreement. The solutions most likely to work required constitutional amendment, making them least likely to be achieved. All that has now changed. What might happen next? There are at least several possible paths. The voters could approve the legislature's proposed constitutional amendment, shifting much power from the governor to the legislature. Whether this would reduce dysfunction is an open question. The authors generally agree with arguments made by the governor and others that the currently proposed amendment would create incentives for late budgets, which are likely to be the norm in New York.

The voters could disapprove the proposed constitutional amendment, and the governor's newly affirmed budget powers could stand. Whether that would reduce dysfunction is also an open question. As the court and others pointed out, the legislature's greatest power in this system would be to delay the budget until the governor agrees to negotiate. But responsibility for late budgets might be more clearly vested in the legislature than before, unlike the old system where it was never clear whom to blame. Under this scenario, however, none of the other issues reformers have proposed to address would be addressed. For example, the legislature still would have a short budget consideration period; the fiscal year still would end in the crush of the tax-filing season; and there would be no constitutional requirement to reach agreement on revenue estimates.

The voters could disapprove the proposed constitutional amendment but the legislature and the governor could reengage and try to agree on alternative reforms. The legislative leaders have already outlined their fallback position. In 2005, the legislature gave first passage to an alternative constitutional amendment that does not include the contingency budget provisions, and might be more palatable to the governor. Second passage could not come before 2007, after a new legislature is elected.

In short, while the Court of Appeals has clarified, at least for the moment, the question of who holds the power in New York's budgeting system, the battle for budget supremacy is not over, and New York could easily revert to the norm of the last two decades—budget dysfunction.

## REFERENCES

Baker, Al, "Budgets in Crisis: Overview; State Legislature Overrides Pataki on Budget Vetoes," *New York Times* (May 16, 2003).

Benjamin, Gerald and Henrik N. Dullea, *Decision 1997: Constitutional Change in New York*. Albany, NY: Rockefeller Institute Press, 1997.

Benjamin, Gerald and T. Norman Hurd, *Rockefeller in Retrospect: the Governor's New York Legacy*. Albany, NY: Rockefeller Institute of Government, 1984.

Benjamin, Gerald and Robert C. Lawton, "New York's Governorship: Back to the Future?" in *Governing New York State*, Jeffrey M. Stonecash (Ed.). State University of New York Press, 2001.

Beyle, Thad, "2002 Gubernatorial Elections, Campaign Costs and Powers," in *The Book of the States*. vol. 35, The Council of State Governments, Lexington, KY, 2003.

Boyd, Donald J. "There is a Way For New York to Adopt a State Budget on Time and Eliminate the Current Upheaval," *Newsday* (August 5, 2001).

Caher, John, "Road to Reform in Albany is a Long One," *New York Journal* (March 15, 2005).

Clynch, Edward J. and Thomas P. Lauth, *Governors, Legislatures and Budgets: Diversity across the American States*. Westport, CT: Greenwood Press, 1991.

Cooper, Michael, "Budget is Job of Governor, Judges Rule," *New York Times* (December 17, 2004).

Cooper, Michael, "Albany Tries to Unmuddy its Budget-making," *New York Times* (March 4, 2005).

Cooper, Michael, "Timing Was Different, Posturing Was Normal," *New York Times* (April 1, 2005).

Dao, James, "Rank and File of Albany Chafing at Their Bit Parts," *New York Times* (January 3, 1998).

DeWitt, Karen, "Court Decision Will Effect Budgetmaking," http://www. publicbroadcasting.net (January 21, 2005).

Forsythe, Dall, *Taxation and Political Change in the Young Nation, 1781–1833*. New York: Columbia University Press, 1977.

Forsythe, Dall, *Memos to the Governor: An Introduction to State Budgeting*. Washington, DC: Georgetown University Press, 1997.

Gallagher, Jay, "Deal Seen Possible on State Budget," *Gannett News* (January 24, 2005).

George E. Pataki, as *Governor of the State of New York v. New York State Assembly/Sheldon Silver v. George E. Pataki, Governor*, No. 171/172 (December 16, 2004), http://www.nycourts.gov/ctapps/decisions/dec04/dec04.htm.

Governor George Pataki, Veto Message No. 5, Senate Bill No. 2 of 2005.

Ginsberg, Benjamin and Martin Shefter, *Politics by Other Means: The Declining Importance of Elections in America*. New York: Basic Books, 1990.

Humbert, Marc, "On-Time State Budget Driven by Politics, Judges and Sunshine," *Associated Press* (April 2, 2005).

Kerker, Robert, *The Executive Budget in New York State: A Half-Century Perspective*. Albany, NY: New York State Division of the Budget, 1981.

Kolbert, Elizabeth, "Accountants in the Sky," *The New Yorker* (May 19, 2003).

Lane, Eric, "Albany's Travesty of Democracy," *City Journal* (Spring 1997).

McKinley Jr., James C., "Budget Showdown," *New York Times* (August 7, 2001).

National Association of State Budget Officers (NASBO), *Budgetary Processes in the States*. Washington, DC: NASBO, 2002.

New York State Court of Appeals, No. 171, *George E. Pataki, as Governor of the State of New York, Respondent, v. New York State Assembly, et al., Appellants*, and No. 172, *Sheldon Silver et al. Appellants v. George E. Pataki, Governor et al. Respondent*, December 2004.

New York State Division of the Budget, *Annual Information Statement for 2001–2002* (0102_Oct.pdf).

New York State Division of the Budget, *Annual Information Statement for 2002–2003* (June 2002 update) (ais0203.pdf).

New York State Division of the Budget, *Annual Information Statement for 2003–2004* (ais0304.pdf).

New York State Division of the Budget, *Executive Budget 2002–2003*, Appendix II (January 2002) (fy0203app2.pdf).

*Newsday* Editorial, "Why Albany Finally Beat the Clock," *Newsday* (April 3, 2005).

Office of Governor Pataki, "Governor: 'I Will Veto the Largest Tax Increase in State History,'" *Press Release* (May 14, 2003).

Pérez-Peña, Richard, "For Albany, the One Constant Is a Late Budget," *New York Times* (July 28, 2001).

Petersen, R. Eric and Jeffrey M. Stonecash, "The Legislature, Parties, and Resolving Conflict," in *Governing New York State*, Jeffrey M. Stonecash, Ed. State University of New York Press, 2001.

Schanberg, Sydney H., "Lies, Damned Lies, and Campaign Promises," *Village Voice* (April 30–May 6, 2003).

Weil, Gotshal and Manges L.L.P., *Litigation Practice* (Winter 2002),http://www.weil.
   com/wgm/cwgmhomep.nsf/Files/LitigationPractice_Win01/
   $file/LitigationPractice_Win01.pdf.

## NOTES

1. *The New York State Executive Budget, 2004–2005* (January 2004), Appendix I,
279, shows 335 full-time-equivalent employees estimated for March 31, 2004.

2. See Kerker, 1981, ix. New York's governorship has long been considered one of
the strongest in the nation, particularly in its budget powers. See, for example, Gerald
Benjamin and Robert C. Lawton, "New York's Governorship: Back to the Future?"
in *Governing New York State*, Jeffrey M. Stonecash, Ed. New York: State University of
New York Press, 2001, p. 126.

3. Benjamin and Dullea, 1997, xv.

4. Kerker, 1997, 96.

5. Ibid., 96.

6. Beyle, 2003, 181.

7. The "more than tripling" is inferred from Figure 8.4 in Eric R. Petersen and
Jeffrey M. Stonecash, "The Legislature, Parties, and Resolving Conflict," in *Governing
New York State*, Jeffrey M. Stonecash, Ed. New York: State University of New York
Press, 2001.

8. Forsythe, 1997, 50–52.

9. Pérez-Peña, July 28, 2001.

10. See Lane, 1997; and Kolbert, 2003.

11. Ginsberg and Shefter, 1990.

12. Benjamin and Hurd, 1984, 213.

13. Ibid., 204–205.

14. Forsythe, 1977.

15. See, for example, responses to a survey by the National Conference of State
Legislature's National Association of Legislative Fiscal Offices, entitled *Legislative-
Executive Budget Relations*, posted to http://www.NCSL.org on June 26, 2002.

16. Dan Morain and Jenifer Warren, "Deadlock at Budget Deadline," *Los Angeles
Times* (June 16, 2003).

17. NASBO, 2002.

18. We are indebted for this point to Louis Raffaele, Chief Budget Examiner, and
New York State Division of the Budget. Private communication (October 4, 2005).

19. *New York State Bankers Association v. Wetzler*, as reported in *McKinney's*
(August 7, 2001).

20. See *Litigation Practice*, Weil, Gotshal, and Manges L.L.P. (Winter 2002),
http://www.weil.com/wgm/cwgmhomep.nsf/Files/LitigationPractice_Win01/$file/
LitigationPractice_Win01.pdf, and *Annual Information Statement for 2003–2004*,
New York State Division of the Budget (ais0304.pdf), p. 98, for descriptions of this
litigation.

21. *McKinney's* (August 7, 2001).

22. Pérez-Peña, July 28, 2001.

23. *McKinney's* (August 7, 2001).

24. *Annual Information Statement for 2001–2002*, New York State Division of the Budget, 5.

25. Schanberg, 2003.

26. Baker, 2003.

27. The discussion and quotes in this section are drawn from New York State Court of Appeals No. 171/172, December 2004.

28. John Caher, 2005. Also, see Michael Cooper, "Budget Is Job of Governor, Judges Rule," *New York Times* (December 17, 2004).

29. Michael Cooper, "Budget Is Job of Governor, Judges Rule," *New York Times* (December 17, 2004).

30. Karen DeWitt, "Court Decision Will Effect Budget-making," http://www. publicbroadcasting.net (January 21, 2005); Jay Gallagher, "Deal Seen Possible on State Budget", *Gannett News* (January 24, 2005).

31. Michael Cooper, "Albany Tries to Unmuddy its Budget-Making," *New York Times* (March 4, 2005).

32. Karen DeWitt, 2005.

33. See Michael Cooper, "Timing Was Different, Posturing Was Normal," *New York Times* (April 1, 2005).

34. See Marc Humbert, "On-Time State Budget Driven by Politics, Judges and Sunshine," *Associated Press* (April 2, 2005); and *Newsday* Editorial, "Why Albany Finally Beat the Clock," *Newsday* (April 3, 2005); and Al Baker and Michael Cooper, "At 11th Hour, Albany Moves to Redo Budget," *New York Times* (April 13, 2005).

35. See Veto Message No. 5, on Senate Bill No.2 of 2005, for discussion of these issues from the governor's perspective.

# CHAPTER 5

# Connecticut: Public Scarcity and Private Wealth

*Carol W. Lewis*

## INTRODUCTION

In an acrimonious budget battle, partisan impasse and ideological gridlock stall negotiations, while proposed coping strategies pit high-income taxpayers and business interests against service recipients, state employees, and state aid to municipalities. Some cooperation and compromise in budget development and adoption ordinarily temper the friction inherent in separation of powers, partisan competition, and class conflict, but these are no ordinary times.

The state endured a shrinking surplus in FY 2001, year-end operating deficits in FY 2002, and FY 2003,[1] repeated gubernatorial vetoes and re-budgeting, cuts in agencies' spending authority and layoffs, special legislative sessions, failed legislative-executive budget summits, an early retirement incentive, a downgraded bond rating, and lawsuits filed by state employee labor unions. Adding to the difficulties, however, is that the FY 2002 deficit was addressed by depleting the rainy day fund and borrowing to finance the remaining operating deficit, steps that reduced the options available in ensuing budget rounds. Reflecting stalemate by beginning FY 2004 without an adopted budget (only the second such occurrence in over a century) and confronting yet another budget gap, the state operated on executive order, issued weekly. Discord and accusation run high, comity is in short supply,[2] and all parties are paying a high price in public opinion polls.[3]

Just how big is the problem? In current dollars, the FY 2002 deficit almost equaled the deficit during the FY 1991 budget crisis, but the budget itself is far larger.[4] A net deficit of $817 million in the general fund in FY 2002 amounted to approximately 6 percent of general fund spending and almost 7 percent of revenues.[5] After repeated adjustments on both sides of the ledger, FY 2003 closed with an estimated $125 million deficit.[6] The estimated gap for FY 2004 stands at $1 billion, or approximately 7 percent of a likely $13.5 billion budget. While these sums are substantial, they suggest as much a political as a fiscal shortfall.

## EXTERNAL BUDGET INFLUENCES

In 1991, the state responded to its second longest economic downturn since before World War II, primarily by adopting a tax on personal earned income, a spending cap, and biennial budgeting.[7] More than a dozen years of experience with the new arrangements make it evident that formal parameters alone do not dictate behavior or policy. Environmental influences—especially income, the business cycle, and electoral politics and public opinion—continue to help shape budgetary politics and outcomes in Connecticut.[8] Their influence also helps explain why, despite the many formal changes introduced more than a decade ago and the informal arrangements that have developed since, many antagonists, policy agendas, budgetary tactics, and gimmicks resurface in response to mounting deficits and recurring budget gaps.

### Income

Because Connecticut relies on income and sales taxes as the leading revenue sources, absolute and relative income levels and income growth are important to understanding state budgeting. Connecticut ranks high in per capita personal income (at 133% or more of the national average in 1991–2000) and per capita capital gains.[9]

Income inequality is politically salient because the gap between high and low income is wide, widening further, greater than for the nation as a whole,[10] and tax progressivity persists as a political issue.[11] Real median household income in the state declined by 3.5 percent in 1991–2000, compared to a 13 percent increase nationally.[12] Still, the state ranks fourth in the country.[13] In 1992, taxpayers above the median adjusted gross income earned 77.4 percent of the total statewide; by 1999, the figure had climbed to 86.5 percent.[14]

The political importance of income disparities within the state has been apparent in every budget round throughout the decade, often as a cleavage between the central cities and affluent suburbs. Many high-income earners are concentrated in certain electoral districts, and the geographic concentration of taxable income is increasing.[15] This pattern is mirrored in the geographic concentration of poverty, unemployment, and other indicators of need, along with needs targeted state programs (including components of state education aid).[16]

### Business Cycle

Budgeting is affected by turns in economic conditions, to which state spending and revenues are sensitive (to different degrees and at varying speeds).

Connecticut's longest recession since the late 1930s (from February 1989 to December 1992) was followed by steady economic growth[17] during what became Connecticut's second longest economic expansion since the Great Depression.[18] Then the economic winds shifted again: the National Bureau of Economic Research designated the beginning of the current recession as March 2001. "Compared with the average Connecticut recession . . . this one seems to be relatively tame—so far."[19] "The current recession still pales in comparison with the downturn a decade ago."[20]

### Electoral Politics and Public Opinion

Both elections and budgeting are decidedly partisan in Connecticut[21] and government is divided along partisan lines. An independent or Republican governor has faced a Democratic legislature for over a decade,[22] and independently elected constitutional officers may represent different parties and voice opposing views.[23] A 2-year legislative election cycle effectively makes every year one of positioning for the upcoming election. Democrats outnumbered Republicans and Independents and others (classified together) among registered voters in every state election from 1976 until 1996, when Independents and others surpassed the major parties.[24]

Public opinion in the state figures strongly in defining policy options and residents appear aware of current state finances.[25] "While majorities feel that both state spending (62%) and state taxes (52%) are 'too high,' those feeling this way are far fewer than in 1991 when Connecticut faced its last major budget crisis. Also, majorities feel they get their money's worth for the state (54%) local (59%) taxes that they pay."[26]

A Connecticut expert in public opinion observes that the governor "is a victim of his own success because people believe state government is efficiently run and understand that cuts will hurt."[27] Nonetheless, the public's confidence in government's capacity is below national levels. When asked, "When government decides to solve a problem, how much confidence do you have that the problem will actually be solved?" a majority of respondents (54%) answered that they have "a lot" or "some" confidence in the state government's ability to solve problems in 2002.[28] This compares to the larger proportion (64% in 2000) reporting a lot or some confidence nationally.[29]

### REVENUES

Over the 5-year period of FY 1998–FY 2002, general fund revenues increased almost 7 percent. Reliance on the income tax increased from almost 36 percent in FY 1998 to 49 percent by FY 2002.[30] This compares to the national average of less than 35 percent in FY 1999.[31] Receipts increased 140 percent from FY 1992 to FY 2001.[32] The state discovered that income tax revenues (and budget surpluses) are more volatile than anticipated, in part because of their link to capital gains. According to the state budget director, the historically "unparalleled" growth in the equity markets from 1995 to 1999 pushed capital gains realizations up 208 percent and was the driver behind the increase in income tax receipts.[33]

Second in importance is the sales tax, which generated about the same share of state revenue (27–28%) in FY 2002 as in FY 1998; the national average was almost 33 percent in FY 1999.[34] Receipts increased more than 50 percent in FY 1992–FY 2001.[35] Yet another way to measure its importance is political: a December 2002 survey shows a majority (53%) of respondents preferring an increase in sales tax to other revenue options, and an even larger majority (70%) judging its level to be "about right."[36]

Unrestricted federal grants, the third most important revenue source, increased from 18 percent to almost 20 percent of general fund revenues in FY 1998–FY 2002. Despite the growth in federal payments, the state is, in fact, financing the rest of the country. For each federal tax dollar paid by Connecticut taxpayers, the state received $0.67 in federal spending in 2001, compared to $0.79 in 1990, and fell from 45th to 49th among all states.[37]

Among the other sources of revenue, the corporate business tax declined almost 14.2 percent in FY 1992–FY 2002, from 8.7 percent to 4.2 percent of general fund revenues in FY 2001.[38] "Of the smaller revenue sources, casino payments have seen the strongest growth advancing at a 5-year average annual compounded rate of 17.4 percent."[39] Slot machine receipts contributed a total of almost $2.4 billion from inception in FY 1993 through FY 2003 as estimated; in FY 2002 alone, almost $369 million came in.[40] The state remits an appropriated portion of the receipts as payments to cities and towns based on statutory formulas. Casinos, tribal recognition, employment, and local opposition have developed into an intertwined, contentious political issue in the state.

### Structural Revenue Problem

General fund revenues fell 9.5 percent in FY 2003 from its historical high the prior year. This development was especially bitter for three reasons. First, when the state became the latest of the now forty-one states to impose a tax on personal earned income,[41] many thought that the state's revenue troubles were over. The prolonged economic expansion that followed, during which the income tax showed the highest rate of increase among general fund revenue sources, helped foster this illusion. Second, the plummet was swift—in a single fiscal year—and income tax receipts dropped almost $500 million. (Note that the current recession affected sales tax receipts first.)[42] Third, the turnabout followed years of numerous tax cuts and handsome surpluses that induced a wholly different approach to budgeting, as exemplified in 1999. "Tax revenues are up, the state's surplus coffers are overflowing and the economy continues to be vigorous, so lawmakers are engaged in the joyful exercise of the politics of plenty—cutting taxes and increasing spending at the same time."[43]

### Revenue Forecasting

The revenue problem cannot reasonably be attributed to the estimating technique. The state's revenue forecasting combines econometric modeling and expert advice. The latter includes the consensus forecast for national economic indicators and the Connecticut Economic Conference Board, created to provide economic advice to the executive and legislature. "[T]he revenue forecast is generated through a consensus interpretation of all available data.... Overall, the process followed in developing Connecticut's revenue forecast is consistent with approaches taken in many other states."[44] According to the state's budget chief, income tax collections are the primary cause of revenue variance in FY 1996–FY 2002.[45] "Nobody could have predicted the type of revenue shortfall that we're having this year."[46]

### Tax Cuts

However, the state's budget problem *is* a revenue problem. According to the OFA analysis,[47] "[r]evenue fluctuations have contributed the most in each year" to general fund surpluses/deficits. Of the more than $1 billion in revenue shortfall (i.e., below budgeted) that OFA identified in FY 2003, much can be traced to the cumulative impact of hundreds of tax changes undertaken in 1991–2002.[48] The two causes of the shortfall are (1) the Wall Street windfall and prolonged economic expansion were used to finance structural revenue changes, and (2) the first two came to an end while the revenue changes remained in place. In 1997, the comptroller warned against using the surplus "to advance permanent changes in the state's revenue base" that, she predicted, "will create long-term structural state deficits."[49] The structural revenue problem and, therefore, the current budget problem, are traceable to public policy as well as to economic conditions.

### Tax Burden

The tax burden imposed by state taxes changed as a result of the revenue changes. Total payments for state and local taxes increased in 1990–2002 in Connecticut from 22 percent to almost 25.6 percent, whereas there was just a fractional increase nationally. However, a true picture of tax burden relates the tax bill to income and to the federal tax system, in which both income and property taxes are allowed as itemized deductions. "On the average, a fifth of all state personal income and individually paid property taxes are 'exported' ... as a result of these deductions. For the best-off state and local taxpayers, close to 40 percent of their state and local income and property tax bills are effectively paid by the federal government."[50]

The tax burden at both extremes of the income range was lower in Connecticut than the national average and close to the average in the middle ranges.[51]

The many changes in the state's tax base and rate since 1995 have affected the whole range of taxpayers in the state.[52] As a result of lower adjusted gross income, lower effective tax rates, and expanded state tax credits for the local property tax, the average state tax paid by taxpayers below the median declined in the late 1990s, while the bill paid by higher income taxpayers increased.[53] Taxpayers below the median reported 13.5 percent of the total adjusted gross income statewide in 1999 and paid little more than 4 percent of the income taxes.

## INSTITUTIONAL CONTOURS

The main institutional contours of the budget process remain just about as they have been since the last major government reorganization in 1978. In the adoption stage of the executive process, the governor is obliged to submit a proposal for a balanced budget to the legislature and is authorized to exercise the line-item veto. When implementing the adopted budget, the chief executive may make limited cuts in appropriations, undertake limited reprogramming,[54] and defer agency spending. With strong formal authority, the governor also is unhampered by term limits and is elected for 4-year terms.[55]

The legislature also is a strong institutional player in the budget process. Its members are elected for 2-year terms, also without term limits. The bicameral legislature operates with joint appropriations and finance committees.[56] It may increase and/or decrease both expenditures and revenues and is required to adopt a balanced budget. Its position is strengthened by its receiving agency estimates and proposals in addition to the governor's recommendations. Nonpartisan, professional staff agencies support the budget function for both the governor (Office of Policy and Management, hereafter OPM) and the legislature (OFA).

Informally, discretionary budgetary issues are hammered out in negotiations between the governor and legislative leadership and between leadership and fiscal committee chairs.[57] Leadership's task is to muster the votes to pass the appropriations act as proposed by the governor and modified by the legislature.[58] The groundwork usually is laid in party caucus and allegiance enforced through choice assignments, selective electoral support, pork barrel, and the like.[59]

According to the General Assembly's fiscal office:[60]

Depending on the division of political power within the legislature and due to the joint committee system, various compromises are reached among the committee chairpersons, legislative leaders and between the legislative and executive branches. The degree of compromise in the legislature is partially dependent on the ratio of one party to the other. The smaller the ratio, the more compromise tends to occur. Also, more compromise tends to occur between branches when the legislative majority is of one party and the Governor is of the other party or a third party. The joint committee system tends to reduce conflict between the House and the Senate. In recent years, moderate and liberal caucuses within the majority party have also played a major part in the process.

These informal practices are what make budgeting possible under conditions of divided government and separation of powers. Since 1991, effective governance and a smooth budget process have depended upon harmony and trust between governmental branches and among executive and legislative leaders from different political parties. Both harmony and trust are delicate and demand continuous nourishment; both dwindled rapidly during budget rounds in 2002–2003.

## PROCEDURAL PARAMETERS

In contrast to stable institutional arrangements, fundamental rules of the game have undergone many changes since 1991 and thereafter. In particular, recission powers, biennial budgeting, balanced budget requirements, and the spending cap play a large role in defining the contours of the process and its outputs.

### Recission

The allotment is foremost among financial controls available during budget implementation. If the comptroller projects a deficit greater than 1 percent of total general fund appropriations, statute requires that the governor then reduce allotments up to 5 percent of an agency's individual appropriation account, but not more than 3 percent of total appropriations in a given fund.[61] With approval of a joint executive-legislative committee with bipartisan representation, the governor can elect to reduce allotments within these same limits, but larger reductions require the legislature's prior approval.[62]

Targeting especially new and expanded programs, the governor notified agencies of budget cuts and holdbacks totaling almost $88 million in October 2001.[63]

A different approach was taken in the special session in May 2002, when legislators used recission powers to evade cutback decisions . . . to pass the buck, so to speak. The legislature expanded this authority to allow the governor to make additional recissions up to $35 million for FY 2003.

### Balanced Budget and Deficit Financing

The governor is required to submit a balanced budget to the legislature. Both the state constitution and statute require that the appropriations bill show revenue estimates, which appropriations may not exceed.[64] Adopted by referendum in 1992, an amendment to the state constitution requires that "the amount of general budget expenditures authorized for any fiscal year shall not exceed the estimate amount of revenue for such fiscal year."[65] What is not required, however, is for the state to end the fiscal year in balance, nor is there a statutory or constitutional prohibition against financing an operating deficit through debt.[66]

Shifting the burden to future taxpayers (and political leaders), deficit financing is a customarily shunned alternative to raising current revenues to finance current operations. Yet, it is nothing new for Connecticut. The state bonded a deficit in 1975 (totaling $71 million) and again in 1991, when $966 million in 5-year economic recovery notes were issued to help resolve the fiscal crisis.[67] The comptroller (2002) labeled such an evasive tactic to cover deficits outside the general fund in FY 2001 a "dubious financial practice." In May 2002, the legislature authorized deficit financing of part of the FY 2002 deficit and, in December 2002, the treasurer issued more than $219 million in economic recovery notes.[68]

### Basis of Accounting

Connecticut's budgetary basis of accounting distorts operating results but still generates the dollar figures most often used in political discourse. Generally Accepted Accounting Principles (GAAP) were mandated as the budgetary basis as of FY 1996, but the statute was never implemented. According to the Comptroller (2002), the state "has not yet adopted GAAP for budget or financial control purposes."

A GAAP basis significantly changes the picture of state finances. FY 2001 is the most recent year for which both modified cash and GAAP figures are available. On a modified cash basis, the deficit totaled more than $222 million, compared to almost $782 million on a GAAP basis.[69]

### Surplus/(Deficit)

After 4 years of deficits, the state turned a surplus in FY 1992, which was by law earmarked to help pay off the debt issued to cover the prior year's deficit.[70] This initiated fully 10 years of surpluses (on a budgetary basis), with the high of $663 million reached in FY 1999.[71] An abrupt turnaround produced a swing of more than $1.4 billion from the FY 2002 surplus of $606.9 million to the FY 2002 estimated deficit of $817.1.[72]

### Rainy Day Fund

The budget reserve fund, created in 1978, authorized a balance equal to 5 percent of net appropriations for the general fund. By law, the fund may only finance year-end deficits; it cannot be used to balance a proposed budget.[73]

By 1987, the fund's balance was $319.6 million, but this sum was depleted over the next 3 years so that nothing was available to help fill the $1 billion chasm in 1991.[74] Deposits to the fund were made annually for 7 years, from 1995 to 2001. When $30.7 million was added at the end of FY 2001 by rescinding supplemental appropriations, the total balance stood at almost $595 million.[75]

The fund was completely drained in 2002 by a single year's deficit. Evidently, the 5 percent standard is an inadequate buffer against economic downturn, fluctuations in intergovernmental resources, and/or emergencies such as natural disasters.[76] In 2002 the maximum allowable target for the fund was increased to 7.5 percent of the net general fund appropriations in the current fiscal year.[77]

### Biennial Budgeting

The state met a fiscal challenge in 1971 by switching from a biennial budget (and biennial legislature) to an annual budget and annual legislative sessions. The idea was to provide more careful decision making and oversight. In response to the 1991 crisis, the state reverted to biennial budgeting, this time to provide a longer time horizon and more planning. Since the cycle for FY 1994, the state has used biennial budgeting, but the idea of annual budgeting resurfaced in 2003. This history suggests that some procedures may serve as placebos—or intended for electoral timing— rather than as real remedies in a broken budget process.[78]

Biennial budgeting in Connecticut requires separate budgets prepared and adopted simultaneously, with revisions and adjustments in the second year.[79] In practice, midterm revisions have not been restricted to technical adjustments but have included policy initiatives as well.[80] For FY 2003, the enacted midterm budget reduced general fund appropriations by $339.6 million.[81] Although this sum is only approximately 3 percent of the almost $12.1 billion adopted for the general fund, it denotes significant change when current services exceed the adopted total and debt service, accrued liabilities, labor contracts, and more constrain decision-making discretion.

### Incremental Decision Making and Reforms

State agencies have been required to submit budgets in a program format since FY 1986. Performance data (e.g., workload, service levels, efficiency, and effectiveness measures) are provided for each program. The so-called program format corresponds to administrative units and omits costs such as pension, leave, and medical benefits.

Over the past decade, the state has taken many steps to revamp decision making, reorient service delivery, and strengthen management capacity. These include automated budget and personnel systems, Total Quality Management, benchmarking, performance measurement, and privatization.[82] The legislature introduced fiscal notes, increased the analytic staff, and required out-year estimates. The OPM began developing Connecticut's strategic business planning model in the mid-1990s.[83] This and all other initiatives were adapted from the corporate world or other jurisdictions.[84]

Despite all these efforts and like the majority of states, budgeting under routine circumstances in Connecticut remains predominately incremental.[85] Incrementalism is structured directly into the formal process. The budget format displays figures from prior years alongside agency requests and recommendations. Change, expressed in percentages and/or dollars, is the analytic focus in most budget narratives.

The budget request forms sent to the agencies by OPM dictate a division into two basic parts. The first and largest dollar component is current services; the automated formulation by OPM, begun in the FY 1993 cycle, has made much of what used to constitute budgeting at the agency level a largely mechanical activity today. Options, the second component, allow for change. They are "[s]ignificant increases or decreases to the 'present level' budget . . . accomplished through an accompanying budget option package which details individual adjustments to agency programs."[86] For most of the past decade, options have been restricted to revenue enhancement and spending reduction. "Still, the budgetary decision-making process tends to be incremental because the base from which the next year's budget is built is the current year's budget and service level, as adjusted for inflation."[87]

## Spending Cap

From 1997 to 2001, the spending cap constrained the growth and nature of spending, but it was *not* a factor in 2002–2003.[88] A part of the 1991 compromise that marshaled the legislative majority behind the income tax, the statutory cap (PA 91–3 JSS)

established a spending cap on general budget expenditures. General budget expenditures cannot exceed expenditures authorized for the previous fiscal year by more than the average increase in personal income in the state over the preceding five years, determined by the U.S. Bureau of Economic Analysis or the percentage increase in inflation during the preceding twelve months as determined by the U.S. Bureau of Labor Statistics, whichever is greater. Funds earmarked for debt service, grants to distressed municipalities in effect on July 1, 1991, first time implementation of court orders or federal mandates (the base expenditure would subsequently be considered in the calculation for the next Fiscal Year) are not included in the cap, nor are expenditures from the Budget Reserve Fund. The legislature can exceed the cap if the Governor declares an emergency or extraordinary circumstances and three-fifths of the General Assembly vote to do so. The same legislation also tightens the limit on the state's bonded indebtedness payable from General Fund tax receipts.[89]

General budget expenditures include all expenditures from the general fund, other appropriated funds, debt service, bond retirement funds, and education activities.[90]

An identical constitutional cap was approved by referendum in 1992. It has yet to be implemented because an agreement on implementing language cannot muster the necessary three-fifths majority in each house. The Connecticut Supreme Court upheld the use of the statutory cap in the interim.[91]

The cap has generated disagreement over what it covers, and also over what it does not. Among the common exemptions to the expenditure limits in effect in twenty-three states are debt service, federal mandates and court order, and state aid to localities.[92] In Connecticut, disagreement over the specifics of some exemptions (e.g., the definition of general budget expenditures) is an obstacle to implementation of the constitutional cap. Controversy also persists over the statutory designation of distressed municipality (eleven are designated) because it involves substantial state aid. (This is one way in which the unequal distribution of wealth and income directly affects budgetary politics.) The exemption of expenditures from the rainy day fund from the cap has encouraged one-time spending.[93] The governor has declared and the legislature approved numerous emergencies or extraordinary circumstances (however weak the reasoning behind such a designation may appear) in order to exceed the cap.

Overall, there has been a noticeable impact on the rate at which spending has increased. In the 9 years before the cap was adopted, the average annual increase in general budget expenditures in current dollars was over 10 percent; in the 9 years since, the rate was less than 6 percent.[94] A limit on annual spending increases has reduced the state's already limited capacity to use fiscal policy to counter the business cycle[95] and, by linking growth to prior years' income growth or inflation, the cap also will limit the state's capacity to respond to programmatic demands even in prosperous times.

## EXPENDITURES

Spending from all appropriated funds in FY 2002 totaled almost $13 billion. Of this, more than one-half was devoted to state grants to towns (primarily aid to education) and other grants. Personal services represent more than 16 percent and debt service 11 percent of all appropriated funds.[96]

The largest fund is the general fund, which amounted to almost $11.9 billion in appropriated expenditures in FY 2002. Total general fund expenditures increased 66.3 percent or almost $8 billion from FY 1992, the first year the income tax was fully instituted, to almost $13.3 billion in FY 2002.[97] Human services, at approximately 29 percent of the total, is the single largest of the ten functions into which general fund expenditures are categorized. This category includes Medicaid payments, Temporary Assistance to Families, and the state's welfare program (General Assistance). The second largest category, at

23 percent, is education, libraries and museums, in which the greatest portion is public education payments. The next largest category (10%) is termed *non-functional* and includes payments for debt service and employees' fringe benefits.[98]

### State Aid

State aid to local governments has served as an increasing source of revenue for Connecticut localities: payments increased a total of more than 41 percent or almost $676 million from FY 1992 to FY 2002, while the annual increase averaged 3.6 percent.[99] It has also been a reliable source of revenue. State aid declined only twice in the last decade: the FY 1993 decrease was only 0.5 percent; the second, in FY 1996, reduced state aid by 5.9 percent or to about what it had been 2 years earlier. Education accounts for 97 percent of all state payments to localities.[100]

State aid may be losing its advantaged position as a sacred cow, but the loss to date has been small and probably temporary. The budget adopted for for FY 2003 cut state aid to localities by $28 million.[101] Furthermore, the governor was authorized for the first time to make recissions in some types of state aid; legislators specified that aid to municipalities would be proportionately reduced if and when appropriations were reduced. In a display of electoral sensitivity, legislators also specifically excluded the largest grant program for public education (Education Cost Sharing), two payments-in-lieu-of taxes (PILOTs) that affected central cities (and other jurisdictions with state facilities), and the grant program for road aid that affects all communities.[102] Some attempts were made in the budget battle to pit contractual givebacks from state employees against cuts in state aid, in what appeared as an effort to reduce legislative support for state employees and their unions.

### Public Employees and the Size of Government

State government employment increased 37 percent over the past quarter century. "Dramatic increases in the number of (state government) jobs occurred in the mid-eighties. Then, employment fell in the early nineties, during the statewide recession, before rebounding to its present level."[103] As of June 30, 2001, full-time state employees numbered 53,218 and part-time, permanent employees numbered 3,074.[104] By 2004, full-time state employment had fallen more than 8 percent, to less than 49,000. (Source: Comptroller, CAFR for FY 2004 at http://www.osc.state.ct.us/2004cafr/statistical/miscellaneous. asp)

According to a report by a research analyst in the Connecticut Department of Labor and published by the Department of Economic and Community Development, wages increased approximately 26 percent in Connecticut's private sector from 1996 to 2000, while wages for state employees increased

**Table 5.1**
**Connecticut Government Employment and Wages**

| Sector | Total Employment | | | Average Wages | | |
|--------|------|------|---------|------|------|--------|
| | 1996 | 2000 | Changes | 1996 | 2000 | Change |
| Private | 1,361,557 | 1,462,534 | 100,977 (7.4%) | $36,469 | $46,027 | 26.2% |
| State | 60,674 | 63,544 | 2,870 (4.7%) | $38,291 | $44,853 | 17.1% |

*Source:* Joo, 2002b.

17 percent; as a result, wages in the private sector exceed state wages.[105] (See Table 5.1.) *The Connecticut Business & Industry Association* (CBIA) offers alternative data: "Average annual salaries in 2001 for state workers and private sector employees were about the same at $48,000, state labor figures show."[106] The CBIA argues that employee benefits increased by almost 73 percent since FY 1996. "In the current fiscal year, $955 million of the $13 billion state budget is earmarked for benefits such as pensions, life insurance, social security and health care, which is the greatest cost."[107]

Are there too many state employees? Are their salaries and benefits too high? These questions are important, and especially so today because they imply other questions. Are state employees to blame for the current fiscal difficulties? But what about the governor, who negotiated the contracts (including the systemwide pension and health care contract in 1997) and the legislature that approved them? Shouldn't they fix what they broke? And, is the system in fact broken?

The fiscal realities are hard to pin down because of political *truths* (e.g., advocacy, passion, and rhetorical techniques such as using selective data) and analytic variations (e.g., differences in classification, timeframes, and comparison groups). In fact, there are many ways to measure government size and spending. For example, when it comes to combined spending by state and local government, Connecticut's seventh highest ranking among the states in FY 1996 is transformed to eleventh lowest when population, average income, and land area are considered.[108] Simple rankings among the states commonly ignore the significant differences among them as to what level of government performs which services and variations in functions and financing (e.g., state aid, contracting out, county government).[109] Using five relative measures of the combined state/local governmental system, a 2002 study ranks Connecticut next to the last and the author concludes, "By any of our measures of government size ... state and local government in Connecticut looks pretty trim. If so, efforts to balance the state's budget by slashing programs or shifting spending commitments to municipalities may be less feasible than selectively raising state taxes."[110]

Fiscal realities need interfere with neither political strategy nor public sentiments. Surveys show that majorities think state spending and taxes are too high,[111] although Connecticut taxpayers spend a relatively small proportion of their income on government. The governor informed the populace that state workers' "wages are the best in the country. . . . Their pension is the best in the Free World."[112]

Whatever the figures, the issue of payroll and benefits relates to the governor's budget-balancing strategy. As described by one observer, "This strategy begins with the governor, hard-pressed to explain why his state budget faces huge impending deficits, accusing state employees of being simultaneously the cause of and the cure for the projected budget shortfalls."[113] Asserting that about $3.3 billion of the total $13 billion budget goes to payroll, pension, and health care combined, Rowland said he believes that "because nearly one-third of the budget is spent on state employees, they should help cover nearly one-third of the deficit."[114] The governor has included union concessions on wage and benefits contracts in his proposal to balance the budget in FY 2003 and fill the gap for FY 2004.

The governor's alternative is employee layoffs, which he threatened as early as May 2002.[115] He issued 3,000 layoff notices in November 2002 and opposition lined up quickly.[116] "Both Republican and Democratic legislators, who have seen similar threats in the past from former [G]overnors Ella T. Grasso and Lowell P. Weicker Jr., said laying off 6 percent of the state's workforce would have a negative effect on state services and be devastating to the families of the laid-off workers."[117] According to Representative William R. Dyson (D– New Haven, CT), cochair of the Appropriations Committee since 1989,

Those layoffs are going to be very hard to come by . . . It makes some assumptions that are unreal. It assumes there's some fat around. You just don't do that in this [economic and budgetary] climate. Then the layoff becomes a threat—a kind of sledgehammer that will be used to get some kind of concessions out of labor.[118]

The impact of layoffs on state services is magnified by the early retirement incentive program offered in Spring 2003.[119]

### Debt Service and Indebtedness

With neither a constitutional debt limit nor a requirement for public referenda, the state is governed solely by statute with respect to incurring debt.[120] In a two-step process, debt first is authorized by the legislature and then allocated by the Bond Commission, a joint executive-legislative body.

The size and growth of bonded indebtedness is an important factor for at least three reasons: they speak to investments in infrastructure; they raise the question of affordability or debt burden; and, as a legal obligation, debt service constrains current discretion over budgetary resources. Connecticut's gross direct general obligation indebtedness totaled more than $8.6 billion by the end of 2002, and debt service on long-term direct general obligation debt in FY 2003 amounted to $809 million. Debt ratios have climbed in recent years, so that gross debt per capita stands at $2,517, or 6 percent of personal income.[121] The ratio of annual debt service for general bonded debt to total general expenditures (including general fund, special revenue, debt service funds, and higher education transfers) increased from 7.2 percent in 1992 to 9.1 percent in 2001.[122] "Connecticut continues to lead the nation in state tax supported debt per capita. Bonded debt per capita has more than doubled over the past decade."[123]

The credit agencies are another set of influential players in the budget process. Moody's, Standard & Poor's, and Fitch assigned ratings of Aa2, AA, and AA, respectively, to the state's Economic Recovery Notes, the general obligation debt issued in December 2002 to finance the FY 2002 deficit. The credit reports note the state's high income levels and underlying economic resources, but also its high debt levels and revenue downturn. As for broader, longer assessments, Moody's and Standard & Poor's retained their negative outlook. The reports emphasize the need to adopt a balanced budget for the upcoming biennium if credit ratings are to be maintained.[124] In July 2003 Moody's downgraded the state's credit rating. "Moody's believes Connecticut's balance sheet will remain weak at least over the next few years as the state grapples with budget challenges."[125]

## CONCLUSION

The relative mildness of the current recession in tandem with recent budgetary and economic experience may encourage political leaders to "wait it out," all the while hoping that economic expansion and a stock market surge will bail out the state. They may hope to survive in the interim through one-shot and/or short-term fiscal remedies. The problem now is that most of the traditional evasive tactics are exhausted and hard choices confront decision makers. The options include confronting unionized labor and cutting services, reducing state aid and shifting costs to the local property tax, and/or fixing the structural problem in the revenue base.

Judging from public opinion polls, stalemate among Connecticut's political leaders is among the less preferred options.[126] Attorney General Richard Blumenthal ruled that the governor's executive orders are a legal substitute for an adopted budget, but said, "Preferably, as happened in 1991, agreement among the legislative and executive branches would be achieved on a temporary spending measure approved by the General Assembly and signed by the governor . . . Such consensus would provide stability and certainty in this critical time."[127] Elected to an unusual third term in Fall 2002, the drop in the once-popular governor's job approval rating in the ensuing months is attributed directly to the budget impasse.[128] The electoral cost of stalemate in 2003 may turn out to be higher than tax reform in 1991.

Connecticut's experience teaches numerous lessons. The parameters of the rainy day fund should be carefully devised to suit the revenue base and its volatility, spending needs such as fixed costs, and economic circumstances. A spending cap can indeed dampen spending growth but, if carefully devised to forestall evasion, it quickly becomes too constraining. There is no silver bullet in budgeting; the income tax panacea mutated into a revenue problem within a single decade. As for the lesson derived from the structural revenue problem—we have seen the enemy and it is us.

A political shortfall as much as a revenue shortfall contributed to making these times extraordinary. Moderation, accommodation, and compromise failed us. The vision of the public interest that ultimately prevailed a decade ago seems to have blurred.

The partisan divide and ideological rhetoric reinforced divisions and amplified conflict among classes, interests, and regions. Positions hardened and accusations and finger pointing continued unabated. Adversaries accused each other of being the real source of the problem and, therefore, solely responsible for its solution. Connecticut began the fiscal year operating on executive orders. Moody's downgraded the state's credit rating and public opinion polls showed that stalemate among Connecticut's political leaders is among the less preferred options.

Another lesson derived from recent experience is that Connecticut needs political leaders with four characteristics. The first is the wisdom to pursue what is good for the Connecticut community rather than what is good for the rich or the poor, for state employees or corporate leaders, or for Democrats or Republicans. The second is political restraint, so that we do not magnify revenue problems when prosperity turns. The third is a commitment to process over and above a desire for winning; in a democracy, the prize is supposed to be participation and fair play, not permanent, all-out victory. And the fourth is the courage to act on the first three.

## REFERENCES

*Associated Press*. Report (December 21, 2002). State Workers Have Big Edge in Benefits. *Connecticut Business & Industry Association*, at http://www.cbia.com/home.htm, accessed December 26, 2002.

Barnes, Christopher E. (2002a). Author's interview (December 10, 2002). Barnes is Associate Director of the Center for Survey Research and Analysis (CSRA), University of Connecticut.

———— (2000b). Registration by Party (1970–2000). 2002 Reapportionment Database, duplicated document, CSRA, University of Connecticut.

Budoff, Carried (2002). Rowland Threatens Layoffs, New Budget Talks about To Begin. *Hartford Courant* (May 31), at http://www.courant.com/, accessed May 31, 2002.

Bureau of Economic Analysis, U.S. (2002a). *Regional Economic Accounts*, at http://www.bea.gov/bea/regional/docs/regional_overview.htm  and  http://www.bea.gov/bea/regional/data.htm, accessed December 20, 2002.

———— (2002b). State BEARFACTS 1991–2001, Connecticut, at http://www.bea.gov/bea/regional/bearfacts/stbf/bf10/b1009000.htm, accessed December 20, 2002.

Census Bureau, U.S. (2002). State Estimates for People of All Ages in Poverty for Connecticut: 1999, Table A99–00, at http://www.census.gov/hhes/www/saipe/stcty/a99_00.htm, accessed December 20, 2002.

Center for Survey Research and Analysis (CSRA) (2002a). News Release. (December 10, 2002), University of Connecticut.

———— (2002b). Surveys (December 4–8, 2002). Data provided courtesy of CSRA, University of Connecticut.

Chedekel, Lisa (2002). Partisan Budget Faces Veto, Millionaire's Tax Part of Democrats' Plan. *HartfordCourant* (April 26), at http://www.courant.com/, accessed April 26, 2002.

Citizens for Tax Justice (CTJ) (1996). *Who Pays? A Distributional Analysis of the Tax Systems in All 50 States* (June), at http://www.ctj.org/whop, accessed December 18, 2002.

Coleman, Tobin A. (2002). Area Shoulders Income Tax Burden. *Greenwich Time* (December 22), at http://www.greenwichtime.com, accessed December 22, 2002.

Comptroller, State of Connecticut (1997). Comptroller Criticizes Governor for Surplus Spending Proposal. Press Release (February 28), at http://www.state.ct.us/otc/pressrl/prrl9705.htm, accessed April 1997.

———— (Annual). Report of the State Comptroller to the Governor (CAFR) for fiscal years 1995, 2000, and 2001, at http://www.osc.state.ct.us/2001cafr, accessed December 20, 2002. CAFR for FY 2004 at http://www.osc.state.ct.us/2004cafr/statistical/miscellaneous.asp, accessed May 23, 2006.

———— (2002). Comptroller's Annual Economic Report: Connecticut's Economic Health (February) (unpaginated), at http://www.osc.state.ct.us/reports/economic/2002cmprpt/indexprint.html, accessed December 13, 2002.

Connecticut Business & Industry Association (CBIA) 2002. Confidence in State Government Declines, CBIA Survey Finds. News release (November 22), at http://www.cbia.com/2News/2002Releases/AnnualSurvey.htm, accessed December 17, 2002.

Connecticut Conference of Municipalities (CCM) (2001). Report on the General Assembly Session, 1992–2001. New Haven, CT: November.

———— (2002b). State Budget Cuts Aid to Municipalities, Gives Governor Power to Cut Even Deeper. *Connecticut Town & City* 30(4) (July–August), 1.

Connecticut Policy and Economic Council (CPEC) (1998). Income Grows in Western CT and Along Shoreline; Slows in Central and Northeastern CT. *CPEC Review*, 2(4) (April), 1, 3.

Department of Economic and Community Development, State of Connecticut (2002). News Release (September 9), at http://www.state.ct.us/ecd, accessed December 20, 2002.

Disputed "Slush Fund" in Budget Melts Away (1999). *Hartford Courant* (June 3), at http://www.courant.com/, accessed June 3, 1999. URL is now http://www.ctnow.com.

Division of Special Revenue, State of Connecticut (2002). Transfers to General Fund, through November 2002, at http://www.dosr.state.ct.us, accessed December 3, 2002.

Fillo, Maryellen (2003). Governor's Weekly Orders OK, Blumenthal: Method "Legally Acceptable,"*Hartford Courant* (July 17), at http://www.courant.com/, accessed July 17, 2003.

Fitch Ratings (2002). Credit Report for State of Connecticut. New York: December.

Haigh, Susan (2002a). Budget Prospects Looking Bleak. *Hartford Courant* (June 15), at http://www.courant.com/, accessed June 15, 2002.

_____ (2002b). Rowland Raises Threat of Layoffs. *Hartford Courant* (November 15), at http://www.courant.com/, accessed November 15, 2002.

Harrison, Chase (2002). Consumer May Think Worst of the Recession is Over, Plan to Save More, Spend Less. *The Connecticut Economy* 10(1) (Winter), 8–9.

Heffley, Dennis (1999). Just How Deep is Connecticut's Public Trough? *The Connecticut Economy* 7(2), 4–5.

_____ (2002a). Can We Reduce Inequality without Hurting Economic Performance? *The Connecticut Economy* 10(1) (Winter), 7–8.

_____ (2002b). My Big Fat State Government? *The Connecticut Economy* 10(4) (Fall), 4–5.

Hamilton, Elizabeth (2003). Capitol Gang Falling Out of Favor. *Hartford Courant* (July 23), at http://www.courant.com/, accessed July 23, 2003.

Hoffman, David (Ed.) (2002). *Facts and Figures on Government Finance*. Washington DC: Tax Foundation.

Jacklin, Michele (2003). The People Behind the Numbers. *Hartford Courant* (June 1), at http://www.courant.com/, accessed June 1, 2003.

Joo, Jungmin Charles (2002a). Greenwich Tops in Wages in 2001, at http://www.state.ct.us/ecd/research/digest/articles/02articles/sep02art1.html, accessed December 28, 2002. The author is an associate research analyst at the Connecticut Department of Labor.

_____ (2002b). Government Sector Trends, at http://www.state.ct.us/ecd/ research, accessed December 10, 2002.

_____ (2002c). Gross State Product Grew 4.7 Percent in 1999, at http://www.state.ct.us/ecd/research/digest/articles/01articles/ jul01art3.html, accessed December 15, 2002.

Joyce, Philip G. (2001). What's So Magical about Five Percent? A Nationwide Look at Factors that Influence the Optimal Size of State Rainy Day Funds. *Public Budgeting and Finance* 21(2) (Summer), 62–87.

Keating, Christopher (1999a). Budget Gains New Tax Cuts, More Spending. *Hartford Courant* (June 3), at http://www.courant.com/, accessed June 3, 1999.

_____ (1999b). Rowland, Democrats Reach Budget Accord. *Hartford Courant* (June 4), at http://www.courant.com/, accessed June 4, 1999.

_____ (2002a). State Budget Compromise Predicted, *Hartford Courant* (November 16), accessed November 16, 2002, at http://www.courant.com/.

_____ (2002b). State Employees Near the Top in Benefits, Pay. *Hartford Courant* (December 5), at http://www.courant.com/, accessed December 5, 2002.

_____ (2003). State's Bond Rating Drops, Debt To Cost Millions More. *Hartford Courant* (July 3), at http://www.courant.com/, accessed July 3, 2003.

Keating, Christopher and Elizabeth Hamilton (2003). State Remains In Fiscal Limbo, Governor Issues Order for Emergency Spending as New Budget Year Begins. *Hartford Courant* (July 1), at http://www.courant.com/, accessed July 1, 2003.

Kennedy, Daniel W. (2000) The Connecticut Business Cycle: A Short History (1939–2002), at http://www.state.ct.us/ecd/research/digest/articles/02articles/jun02art1.html, accessed December 15, 2002. The author is a senior economist at the Connecticut Department of Labor.

Lanza, Steven P. (1997). Connecticut's Surprisingly Low Price Burden. *The Connecticut Economy* 5(4) (Fall), 7.

_____ (2001). The Ups and Downs of the Connecticut Income Tax. *The Connecticut Economy* 9(2) (Spring), 12–13.

Lender, Jon and Mark Pazniokas (2000). Andrews Charged in Scandal. *Hartford Courant* (October 11), at http://www.courant.com/, accessed October 11, 2002.

Leonard, Ira M. (2002). Once Again, State Workers Are Budget Scapegoats. *Hartford Courant* (November 23), opinion, at http://www.courant.com/, accessed November 23, 2002. The author is a professor of history in the state university system.

Lewis, Carol W. (1991). Connecticut: Prosperity, Frugality, and Stability in E. J. Clynch and T. P. Lauth (eds.) *Governors, Legislatures, and Budgets, Diversity Across the American States*. Contributions in Political Science, No. 265, CT: Greenwood Press, 1991, pp. 41–52.

_____ (1995). "Connecticut: Surviving Tax Reform," in *The Fiscal Crisis of the States*, Steven Gold (Ed.). Washington DC: Georgetown University Press, 1995, pp. 141–196.

Lohman, Judith. (2002). Tax Changes 1991–2002. Office of Legislative Research, Connecticut General Assembly (November 1), at http://www.cga.state.ct.us/olr, accessed December 17, 2002. The author is a chief analyst.

McEachern, William A. (1998). Changes in Connecticut's Median Household Help Explain the Income Decline. *The Connecticut Economy* 6(1) (Winter), 5.

_____ (2002). State Budget Shortfall Takes Us Back to the Future. *The Connecticut Economy* 10(1) (Winter), 4–5.

Moody's Investors Service (2002). Credit Report for State of Connecticut. New York: December 11.

Nagy, Barbara (2002). State's Job Picture Looking Gloomier. *Hartford Courant* (November 19), at http://www.courant.com/, accessed November 19, 2002.

National Conference of State Legislatures (NCSL) (1999). *Legislative Budget Procedures: A Guide to Appropriations and Budget Processes in the States, Commonwealths and Territories* (May), at http://www.ncsl.org, accessed October 29, 1999.

Office of Fiscal Analysis (OFA), Connecticut General Assembly (1992 and 1998 revised). Connecticut's Budget Process (undated) at http://www.cga.state.ct.us/ofa, accessed August 2001. Although no publication date is given, reference is made to the current fiscal year as 1992–1993 and the final screen notes that the document was last updated in December 1998.

_____ (2001a). The Constitutional Spending Cap, at http://www.cga.state.ct.us/ofa/documents/MajorIssues/2001/ConnecticutSpendingCap.htm, accessed December 17, 2002.

———— (2001b). Survey of 50 States Re: Expenditure Limit Exemptions, at http://www.
cga.state.ct.us/ofa/documents/MajorIssues/2001/Survey50States Expenditure-
LimitExemptions.htm, accessed December 17, 2002.

———— (2002a). Connecticut State Budget 2001–2003 Revisions. A Summary of Revenue, Appropriations and Bonds Authorized by the General Assembly, at http://www.cga.state.ct.us/ofa, accessed December 13,
2002.

———— (2002b). Connecticut Tax Expenditure Report (January), at http://www.
cga.state.ct.us/ofa, accessed December 17, 2002.

———— (2002c). FY 2003 General Fund Budget Projection Fund Update, December 17.

———— (2002d). OFA Budget Book for FY 2003, at http://www.cga.state.ct.us/
ofa/documents/OFABudget/2002/Book/OpenBook.htm, accessed December 17, 2002.

———— (2002e). Overview of the State Budget Process, at http://www.cga.state.
ct.us/ofa/documents/Misc/2002/BudgetProcess.pdf, accessed December 10,
2002.

Office of Policy and Management, State of Connecticut (OPM) (1998).
Strategic Business Planning, A Guide for Executive Branch Agencies,
at http://www.opm.state.ct.us/mgmt/busguide/busplan.pdf, accessed December 15, 2002.

———— (2002). Governor's Midterm Budget Adjustments FY 2002–2003, at
http://www.opm.state.ct.us/budget/2003MidTerm/MidTermHome.htm, accessed December 10, 2002.

Packman, Lauren (2002). Yankee Reserve: Connecticut Rates Governments. *The Connecticut Economy* 10(4) (Fall), 9.

Perna, Nicholas S. and Patrick J. Flaherty (1997). Connecticut's Wealth. *The Connecticut Economy* 5(2) (Spring), 12.

Rowland, John G., Governor, State of Connecticut. (2001) Governor Rowland Noti-
fies Agencies of Budget Rescissions to Keep Budget in Balance. Press Release.
Hartford, CT: October 1, 2001.

———— (2002). Governor's Address (December 15), at http://www.state.ct.us/
governor/news/120502budget.htm, accessed December 20, 2002.

Ryan, Marc S. (2002a). Exhibits presented by Marc S. Ryan, Secretary of the Office
of Policy and Management, in connection with *Sheff v. O'Neill*. Hartford, CT:
March 25.

———— (2002b). Nobody Could Have Predicted This. Q & A with Marc S. Ryan on
the State Budget Crisis. *Hartford Courant* (June 2), C1, C4.

Satter, Robert (2002). State Elections Are Stacked Against Challengers. *Hartford
Courant* (December 6), opinion.

Secretary of the State, Office of, State of Connecticut (1992). Proposed Amendments
to the Constitution. Hartford, CT.

Standard & Poor's (2002). Credit Report for State of Connecticut. New York: December 11.

Stodder, James (1998). Have Most People Benefited from the Recovery? *The Connecticut
Economy* 6(1) (Winter), 4.

Stokes, Charles J. (1995). Poverty in Connecticut: A Reality Check. *The Connecticut
Economy* 3 (October 4), 5.

Swift, Mike and Dan Haar (1998). Connecticut Poverty Rate Shows Increase. *Hartford*

*Courant* (September 16), at http://www.courant.com/, accessed September 16, 1998.

Tax Foundation (2002). Federal Tax and Spending Patterns Benefit Some States, Leaves Others Footing the Bill. *Tax Features* 46(3) (Summer), 1–3.

Treasurer, State of Connecticut (1997). Official Statement, General Obligation Bonds. Hartford, CT: September 15.

———— (2002). Official Statement, General Obligation Economic Recovery Notes. Hartford, CT: December 1, at http://www.state.ct.us/ott.

Williams, Barry (2002). Electronic communication of December 17, 2002. The author is principal of Government Relations Consulting and lobbyist for labor and nonprofit organizations.

Williams, Larry (1992). The State Surplus Isn't, and That's the Way It Is. *Hartford Courant* (August 26), A1, A10.

Wolkoff, Michael (1987). An Evaluation of Rainy Day Funds. *Public Budgeting and Finance* 7 (Summer), 52–63.

## NOTES

1. The FY 2003 deficit was developing even as the budget was being adopted. The governor vetoed the budget initially adopted for FY 2003 and agreement was reached only as the new fiscal year was about to begin. Then followed a series of postadoption special legislative sessions devoted to budget matters.

2. Keating and Hamilton, 2003.

3. Hamilton, 2003.

4. The state faced a gap of about one-third the total budget for FY 1992, which began without a budget in place for the first time in over a century. Instead, the state saw special sessions, agency closings, employee furloughs, and minibudgets (Lewis, 1995).

5. Calculated from Treasurer, 2002, III-D-5, 7.

6. Midyear estimates put the FY 2003 deficit at $581 million, representing 4.7 percent of almost $12.3 billion in spending and 5 percent of the almost $11.7 billion in estimated general fund revenues for FY 2003 (calculated from Office of Fiscal Analysis, 2002b, 5; hereafter, OFA).

7. Lewis, 1991 and 1995.

8. For the sake of parsimony, other factors such as demographics are omitted from this discussion.

9. Perna and Flaherty, 1997.

10. Lanza, 2001, 13; McEachern, 1998, 5; Stodder, 1998, 4.

11. Governor Rowland vetoed the FY 2003 budget because he opposed its including tax surcharge on incomes in excess of $1 million, and months later endorsed the surcharge as part of his proposed solution to the FY 2003 deficit (Treasurer, 2002, II-1). Many participants in the current budget fray may recall that Governor Lowell P. Weicker Jr., abandoned his opposition to an income tax after many months of hard bargaining and uncomfortable confrontations with fiscal realities (Lewis, 1995, 148–149).

12. Comptroller, CAFR, FY 2001.

13. Comptroller, 2002.

14. Lanza, 2001, 12.

15. Connecticut Policy and Economic Council, 1998; Lanza, 2001, 13; Joo, 2002a.

16. A majority (52 percent) of the state's impoverished residents live outside the large cities (Stokes, 1995, 12).

17. Joo, 2002c.

18. Kennedy, 2002.

19. Kennedy, 2002.

20. Nagy, 2002.

21. For example, Chedekel, 2002, OFA, 1992.

22. A Democratic majority has ruled the General Assembly's House since 1986 and the Senate likewise, except for a one-term Republican majority in 1994. Currently, the governor and lieutenant governor are Republicans, while the attorney general, treasurer, and comptroller are Democrats.

23. For example, Comptroller, 1997.

24. Barnes, 2002b.

25. Center Survey Research & Analysis 2002b, hereafter CSRA; Hamilton, 2003.

26. CSRA, 2002a.

27. Barnes, 2002a.

28. Packman, 2002, 9.

29. A business advocacy organization reports that their survey shows a decline in confidence in state government, *Connecticut Business & Industry Association* (2002).

30. Comptroller, 2002, Schedule B-2; the income tax was adopted in 1991 in response to the state's budget crisis. In FY 1992, the income tax generated almost 27 percent of general fund revenues (Treasurer, 1997, III-15). Connecticut first adopted a tax on earned income in 1971, but rescinded it before the state collected any receipts.

31. Hoffman, 2002, 205.

32. Treasurer, CAFR for FY 2001.

33. Ryan, 2002a, 2–3.

34. Hoffman, 2002, 205.

35. Comptroller, 2002.

36. CSRA, 2002b.

37. Hoffman, 2002, 3.

38. Comptroller, 2002.

39. Comptroller, 2002.

40. Division of Special Revenue, 2002.

41. Another two states tax interest and dividends, as did Connecticut prior to the 1991 adoption of the personal income tax on earned income (Hoffman, 2002, 229).

42. Comptroller, 2002.

43. Keating, 1999a.

44. Treasurer, 2002, III-2; see also NCSL, 1999.

45. Ryan, 2002a, 4.

46. Ryan, 2002b, C1.

47. 2002a, 25.

48. Lohman, 2002 and OFA, 2002b; The only outright income tax increase from 1991 to 2002 was to tax nonresident winners of the state's lottery if winnings exceed $5,000 (Lohman, 2002).

49. Comptroller, 1997.

50. Citizens for Tax Justice, 1996, 10, hereafter CTJ.

51. CJT, 1996, Appendix I, 7.

52. Lohman, 2002.

53. Lanza, 2001, 12.

54. "If a transfer of funds from one appropriation account to another exceeds 10% of the original appropriation or $50,000, whichever is less, it must be approved by the Finance Advisory Committee" (OFA, 1992, 3).

55. Lewis, 1991 and 1995.

56. The composition is 36 senators and 151 representatives.

57. Haigh, 2002a; Keating, 1999b; and Williams, 2002.

58. Williams, 2002.

59. For example, Disputed "Slush Fund," 1999.

60. OFA, 1992.

61. OFA, 1992, 3.

62. OFA, 1992, 3.

63. Rowland, 2001.

64. OFA, 1992, 2.

65. Secretary, 1992; This constitutional provision was triggered in 1995 and the legislature responded by authorizing transfers among agencies (National Conference of State Legislatures, 1999, Revenue Forecast, 9; hereafter NCSL).

66. Treasurer, 2002, III-5.

67. In effect, the "legislature expressed disapproval of its own action by adopting a more restrictive debt limit in 1991" but it has yet to have a restraining effect (Lewis, 1995, 152–153).

68. Treasurer, 2002.

69. Treasurer, 2002, III-26-III-27.

70. Williams, 1992.

71. OFA, 2002d, 11.

72. Calculated from OFA, 2002d, 11.

73. OFA, 1992, 4.

74. Comptroller, 2002.

75. Comptroller, CAFR for FY 2001, transmittal letter.

76. This issue is the subject of much research and debate (e.g., Joyce, 2001 and Wolkoff, 1987).

77. OFA, 2002d, 4.

78. Keating, 2003.

79. OFA, 1992, 4; OPM, 2002.

80. OFA, 2002d, 10–11.

81. Treasurer, 2002, III-22–23.

82. Lewis, 1995, 166–172.

83. OPM, 1998, 1.

84. For example, OPM, 1998, p. v.

85. National Conference of State Legislatures, 1999.

86. OFA, 1992, 6.

87. OFA, 1992, 4.

88. OFA, 2002d, 5; Initially the FY 2003 budget was $63 million under and the revised budget was $363 million under the cap (OFA, 2002, 5).

89. OFA, 1992, 4–5.

90. OFA, 2002d, 5.

91. Treasurer, 2002, III-5.

92. OFA, 2001b, 1.

93. OFA, 2002d, 5.

94. Calculated from OFA, 2002d, 5.

95. Connecticut accounts for just 1.6 percent of national gross domestic product (Heffley, 2002a, 7).

96. OFA, 2002e.

97. Treasurer, 1997, III-D-7 and 2002, III-D-7.

98. Treasurer, 2002, III-17–19.

99. Calculated from Connecticut Conference of Municipalities, 2001, hereafter CCM.

100. Calculated from Treasurer, 2002, III-21; Public schools are included in city and town budgets on a bottom-line basis, and education assistance is included among payments to local governments and/or state aid to municipalities.

101. CCM, 2002b, 1.

102. OFA, 2002a.

103. Joo, 2000b.

104. Comptroller, CAFR for FY 2001.

105. Joo, 2002b.

106. Unlike some other counts, Joo's (2000b) classifies Indian tribal business employment, including casinos, in the private sector. This is important because the Mashantucket Pequot Tribal Nation (i.e., Foxwoods Casino) ranked second in 2000 among the top twenty nongovernmental employers in the state, and the Mogehan Sun Casino ranked sixteenth (Comptroller, CAFR for FY 2001); also, in 1996, the annual average wage per worker in *all* levels of government was higher than the annual average wage in the private sector but the opposite was true by 2000 (Joo, 2000b).

107. Associated Press, 2002.

108. Associated Press, 2002; see also Keating, 2002b.

109. Heffley, 1999.

110. Counties do not exist as political/administrative units in Connecticut.

111. Heffley, 2002b.

112. CSRA, 2002b.

113. Associated Press, 2002.

114. Leonard, 2002.

115. Haigh, 2002b.

116. Budoff, 2002.

117. During the 1991 fiscal crisis, Governor Weicker issued 8,000 layoff notices.

118. Keating, 2002a.

119. Keating, 2002a.

120. Jacklin, 2003.

121. Treasurer, 2002, III-29.

122. Treasurer, 2002, III-36–37.

123. Comptroller, CAFR for FY 2001.

124. Comptroller, 2002.

125. Fitch, 2002; Moody's, 2002; Standard & Poor's, 2002.

126. Keating, 2003.

127. Hamilton, 2003.

128. Fillo, 2003.

129. Hamilton, 2003.

# CHAPTER 6

# Illinois: Constitutional versus Negotiated Powers

*Douglas R. Snow and Irene S. Rubin*

## INTRODUCTION

In 1991, Rubin, King, Wagner, and Dran described an Illinois budget process firmly in control of the chief executive.[1] Constitutional powers in the form of the line item, reduction, and amendatory vetoes, plus control over budget implementation and release of capital expenditures allowed Illinois governors to dominate budgetary decisions at all points in the budget cycle. Through the powerful Bureau of the Budget (BoB), Illinois governors possess the institutional strength to monitor and control agencies during legislative deliberations, to identify budget changes that are not in line with policy, and to shape the budget by working closely with legislative leaders and their staffs as budget bills are drafted. By all standards in use today, Illinois is an executive dominant state.[2]

Reexamination of the Illinois budget process 10 years down the road has given us new insights that inform a richer description of budgeting in a state characterized as "executive dominant." Illinois governors still have the same constitutional powers and institutional advantages that they had a decade ago. We find, however, that strong constitutional powers do not always necessarily shape the budget process over time. Political and fiscal conditions can change the relationship between the executive and legislative branches. In the 1990s, Republican Governors and legislative leaders found that negotiating the budget early in the budget session was superior to vetoes and inevitable override sessions after the budget was passed. Vetoes say only "no," while negotiations open up the possibility of "yes."

From at least as early as 1993 and through 2001, budgeting in Illinois could best be described as a process of negotiation administered by the governor and the leaders of the four General Assembly caucuses (House and Senate Democrats; House and Senate Republicans). This is very different from the model described over 10 years ago when a Republican governor used both the threat and extensive use of the veto to keep the Democratic General Assembly in line with his own budget priorities. The new practice of budgeting by negotiation enhanced the role of legislative leaders, diminished the role of appropriations committees, and served to further strengthen the Bureau of the Budget. Appropriations committees, which at one time marked up some eighty budget bills every budget cycle, had little to do but hear agency presentations. In the Illinois General Assembly, the real budget work was managed by leadership of the party caucuses in each house, working in concert with the Governor's budget staff. Authority became much less fragmented than in the past, but the price was weaker committees.

Illinois, as of this writing, is again on the cusp of change. Budgeting by veto in the 1980s gave way to budgeting by negotiation for a 9-year period, 1993–2001. By the end of the 2002 session of the General Assembly, the incentives that supported budgeting by negotiation had broken down. Fiscal stress and *the prospect of political change brought a return to heavy use of the governor's veto powers. In 2003 divided government ended when Democrats took control of the governor's office and both legislative chambers.* In this chapter we examine the political and fiscal forces that changed the landscape of budgeting in Illinois in the 1990s and in the first years of the new millennium. We first examine fiscal and political trends that we believe contributed to budgeting by negotiation, describe budgeting by negotiation, discuss the effects of budgeting by negotiation on legislative and executive institutions, *compare budgeting by negotiation to budget by one dominate political party*, and conclude with a discussion of the significance of our findings.

## FISCAL TRENDS

In Illinois, the early 1990s were defined by slow recovery from economic recession. Strong economic growth followed in the mid- to late 1990s, only to end with a second recession in 2001. Cost pressures, ambitious spending, and reluctance to increase taxes added to budget pressures when recession returned in 2001. By early 2002, fiscal constraints had significantly reduced the maneuverability of all actors in the Illinois budget process.

An examination of the General Fund balance sheets for the fiscal years 1991–2001 indicates that state finances did not fully recover from the 1990–1991 recession before recession returned again in 2001. General Fund balances, based on Generally Accepted Accounting Principles (GAAP), are summarized in Table 6.1. On a GAAP basis, Illinois began the 1990s with a large, negative General Fund balance. Beginning in fiscal year 1994, the General Fund balance sheet began to improve. The state was generating surpluses and gradually bringing the balance sheet out of the red. Before the General Fund could

**Table 6.1**
**Fund Balance History (GAAP Basis) for**
**the General Funds**

| Fiscal Year | Fund Balance ($ in Millions) |
|---|---|
| 1991 | (1,368) |
| 1992 | (1,656) |
| 1993 | (1,916) |
| 1994 | (1,595) |
| 1995 | (1,204) |
| 1996 | (951) |
| 1997 | (443) |
| 1998 | (213) |
| 1999 | (303) |
| 2000 | (315) |
| 2001 | (1,278) |

*Source:* Illinois FY 2000 & 2001, Comprehensive
Annual Financial Report (CAFR).

climb completely out of the red, another recession, beginning in 2001, reversed the trend. The negative balance in the General Fund, by the end of FY 2001, was as large as it had been in 1995. Illinois's General Fund balance sheet carried a negative fund balance through the 1990s and into the new millenium.

While fund balances inched back toward the black in the late 1990s, major categories of spending grew at rates exceeding growth in income and sales tax revenues. Three major government functions—education, human services, and corrections—grew at rates faster than personal income and sales tax revenues. Other functions grew more slowly, as evidenced by the much slower rate of growth in total expenditures. The two fastest growing functions—education and human services—increased from 43 percent to 59 percent of total expenditures. Growth rates for major revenue sources and categories of expenditure are summarized in Table 6.2. Meanwhile, Illinois grew somewhat more dependent on federal grants-in-aid than on personal income and sales taxes, and reduced its overall reliance on all three revenue sources. Relative reliance on these revenue sources is summarized in Table 6.3.

Growth in Education and Human Services occurred for different reasons. In the education function, Governor George Ryan—elected in 1998—made it a policy to allocate 51 percent of new revenues each year to K-12 education. In human services, "cost push" in the Medicaid program was the primary factor, a condition lamented by Governor Ryan in his February 21, 2001, budget address.

**Table 6.2**
**Summary of Major Fiscal Indicators: 1991–2001**

| Indicator | Rate of Growth in Constant Dollars (1982–1984 = 100) |
|---|---|
| Per Capita Personal Income | 1.7% |
| Revenues: | |
|    Income Tax | 3.0% |
|    Sales Tax | 1.9% |
|    Federal Grants-in-Aid | 3.9% |
| Expenditures: | |
|    Education | 4.0% |
|    Human Services* | 3.8% |
|    Public Protection and Justice | 3.3% |
|    All Functions | 2.8% |
|    Bonded Debt (General and Special Obligation) | 2.5% |

*The sum of the Health and Social Services and Social Assistance functions in CAFR.
Source: Illinois FY 2000 & 2001 CAFR, Bond Rating April 2002: Moody's Aa2.

**Table 6.3**
**Reliance on Major Revenue Sources: FY 1991–2001**

| Source | 2001 | 1991 |
|---|---|---|
| Income Tax | 24.4% | 25.1% |
| Sales Tax | 21.1% | 24.2% |
| Federal Grants-in-Aid | 27.2% | 25.7% |
| Total | 72.7% | 75.0% |

Source: Illinois FY 2000 & 2001 CAFR.

The continuous, negative General Fund balance had significant fiscal and, ultimately, political consequences. During a period when many states were building reserves, Illinois was trying to get its fund balances back out of the red.[3] By 2001, Illinois was again, with the rest of the country, in recessionary mode and the state was in no position to make up for what eventually became a $1.6 billion revenue shortfall for FY 2003.

At the end of FY 1993, thirty-one states had set aside funds for budget stabilization averaging 2.25 percent of appropriations. By FY 1999, The National Conference of State Legislatures projected thirty-nine states would have stabilization funds averaging 6.75 percent of appropriations.[4] The Illinois General Assembly did not enact stabilization fund legislation until the Spring 2000 legislative session. The legislation authorized a one-time transfer of leftover money from the State's Tobacco Settlement Recovery Fund after June 30, 2001.[5] As of October 2001, $226 million was available in the new Budget Stabilization Fund, about one-half of 1 percent of appropriations.[6] In budgeting for FY 2003 in the 2002 legislative session, the stabilization fund was grossly inadequate. Because of the small size of the Fund, it was not used to balance the 2002–2003 budget, but the General Assembly did authorize borrowing from the Fund for cash flow purposes.

## POLITICAL ENVIRONMENT

Until the 2002 general election, when Democrats captured the governor's mansion and both houses of the General Assembly, divided government had been a fact of life in Illinois for three decades. A Republican executive and Democratic legislature was the rule for the 1980s. While a Republican governor remained the rule up through 2002, Democratic majorities in the General Assembly did not. Party competition intensified in the 1990s. Republicans gained control of the Senate in 1992 elections and maintained that control into the new millennium. Landmark 1994 elections brought a landslide reelection victory to Republican Governor Jim Edgar. The same election brought a Republican majority to the Illinois House for the first time in over a decade. A humbled Democratic majority was returned to the House in 1996. In 1998, Republican Governor George Ryan won office by only a slim 51 percent majority. Party control of the General Assembly is depicted in Figures 6.1 and 6.2.

This intense party competition helped change a relationship that had become familiar through the 1980s. The Republican executive would use his veto powers to discipline a strong but not veto-proof Democratic majority in the General Assembly. By the mid- to late-1990s, the situation was more fluid. Governor Edgar enjoyed a Republican controlled Senate after 1992, while a narrow Democratic majority controlled the House. He had a majority in both houses for 2 years—1995–1997. From 1993 onward, control of the Senate was a plus for Republicans, but the narrow margin of Republican Governor Ryan's victory in 1998, and Ryan's subsequent alienation from more conservative Senate Republicans because of his ambitious spending agenda meant that House Democrats were still very important. To enact a budget, bipartisan cooperation was essential. A further political constraint at this time was popular opposition to sales and personal income tax increases.[7] The line-item veto was not the tool that Governor Ryan needed.

**Figure 6.1**
**Party Control of the Illinois House of Representatives**

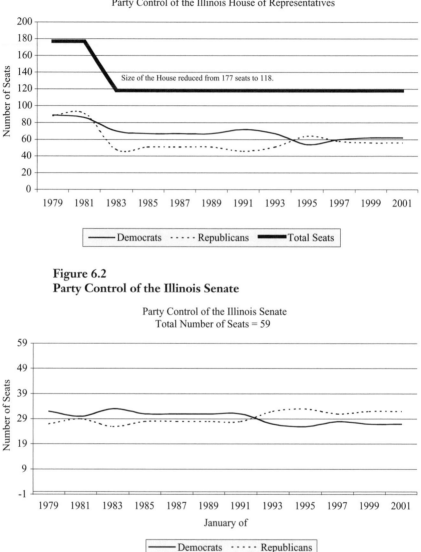

Party Control of the Illinois House of Representatives

Size of the House reduced from 177 seats to 118.

——Democrats · · · · · Republicans ▬▬Total Seats

**Figure 6.2**
**Party Control of the Illinois Senate**

Party Control of the Illinois Senate
Total Number of Seats = 59

January of

——Democrats · · · · · Republicans

By 2002, Governor Ryan had been weakened by a scandal that had taken place while he was Illinois Secretary of State. Top aides had been indicted for selling driver's licenses for bribes. While Ryan was not charged with any crimes, his associates were. Meanwhile, severe fiscal stress undermined his fiscal agenda. He announced that he would not seek a second term. Democrats sensed the opportunity to retake the Governor's mansion, and, possibly, the Senate. When the General Assembly met in 2002, Democrats had an incentive to stop cooperating with the lame duck Republican governor. Democratic optimism was borne out by the November 5, 2002 elections. A Democrat was elected governor and Democratic majorities were won in both the House and the Senate.

## BUDGETING BY NEGOTIATION

The context for budgeting in Illinois in the 1980s was divided government. A Republican governor used strong constitutional and institutional powers to dominate a Democratic legislature. Budgeting by veto characterized the period. In the 1990s, a new way of making budget decisions evolved. From around 1993 to 2001, a 9-year period, budget decisions were negotiated by the governor and legislative leaders. Budgeting by negotiation had three distinct features. First, reduction and item vetoes virtually disappeared, while amendatory vetoes declined as shown in Table 6.4. Because the budget was negotiated in advance, the governor had no need to exercise the strong veto powers granted by the Illinois constitution. Second, legislative leaders of all four caucuses met with the governor at various times throughout the budget process to negotiate budget targets, or "set the marks." The Bureau of the Budget was an important partner in the negotiation process, often being the agency that drafted the main budget bill. As a result, appropriations committees became unimportant in the budget process. Third, the budget was enacted in a few large appropriations bills. An informal search of session laws back as far as 1992 by the Illinois General Assembly's Legislative Research Unit found just two or three appropriations bills each year. General Assembly staff responses to a 1998 survey by the National Conference of State Legislatures indicate that two to eight bills were generally used to enact the budget.[8] This is very different from the eighty or so bills used in the 1980s.

Budgeting by negotiation did not come into being overnight. It evolved in response to changing political and economic circumstances. To exist, it required a system of incentives. It was an informal process that existed within the context of the governor's constitutional and institutional advantages. Two Republican governors, Jim Edgar (January 1991 through 1998) and George Ryan (January 1999 through 2002) used the process.

By our criteria, budgeting by negotiation began when the new Senate Republican majority, elected in 1992, took power in 1993. All three characteristics of budgeting by negotiation, as we have defined it, were present that year—absence of reduction and line-item vetoes, negotiation of the budget by a small group of legislative leaders and executive officials, and a greatly reduced number of appropriations bills. Two of the characteristics, negotiation by a few elites and reduced number of appropriations bills, were present at least as early as 1992, but the continued—but somewhat reduced—use of item and

**Table 6.4**
**Exercise of Reduction, Item, and Amendatory Veto**

| General Assembly Session | Reduction or Item-Vetoed | Amendatory Vetoed | Total |
|---|---|---|---|
| 1973–1974 | 99 | 60 | 159 |
| 1975–1976 | 104 | 98 | 202 |
| 1977–1978 | 39 | 116 | 155 |
| 1979–1980 | 49 | 123 | 172 |
| 1981–1982 | 131 | 102 | 233 |
| 1983–1984 | 68 | 187 | 255 |
| 1985–1986 | 135 | 115 | 250 |
| 1987–1988 | 107 | 133 | 240 |
| 1989–1990 | 40 | 140 | 180 |
| 1991–1992 | 26 | 90 | 116 |
| 1993–1994 | 0 | 50 | 50 |
| 1995–1996 | 0 | 46 | 46 |
| 1997–1998 | 0 | 53 | 53 |
| 1999–2000 | 1 | 40 | 41 |
| 2001–2002 (First Year Only) | 0 | 19 | 19 |
| 2001–2002 (Second Year Only) | 234 | Unavailable | 234 |

*Source:* Table created by the authors from data provided by Illinois General Assembly Legislative Research Unit. A count of amendatory vetoes for the second year of the 2001–2002 General Assembly was unavailable as of this writing.

reduction vetoes would seem to indicate that the system was less effective than in subsequent years. It was after the Republican Senate took office in 1993 that the number of item and reduction vetoes dropped to zero.

To cope with budget shortfalls, Governor Jim Edgar, who took office in 1991, developed a policy of meeting with legislative leaders early in the budget process in order to avoid confrontations, budget delays, and veto threats late in the session. As shown in Table 6.1, a negative General Fund balance at the end of FY 1991, 6 months after Edgar took office, continued to get worse in 1992 and 1993. Still, Governor Edgar used vetoes in the first 2 years of his first term. After the 1992 general election, a Republican Senate majority gave Edgar a more congenial relationship with at least one General Assembly chamber. Always difficult, overrides were now going to be impossible for House Democrats, who still retained a majority. Democrats now had an incentive to get what they wanted through negotiations. They could negotiate and become participants in the process, for which there was now a precedent, or they could be sidelined.

We also examined another possible contribution to the phenomenon of budgeting by negotiation. This was a feature of the 1970 Illinois Constitution that required a three-fifths majority to enact a budget after June 30. This date was moved up to May 30 in a 1994 amendment to the state constitution. It is possible that the shortened time frame in 1994 contributed to budgeting by negotiation in the 1990s by shortening the legislative budget process. However, budgeting by negotiation had already begun before the amendment.

At the same time that budgeting by negotiation was beginning to evolve, the legislature began enacting the budget in a few omnibus appropriations bills, a different strategy from the pattern of the 1980s. But the omnibus bill fits the budgeting by negotiation model. It is difficult to manage a negotiated agreement if it is enacted piecemeal. Multiple bills require multiple votes, any one of which could fail, and failure of the leadership to win on any one of many bills could unravel a negotiated budget. Breaking the budget up into a few bills—operating, capital, and education finance, for example—reduces the number of votes that must be taken. Still, failure to enact the negotiated budget on a floor vote or amendments to the bill on the floor could contribute to failure of the negotiated budget.

To protect leadership's budget bills and make budgeting by negotiation workable, tools were needed to satisfy the rank and file who had been excluded from the process. Illinois had several tools available. These tools allowed the governor and legislative leaders to reward legislators with funds for their districts. *Member Initiative Grants* were available to individual legislators to send to their districts at their discretion. The funds were allocated to the rank and file by the leadership. Legislators came to rely on these grants to demonstrate to their constituents that they had clout in Springfield.[9] The Governor was also able to award funds from various state grant-in-aid programs and controlled the release of capital development funds. All of these tools could be used to reward the faithful rank and file with funds that could be used to benefit their districts. Voting against the leadership's negotiated budget could mean losing access to funds beneficial to a legislator's district and thereby endanger a legislator's chances of reelection.

Budgeting by negotiation reduced agency influence in the budget process. The system was highly centralized, virtually eliminating any influence by the appropriations committees (especially in the House). Budget hearings became pro forma exercises. State agencies were not testifying in front of the real decision makers. For the executive branch, control over agencies became easier. The governor had enjoyed substantial control over agency behavior even before the negotiated budget system became the model. Responses to two NCSL surveys published in 1988 and 1998 indicate that, historically, Illinois General Assembly appropriations committees have not even received copies of agency budget requests, only the Governor's recommendations.[10] But, by making agency testimony ineffective, budgeting by negotiation increased executive control over agencies.

The political landscape grew more competitive as the fiscal situation improved in the 1990s. Republicans gained control of the Senate in 1993.

Democrats lost control of the House for 2 years (1995–1996) and, after regaining control, were more eager for bipartisan legislating.

Republican Governor George Ryan came into office in 1999 on the heels of a very close election. His margin of victory was a bare 51 percent. Ryan's platform included ambitious plans for capital improvements and public education—51 percent of new revenues were to be committed to public education and a $12 billion program of public works, *Illinois First*, would require new bonding authority.[11] While the state's fiscal condition had improved, the Republican Senate, which should have given Governor Ryan ample power to dominate the Democratic House, remained fiscally conservative. And, according to GAAP measures, the General Fund still had a negative balance. There was no way Ryan could accomplish his costly agenda without negotiating with legislative leaders, especially Democrats. His veto powers became irrelevant to the budget issues at hand. Instead, he continued and enhanced the negotiating process initiated by his Republican predecessor, Jim Edgar. He met with the leaders of each caucus at the beginning of the legislative process to "set the marks," i.e., set spending targets for government functions and make policy on major budget items, such as Medicaid reimbursement rates, for example. It was a bipartisan process. The negotiation process enabled give and take between a small group of people. The agendas of the major actors were not the same, but the effect was a kind of before-the-fact conference committee. The conference would normally be the most important feature of the budget process in a state legislature with a caucus-oriented budget system, like the Illinois General Assembly.[12] The effect on the executive process and on legislative institutions was profound.

### The Effect of Budgeting by Negotiation on the Formal Budgetary Process

While the center of decision making in the General Assembly is the party caucus, committee structures exist to deliberate policy and make appropriations. As of 2002, there were five appropriations committees, plus a property tax and school funding committee, and a revenue committee in the House. The Senate had a single appropriations committee and a revenue committee as shown in Table 6.5. Each party caucus in each chamber has a staff, including budget analysts, which reports to the party leadership. The fiscal staff directors assign staff members to the various appropriations committees. Separate majority and minority staffs serve each committee. Formally, direction to committees comes from the party caucus and its leadership. In turn, committees are supposed to draft the various appropriations bills and report them to the floor of their respective chambers. In addition to partisan staff, the Economic and Fiscal Commission, a bipartisan legislative agency, provides technical support in the form of revenue forecasts, fiscal notes, and special studies, to both chambers.

**Table 6.5**
**General Assembly Money Committees**

| House | Senate |
| --- | --- |
| Appropriations: Elementary and Secondary Education | Appropriations |
| Appropriations: General Services | Revenue |
| Appropriations: Higher Education | |
| Appropriations: Human Services | |
| Appropriations: Public Safety | |
| Property Tax and School Funding | |
| Revenue Committee | |

*Source:* Illinois General Assembly Web site, http://www.legis.state.il.us. (Accessed April 2002).

The informal process of budgeting by negotiation, however, diverted authority from the committees, and even from the caucuses. To deliver on the negotiated budget, legislative leaders needed more control. Committees could not be trusted to deliver a negotiated budget piecemeal, so legislative leaders appointed a group of loyal supporters to mark up the budget. When Ryan became governor, this small group of the leadership's designees came to be called the "budgeteers" by Springfield insiders and the press. Caucus appropriations staff and the Bureau of the Budget provided staff support. Under the formal process, caucus appropriations staff members are allocated to the various appropriations committees by the staff directors to support the work of the committees. In the informal process, the caucus staff supported the work of their respective budgeteers. In the 2002 session, there were just four budgeteers, one from each party caucus in each chamber.

While appropriations committees went through the motions of budget hearings, the budgeteers did the real work of marking up the budget. Acting upon the negotiated targets set by leadership and the governor, the budgeteers, supported by caucus and BoB staffs, created the budget, line by line. Generally, it was BoB that drafted the budget bills.

On the surface, the House committee structure would appear to increase member participation. Where there were only two appropriations committees in the 1980s there are now five. The Senate has dropped from two appropriations committees to one. But the rise of an informal process made appropriations committees, especially in the House of Representatives, irrelevant. The informal process significantly reduced the influence and participation of rank and file legislators in the budget process. The number of appropriations bills used to enact the budget was also reduced, from multiple bills, as many as eighty, to an omnibus format with the budget enacted in just a few large bills.

Budgeting by negotiation greatly reduced the exercise of item, reduction, and amendatory vetoes. Item and reduction vetoes disappeared in the 1993–1994 General Assembly (when Republicans took control of the Senate) and only one such veto was exercised until 2002. Yet, in previous years these vetoes were numerous. Amendatory vetoes also dropped (Table 6.4). Clearly, legislative leaders were able to hold negotiated budgets together.

During the 1990s, the formal executive budget process described in 1991 by Rubin et al. changed very little. But after the Governor delivered the budget to the General Assembly, things did change. BoB's director and staff worked closely with legislative leaders and/or designees to mark up the budget and draft the omnibus appropriations bill. Since legislative appropriations committees did not mark up separate bills, BoB's attention was on the small group of people—the budgeteers—who were designated by leadership to mark up the bills.

The effect of budgeting by negotiation on agencies and executive power was profound. Agency testimony before committees can be of little effect if the committees are not making budget decisions. This placed even more importance on agency success in the executive budget process. This process strengthened the BoB.

Budgeting by negotiation offered a number of advantages to the executive. It increased executive influence in marking up omnibus appropriations bills. The Bureau of the Budget did not have to keep track of the work of a number of committees; it had only to support the work of a few key people selected by leadership. By moving real decisions away from committees, it became harder for agencies to make an end run around executive priorities. The process also contributed to an image of bipartisanship in the budget process. Both Democrats and Republicans worked together, up front, in setting budget targets. Strong leaders could then ensure that the negotiated budgets were implemented by maintaining control of appropriations bills.

Ironically, perhaps, given the powerful constitutional tools possessed by the governor, budgeting by negotiation strengthened the executive branch in ways that the veto power could not. The BoB did not have to keep track of several legislative committees to monitor the budget process. It had only to serve the handful of legislative leaders and their designees who were directly involved in the negotiation process. The BoB even dominated bill drafting. Drafting a few large bills placed BoB in a more powerful position than it would have been in had it been forced to review dozens of bills for language to be amended and items to be reduced or vetoed.

### The End of Budgeting by Negotiation

Our conversations with executive and legislative branch staff, as well as the item and reduction veto trend, indicate that budgeting by negotiation lasted from at least as early as 1993 through the 2001 legislative session. While the system was tried in the 2002 budget process, stresses on the system were too great. The system broke down in the House of Representatives when committees reasserted control over the budget.

When the General Assembly convened in January of 2002, Illinois was facing a budget shortfall and the economy was in recession. Governor Ryan, weakened by a scandal that had occurred years before when he was Secretary of State, decided not to run for a second term. There was no money available for the Governor's fiscal agenda so the Governor no longer had anything to gain from negotiation. For legislators, the Governor would not be around to punish them by withholding funds from their districts if they did not support him. The Governor and the Senate would not accept tax increases and House members did not wish to make the deep reductions in the budget that would be necessary without a tax increase. In fact, it was seen as advantageous to House Democrats to speak out and vote against budget reductions.

The General Assembly passed a budget some $500 million out of balance (as defined by the Governor), most of which had been added to the bill by the House. Rather than deal with the issue in conference committee, the Senate concurred with House amendments and the bill went to the Governor. The House appropriations committees had reasserted their role in the budget process, undercutting the role of the budgeteers. Budgeting by negotiation broke down. The Governor issued 234 item and reduction vetoes to bring the budget into balance.[13] There had been only one item veto issued in the years 1993 through 2001. The budget bill was returned to the house of origin, the Senate, which, with its Republican majority, was able to sustain 90 percent of the actual dollar amount vetoed.[14] Only twenty-five vetoes were overridden.[15] The number of vetoes issued by Ryan in 2002 is consistent with the kinds of numbers seen in the 1980s.

It would be naïve to assert that the item and reduction vetoes were unimportant during the period of budgeting by negotiation. The threat was always there, stated or not. As with the system of financial rewards, the extensive veto powers of the governor probably helped sustain the system. With Republican control of the Senate, the Governor would have the last word, even if it meant that all parties would not get what they wanted.

In 2003 Democratic Governor George Blagojevich took office with his party also controlling both legislative chambers. Illinois continued to move away from budgeting by negotiation and returned to the strong gubernatorial pattern observed in the 1980s. The governor used the item and amendatory veto extensively in the 2003 budget cycle. The budget was enacted as twenty-six separate bills rather than a single omnibus appropriation bill. Item, reduction, and amendatory vetoes were used in fifteen of the bills. In fact 135 veto items occurred in three of the bills.

## CONCLUSION

Formal powers granted by constitution or by statute are not always operational. In the case of Illinois in the 1980s, extensive veto powers were useful to a conservative governor facing a Democratic General Assembly. Those same powers became less useful to Republican governors when control of the General Assembly itself became divided, when legislative majorities and electoral margins became thin, and when getting the legislature to say "yes" to the governor's own priorities became more important than just saying "no" to legislative priorities.

Budgeting by negotiation eliminated the need for extensive use of vetoes, encouraged bipartisanship, and avoided gamesmanship by executive agencies. It strengthened the executive's hand through upfront access to the bill drafting process and by reducing the influence of agencies in committee processes that became irrelevant. It also weakened legislative committees and concentrated legislative budget power in a much smaller group of people than in the 1980s.

Will budgeting by negotiation return, or will executives again rely on the veto? We do know that executive and legislative relationships are fluid. Politics can make formal institutions and constitutional powers more or less important. Still, budgeting by negotiation may not be robust over time. Even if not in use, formal institutions and constitutional powers remain in the background, even forming a part of the negotiation system. When the incentives that support an informal system fail, formal powers can easily become operational again. Legislators were certainly aware that a failed negotiation would be that all parties would revert to their formal roles.

It is fairly easy to describe the evolution of budgeting by negotiation. Executive and legislative branch staff members spoke to us freely and candidly about the system. Pinpointing the causes behind the evolution of the system is much more difficult. Fiscal stress seems to be what first prompted Governor Edgar to begin negotiating the budget with legislative leaders, even though it was a Republican Senate majority that allowed the process to flourish. Governor Edgar needed bipartisan support to deal with severe fiscal stress—as illustrated by the increasingly large, negative General Fund balances of the first 3 years of his first term. Even before the use of the item and reduction vetoes ceased, it had become advantageous to negotiate with legislative leaders and use omnibus appropriations bills.

Ironically, it also appears that fiscal stress was a contributing factor in the demise of budgeting by negotiation. Severe fiscal constraints forced budget decisions unacceptable to House Democrats. For Governor Ryan budgeting by negotiation was necessary to pursue his own ambitious fiscal agenda. Ryan was able to secure an ambitious program of spending on education and capital improvements, while legislators were able to bring grants and capital projects to their constituencies. The system, at least in the Ryan years, had come to depend on money. But another important factor in the demise of budgeting by negotiation was political change. Election year politics, Ryan's decision to not seek another term, and the potential opportunity to elect a Democratic governor meant that House Democrats had another incentive not to negotiate with Ryan. It was better to be against budget cuts that might endanger their reelection campaigns. After nearly a decade of use, budgeting by negotiation fell apart.

Budgeting by negotiation existed as a phenomenon born of the political needs of two governors and legislative leaders who developed the strategy to reduce budget conflict. The incentives to budget by negotiation ended in the last year of Governor Ryan's term. At the present time, it appears that Governor Blagojevich will not be shy about using the extensive constitutional powers that were set aside by his two predecessors, especially given his campaign commitment to restore the state's fiscal health.

## NOTES

1. I. Rubin, J. King, S. C. Wagner, and E. M. Dran (1991), "Illinois: Executive Reform and Fiscal Condition," in *Governors, Legislatures, and Budgets: Diversity Across American States*, chapter 3, pp. 17–29, Edward J. Clynch and Thomas P. Lauth, Eds. Westport, CT: Greenwood.

2. E. J. Clynch and T. P. Lauth (1991), *Governors, Legislatures, and Budgets: Diversity Across American States*. Westport, CT: Greenwood, pp. 152–153.

3. National Association of State Budget Officers, *The Fiscal Survey of States: December 2001* and *The Fiscal Survey of States: December 2000*. Washington, DC.

4. National Conference of State Legislatures 1993–1998 (series), *State Budget Actions*, Denver, CO.

5. Comptroller of Illinois, *FY 2000 Comprehensive Annual Financial Report*, pp. I-13–I-14.

6. Comptroller of Illinois, *Fiscal Focus Quarterly*, p. 17, at http://www.ioc.state.il.us. Percentage calculation by the authors based on $41 billion in FY 2000 appropriations.

7. *Chicago Tribune*, May 5, 2002.

8. J. Grooters and C. Eckl (1998), *Legislative Budget Procedures: A Guide to Appropriations and Budget Processes in the States, Commonwealths and Territories*. Denver, CO: National Conference of State Legislatures.

9. *Chicago Tribune* (February 3, 2002). *The Tribune* reported that grants had totaled $1.5 billion.

10. T. Hutchison and K. James (1988), *Legislative Budget Procedures in the 50 States: A Guide to Appropriations and Budget Processes*. Denver, CO: National Conference of State Legislatures. J. Grooters and C. Eckl (1998), *Legislative Budget Procedures: A Guide to Appropriations and Budget Processes in the States, Commonwealths and Territories*. Denver, CO: National Conference of State Legislatures.

11. Office of the Governor, *For The Record: Administrative and Legislative Accomplishments, George H. Ryan, Governor, Spring 2001*.

12. D. R. Snow and W. Clarke (1999), *Legislative Budget Staffs in the States: A Typology*. Paper presented at the annual conference of the Association for Budgeting and Financial Management, Washington DC, October 9.

13. Office of the Governor, *Veto Message, June 10, 2002, SB 2393*.

14. Office of the Governor, *Governor Ryan Commends Senate for Special Session Action*, Press Release, June 11, 2002.

15. Illinois General Assembly, *Legislative Status Reports, SB 2393*, http://www.legis.state.il.us.

CHAPTER 7

# Oregon: The Influence of Direct Democracy on Budget Outcomes

*Bill Simonsen*

This chapter looks at the State of Oregon budget process and the environment in which resource allocation and revenue raising decisions are made. Oregon is a state where initiative and referenda are arguably the most important factors shaping resource allocation trends. It is one of the few states that do not employ a general retail sales tax resulting in an extreme reliance upon the personal income tax. Further, the economy of the state is transforming from a resource-based timber dominated economy to a service and high technology driven one. As will be shown, these environmental factors have important impacts on budget outcomes.

This chapter is organized as follows. First, I discuss the changing economy and demographics in the state. Next, I provide an overview of Oregon's revenues and expenditures. I then describe the initiative and referendum process and its impact upon the state budget. I next provide an overview of the state's strategic plan and benchmarks. This is followed by a description of the technical budget process.

## ECONOMY AND DEMOGRAPHICS

The Oregon economy has historically been based on natural resource extraction, particularly timber. The recession in the early 1980s hit Oregon harder than the rest of the country, especially the construction and the timber industries. Between 1979 and 1982 about 9 percent of all nonfarm jobs were lost (State of Oregon, Preliminary Official Statement, 2001). The expansion in the 1980s saw the Oregon economy begin to diversify. Wood products continued to decline, the high technology sector began to emerge, and there was strong growth in the service and trade sectors.

These trends continued into the 1990s as the importance of the lumber and wood products industry declined, while high technology and services grew considerably (State of Oregon, Secretary of State, 2000). Table 7.1 shows the change in Oregon nonfarm employment from 1991 to 2001. The economy of the state continued its transformation from lumber to a high technology, service, and trade-based economy. Government employment also fell from 18.1 percent of employment to 16.9 percent of overall nonfarm employment.

Just like the national economy, financial services, business services (including temporary employment companies) and other services all showed strong growth during the 1990s. The service sector is now a larger part of the Oregon economy than the goods producing sector (including wood products) (State of Oregon, Secretary of State, 2000). Per capita income growth also outstripped the nation during the 1990s. In 1988, per capita income was 92.2 percent of the United States average, and by 1996 it had grown to 96.2 percent (State of Oregon, Preliminary Official Statement, 2002).

Recent economic times have not been as good, however. The Asian financial crisis hurt Oregon's economic growth: job growth fell to about 2 percent annually in 1998 and 1999, from 4 percent during much of the 1990s (State of Oregon, Preliminary Official Statement, 2001). Many high technology firms cancelled or postponed expansions and reduced employment. During this period exports to Canada grew steadily and now represents Oregon's largest export market. However, the recent weak economy hurt Oregon exports, including exports to Canada. Oregon exports declined 22.2 percent from 2000 to 2001 (State of Oregon Department of Administrative Services, 2002, p. 26). Table 7.1 shows that total nonfarm jobs fell 0.7 percent between 2000 and 2001. Certain industries saw precipitous declines from 2000 to 2001, including construction and lumber and wood products. Per capita income has fallen relative to the nation since 1997 and now stands at about 93 percent of the national average, erasing the gains made through much of the 1990s (State of Oregon, Preliminary Official Statement, 2002). The weak economy led to severe state budget crises during the 2001–2003 biennium (see Budget Problems in the 2001–2003 Biennium).

Population in the state grew by 18.3 percent from 1989 to 1999 to 3,300,800 people. About 64 percent of this growth was because of in-migration, the rest due to natural changes (births-deaths) (State of Oregon Legislative Revenue Office, 2001). Since 1990, Oregon has numbered among the top ten fastest growing states (State of Oregon, Secretary of State, 2000). This strong population growth has been accompanied by changing demographics. School age population (K-12) grew substantially in the 1990s (19.2%) as did the 45 to 65 age group, which rose by 48.1 percent (State of Oregon Legislative Revenue Office, 2001). The Asian and Black racial groups and the Hispanic ethnic group increased rapidly during the 1990s. Oregon remains overwhelmingly white, however.

# Table 7.1
## Oregon Nonfarm Payroll Employment, Calendar Year Averages. (Nos. in 000s)

| Industry | 1991 | 1991, % of Total | 2000 | 2001 | 2001, % of Total | % Change, 1991–2000 | % Change, 2000–2001 |
|---|---|---|---|---|---|---|---|
| Total All Industries | 1,250.8 | 100 | 1,606.8 | 1,596.1 | 100 | 28.5 | -0.7 |
| Manufacturing | 211.7 | 16.9 | 243.6 | 236.2 | 14.8 | 15.1 | -3.0 |
| Durable Goods | 150.1 | 12.0 | 180.1 | 174.1 | 10.9 | 20.0 | -3.3 |
| Lumber and Wood Products | 56.6 | 4.5 | 49.0 | 46.0 | 2.9 | -13.4 | -6.1 |
| Nondurable Goods | 61.6 | 4.9 | 63.5 | 62.1 | 3.9 | 3.1 | -2.2 |
| Food and Kindred Products | 25.0 | 2.0 | 24.9 | 23.8 | 1.5 | -0.4 | -4.4 |
| Textile Mill Products | 1.6 | 0.1 | 0.9 | 0.9 | 0.1 | -43.8 | 0.0 |
| Apparel | 2.7 | 0.2 | 2.6 | 2.7 | 0.2 | -3.7 | 3.8 |
| Paper and Allied Products | 9.2 | 0.7 | 7.8 | 7.5 | 0.5 | -15.2 | -3.8 |
| Printing and Publishing | 15.0 | 1.2 | 17.0 | 16.3 | 1.0 | 13.3 | -4.1 |
| Chemicals and Allied Products | 2.6 | 0.2 | 3.5 | 3.7 | 0.2 | 34.6 | 5.7 |
| Petroleum and Asphalt Products | 0.6 | 0.0 | 0.4 | 0.4 | 0.0 | -33.3 | 0.0 |
| Rubber and Plastic Products | 4.6 | 0.4 | 6.9 | 6.5 | 0.4 | 50.0 | -5.8 |
| Leather Products | 0.4 | 0.0 | 0.4 | 0.4 | 0.0 | 0.0 | 0.0 |
| Nonmanufacturing | 1,039.0 | 83.1 | 1,363.3 | 1,360.0 | 85.2 | 31.2 | -0.2 |
| Mining and Quarrying | 1.6 | 0.1 | 1.9 | 1.8 | 0.1 | 18.8 | -5.3 |
| Construction | 51.4 | 4.1 | 84.3 | 78.9 | 4.9 | 64.0 | -6.4 |
| Transportation and Public Utilities | 65.2 | 5.2 | 80.0 | 79.3 | 5.0 | 22.7 | -0.9 |
| Trade | 314.3 | 25.1 | 395.3 | 390.5 | 24.5 | 25.8 | -1.2 |
| Finance, Insurance, and Real Estate | 83.2 | 6.7 | 94.0 | 95.0 | 6.0 | 13.0 | 1.1 |
| Services | 296.9 | 23.7 | 440.6 | 445.3 | 27.9 | 48.4 | 1.1 |
| Government | 226.4 | 18.1 | 267.3 | 269.2 | 16.9 | 18.1 | 0.7 |

Source: State of Oregon Preliminary Official Statement, 2002. (Their source: Oregon Employment Department)

## OVERVIEW OF OREGON REVENUES AND EXPENDITURES

Oregon is one of only five states that do not have a general retail sales tax. The Oregon electorate has voted upon a sales tax nine times in the past. Each time the sales tax measure failed to pass, often by large margins. Therefore, because the state also receives no property taxes, the principle source of revenue for the state's general fund is the personal income tax. Table 7.2 shows the mix of general and lottery fund revenue sources, and how it has changed from the 1988–1989 biennium (as described in the "Oregon Budget Process" section, the state operates on a 2-year budget cycle). There was strong growth in the personal income tax during the 1989–2001 period, fuelled by a strong and growing economy. The personal income tax lost ground during the 2001–2003 biennium as the economy weakened. The state is now more dependent upon personal income taxes than it was a decade ago. Corporate income tax has fallen in importance over the 10-year period. Lottery funds have increased significantly from 1989–1991 biennium to the 2001–2002 biennium, growing by 571 percent. The use of lottery funds are limited by the state constitution to economic development, education, and protecting parks, beaches, watersheds, and critical fish and wildlife habitats.

The marginal tax rates for the individual income tax are progressively structured ranging from 5 percent to 9 percent of taxable income (tied to the federal definition of taxable income). Since 1993 the tax brackets have been tied to the U.S. Consumer Price Index. The effective tax rate in 2000 was about 5.5 percent of adjusted gross income because of deductions and credits (State of Oregon Legislative Revenue Office, 2001). As of 2001, the marginal tax brackets were as shown in Table 7.3.

Like many states, Oregon's general and lottery fund is dominated by expenditures on K-12 education, which accounts for nearly three out of every five dollars of spending. Figure 7.1 shows the relative importance of general lottery fund categories of expenditures.

Spending has grown significantly in the areas of public safety and K-12 education, due to voter approved mandates (see Referendum, Initiative and Budgeting in Oregon).

### Budget Problems in the 2001–2003 Biennium

Oregon was hit with severe budget problems in the 2001–2003 biennium due to the weak state and national economy. Table 7.4 shows the personal income growth in the state and the growth in personal income tax collections.

Personal income taxes showed terrific growth from 1989–1991 biennium to the 1999–2001 biennium. Some of this growth in personal income taxes in this period was due to indexing the tax brackets to the Consumer Price Index since 1993. However, the progressive nature of the personal income tax is also a key reason it has historically grown faster than State personal income

**Table 7.2**
**General and Lottery Fund Revenue Sources ($ in Millions)**

| Revenue source | 1987–1989 Biennium | % of Total | 1997–1999 Biennium | % of Total | 1999–2001 Biennium | % of Total | Est.* 2001–2003 Biennium | % of Total | % Change, 1987–1989/ 1997–1999 | % Change, 1997–1999/ 1999–2001 | % Change, 1999–2001/ 2001–2003 |
|---|---|---|---|---|---|---|---|---|---|---|---|
| Personal Income Tax | 3,009 | 79.2 | 7,123.1 | 85.5 | 8,737.00 | 86.3 | 8,440.0 | 86.7 | 136.7 | 22.7 | –3.4 |
| Corporate Income Tax | 324.5 | 8.5 | 589.1 | 7.1 | 754.9 | 7.5 | 524.5 | 5.4 | 81.5 | 28.1 | –30.5 |
| Insurance Premium Tax | 108.4 | 2.9 | 102 | 1.2 | 102.8 | 1.0 | 105.4 | 1.1 | –5.9 | 0.8 | 2.5 |
| Inheritance Tax | 23.2 | 0.6 | 89 | 1.1 | 91.4 | 0.9 | 100.7 | 1.0 | 283.6 | 2.7 | 10.2 |
| Cigarette Tax | 128 | 3.4 | 119.7 | 1.4 | 104.3 | 1.0 | 98.2 | 1.0 | –6.5 | –12.9 | –5.8 |
| Other Tobacco Tax | 10 | 0.2 | 21.2 | 0.3 | 22.1 | 0.2 | 22.6 | 0.2 | 112.0 | 4.2 | 2.3 |
| Other Taxes | 5.1 | 0.1 | 4.9 | 0.1 | 4.4 | 0.04 | 4.3 | 0.04 | –3.9 | –10.2 | –2.3 |
| Non-Tax Revenue | 193.5 | 5.1 | 285.6 | 3.3 | 304.9 | 3.0 | 439.5 | 4.5 | 47.6 | 6.8 | 44.1 |
| Total | 3,801.7 | 100 | 8,334.6 | 100 | 10,121.90 | 100.0 | 9735.2 | 100.0 | 119.2 | 21.4 | –3.8 |
| Lottery Fund Revenue | 106 | N/A | 612.9 | N/A | 630.6 | N/A | 711.1 | N/A | 478.2 | 2.9 | 12.8 |

* Estimate as of June 2002. Personal income taxes later (December 2002) expected to decline 7.7 percent from 1999–2001 close of session forecast (State of Oregon Department of Administrative Services, 2002. *Oregon Economic and Revenue Forecast*, December 2002, XXII(4)).

*Source:* Years 1987–1989 and 1997–1999—State of Oregon Legislative Revenue Office, 2001. *Oregon Public Finance: Basic Facts*. Salem, OR: Legislative Revenue Office, pp. A6 and A7. (Their Source: Department of Administrative Services). Years 1999–2001 and 2001–2003 estimate—State of Oregon Department of Administrative Services, 2002. *Oregon Economic and Revenue Forecast*, June 2002, XXII(2), Salem, OR: Department of Administrative Services, Tables B2 and R.2, p. 86.

**Table 7.3**
**2001 Tax Year Rate Schedule**

| Single Returns | | Joint Returns | |
|---|---|---|---|
| *Taxable Income* | *Tax Before Credits* | *Taxable Income* | *Tax Before Credits* |
| Not Over $2,500 | 5% of Taxable Income | Not Over $5,000 | 5% of Taxable Income |
| $2,500 to $6,300 | $125 + 7% of Income Over $2,500 | $5,000 to $12,600 | $250 + 7% of Income Over $5,000 |
| Over $6,300 | $391 + 9% of Income Over $6,300 | Over $12,600 | $782 + 9% of Income Over $12,600 |

*Source:* State of Oregon Department of Revenue Web site. *Personal Income Taxes.* URL: http://www.dor.state.or.us/personal.html. Downloaded on December 20, 2002.

**Figure 7.1**
**General and Lottery Fund Budget, 2001–2003.**
*Source*: State of Oregon Legislative Revenue Office, 2002. Budget Highlights Revised 2001–2003, Legislatively Approved Budget, Based on September 1–18, 2002, Special Session Actions. Salem, OR: Legislative Revenue Office, p. iv

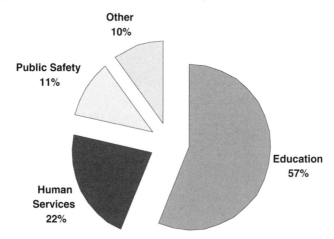

(Governor's Tax Review Technical Advisory Committee, 1998). Although the progressive nature of the personal income tax allowed it to grow faster than personal income while the economy was strong, the state's economic problems have led to personal income growth in 2001 and 2002 that is about half what it was throughout the 1990s. This has led to very weak personal income tax collections in the 2001–2003 biennium. In addition, the voters in November

Table 7.4
**Personal Income and Personal Income Taxes**

| Year | Oregon Personal Income ($ in Millions) | Percent Change | Biennium Year | Oregon Personal Income Tax Collections ($ in Millions) | Percent Change |
|------|------|------|------|------|------|
| 1990 | 52.2 | | | | |
| 1991 | 54.9 | 5.2 | 1989–1991 | 3,854 | |
| 1992 | 58.2 | 6.0 | | | |
| 1993 | 61.9 | 6.4 | 1991–1993 | 4,562 | 18.4 |
| 1994 | 66.1 | 6.8 | | | |
| 1995 | 71.2 | 7.7 | 1993–1995 | 5,381 | 18.0 |
| 1996 | 75.6 | 6.2 | | | |
| 1997 | 80.6 | 6.6 | 1995–1997 | 6,303 | 17.1 |
| 1998 | 85.3 | 5.8 | | | |
| 1999 | 89.1 | 4.5 | 1997–1999 | 7,123 | 13.0 |
| 2000 | 95.4 | 7.1 | | | |
| 2001 | 97.8 | 2.5 | 1999–2001 | 8,737 | 22.7 |
| Est. 2002 | 101.1 | 3.4 | Est. 2001–2003 | 8,061 | −7.7 |

*Source:* State of Oregon POS (2002), p. A-10, A-21. 2002 Estimate from State of Oregon, Department of Administrative Services, 2002. *Oregon Economic and Revenue Forecast* (December 2002) XXII(4), pp. 53, 81.

2000 passed Measure 88, which increased the maximum deduction of federal income taxes paid from $3,000 to $5,000 (State of Oregon, Secretary of State, 2000b). The reduction in taxes due to Measure 88 was estimated at the time of the vote at $168 million for the 2001–2003 biennium (State of Oregon, Secretary of State, 2000b). This Measure was referred by the Legislature.

Personal income taxes are now projected to *decline* 7.7 percent. This creates substantial problems for the state budget because there is no sales tax, and personal income tax comprises about 87 percent of General and Lottery Fund revenues. Continued downward revised revenue forecasts through the biennium led to *five* special sessions of the state legislature. The revenue problems are compounded by the expenditure inflexibility created by voter-approved initiatives (see Referendum, Initiative and Budgeting in Oregon).

Table 7.5 shows the dates of the special sessions, the revised revenue forecasts, and the key actions taken.

As the above Table 7.5 indicates, the State used a variety of expenditure cuts and recurring or one-time revenue increases to maintain budget balance. On January 28, 2003, the Oregon electorate defeated the Measure 28, the proposed income tax increase, by a 54 percent ("no") to 46 percent ("yes")

**Table 7.5**
**Special Session Highlights**

| Dates | General Fund Revenue Projections | Special Session Highlights |
|---|---|---|
| Number 1, February 8–11, 2002 | Forecast of $720 million less in revenues than the 2001 close-of-session estimate. Based on December 2001 revenue forecast | Prior to the special session the State Emergency Board implemented some reductions in the Department of Human Services and the Department of Corrections. The Legislature reduced spending by $641 million during the special session and increased revenues from various sources. The Governor subsequently vetoed (or didn't sign) the legislative rebalancing plan |
| Number 2, February 25– March 2, 2002 | Additional $144 million general fund revenue loss. Total of $864 million less than the 2001 close-of-session estimate, somewhat offset by a $31 million lottery fund increase. Based on March 2002 revenue forecast | During the special session the legislature raised about $480 million in revenue from direct increases to the general fund and transfers from other funds. The revenue plan included the use of unallocated Medicaid Upper Payment Limit (MUPL) Account Funds, Tobacco Master Settlement Funds, and transfers from a separate education fund. The education transfer required a constitutional amendment changing the Education Endowment Fund to the Education Stability Fund that was later defeated by the voters at a May election. Subsequently, the Governor vetoed portions of the plan resulting in a $81 million shortfall. The Governor directed the Department of Administrative Services to make selective allotment reductions |
| Number 3, June 12–30, 2002 | Additional $545 million, $1.409 billion below than the 2001 close-of-session estimate. Based on June 2002 revenue forecast | The plan consisted of $835 million of revenue changes and $54 million in expenditure reductions. The increased revenues included raising the cigarette tax and various one-time revenue sources such as shifts from other funds, revenue bonds on future cigarette taxes, and delayed education payments. The voters at September election approved the education transfer through approval of the Education Stability Fund |

| Dates | General Fund Revenue Projections | Special Session Highlights |
|-------|----------------------------------|----------------------------|
| Number 4, August 16–20, 2002 | No new revenue estimate | The Governor vetoed three bills from the 3rd special session, including two key ones: issuance of revenue bonds based on cigarette tax and the delayed education payments. The purpose of the 4th special session was to allow the Legislature to override or sustain the veto. The veto was sustained for the revenue bonds and overridden for the delayed education payments |
| Number 5, September 1–18, 2002 | Estimate of $482 million below the June 2002 forecast. Total of $1.891 billion less than the 2001 close-of-session estimate. Based on September 2002 revenue forecast | The 5th special session included expenditure cuts of $43.7 million and $150 million in tobacco revenue bonds. It also included $303 million of increased income taxes or $310 million of across the board cuts if the income tax is not approved by the voters (vote was held on January 28, 2003). The income tax increase would change the top personal income tax rate from 9% to 9.5% and increase the corporate rate from 6.6% to 6.93%. Rates would return to 9% after 3 years |

*Sources:* State of Oregon Legislative Revenue Office, 2002, *Budget Highlights.*
*Revised 2001–2003, Legislatively Approved Budget, Based on September 1–18, 2002.*
*Special Session Actions.* Salem, OR: Legislative Revenue Office, pp. i–iii, State of Oregon Secretary of State, 2003, *January Special Election Online Voters' Guide,* Measure 28, http://www.sos.state. or.us/elections/jan282003/guide/m28.htm. Downloaded on December 28, 2002.

margin (State of Oregon, Secretary of State, 2003). The State implemented a plan to balance the budget after the voters rejected the income tax increase. The plan included, among other items, cuts to state programs and a $95 million funding decrease for K-12 education (Hogan and Carter, 2003). The education cuts have prompted several school districts in the state to reduce the number of school days in order to balance their budgets, resulting in thirteen districts (amounting to one in seven school children) in violation of state minimum requirements (Hammond, 2003).

## REFERENDUM, INITIATIVE, AND BUDGETING IN OREGON

Oregon has a long history of direct citizen participation in decision making. Initiatives and referendum were instituted in 1902 through a ballot measure approved by Oregon voters (the first state to establish the initiative process was South Dakota in 1898) (Moore and Greiss, 1997). The initiative process allows the citizens to directly enact new laws or amend the constitution, while a referendum gives voters the opportunity to consider legislation passed by the legislature. In 1908, the State constitution was amended to allow for voter recall of public officials.

Since its inception until 2000, voters in Oregon have passed 124 out of 349 (about 36%) of initiative and referenda that have been placed on the ballot by citizens, and 206 out of 363 (about 57%) of the measures referred by the legislature (State of Oregon Elections Division, 2000). The numbers of initiative and referenda on the ballot has been very high in recent years; for instance, the Oregon electorate voted on twenty citizen-developed initiatives or referenda in 2000.

One could easily argue that the key factor shaping the State of Oregon budget over the past 10 years has been the citizen initiative process. Of course, the changing nature of the economy and demographic shifts have also had impacts. However, two types of citizen-led initiatives, for property tax limits and corrections, have had a profound affect on the structure of the state's budget. First, I turn to property tax limitation initiatives.

### Property Tax Initiatives

In November of 1990, the voters passed Measure 5 that amended the constitution to limit property taxes. Measure 5 separated local governments into two categories, schools and nonschools, and set separate limits for each of them. Schools include K-12 education and community colleges. The limit for schools was set initially at $15 per $1000 of assessed value, declining by $2.50 per $1000 over 5 years until the phase-in ended in 1995 at $5 per $1000. Measure 5 also required that the state replace all revenues that schools would lose due to the enactment of the limit. Nonschools are defined as all other local governments (cities, counties, and special districts, etc.) and their limit was set at $10 per $1000 of assessed value with no phase-in or state replacement obligation. Further, Measure 5 required that assessed value be set at real market value. Voters cannot override these limits except for debt service for voter approved municipal bond sales.

Measure 5 deeply changed public finance in the state by placing the primary responsibility for financing schools with the state. Although Measure 5 required the state to replace lost revenue, it did not require that existing state aid be maintained. Further, the measure did not require that each district be made whole, just that the aggregate amount be provided by the state. The state decided to allocate funds primarily on a per pupil basis, and to reduce the amount it was already providing to schools. This forced many of the higher spending school districts to significantly reduce their budgets in the early years of Measure 5.

For many households, Measure 5 did not appear to deliver the tax relief that it promised. There were two main reasons this occurred. First, Measure 5 required that assessed value be set to market value, which in much of Oregon was undergoing strong growth. From 1988 to 1994 the value of taxable property in Oregon grew by 65 percent, with the value of residential property growing by 86 percent and nonresidential property by 49 percent (Oregon Fiscal Choices, 1994). This rapid growth in assessed value was due to strong population and economic growth and an effort by assessors to bring the assessed values to market values where they had fallen behind.

By 1994, the amount of property tax revenue had fallen by 2.7 percent due to Measure 5, but this aggregate number masks regional differences where some counties had double digit declines and other revenue increases. In addition, because of the differential growth in assessed values, residential property taxes grew statewide by 8 percent between 1991 and 1994, while nonresidential property tax fell by 12 percent (Oregon Fiscal Choices, 1994).

Thus, a paradoxical situation emerged (1) governments lost revenue due to Measure 5 (some school districts had significant funding decreases), while (2) residential property taxes increased. This set the stage for the next property tax limit, Measure 47.

Measure 47 was passed in November 1996. When the legislature set out to interpret the new constitutional property tax limit, they found it difficult to write consistent implementing language. As a response, the legislature proposed Measure 50, which Oregon voters enacted in May of 1997. Measure 50 addressed the escalating residential property growth by establishing different assessed and market values for most property and establishing a permanent tax rate. After Measure 50, in 1998 each property's assessed value was rolled back to 1996 values less 10 percent and frozen. These values can grow only 3 percent per year plus new construction and a small number of other adjustments. The combination of assessed value rollback and a permanent tax rate were designed to decrease taxes by 13.2 percent (Legislative Revenue Office, 1999). Temporary operating levies can be approved by the voters, up to the Measure 5 limits and only if passed during a general election or other election where 50 percent of the registered voters cast ballots.

The effect of these property tax measures has been to transfer the bulk of the responsibility for school funding to the state, in effect creating a new mandate. This can easily be seen in the shift of school revenue sources (see Table 7.6). Prior to Measure 5, 25.5 percent of school operating revenue came form the state. By 1999–2000, the state was providing 58.2 percent of school operating revenue.

## Public Safety Initiative

Like many other states, spending on jails and corrections has increased significantly in Oregon. One of the key reasons for this increase was the passage

**Table 7.6**
**School Operating Revenue By Source ($ in Millions)**

| Source of Revenue | 1989–1990 | 1999–2000 |
|---|---|---|
| Total from All Sources | $2,435,701,000 | $4,010,900,000 |
| % From Local Sources | 66.8 | 34.0 |
| % From State Sources | 25.5 | 58.2 |
| % From Federal Sources | 5.9 | 6.4 |
| % From Intermediate Sources | 1.8 | 1.4 |

Source: Legislative Revenue Office, 2001. Oregon Public Finance: Basic Facts. Salem, OR: Legislative Revenue Office, p. 14. (Their Source: Oregon Department of Education).

of Measure 11 in 1994 that provides for mandatory minimum sentences, ranging from 70 to 300 months, for twenty-one violent crimes and treats minors 15-years-old and above as adults for these crimes. In 1990 the prison population in Oregon totaled 5,800 (Office of Economic Analysis, 2000). This number grew to 10,219 by January 1, 2001 and is expected to rise to 14,949 by 2011 (Office of Economic Analysis, 2001). "Measure 11 is responsible for most prison population growth since 1995" (State of Oregon Office of Economic Analysis, 2001, p. 17).

### Impact on the State Budget

The growth in these two voter-enacted mandates, public safety (corrections) and education has far outpaced the rest of the state's budget. School spending made up 41 percent of the General and Lottery fund budgets in the 1989–1991 biennium. By the 1999–2001 biennium this figure climbed to 57 percent (State of Oregon, Secretary of State, 2000; State of Oregon, Legislative Revenue Office, 2002). As Figure 7.2 shows, from the 1989–1991 biennium to the 1999–2001 biennium, the growth in K-12 and community college spending increased 291.1 percent and public safety 151.1 percent. This growth has come at the expense of other budget categories, particularly higher education.

### OREGON BUDGET PROCESS

### Benchmarks

In 1989, the Oregon Progress Board was created to oversee and promote *Oregon Shines*, the state's strategic plan. A series of benchmarks were developed by the Progress Board to measure progress on key issues. There are currently ninety benchmarks covering everything from poverty to protection of rivers and streams. The three core areas are: quality jobs for all Oregonians;

**Figure 7.2**
**Changes in State Spending.**
*Source:* General Fund and Lottery Budgets, 1989–1991 to 1999–2001. Reprinted from: State of Oregon, Secretary of State, 2000, *1999–2000, Oregon Blue Book* (Figure on p. 150)

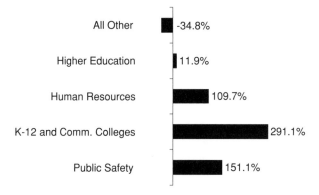

safe, caring, and engaged communities; and healthy, sustainable, surroundings (State of Oregon Progress Board, 2000, 2001).

The Progress Board collects and analyzes data on these benchmarks in order to make recommendations to the legislature and to the Governor. The Progress Board also works with local and county governments to help them develop benchmarks for their specific jurisdictions. The Oregon benchmarks do not carry the force of law (State of Oregon Progress Board, 2001).

As part of the narrative portion of their budget requests, agencies must provide information regarding how their programs and activities relate to Oregon's benchmarks (BAM, 2002). The governor may also request more information on specific benchmarks from any given agency (BAM, 2002). This information is then used in developing funding and program priorities for the governor's budget and may guide legislative debate and appropriations decisions. Therefore, the benchmark system is only loosely tied to the budgeting process.

## Process

The State of Oregon operates on a 2-year budget cycle. The biennium begins July 1 and ends June 30 of odd-numbered years. Budget preparation begins in February of even numbered years. Based on current funding levels, projections for growth, inflation, and new or discontinued programs, state agencies present the governor with a budget request. The governor then reviews the budget requests and develops the overall state budget. This budget is then submitted to the state legislature, which then passes multiple budget bills that the governor can sign, veto, or veto specific provisions thereof (State of Oregon POS, 2001). (A veto may be overridden by a two-thirds vote of the legislature.) The governor and legislature are required by the Oregon Constitution to pass a budget that does not exceed projected revenues for that biennium (Oregon Constitution, Article IX, Section 6). State agencies then spend according to their approved budgets, with the Secretary of State performing audits as required by law. The Legislature enacted a general fund spending limit of 8 percent of the State's personal income (beginning 2001–2003 biennium). This limit can be overridden if the Governor declares an emergency and a three-fifths vote of each house of the Legislature (State of Oregon POS, 2002).

## Preparation

Budget preparation for the following biennium begins in February of even-numbered years with the state Budget and Management (BAM) Division developing tentative budget estimates and producing instructions for agency budget requests. Each agency begins with their current budget and then adjusts for changes in service or personnel levels, addition or cessation of programs, inflation, mandated programs, and other factors that affect the agency's financial needs. Each agency prepares three different budget packages as follows for the 2003–2005 biennium (BAM, 2002, p. 1):

1. The base budget is built on the 2001–2003 Legislatively Adopted Budget. That adopted budget is adjusted for Emergency Board, special session, and nonlimited administrative actions through April 2002, resulting in the legislatively approved budget. It is also adjusted for projected Personal Services, scheduled debt service, and capital construction in the 2003–2005 biennium.
2. Essential packages describe budget adjustments that bring the base to a current service level. Inflation and legislatively approved program changes are examples.
3. Policy packages reflect other program and policy changes that will affect the budget if adopted. *Standardized policy packages will be created for Emergency Board actions after April 2002 (Policy Package No. 080, page 25) and for expenditure reductions needed to balance to available revenues (Policy Package No. 070, page 24).* (Emphasis not added.)

Additionally, to provide the governor and legislature more information regarding potential areas for funding cuts, each agency must propose reduction options of at least 10 percent of its current budget.

The agency requests are compiled by the Budget and Management Division, which then makes recommendations to the governor. At this point, each agency then has the opportunity to appeal the BAM recommendations. The governor's recommended budget is then printed and submitted to the state legislature for consideration during the session that begins January of each odd-numbered year (BAM, 2002).

**Table 7.7**
**State Leadership by Party**

| Year | Senate | House | Governor |
|------|--------|-------|----------|
| 1985 | Democrat | Democrat | Republican |
| 1987 | Democrat | Democrat | Democrat |
| 1989 | Democrat | Democrat | Democrat |
| 1991 | Democrat | Republican | Democrat |
| 1993 | Democrat | Republican | Democrat |
| 1995 | Republican | Republican | Democrat |
| 1997 | Republican | Republican | Democrat |
| 1999 | Republican | Republican | Democrat |
| 2001 | Republican | Republican | Democrat |

*Source:* State of Oregon 2001–2002 Blue Book, http://bluebook.state.or.us/state/elections/elections23.htm. Downloaded on December 20, 2002.

## Approval

Oregon has a bicameral legislature with a Senate and House of Representatives. The Senate has thirty members elected to 4-year terms with half of the seats filled every 2 years. There are sixty representatives that serve 2-year terms in the House. Legislators are elected in even-numbered years from single-member districts. In November 1992, the Constitution was amended to limit terms for the Legislature, statewide offices, and congressional offices. Oregon Legislature limits are 6 years in the House of Representatives, 8 years in the Senate, and 12 years total. The limit is 8 years for each statewide elected office (State of Oregon, Secretary of State, 2000).

Since 1985, both major parties have held leadership in the executive and legislative branches. During most of this time there has not been one party controlling both the legislature and the governorship. Table 7.7 shows the parties of the house and senate leadership and the governor.

Each agency's budget is presented as a separate bill. The Legislative Fiscal Office analyzes the appropriation bills for the Ways and Means Committee. Public hearings are scheduled for comment on the proposed budget for each agency, after which appropriations bills are submitted to the full legislature for a vote. The Governor may veto any bill, or portion of a bill without affecting its remaining provisions (State of Oregon POS, 2001; BAM, 2000).

Revenues are forecast by the State's Office of Economic Analysis (OEA). The OEA revenue forecasts are used by both the legislature and the governor in the budget. If revenues exceed projections by 2 percent or more, the excess is refunded to taxpayers. The amount of the refund is not only the excess over the 2 percent, but also all excess including the 2 percent trigger. The kicker is a statute (ORS 291.349(6)(d)) (State of Oregon, Secretary of State, 2000a). It is not written into the constitution so it can be changed or modified like any other statute.

### Execution

Agencies receive individual allocations for each of the eight quarters of the biennium through the BAM (State of Oregon POS, 2002). The BAM has ability to increase or decrease allotments by administrative action. All government funds are accounted for using the modified accrual basis of accounting and financial statements are prepared according to the generally accepted accounting principles (GAAP). The Department of Administrative Services publishes the Oregon Accounting Manual, which state agencies are required to follow in their financial reporting. The DAS is required to prepare a financial report for the state each year.

During the approximately 18 months per biennium that the legislature is out of session, the Emergency Board, a joint legislative committee of seventeen members, typically meets every other month during the period between sessions. During an emergency, the Board has the authority to allocate to any state agency funds appropriated to the Board for that purpose as well as take other actions deemed appropriate and approved under Oregon law. This provides the legislature the ability to respond to changing circumstances during legislative recesses.

### Audit

The Secretary of State conducts the audit of the state's finances after the end of the biennium. The Secretary of State serves as chief auditor for the state and conducts the financial audit through his or her office or by contracting with state-certified accountants.

Additionally, the Secretary of State must conduct an audit of any agency or department upon the departure of the head of the agency of department. Upon completion of an audit, the Secretary of State must submit to the governor a report of his or her findings (Oregon Revised Statutes 297.210).

### CONCLUSION

As we have seen, Oregon is a state where citizen initiative and referenda have a significant impact on resource allocation decisions. In particular, citizen initiated measures to limit property taxes and provide mandatory jail sentences have been driving forces shaping the State budget. These mandates substantially limit spending flexibility. Further, the lack of a sales tax and the consequent lack of a diversified revenue stream limits revenue raising flexibility, while the volatile nature of the tax system makes the state very vulnerable to economic downturns.

States have choices about their tax and revenue system. Voters in Oregon have chosen a system that relies very heavily on personal income taxes. The progressive nature of Oregon's personal income tax structure has led to very strong revenue growth during good economic times. Unfortunately, you "live by the sword and die by the sword." The downside of the strong growth during good times is precipitous declines during bad times.

## ACKNOWLEDGMENT

The author would like to thank Seth Skinner for his research support for this chapter.

## REFERENCES

Brian Moore and Jill Greiss. 1997. "The Good and Bad of Voter Initiatives." *Government Finance Review* (December), 21–24.

Governor's Tax Review Technical Advisory Committee. 1998. *Review of Oregon's Tax System* (June). Salem, OR: Governor's Office.

Betsy Hammond. 2003. "13 School Districts Won't Meet State Rules," *The Oregonian* (March 21, 2003), http://www.oregonlive.com/search/index.ssf?/base/news/104825154414540.xml?oregonian?lced. Downloaded on April 1, 2003.

Dave Hogan and Steven Carter. 2003. "The $310 Million in Cuts Will Come Swiftly," *The Oregonian* (January 29, 2003), A11.

Oregon Fiscal Choices. 1994. *Why Haven't My Property Taxes Gone Down Yet?* Corvallis, OR: Oregon State University Extension Service.

Oregon Revised Statutes 297.210. Regular auditing of accounts of state agencies and state-aided institutions and agencies; subpoena; auditing on retirement of executive head of institution or department; terms and compensation of auditors, http://www.oregonlawyer.com/ors/Statute Details.cfm?Statute=297.210.

State of Oregon Constitution, article IX, section 6.

State of Oregon Department of Administrative Services, Budget and Management Division (BAM). 1999. *Budget and Legislative Concept Instructions*. Salem, OR: Budget and Management Division.

State of Oregon Department of Administrative Services, Budget and Management Division (BAM). 2000. *Budget Process Flowcharts*. Salem, OR: Budget and Management Division.

State of Oregon Department of Administrative Services, Budget and Management Division (BAM). 2001. *Executive Summary*, http://www.bam.das.state.or.us/budinstr/pdf_file/execsum.pdf.

State of Oregon Department of Administrative Services, Budget and Management Division (BAM). 2002. *2003–2005 Budget and Legislative Concept Instructions*. Salem, OR: Budget and Management Division.

State of Oregon Department of Human Services, Adult and Family Services Division. 1999. *An Introduction to Adult and Family Services*. Salem, OR: Adult and Family Services Division.

State of Oregon Department of Human Services. 2000. *Progress Report*. Salem, OR: Oregon Department of Human Services.

State of Oregon Department of Land Conservation and Development. 2000. *Department of Land Conservation and Development: Fast Facts*. Salem, OR: Department of Land Conservation and Development.

State of Oregon Elections Division. 2000. *State Initiative and Referendum Manual*. Salem, OR: State of Oregon Elections Division.

State of Oregon Governor's Office. 2001. *2001–2003 Budget in Brief*. Salem, OR: Governor's Office.

State of Oregon Legislative Revenue Office. 1999. *1999 School Finance Legislation: Funding and Distribution (1999) (Report Nos. 4–99)*. Salem, OR: State of Oregon Legislative Revenue Office.

State of Oregon Legislative Revenue Office. 2001. *Oregon Public Finance: Basic Facts*. Salem, OR: Legislative Revenue Office.

State of Oregon Office of Economic Analysis. 2001. *April 2001 Corrections Population Forecast*. Salem, OR: State of Oregon Office of Economic Analysis.

State of Oregon Office of Economic Analysis. 2000. *Oregon Economic and Revenue Forecast* (September). Salem, OR: State of Oregon Office of Economic Analysis.

State of Oregon Preliminary Official Statement (POS). 2001. *Preliminary Official Statement Dated March 30, 2001*. Salem, OR: Oregon State Treasury.

State of Oregon Preliminary Official Statement (POS). 2002. *Preliminary Official Statement Dated December 10, 2002*. Salem, OR: Oregon State Treasury.

State of Oregon Progress Board. 2000. *The Oregon Progress Board At-A-Glance*. Salem, OR: Oregon Progress Board.

State of Oregon Progress Board. 2001. *A Brief History of the Oregon Progress Board*. Salem, OR: Oregon Progress Board.

State of Oregon Progress Board. 2001a. *Achieving the Oregon Shines Vision: The 2001 Benchmark Performance Report Highlights*. Salem, OR: Oregon Progress Board.

State of Oregon Secretary of State. 2000. *1999–2000 Oregon Blue Book*. Salem, OR: Office of the Secretary of State.

State of Oregon Secretary of State. 2002. *2001–2002 Oregon Blue Book*. Salem, OR: Office of the Secretary of State.

State of Oregon Secretary of State. 2000a. *Oregon Revised Statutes*. Salem, OR: Office of the Secretary of State.

State of Oregon Secretary of State. 2000b. *Measure 88 Explanatory Statement*. Salem, OR: Office of the Secretary of State, http://www.sos.state.or.us/elections/nov72000/guide/mea/m88/88ex.htm. Downloaded on January 6, 2003.

State of Oregon Secretary of State. 2003. *January 28, 2003, Special Election, State Measure No. 28*. Salem, OR: Office of the Secretary of State, http://www.sos.state.or.us/elections/jan282003/s03abstract.pdf. Downloaded on April 1, 2003.

# CHAPTER 8

# Florida: Ebb and Flow in Executive–Legislative Relations

*Robert B. Bradley*

Years ago, Allen Schick argued that budgeting systems have three major functions: planning, control, and management. It was his contention that budget systems had relative orientations, emphasizing one function more than the others. For him, the significant issue was "the balance among these vital functions at the central level."[1] Tyer and Willand extended this idea recently, adding two additional emphases suggested by Irene Rubin: prioritization and accountability.[2] However, they noted that characterizing a budget system by such emphases is more difficult than it might first appear. The contextual understanding of budgeting emphasized by Rubin, they insist, is necessary to any explanation of a budgeting system. In Florida, context is vital.

This article examines various contextual factors that shape state budgeting in Florida. It provides a brief glimpse at the way in which the ongoing struggle between the two branches affects the way in which budgeting is done, the challenges it faces, and the prospects for improving it in the future.

## GOVERNMENTAL AND POLITICAL CONTEXT

V.O. Key long provided the touchstone by which politics in Florida was understood. Fifty years ago, Florida was part of the solidly Democratic South. For all its similarities to other states in the region, Florida, Key argued, remained a "political curiosity."[3] In Florida, Key famously noted, it is "every man for himself." Focusing on features such as the state's geography, the distances between population centers, and its social composition, Key pictured a state with many factions whose political leadership was fractured in important ways. "Florida," he observed, "is not only unbossed, it is also unled." Assessing the state's political history, Key suggested, "anything can happen in elections and does."[4]

Florida has changed considerably since Key penned his observations. It has become more populous, less rural, increasingly suburban, and more diverse. In 1900, Florida was the least populous Southern state, with just over a half a million residents. By 2000, the state's population had grown to nearly 16 million.[5] In 2002, it was the fourth largest state, with 16.7 million residents.[6] Each year for the last decade, Florida's population has grown by more than a quarter million people. This growth and the changes that accompany it are the most important challenges facing policymakers and governments in the state.

Most of Florida's population growth comes from net migration. During the 1990s, migration accounted for over 85 percent of the total population increase. And this statistic only begins to capture the population movements underway in the state. In 2000, more than 51 percent of the population age 5 years or older lived in a different house 5 years before the Census. During the 1990s, Florida's Hispanic population grew by over 1.1 million. During the same period, non-Hispanic African Americans increased by more than 560,000. The state has become conspicuously more diverse over the last half century.

In the face of sustained growth and stunning movements of population to, from, and within the state, Florida has remained a conservative state. The Florida Annual Policy Survey conducted by Florida State University records a striking constancy of opinion. Between 1980 and 2001, the percentage of respondents classifying themselves as liberal has typically ranged between 11 percent and 14 percent. Self-identified conservative respondents, on the other hand, have typically ranged between 28 percent and 32 percent. Self-identified middle-of-the-road respondents generally fall between 28 percent and 33 percent.[7] Overall, the groupings of political ideology have not changed much.[8] Instead, there has been change in the numbers of those surveyed that indicate "they do not think in those terms." The percentages of this group grew first in the eighties at the expense of liberals and middle-of-the-road identifiers and later at the expense of conservatives, reaching more than 30 percent of those polled in 2001.[9]

The partisan character of Florida has changed markedly over the last 30 years. In 1970, Democrats amounted to 72 percent of registered voters; Republicans to 25 percent. By 2002, registered Democrats still outnumbered registered Republicans by nearly 350,000 voters. However, Democrats constituted 43 percent of registered voters and Republicans 39 percent.[10] Democrats controlled both houses of the state legislature for the entire post-World War II period until 1990. By 1997, Republicans controlled both Houses of the Legislature. In 1998, a Republican, Jeb Bush, was elected Governor convincingly. Republican dominance was cemented with his reelection.[11] Republicans now hold total control of the Legislature and Executive.

Despite the Republicans' success, over 40 percent of voters registering since 1996 have been recorded as something other than Republican or Democratic. The emergence of nonideological voters and nonpartisan shifts of the electorate lend volatility to politics in the state that can yield unexpected results.[12] This is most obvious in the politics of the initiative process.[13]

Prior to the nineties, the constitutional direct initiative process was used sparingly. Beginning in 1992, the popularity and successful use of the popular direct initiative increased.[14] Initially, it was used to restrict government in a variety of ways, ranging from limits on property valuations for tax purposes and term limits (1992) to revenue ceilings (1994) and tax limitations (1996). More recently, the initiative has been used to promote a more expansive agenda through constitutional expenditure mandates. During the same 2002 election that witnessed a sweep of statewide offices and controlling majorities in both houses of the Legislature by conservative Republicans, the electorate also approved amendments supported by Democrats mandating voluntary universal prekindergarten and a reduction in public school class size estimated to cost billions of dollars.

The juxtaposition of results from the 2002 elections testifies to the underlying instability of the coalitions forged throughout the state. But the influence of such partisan developments must be weighed against other significant changes in the political system. Perhaps none is more important than the imposition of legislative term limits through the initiative process. Term limits have altered the depth of expertise in the Legislature, especially in the House of Representatives. They have promoted movement of House members to the Senate. They have increased the role of lobbyists in the legislative process. More importantly, they have accelerated races for leadership (Speaker and President) in both houses, which in Florida are limited by tradition and practice to a single term. Races, along with the fundraising they entail, can now begin even before a legislator first runs for office. While terms are limited to 8 years, practically members have 6 years to make their mark.

The policymaking horizon has been foreshortened by a politics that limits accommodation and long-term compromise. It has become part of a political landscape scoured by population movements and riven by uncertain ideological and partisan sentiments. Budgeting in this climate is more reactive and tentative. It faces enormous challenges from several constitutional mandates directing increased spending for the courts, transportation, and education.

## ECONOMIC CONTEXT

In 2001, Florida was the most populous state in the Southeast and one of seven states with more than 10 million residents. It has a large, complex economy. The gross state product (GSP)—the value of goods and services produced by a state—is nearing a half trillion dollars. At $491.5 billion in 2001, it ranked fourth in the nation. But size can be misleading. When viewed in GSP per capita, Florida ranked 39th in 2001.[15] In these terms, the state performs much more poorly than other large states. Of the top 10 most populous states, it was the only state with GSP per capita under $32,000 at $30,018.

The economy influences what policymakers can do, what they are interested in doing and, to some extent, what they must do. The relatively poor performance of the GSP places limits on state policymakers, but it is not the whole story.

From another perspective, total personal income, Florida's prospects look better.[16] Florida ranked fourth in the nation in total personal income in 2002 and 22nd in per capita personal income.[17] It must be noted, however, that *per capita personal income actually declined* with respect to the rest of the nation—going from 3 percent above the rest of the country to more than 5 percent below between 1989 and 2001.[18]

Florida has done well in job growth. Florida ranked 2nd behind Alaska in percent change in seasonally adjusted state employment growth from December 2000 to December 2001; it was 11th from August 2001 until August 2002.[19] For years it has been among the leaders of the large states. Regrettably, the state's employment growth has come disproportionately in low wage jobs. Per capita wage income continues to lag the nation by almost 18 percent. Average wages are substantially below those of the nation.[20]

In part, Florida's poor wage ranking is a reflection of the industrial mix within the state. Florida's economy is concentrated in low productivity sectors such as services and trade. In 2000, Florida's relative portion of GSP from service was 23.5 percent compared to 19.8 percent nationally. Its high-productivity sectors, agriculture, finance, insurance, and real estate are not high employment generators.[21] Strikingly, the state produces almost 10 percent less of its GSP in manufacturing than the nation as a whole.

The state continues to rely heavily upon its destination status for tourists, retirees, and others seeking the opportunities that growth entails. It remains sensitive to developments that alter such factors. Tourism, for example, now attracts almost 70 million visitors annually, but is susceptible to both economic conditions outside the state and to uncertainty over such matters as the willingness of visitors to travel by air. Increasingly, the state is also linked to national and international developments. International trade, encompassing exports and imports, amounted to just over $2 billion in 1971. In 2000, it exceeded $73 billion.[22]

Under the sustained influence of what Wilbur Thompson once termed as the population growth ratchet, Florida has avoided the dramatic downturns of many other states.[23] It did comparatively well in the prolonged slump of 2001–2002, even though statewide unemployment increased and growth slowed. The economy became slightly more diversified in the nineties, led by the growth in business services. But productivity is low in the state. Personal income is more poorly distributed in Florida than in the rest of nation, and this inequality has increased over the last two decades.[24] The gap between the best-off families and those in the middle is especially large.

Such features shape the prospects for state finances and help create demands on policymakers in a variety of ways. For example, the revenue structure has long been tailored to the exigencies of a state hoping to attract tourists, retirees, and settlers. As early as the 1920s, the state foreswore the personal income tax (1924) along with the inheritance tax (1924).[25] Since the late 1940s, the sales tax has aimed to shield necessities of a retirement population from taxation, while capturing a portion of tourist spending. But the state's tax structure has not been retooled to capture the benefits the burgeoning service economy produces. The relative success of the current economic system, resting in important ways on climate, location, and a low cost of living makes it difficult to promote change even if that change holds the promise to improve the wellbeing of most Floridians.

## EXECUTIVE–LEGISLATIVE RELATIONS

Like many Southern states, Florida emerged from Reconstruction intent on diffusing executive power. Under the 1885 post-Reconstruction Constitution, the state had approximately 150 executive agencies, boards, and commissions until late in the sixties.[26] Perhaps as important, authority was vested in a collegial Executive consisting of the Governor and six cabinet officers (Secretary of State, Attorney General, Comptroller, Treasurer, Superintendent of Public Instruction, and Commissioner of Agriculture) all elected statewide.[27] The Governor was limited to a single 4-year term. The terms of cabinet officers were not limited.

Well into the 1960s, Florida's Executive was marked by the significant role of the cabinet, the extensive use of boards and commissions, and the paucity of large departments. Joseph Schlesinger judged the formal powers of Florida's Governor as 47th among the states just before the Constitutional revision of 1968.[28]

Legislative dominance was the hallmark of Florida state government throughout the 20th century, but both the Legislature and the Executive were transformed over the period. In the process, their relationship to one another gradually changed, with the Executive becoming increasingly important. These changes often emerged in the contention between the two branches over state budgeting.[29]

In the reorganization struggle that followed the approval of the 1968 Constitution, the Governor was given sole authority to propose a budget in 1969, and agencies were required to submit so called "legislative budget requests" to the Governor. The Governor administered the budget through the Department of Administration that included a newly formed Division of Planning and Budgeting. Staff of the Division continued to staff legislative appropriations committees until, in the mid-seventies, appropriations committees in both chambers acquired professional staff.[30]

Further changes were made in the late seventies. Governor Bob Graham, elected in 1978, championed an effort to make planning preeminent in the budget preparation phase. A newly modified program structure was developed and implemented. Statewide planning and budgeting were removed from the Department of Administration and made part of a newly created Executive Office of the Governor in 1979 as the Office of Planning and Budgeting. The Governor's role in appropriations was expanded.[31]

During its 1980 session, however, the legislature moved quickly to ensure the decision-making process it was familiar with remained in place. It required that each agency's legislative budget request be submitted to the legislature and Governor simultaneously and in a common format.[32] It also mandated that agency requests be based, not on gubernatorial direction, but on the "agency's independent judgment of its needs."[33] Executive authority in the budget preparation was restricted. The Legislature reasserted its preeminence in the preparation phase of the budget and maintained strict controls over budget execution and implementation.

Legislative preeminence continued throughout the eighties and during much of the nineties even as the political complexion of state government changed and the demands for reform of the state budgetary process grew. In 1990, Lawton Chiles, a Democrat, was elected Governor. Drawing on his long experience as a state legislator, U.S. Senator, and Chairman of the Congressional Budget Committee, Governor Chiles called for an end to so-called "micromanagement" by the Legislature in his first State of the State address, and asked that the Executive be provided greater flexibility in administration of the budget.

The Government Performance and Accountability Act of 1994[34] that emerged from a 2-year collaboration between the branches embraced several of the Governor's concerns. The legislation relaxed some of the restrictions on state agencies, but it did not alter in fundamental ways the relationship between the two branches. The Republican-dominated Legislature did not authorize ongoing grants of flexibility to the Executive. In 1995, the Senate Appropriations Committee even requested Executive agencies to prepare budget recommendations outside the statutorily authorized budget process. Gains proceeded in a piecemeal and contingent fashion. Still, the collaboration over performance budgeting did crystallize many of the limitations on Executive authority in ways that had not been generally understood before. It helped provide the basis on which change might continue.

The election of Jeb Bush as Governor in 1998 put the Republicans in charge of the Executive Branch and both Chambers of the legislature for the first time since Reconstruction. As important, it created a climate in which legislators wanted the Governor to succeed and were willing to concede power.

The Bush Administration proposed a number of modifications to the budgeting system in January, 2000. These proposals dramatically reduced the number of budgetary line items, eliminated appropriation categories for several budget entities, and extended considerable budget flexibility to state agencies. In doing so, they aimed to reduce the number of midyear budget amendments, reducing legislative control both in the preparation and implementation phases of the budget.

The Legislature enacted many of the Governor's recommendations as part of a major rewrite of the budget.[35] In doing so, it substantially shifted the balance of Executive–Legislative authority toward the Governor. For example, it increased the amount of funds agency heads might transfer between appropriation categories and budget entities without legislative approval. It restructured the budget format into policy areas, programs, services, and activities, thereby increasing administrative flexibility in many agencies. It removed the requirement that agencies submit preliminary Legislative Budget Requests, and thus limited opportunities for legislative intervention in framing departmental submissions. The legislation also altered the planning process in a way that allows the Governor to shape each agency's "independent assessment of its need" so that it conforms to legislative mandate but allows for gubernatorial direction. And it created a community budget request process that requires legislators to submit projects designated for their communities in a separate application that is subsequently folded into the general appropriations act. Significantly, it largely eliminated the role of the elected cabinet in the budget process.

The legislation strengthened the Governor's hand, but it created some venues for Legislative influence as well. It created the Legislative Budget Commission, consisting of fourteen members of both Houses including the chairs of the appropriations committees. The Commission actually expands the formal role of the Legislature in the budget implementation process. More importantly, it establishes a new budgetary activity. The Commission is assigned the role of reviewing the budget of each state agency at least once every 8 years using zero-based budgeting principles.

Historically in Florida, when the Executive pressed for greater authority in the state budgeting process, the Legislature responded by increasing its emphasis on control. The current transformation is different. The Executive's formal powers are greater. Thad Beyle ranked Florida's Governor 18th on his institutional power scale in 2003, up considerably from Schlesinger's estimate 35 years earlier.[36] The cabinet has been restructured and the constitutional status of the Commission enhanced.[37] Now, the Republican Legislature working with a Republican Governor is more closely attuned to Executive direction. Practically, the legislature has deferred more than the formal powers would indicate.[38] It has expanded Executive prerogatives in budgetary arenas over which the Legislature traditionally held sway. Under the current political alignment, the Governor is stronger than ever before in Florida.

It is worth noting that the Legislature has reinvented its role amidst the transformation by creating a Legislative Budget Commission to involve leadership on a continuing basis directly in budgetary matters. The Legislative Budget Commission has the potential to involve the legislature in the most basic agency administrative and programmatic processes through periodic zero-based budgeting examinations. Its long-term prospects are uncertain. For now, the Legislature has granted the Executive more latitude in budgeting, but it retains the tools to reassert itself as circumstances change.

## REVENUE SOURCES AND TRENDS

Most of Florida's annual appropriations are made in a single bill, the General Appropriations Act. General Appropriations amounted to approximately $50.3 billion for fiscal year 2002–2003, when adjusted for vetoes. Under the Constitution the state budget must be balanced. The state's appropriations are supported by $48.7 in revenues.[39]

All moneys received by the state are deposited in the treasury unless otherwise dedicated. The Treasury maintains four funds: Trust Funds, the General Revenue (GR) Fund, the Working Capital Fund, and the Budget Stabilization Fund. They are subject to a constitutional provision, approved in 1994, that limits state revenue growth.[40]

In fiscal year 2002–2003, it was anticipated that a little less than 60 percent of the state's current year revenues would be dedicated to various trust funds. The remaining portion of total revenues, accounting for just over 40 percent of the total, was deposited in the General Revenue Fund. Florida is only one of seven states in the country prohibited from imposing a personal income tax. The intangible personal property tax as well as Florida's corporate income and emergency excise tax are also constitutionally limited. And, constitutionally, state government cannot levy a tangible personal property tax. As a result, approximately 75 percent of the General Revenue is derived from the sales and use tax.[41]

More than two dozen taxes of various types comprise the General Revenue Fund in addition to the sales tax. Of these the corporation income tax is the largest, accounting for less than 5 percent of General Revenue (GR).[42] The tax on intangible personal property and the estate tax allowed as a credit against federal estate tax rank next. Both have been diminished in recent years. The intangible tax has been reduced as a matter of state policy, the estate tax through federal action. Only a few other substantial sources remain.

Since the mid-sixties Florida has ranked below most other state governments in the burden it places on taxpayers. In 1994, for example, it ranked 36th on state taxes per capita, while as a percentage of personal income it was 41st.[43] By 2000, it was 43rd and 45th, respectively.[44] State taxes have been reduced every year since 1994.[45] Overall, state taxes amounted to 5.9 percent of personal income in 2000, compared to 6.95 percent nationally.[46]

It is difficult to assess either Florida's tax effort or tax capacity from such statistics. As noted earlier, wages in the state substantially lag those nationally. While average personal income is near the national average, it declined in the late nineties and has only rebounded recently. Perhaps most telling, the per capita gross state product is near the bottom quartile. Tannenwald reported in 1997 that Florida was at 91 percent of national state and local tax effort, while at 98 percent average tax capacity.[47] This suggests Florida underinvests slightly in state government.[48]

Over two-thirds of the state's taxes are consumption taxes. The great majority is sales tax. Approximately 75 percent of sales taxes are levied against goods; about 20 percent are placed on admissions, leases, and rentals; less than 5 percent is imposed on services. Services, as noted earlier, constitute a growing portion of the economy. While a substantial portion of the sales tax burden, as much as 24.8 percent by some estimates, is exported through out-of-state visitors, business, and labor, the shifting structural character of the economy undermines the long-term robustness of the current structure.[49] At the same time, the large and increasing share of tax borne by business creates pressure for additional exemptions. There were more sales tax exemptions (106) enacted by the legislature in the nineties than in the previous four decades put together (101).[50]

Florida's state revenue structure is unlike that of most other states.[51] Much of it was shaped years ago during the boom days of the twenties, the bust of the Depression, and the pivotal years following World War II. It is highly skewed toward consumption taxes, especially general and selective sales. That emphasis avoids the swings associated with systems more heavily dependent on personal or corporate income, but it leaves the state vulnerable to changes in consumption patterns and creates ongoing problems of regressivity and pyramiding. It is geared towards consumption of goods in an economy that increasingly values services. Florida has attempted to secure a bit of equity in the sales tax by exempting various necessities such as food and medicine. It has been less successful ensuring overall vertical and horizontal efficiency.

During 2001 and 2002, both Houses of the Legislature conducted separate studies of the state's tax system. State leaders remain chastened by the failure to sustain the unitary tax and the sales tax on services enacted in the late eighties. Others remember the failed effort to galvanize support for a value added tax or even a modified sales tax on services in 1992. After nearly a decade of tax reduction, the sentiment for reform is not widespread.

## FISCAL FEDERALISM

A substantial portion of the state's budget reflects the character and demands of fiscal federalism. The operating portion of the budget for FY 2002–2003 consists of approximately $42.1 billion out of the $50.3 billion appropriated. Of this, just $11.4 billion is for distinctly state operations. The remaining $30.7 billion is targeted at schools, municipalities, counties, retirees, Medicaid, Temporary Assistance for Needy Families (TANF), and a host of federal programs. Over 35 percent is designated for local governments, mostly schools. Approximately 29 percent is set aside for Medicaid and TANF.[52]

These percentages fail to capture the texture of historical reality. Florida has long had a strong local fiscal system. It long resisted participating fully in federal programs. In 1991–1992, for example, Florida ranked 49th in the share of its state and local revenues obtained from the federal government. In 2000, it was still only 46th.[53] For years it has ranked near the bottom of states, receiving the fewest federal grant dollars per capita.

Nevertheless, Florida and its citizens receive considerable federal funds. It ranked 4th in total dollars and 23rd in per capita federal direct expenditures in FY 1999–2000. The lion's share of the nearly $93 billion was in social security payments ($20.1 billion) and Medicare ($17.8 billion) benefits.[54]

In part, Florida's poor showing in per capita federal grant awards is the result of its growth. Program formulas often employ population statistics, which, in the context of the state's growth, are hopelessly outdated. Perhaps as important, though, policymakers have often been wary of federal largesse, even though the state's movement from the least populous Southern state in 1930 to its most populous in 1960 had been fueled in large measure by federal funds aimed at infrastructure, the military, and retirees.[55] Federal funds were subjected to the legislative appropriations process in the late seventies, in part to ensure that each funding opportunity was scrutinized thoroughly and with an eye toward latent difficulties.

This has changed in recent years. Following the state's successful collaboration with the federal government in the wake of Hurricane Andrew in the early nineties, and with the familial relationship between the Governor and President Bush, the state's receptivity to federal funding in areas ranging from reading to electoral reform and homeland security has increased.

While state policy has long discouraged overreliance on federal funds, it has encouraged the decentralization of services and funding. Although state taxes rank in the bottom quintile nationally, Florida's combined state and local per capita ranking on revenues was estimated to be 33rd in 2000. Local government taxes rank 20th. State taxes are 15 percent below the national average personal income. Local taxes are just 4 percent under the national average. Local effort on charges for services has long surpassed national averages.[56]

There are more than a dozen state shared revenue programs. Most are relatively small. For example, the Phosphate Rock Severance tax allocates little more than $2 million. Others like the half-cent sales tax distribute more than $1 billion. Typically, state collected funds in state shared revenue are allocated to specific jurisdictions based on eligibility criteria using a statutorily determined formula.

Two facets of shared revenues are especially important in the budgeting process. First, the Legislature has allowed several of the sources to be bonded locally and thus attempts to modify the programs' risk of running afoul of constitutional prohibitions concerning impairment of contracts. Second, several state shared revenues are covered by a constitutional provision limiting the ability of the Legislature to reduce the funds they provide.[57]

State shared revenues provide the largest single transfer of funds to cities and counties. They pale, of course, alongside the annual appropriation from other state sources for public schools, community colleges, and universities. Education funding exceeded $15.6 billion in 2002 with $9.8 dedicated to local school districts. Approximately 60 percent of the funding for public schools comes from the state. Well over 50 percent of the state's general revenue is devoted to education.[58]

Intergovernmental concerns lie at the heart of the state budget. In FY 2002–2003, federal funds accounted for over 30 percent of the budget; the state match of federal dollars totaled nearly another 14 percent; and 30 percent went into aid for local cities, counties, and schools, including federal funds.[59] As a rule, though, the real budgeting effort in fiscal federalism swirls around a handful of large federal programs, state programs of local note, major transfers such as the funds for public education, and hometown projects sponsored by various members.

## PERFORMANCE MEASURES AND OTHER BUDGET PROCESS REFORMS

Florida first introduced program budgeting into its appropriations process in the late sixties. It was integrally linked to the reorganization of state government accomplished by the 1968 Constitution and the creation of the Governor's Office of Planning and Budgeting. While these early efforts were largely unsuccessful, the legacy of the effort and interest in the approach did not die.

The recession of 1989–1991 helped crystallize the call for budget reforms, and in 1992 the Constitutional Commission on Taxation and Budget Reform gave them form. The Commission certified a series of constitutional amendments to the statewide ballot that were approved overwhelmingly by the electorate.[60] They included changes in the treatment of trust funds, in budget format, in the transmission of information, and in the level of state reserves. They also mandated development of an accountability program.

The Governmental Performance and Accountability Act enacted in 1994 was the first major response to this call for additional accountability. The Act called for Performance-Based Program Budgeting (commonly referred to as PB2 in Florida, chapter 94–249, *Laws of Florida*) by all of Florida's state agencies. The reform was intended to provide a greater focus on the results of governmental action. While the legislation was designed to be phased in over a number of years, it held the promise of a major shift in the way state business was conducted. From the beginning, there was widespread acknowledgement that successful implementation would require active collaboration between the Executive and Legislature.

While there was general agreement on the principles in the legislation between the Executive and Legislature, large, often unspoken differences remained. At issue were the prerogatives of each Branch in the various budget processes.

Schick has argued that budgets involve three major processes: conserving, claiming, and allocating.[61] The Executive approached budget reform with the idea that performance measures would serve as a diagnostic to help improve the business processes of agencies as well as their programs. The focus was on improvements to the claiming or justification processes of the budgetary system. Among many in the Legislature, the central concern of reform was for improved mechanisms of allocation. Results had to drive allocation and not merely constitute an improvement in the process by which claims on resources were justified.

Curiously, neither the Executive nor the Legislature gave much thought during the initial design period to conservation processes within the budgetary scheme. Issues of efficiency were neglected, for the most part, in favor of issues of effectiveness. Unit cost performance and notions of return on investment were deferred. Conservation processes took a back seat.[62]

As with many significant reforms, implementation of PB2 was not without its difficulties or detractors. Florida, like most governments, faced problems of measurement, program identification, poor data, and misaligned accounting systems. Many of those officials directly involved found much to criticize. Agency officials worried that the promise of the flexibility and incentives had not been forthcoming. Legislative members sagged under the demands of reviewing and approving measures and decried the minor contribution of the reform to budgeting decisions.[63] Nonetheless, state leaders continued their commitment throughout the nineties.

During the 2000 Legislative session, Governor Bush supported and the Legislature expanded, the budget reforms.[64] In 2001, the Legislature added to the budgeting reform, indicating its intent that all funds within an agency be allocated to an appropriate activity. It adopted activity-based planning and budgeting in order to link costs to performance.[65] Reform has been extended to deal with each of the major budgetary processes identified by Schick; however, it is increasingly clear that the early hopes for performance-based budgeting have not been realized.

## COURT DECISIONS

Under the state Constitution, money may only be drawn from the Treasury through appropriations made by law.[66] The Legislature has the exclusive power of appropriating public funds and this power is exercised through statutes approved by both Chambers. In Florida, as noted earlier, most appropriations are made as part of the General Appropriations Act. However, substantive bills enacted by the Legislature may also contain appropriations for any proper purpose.[67] The courts have given the Legislature broad latitude in determining when the Legislature has exercised its power to appropriate revenues properly.[68] However, they have applied limitations in several instances.

Often such limitations have revolved around the Constitutional provisions that hold "Laws making appropriations for salaries of public officers and other current expenses of the state shall contain provisions on no other subject"[69] and "The Governor may veto any specific appropriation in a general appropriation bill, but may not veto any qualification or restriction without also vetoing the appropriation to which it relates."[70]

In *Brown v. Firestone*, the Court established the principles for many of the subsequent interpretations of such provisions. *Brown* found that a "general appropriations bill must deal only with appropriations and matters properly connected therewith."[71] An appropriations bill should not change or amend existing law on subjects other than appropriations. The Court further held that a specific appropriation is an integrated fund that the Legislature has allocated for a "specific purpose."[72] More importantly, it "is the smallest identifiable fund to which a qualification or restriction is or can be directly and logically related."[73] In Florida, such qualifications and restrictions are called "proviso" language. Under *Brown*, if the Governor wants to veto any qualification or restriction in a general appropriations bill, he must also veto the appropriation to which it relates. He cannot legitimately veto unconstitutional proviso unless he also vetoes the specific appropriation to which it is related. Nor can the Governor veto a proviso that does not contain express identifiable funds without vetoing the appropriation to which it also relates. His only remedy in both cases is to seek a declaratory judgment nullifying the proviso if he wants to avoid striking the appropriation.

These principles are key to the adoption phase of the budget process in which both the Legislature and the Governor have a stake. They have been tested repeatedly in recent years from a variety of perspectives. Following *Brown*, the Courts have consistently argued that an appropriations bill must not change or amend existing law on subjects other than appropriations.[74] For years, this was generally understood to mean that appropriation bills could not modify or amend statutory formula for distribution of funds.[75] In 1995, the Court in *Chiles v. Milligan* found that such formula must be quite explicit to qualify.[76] It argued that proviso attached to the state's educational finance program was a clarification of general provisions in law. It made a similar finding in *Moreau v. Lewis* regarding Medicaid co-payments whose statutory basis the Court found too nebulous.[77]

The Court's interest in the adoption phase typically revolves around the on-going struggle between the Executive and Legislature to assert their respective prerogatives. They have less often dealt with the administration of the budget. In 1991, however, *Chiles v. Children* took up one facet of this issue.[78] Again, it centered on the relative roles of the Executive and the Legislative Branches. In accordance with then existing state law, Governor Chiles directed all state agencies, which by definition included the judicial branch, to prepare revised financial plans to reduce their operating budgets. Based on these plans, the Governor and Cabinet (functioning as the Administration Commission) reduced agency budgets by over $600 million. The *Chiles* Court found existing law was "an impermissible attempt by the Legislature to abdicate a portion of its lawmaking authority and to vest in an executive entity."[79] In the strongest terms, the Court reasserted the principle of separation of powers, establishing both the inability of the Legislature to delegate its appropriation powers and the inability of the Executive to exercise budgetary oversight over the Judiciary. The Court held these concerns outweighed the obligation the Constitution imposes on the Governor to operate within a balanced budget.

## CONCLUSION AND IMPLICATIONS

Florida is no longer the state V.O. Key characterized so aptly in the late forties. It is large, diverse, complex, and thriving in ways not envisioned in the middle of the twentieth century. Still, it is a state given to electoral volatility and unexpected developments.

Executive–Legislative relations lie at the heart of many of the budgeting changes undertaken in the state. They are grounded in longstanding Constitutional and statutory provisions. These relations are not immune to the larger forces sweeping over the state, however. In recent years the Executive has assumed greater influence in the budgeting process.

Florida's budget has been reinvented several times. It is supported by a revenue structure that has remained largely the same for half a century. It grapples annually with the effects of growth encouraged by both its tax structure and those who cherish the opportunities growth entails. Constrained by the revenues the tax structure generates, for years the budgeting process has aimed to improve the performance of state government and to wring ever greater efficiencies out of every program.

More recently, the budgeting process has been given a wholly new task. It has been asked to resolve demands for increased services placed on the state in a series of unprecedented Constitutional initiatives approved by the electorate. Its ability to do so is questionable. Experience suggests, however, that its capacity to meet the challenge should not be underestimated.

## NOTES

1. Allen Schick, "The Road to PBB: The Stages of Budget Reform," *Public Administration Review*, 26 (December 1966), 245.

2. Charlie Tyer and Jennifer Willand, "Public Budgeting in America: A Twentieth Century Retrospective," *Journal of Public Budgeting, Accounting and Financial Management*, 9 (Summer 1997), 189–219; Irene Rubin, "Budgeting for Accountability: Municipal Budgeting for the 1990s," *Public Budgeting and Finance*, 16 (Summer 1996), 112–132.

3. V. O. Key, *Southern Politics in the State and Nation.* New York: Vintage, 1949, p. 83.

4. Ibid.

5. David Colburn and Lance deHaven-Smith, *Florida's Megatrends: Critical Issues in Florida.* Gainesville, FL: University Press of Florida, 2002, p. 15.

6. Florida. Legislature, Office of Economic and Demographic Research, "Florida's Population," *Demographic Newsletter.* Tallahassee, FL: January 2002.

7. Florida State University, College of Social Sciences, "Florida Annual Policy Survey: 1979–2001," database on-line, http://www.fsu.edu/~survey/FAPS/index.htm (accessed November 20, 2002).

8. Lance DeHaven Smith, *Atlas of Florida Voting and Public Opinion.* Tallahassee, FL: Florida Institute of Government, 1998, p. 41.

9. Florida State University, College of Social Sciences, "Florida Annual Policy Survey: 1979–2001," database on-line, http://www.fsu.edu/~survey/FAPS/index.htm (accessed November 20, 2002).

10. State of Florida, Department of State, Division of Elections, "Voter Registration Statistics," database on-line, http://election,dos.state,fl.us/voterreg/index.shtml (accessed November 9, 2002).

11. Allen Morris and Joan Perry Morris (Eds.), *The Florida Handbook: 2000–2001*, 28th biennial edition. Tallahassee, FL: Peninsular Publishing Co., 2001, p. 152.

12. Joan Carver and Tom Fiedler, "Florida: A Volatile National Microcosm," in Alexander Lamis (Ed.), *Southern Politics in the 1990s*, e-Book, Net Library, http//: emedia.netlibrary.com/nlreader.dll?/bookid=47679&filename=Page_343.html #(8D9), Baton Rouge, LA: Louisiana State University Press, 1999.

13. State of Florida, Department of State, Division of Elections, "Initiatives, Amendments and Petitions," database on-line, http://election.dos.state.fl.us/ initiatives/initiativelist.asp (accessed November 9, 2002).

14. P. K. Jameson and Marsha Hosack, "Citizen Initiative in Florida: An Analysis of Florida's Constitutional Initiative Process, Issues, and Statutory Initiative Alternatives," *Florida State University Law Review*, 23 (Winter 1995), 417–459.

15. Kendra A. Hovey and Harold A. Hovey (Eds.), *CQ's State Fact Finder, 2002: Rankings Across America.* Washington, DC: Congressional Quarterly Press, 2002, Table B-2.

16. Data on this measure reflect the income of residents of the state including their pensions, dividends, interest, and rent as well as amounts received from employers as wages and salaries. Total personal income typically bears a close but not identical relationship with GSP. For Florida, however, the two measures differ because total personal income includes the interest, dividend, and transfer payment income earned by Florida's large retiree population.

17. Hovey and Hovey, *State Fact Finder, 2004*, Table B-3.

18. "Reversal of Fortune," *State Policy Reports*, 20(17) (2002), 18.

19. "Index of Economic Momentum," *State Policy Reports*, 20(8) (2002), 2.

20. Kendra A. Hovey and Harold A. Hovey (Eds.), *CQ's State Fact Finder, 2002: Rankings Across America.* Washington, DC: Congressional Quarterly Press, 2002, Table B-5.

21. Florida Chamber of Commerce, "Florida's Economic Outlook: Trends, Opportunities, and Risks," *Cornerstone Report.* Tallahassee, FL: Florida Chamber Foundation, November 2001, pp. 2–23.

22. Enterprise Florida, "Florida: An Economic Overview," Orlando, FL: Enterprise Florida, July 2001, pp. 11–12.

23. Wilbur R. Thompson, *A Preface to Urban Economics*. Baltimore, MD: Resources for the Future and The Johns Hopkins Press, 1965, p. 22.

24. Jared Bernstein, Heather Boushey, Elizabeth McNichol, and Robert Zahradnik, *Pulling Apart: A State-by-State Analysis of Income Trends, Florida*. Washington, DC: Economic Policy Institute and Center on Budget and Policy Priorities (April 2002), database on-line, http://www.cbpp.org./1–18–00, sfp.fl.pdf.

25. Florida Senate, *2002 Florida Tax Handbook Including Fiscal Impact of Potential Changes*. Tallahassee, FL: 2002.

26. Manning J. Dauer, "Florida: The Different State," from *The Changing Politics of the South* by W. C. Harvard, Louisiana State Press, 1972 reprinted in *Reapportionment and Representation in Florida: A Historical Collection*, Susan A. MacManus (Ed.), Tampa, FL: University of South Florida, 1991, p. 96.

27. *Florida Constitution*, 2002, art. IV, s. 4.

28. Joseph Schlesinger, "The Politics of the Executive," in Herbert Jacob and Kenneth N. Vines (Eds.), *Politics in the American States*, 2nd edition. Boston, MA: Little Brown, 1971, p. 230.

29. Tracy E. Danese, "The Florida Political System To Mid-Twentieth Century: Motion Without Movement," Masters Thesis, Florida State University, 1994, p. 1. Wilson Doyle, Angus Laird, and Sherman Weiss, *The Government and Administration of Florida*. New York: Thomas Crowell Co., 1954, p. 124.

30. Richard Scher, "The Governor and Cabinet: Executive Policy-Making and Policy Management," in *The Florida Public Policy Management System*, 2nd edition, Richard Chackerian (Ed.). Dubuque, IA: Kendall/Hunt Publishing Co., 1998, pp. 77–78.

31. W. E. Klay, "Planning and Budgeting," in *The Florida Public Policy Management System*, 2nd edition, Richard Chackerian (Ed.). Dubuque, IA: Kendall/Hunt Publishing Co., 1998, pp. 189–214.

32. Robert B. Bradley and Geraldo Flowers, "Getting to Results in Florida," *Quicker, Better, Cheaper: Managing Performance in American Government*, Dall Forsythe, (Ed.). Albany, NY: Rockefeller Institute Press, 2001, pp. 370–371.

33. *Laws of Florida*, 1980, ch. 1980–45; *Florida Statutes*, 2002, s. 216.023.

34. *Laws of Florida*, 1994, ch. 1994–249.

35. *Laws of Florida*, 2000, ch. 2000–371.

36. Kendra A. Hovey and Harold A. Hovey (Eds.), *CQ's State Fact Finder, 2004: Rankings Across America*. Washington, DC: Congressional Quarterly Press, 2004, Table D-11.

37. See *Florida Constitution*, 2002. art. IV, ss. 4 (a), (c), (e), (f), and (g).

38. Steve Bousquet, "A Strong Hand," *St. Petersburg Times* (December 8, 2002).

39. Florida Legislature, Office of Economic and Demographic Research, *Florida Consensus Estimating Conference: Revenue Analysis, FY 1970–71 Through FY 2011–12*, vol. 18. Tallahassee, Fl: 2002, p. 33. The state appropriated $50.3 billion in FY 2002–2003, but another $6.7 billion in continuing appropriations are noted in the General Appropriation Act. Revenues are estimated to total only $48.7 billion. The difference is accounted for by the use of accumulated balances, borrowed funds, and interfund transfers.

40. *Florida Constitution*, 2002, art. VII, s. 1(e). For FY 2002–2003, the constitutional limit is approximately $30.2 billion, while the amount of actual state revenues covered

is anticipated to be $25.0, putting the state more than $5.2 billion under its constitutional limit. Florida Legislature, Office of Economic and Demographic Research, "Florida Consensus Estimating Conference: Five Year Projection—Revenue Subject to Constitutional Limitation, 2002." Tallahassee, FL: November 2002.

41. Florida Legislature, Office of Economic and Demographic Research, *Florida Consensus Estimating Conference: Revenue Analysis, FY 1970–71 Through FY 2011–12*, vol. 18. Tallahassee, FL: 2002, p. 33.

42. Ibid.

43. Florida Tax Watch, *How Florida Compares: State and Local Taxes in Florida and the Nation*. Tallahassee, FL: January 1996, p. 2.

44. Florida Tax Watch, *How Florida Compares: State and Local Taxes in Florida and the Nation*. Tallahassee, FL: February 2002, p. 3.

45. Florida Senate, Committee on Finance and Taxation, "Historical Legislative Revenue and Appropriations Decisions," Committee Handout, February 1997 and Florida Legislature, *Fiscal Analysis in Brief for Fiscal Year 2002–2003*, "Measures Affecting Revenues and Tax Administration." Tallahassee, FL: August 2002, p. 41.

46. Florida Tax Watch, *How Florida Compares: State and Local Taxes in Florida and the Nation*. Tallahassee, FL: February 2002, p. 3.

47. Kendra A. Hovey and Harold A. Hovey (Eds.), *CQ's State Fact Finder, 2004: Rankings Across America*. Washington, DC: Congressional Quarterly Press, 2004, Tables F-3 and 4.

48. Gloria Grizzle, "Florida: Miles to Go and Promises to Keep," *in Governors, Legislatures and Budgets: Diversity Across the American States*," Edward J. Clynch and Thomas P. Lauth (Eds.). New York: Greenwood Press, 1991, pp. 93–102.

49. Florida Legislature, Office of Economic and Demographic Research, "Who Pays Florida's Sales Tax? An Examination of Florida's Sales Tax." Tallahassee, FL: July 1992, p. 13.

50. Florida Senate, Office of the President, "Reforming Florida's Tax System: Building a Foundation for Florida's Future." Tallahassee, FL: 2002, pp. 4–5.

51. In general structure, Florida's revenue system closely resembles that of Tennessee and Washington in the share raised from the major revenue bases.

52. Florida, *Laws of Florida*, 2002, ch. 2002–394.

53. Kendra A. Hovey and Harold A. Hovey (Eds.), *CQ's State Fact Finder, 2004: Rankings Across America*. Washington, DC: Congressional Quarterly Press, 2004, Tables E-12.

54. Florida Legislature, Legislative Committee on Intergovernmental Relations, *Review of Federal Expenditures to Florida in Fiscal Year 1999–2000 With Particular Emphasis on Federal Grants to Florida's State and Local Governments*. Tallahassee, FL: September 2001, p. 5.

55. David Colburn and Lance deHaven-Smith, *Florida's Megatrends: Critical Issues in Florida*. Gainesville, FL: University Press of Florida, 2002, pp. 35–61.

56. Florida Tax Watch, *How Florida Compares: State and Local Taxes in Florida and the Nation*. Tallahassee, FL: February 2002, p. 3.

57. *Florida Constitution*, 2002, art. VIII, s. 18.

58. *Laws of Florida*, 2002, ch. 2002–394.

59. Ibid.

60. *Florida Constitution*, 2002, art. III, s. 19.

61. Allen Schick, "An Inquiry into the Possibility of a Budgetary Theory," in Irene S. Rubin (Ed.), *New Directions in Budget Theory*. Albany, New York: State University Press of New York, 1988, pp. 59–69.

62. Robert Bradley, "The Transformation of Performance Based Program Budgeting in Florida," 22nd Annual Research Conference, Association for Public Policy Analysis and Management. Seattle, WA: November 4, 2000, p. 11.

63. Ibid.

64. *Laws of Florida*, 2002, ch. 2000–371.

65. *Laws of Florida*, 2002, ch. 2001–56.

66. *Florida Constitution*, 2002, art. VII, s. 1(c).

67. Florida Legislature, *Fiscal Analysis in Brief for Fiscal Year 2002–2003*, "Measures Affecting Revenues and Tax Administration." Tallahassee, FL: August 2002, p. 41.

68. *Dickinson v. Bradley*, 298 So. 2nd 353 (Fla. 1974).

69. *Florida Constitution*, 2002, art III, s 12.

70. *Florida Constitution*, 2002, art III, s 8. See Florida, *Constitution*, art III, s. 19 for veto of appropriations in substantive legislation.

71. *Brown v. Firestone*, 382 So.2d 663 (Fla. 1980).

72. Ibid., 668.

73. Ibid.

74. *Brown v. Firestone*, 382 So.2d 664 (Fla. 1980).

75. *Gindl v. Department of Education*, 396 So.2d 1105 (Fla. 1981).

76. *Chiles v. Milligan*, 659 So.2d 1055 (Fla. 1995).

77. *Moreau v. Lewis*, 648 So.2d 124 (Fla. 1995).

78. *Chiles v. Children*, 589 So.2d 260 (Fla. 1991).

79. Ibid., 267.

# CHAPTER 9

# Kentucky: The Executive/ Legislative Budget Role Transition Continues

*Merl M. Hackbart and James R. Ramsey*

## INTRODUCTION

The nature and character of budget processes in the states has evolved in response to a variety of factors including budget process innovations, efforts to insure financial accountability, changing economic conditions, and political factors including the changing roles of the executive and legislative branches in the budget process. In some states, budgetary process adjustments have been institutionalized through legislation or through court decisions focusing on issues such as separation of powers, among others. Meanwhile, in other states, budget process changes have emanated from legislative or administrative policy decisions designed to respond to public concerns regarding performance, accountability, or greater public demands for information regarding public budget decision-making process.[1]

Budget process changes have taken many forms during the last century. Early process changes were directed toward insuring greater fiscal accountability, while later budget system adjustments focused on performance and included changes designed to implement Hoover Commission recommendations, among others. Other changes had a managerial focus (PPBS or ZBB) and were principally designed to enhance the information available to budget makers. Still other state budget process changes, including those that adjusted the roles of the legislative and executive branches, resulted from local political considerations. Regardless of origin, the nature of the budget process change tends to dictate the impact of the change on budget "decision-making," the critical or "real" state budget process issue.[2]

While formal state budget process changes may force adjustments in the information provided by agencies in their budget requests, and in the packaging and marketing of budget proposals, the "real" budget decisions involved in "tradeoffs" and budget allocation decisions may be unaffected. Still other budget process changes can modify the balance of power between the executive and legislative branches of state government and, as a result, the "real" budget decision-making process may be impacted. Meanwhile, political power shifts can also impact the "real" budgetary process by changing the dynamics and nature of both the formal and the informal negotiations critical to the state budgetary process. Political power shifts, such as those experienced in Washington in the early 1990s leading to the Republican takeover of Congress can fundamentally change the dynamics of the "real" budgetary decision-making process, while leaving the formal and technical or operational aspects of budget making largely unaffected.

## FOCUS OF PAPER

This paper focuses on reviewing, analyzing, and synthesizing the factors that influenced changes in Kentucky's budgetary processes in the decade of the "1990s" (more specifically, from 1987 to 2003). In the analysis, special emphasis is devoted to the budget process changes that were associated with the evolving "new" relationship between Kentucky's executive and legislative branches. This paper builds on an earlier article that reviewed the factors that influenced budget processes and budget process roles during the 1972–1987 period.[3] Like the earlier period, Kentucky's legislative/executive branch budget policy and process roles in the 1990s were influenced by legal as well as economic and political considerations.

This review of the "1990s" period begins with an overview of the period in terms of gubernatorial leadership and political party control. This overview is followed by an assessment of the budget process and policy changes that evolved during the terms of three Kentucky Governors. Finally, the last section considers the potential implications of the changing roles of the executive and legislative branches in budget making. It is noted that the changing roles were part of a continuous evolution of executive/legislative budget making relationships and policymaking authority that began in the 1970s.

## POLITICAL LEADERSHIP AND BUDGET POLICY IN THE 1990s

Following the trend of the previous two decades, the Democrat party maintained control of the Governors Office in the 1990s. Governor Wallace Wilkinson was elected in 1987 and served one 4-year term followed by Governor Brereton Jones who was elected in 1991 and served through 1995. Governor Paul Patton was elected in 1995 with the opportunity to serve two terms due to a constitutional amendment, which passed in 1992. That

Figure 9.1
Kentucky Senate Party Affiliation (1990–2002) by Session. *Source*:
Kentucky Legislative Research Commission.

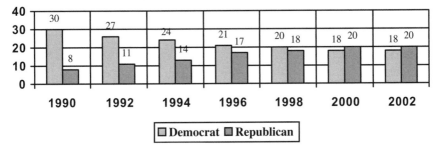

amendment permitted Kentucky governors to serve two consecutive 4-year
terms rather than a single 4-year term under the previous constitutional provision. He was reelected in 1999, and his second term was completed in
December 2003.

The Democrats also maintained control of both houses of the General
Assembly throughout the 1990s, although their margin of control declined.
The Democrats' margin in the Senate dropped from thirty to eight in the
1990 Session to twenty Democrats and eighteen Republicans in the 1998
Session of the Kentucky General Assembly. Due to the "party switches" of
two Senate Democrats, the Republican Party gained control of the Senate
after the 2000 election. The Republicans maintained their two-seat margin
in the 2002 regular session of the Kentucky General Assembly and expanded
their margin to twenty-two to sixteen in the 2002 election, reinforcing the
resurgence of the Republican Party in the Kentucky Legislature. While the
Democrat House majority also declined, the slippage was not as significant
as in the Senate (71 Democrats to 29 Republicans in the 1990 session v. 66
Democrats to 34 Republicans in the 2002 session), and they maintained a
strong majority. The party affiliations for both houses for the 1990 to 2002
sessions are shown in Figure 9.1 and Figure 9.2. With the changing majorities
in the Kentucky House and Senate, the working relationships between the
executive and legislative branches adjusted to reflect the power shifts. This
change was particularly evident during Governor Patton's first term where he
emphasized consultation and collaboration regarding the preparation of his
budget with leaders of both parties—a change from previous sessions when
the Democrats had strong majorities in both houses.

Kentucky's economic and fiscal conditions and predominant budget
policy issues changed over the period as well. Meanwhile, court decrees, policy
initiatives, and partisan "politics" rotated as the driving forces in Kentucky's
changing budget policy and budget processes. In the sections that follow,

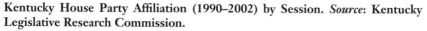

**Figure 9.2**
**Kentucky House Party Affiliation (1990–2002) by Session.** *Source*: Kentucky
Legislative Research Commission.

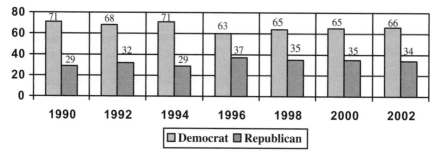

each Governor's term during the 1987–2003 period is reviewed to highlight
the fiscal, political, legal, and policy factors that influenced budget process or
budget policy changes.

### Governor Wilkinson (1987–1991)

Governor Wilkinson was elected with the public image of a businessman
who was fiscally conservative and opposed to higher taxes. During his campaign, he advocated a constitutional amendment to permit the establishment of
a state lottery as an alternative means of providing additional funds for elementary and secondary education and for his economic development initiatives.
After his election, the constitutional amendment passed and he actively pursued a variety of state economic development initiatives. Consistent with his
stated philosophy and required by tight revenue conditions, his first budget
was a fiscally conservative, "continuation" budget. To stretch revenues, his
budget proposal included initiatives designed to speed up tax receipts and a
"tax amnesty" program. The amnesty initiative permitted delinquent taxpayers to voluntarily pay taxes due without penalty as a means of increasing tax
compliance and accelerating the payment of taxes that were due to the state.
As an independent and successful businessman, Governor Wilkinson acted
aggressively and independently of the General Assembly. His personal style
and approach to governing generated significant animosity among legislators
of both parties.

The far-reaching Kentucky Supreme Court decision of 1989, *Rose v. Council
for Better Education*,[4] which declared Kentucky's system of public schools unconstitutional, dramatically altered Governor Wilkinson's term and the policy
focus on his administration. After the Supreme Court's decision was rendered,
Governor Wilkinson and the legislative leadership vowed to effectively deal
with the issues raised in the case. A joint legislative/executive branch Task

Force comprised of twelve legislative members and six executive branch members was formed in July, following the June 1989 Supreme Court decision. The Task Force was charged with the responsibility to develop a plan to comply with the dictates of the Supreme Court and to reform Kentucky's system of public education by the start of the 1990 Session of the General Assembly. In carrying out its responsibilities, the Task Force established subgroups that focused on curriculum, governance, and financial concerns as it developed recommendations to deal with the Supreme Court mandates as well as other reform issues identified by the Task Force.

As the 1990 Session approached, it became obvious that the court's mandate to correct the inefficiency and inadequacy conditions of Kentucky's school financing system could not be dealt with without significant new revenues. Notwithstanding his "no new tax" campaign pledge, Governor Wilkinson proposed a sweeping tax reform package, which raised 18 percent more General Fund revenue to support educational and other initiatives. The revenue increase resulted from several tax changes that were included in the tax bill passed by the Kentucky General Assembly. Among the measures included in the bill were an increase in the sales tax from 5 to 6 percent, the elimination of the deductibility of federal income tax payments, an increase in the corporate tax rate, the enactment of a low income tax credit and the updating of the Kentucky tax code to reflect changes in the Internal Revenue Service tax code. Thus, the court's decision changed the budget policy environment from what would have been another "continuation" budget into an aggressive expansion budget. The enhanced budget that the tax increase permitted received the support of the General Assembly in a contentious legislative session.

A key element of the legislative session was the ownership that the legislative branch assumed for the education reform issue. The original suit (*Rose v. Council for Better Education*) named legislative leaders as defendants. After hearing the case, the Kentucky Supreme Court found that the Kentucky legislature had not met its constitutional responsibility to provide an efficient (or equitable) and adequate system of school finance. The Court directed the Legislature to take action to remedy the unacceptable conditions existent in Kentucky's educational system. Accepting that responsibility, members of the Kentucky General Assembly became major players on the Task Force. They played strong roles in fashioning the curriculum and governance components of the Kentucky Educational Reform Act (KERA) and shared responsibilities with the executive branch for fashioning the financial aspects of the Act.

The KERA was considered to be, by many observers, the major legislative initiative of the decade. As a result of its role in KERA, the Legislature gained stature as a program initiator rather than being, simply, a modifier of executive branch initiatives. At the same time, the Governor made a major contribution to the effort by actively participating in the Task Force and helping craft the recommendations of the Task Force. More importantly, he is credited for taking the "politically risky" initiative to propose a major tax increase that was sufficient to deal with both the efficiency (or equity) and adequacy concerns of the Kentucky Supreme Court.

While in-state issues dominated the Wilkinson era, federal/state fiscal relations also claimed a spot on the policy agenda. The Reagan administration has been recognized for its efforts to begin the implementation of a policy of "shifting fiscal federalism;" that is, shifting expenditure responsibilities for many programs from the federal government to state and local governments, often without the corresponding revenue sources to finance such programs. The Wilkinson administration realized during its transition into office that it should view shifting fiscal federalism as an opportunity to achieve some of its policy objectives. For example, as indicated, the Wilkinson administration, in addition to its focus on elementary and secondary education, identified economic development as a major policy focus. Consequently, when the U.S. Environmental Protection Agency (EPA) shifted its emphasis from a wastewater grant program that directly funded local wastewater projects to a "capitalization grant program," the Wilkinson administration recognized a unique opportunity to develop an innovative approach for addressing existing infrastructure issues associated with the state's economic development efforts.

The theory of the new capitalization program was that, over time, the Federal government would eliminate annual payments to wastewater treatment facilities and replace the payments with capitalization grants. The grants would support state infrastructure loan programs that could become self-supporting. Taking advantage of the new federal program flexibility, the Wilkinson administration implemented Kentucky's "capitalization" program as part of a broader economic development initiative, by combining an existing infrastructure bonding program with direct cash appropriations to create a broad-based Kentucky infrastructure authority financing program.

In addition to this innovative effort, the Wilkinson administration was active through the National Governor's Association and other state lobbying groups to try to influence Federal policy with regard to the Federal Highway Trust Fund and other programs that provide vital support to state governments.

While the Wilkinson period is remembered for Kentucky's progress in public education, it is also recognized as a period when the Kentucky General Assembly took another step toward greater independence. Earlier efforts to enhance legislative independence focused on largely process issues, such as the right of the General Assembly to promulgate budget instructions as a result of *L.R.C. v. Brown,*[5] and the establishment of a more professional staff to assist in reacting to the Governor's budget recommendations and the like.[6] With the KERA legislation, the General Assembly displayed the ability to work closely with and to provide leadership in the development and enactment of major reform legislation. The use of the joint executive/legislative Task Force to develop policy options also became the model for future legislative/executive reform efforts.

## Brereton Jones (1991–1995)

Following the contentious legislative/executive branch years of the Wilkinson administration, Governor Jones was elected in an "era of good feeling" between the executive and legislative branches. Having served as Lieutenant Governor and therefore having presided over the Senate at times, Jones had established good relations with legislators and had focused efforts on improving executive/legislative relations during his campaign for Governor. He identified healthcare as his major policy initiative and pursued the issue with vigor, although unsuccessfully, throughout his term.

During his first budget session in 1992, Governor Jones' budget was well received and essentially passed as presented. The good will and working relationship that he had fostered during his gubernatorial campaign created an environment that was in sharp contrast to his predecessor. In addition to his successful budget initiative, he pursued and received support to place a constitutional amendment on the 1992 General Election ballot for gubernatorial succession. He also supported an initiative to place the Economic Development Cabinet under a separate board to remove it from "politics." This initiative, to some extent, was a reaction to Governor Wilkinson's approach to economic development and his relationship with the Legislature regarding economic development activities.

The legislative/executive era of good feeling began to disentangle with the arrival of federal "corruption in government" authorities in March 1992 to begin an investigation that became known as "Boptrot" (an investigation that focused on issues involving the Business Occupations and Professions Committee and the harness racing industry). Eventually, several legislators were indicted for matters related to legislative ethical conduct. As a result of the indictments and the associated negative publicity, the morale of the General Assembly was depleted and Governor Jones drew a strong negative reaction when he began to criticize the legislature for their ethical lapses and/or for guilt by association. His criticism led to a deterioration of executive/legislative relations reminiscent of Governor Wilkinson's term as Governor.

A political repercussion of the executive/legislative branch friction was the defeat of Governor Jones' universal health care initiative that was considered in a special session of the General Assembly in May 1993. The defeat of the Governor's initiative led to a further deterioration of relations and carried over to the next regular legislative session in January 1994. During that session, significant disputes arose regarding the budget that led to Governor Jones vetoing the appropriation bill on the last day of the session. The veto forced a special session to approve a budget for the next biennium that occurred in May 1994.

While communication and personality issues led to significant conflict and tension for the latter half of Governor Jones' administration, cooperative legislative/executive efforts did emerge in budget related issues. First,

Kentucky established a "consensus revenue forecasting initiative" including legislative and executive branch appointees by executive order, which was later legislatively confirmed in the 1996 Session of the General Assembly. The Consensus Forecasting Group was charged with providing both branches with the "official" revenue forecast for consideration by the executive and legislative branches as part of the budgetary process. Second, a legislative/executive Tax Study Commission was formed to develop a "blueprint" for tax reform.[7] The Commission held hearings, conducted research, and produced a comprehensive set of tax reform recommendations that were referenced by both branches when tax reform initiatives were proposed and considered during the last half of the 1990s.

As previously mentioned, a major policy initiative of Governor Jones was health care. However, his state policy efforts were hindered by Federal policy discussions, led by the Clinton administration, to revamp health care nationally. The debate and discussions at the national level created a perception that Kentucky's reform efforts should be more limited in scope because the major health care issues were going to be addressed from a national perspective.

Compared to the previous Wilkinson administration, Governor Jones' administration was much less actively involved in intergovernmental issues. His administration had limited involvement with the National Governor's Association and other state interest groups that focus on influencing Federal policy. Such limited involvement, apparently, reflected his stronger interest in "in-state" issues rather than national federal/state government policy conflicts and concerns.

### Paul Patton (1995–2003)

Elected the first Governor with the possibility of succession, Governor Patton took both a long-term (8 year) as well as a short-term (next biennium) view of his programs and policy initiatives. Having observed two administrations where the executive/legislative relations were strained, he realized the importance of good relations between the two branches in getting programs approved. Therefore, he indicated to the members of the General Assembly that he wanted to establish and maintain a good working relationship with the Legislature. He acknowledged their "policy making" role and pledged to work closely with them during his tenure as Governor. He maintained that commitment and held numerous meetings with the legislative leadership of both parties during and between sessions and held many "one on one" meetings with individual legislators to discuss his programs and initiatives.

In his inaugural address, he indicated that higher education would be the first priority of his administration. In addition, he cited workers' compensation reform and sound financial management as priority policy initiatives. These issues dominated his first term and he enjoyed success in pursuing these objectives.

Soon after his election, Governor Patton met with his financial advisors and determined that he was facing a structural budget deficit implying that projected continuing expenditures exceeded continuing revenues. At the same time, ironically, there was a temporary surplus in the General Fund resulting from budget cuts and other actions of the Jones' administration.[8]

Governor Patton established as one of his financial management principles the maintenance of a structurally balanced budget. He also stressed the financial management principles of: (1) the use of the consensus revenue forecast; (2) maintaining an adequate budget reserve fund; and (3) utilizing a "surplus expenditure plan" as a means of reducing the tendency of state policymakers to utilize unanticipated or "surplus" state revenues to expand the state's continuing expenditure base.

As a result of the financial conditions he faced, Governor Patton's first budget was a "continuation" budget with limited capital investment projects and few expansion programs. He also recommended the codification of the consensus forecasting initiative that had been developed by the Jones administration by Executive Order.

Upon completion of the first session of his administration, Governor Patton began to focus on his principal policy issues: workers' compensation and higher education. Changes in Kentucky's workers compensation statutes were considered by the Workers Compensation Advisory Board in 1996 that was unable to develop a set of consensus recommendations due to the makeup of the board, which consisted of labor and business representatives. As a result, Governor Patton developed a workers' compensation reform package and presented it to the General Assembly at a special session in December 1996. After considerable debate, the bill passed over the objection of labor leaders and eastern Kentucky legislators. This issue became the source of legislative/executive tension that affected future policy initiatives to a limited extent.

As indicated, Governor Patton had acknowledged the importance of establishing a close working relationship with members of the General Assembly in major policy initiatives early in his administration. As a result, he worked with members of the General Assembly to establish a Task Force on Postsecondary Education Reform during the 1996 regular session. The Task Force began meeting in June 1996 and consisted of twelve legislators and six members of the executive branch, including Governor Patton as Chairperson. The joint executive/legislative Task Force on Postsecondary Education reform was patterned after the successful KERA Task Force that developed the elementary and secondary education reform package in 1989. The Task Force reviewed the status of postsecondary education, trends and future challenges for postsecondary education, and developed reform goals.

Governor Patton called a special session of the General Assembly in May 1997 to consider proposals for reforming Kentucky's postsecondary educational system. The session was successful and benefited from the involvement of both branches in the development of the reform recommendations. The legislation created the Council on Postsecondary Education (CPE) to replace the previous Council on Higher Education, changed the system of higher education finance, established trust funds to support higher education initiatives, established a virtual university and separated the Community College System from the University of Kentucky and merged it with the postsecondary technology schools (vocational schools) to form the Kentucky Community and Technical College System. In addition, the legislation called for the establishment of SCOPE (the Strategic Committee on Postsecondary Education) a joint legislative/executive and CPE group charged with reviewing CPE plans and anticipated budget requests prior to submission to the General Assembly and the Governor, along with other policy discussions with CPE.

Governor Patton's second regular legislative session (1998) contrasted sharply with his first "continuation" budget session. Focusing on his strategic vision of raising Kentucky's economic wellbeing level to the national average within 20 years, which he articulated during his first legislative session, he proposed aggressive initiatives in five policy areas including: (1) improving Kentucky's education product; (2) promoting economic development; (3) reducing crime and its cost to society; (4) building self-sustaining families; and (5) strengthening Kentucky's financial condition and responsiveness of government. Postsecondary education initiatives included funding for a $100 million endowment for faculty chairs and professorships at the state's two research universities (referred to as the "Bucks for Brains" program), funding for a new merit scholarship program that provides college scholarship support for high school graduates depending on academic achievement in high school and college (funded with lottery proceeds), funding for the establishment of a virtual university, special funding for the comprehensive universities and the new community college/technical college system, as well as significant new funding for new university facilities and maintenance. Other budget initiatives included major funding for correctional facilities, affordable housing, tourism, "Empower Kentucky" (a major process reengineering effort), and economic development related capital investments. The budget proposals were developed with significant legislative input. As a consequence, the Governors' budget proposals were passed largely intact.

The joint legislative/executive Task Force model was again relied upon during the last 2 years of Governor Patton's first term to increase public awareness of emerging issues and to develop legislative packages for the 2000 session when issue consensus was attainable. Among the joint Task Forces created were: (1) the Task Force on Utility Tax Policy; (2) the Electricity Restructuring Task Force; (3) the Early Childhood Education Task Force; and (4) the Tobacco Settlement Task Force. Established by legislative resolution by the 1998 session of the General Assembly, the Utility Tax, the Electricity Restructuring, and the Early Childhood Task Forces met regularly during the interim in an effort to develop state policy direction and draft legislation for consideration by the 2000 session of the Kentucky General Assembly.

While the Utility Tax Task Force failed to issue legislative recommendations, it did prepare recommendations for changes in the manner that public service companies are taxed. Some of those recommendations were incorporated in the tax proposals that Governor Patton presented to the 2000 session of the Kentucky General Assembly. The Energy Deregulation Task Force deliberated deregulation but concluded that deregulation was not in Kentucky's best interest at this time. The Early Childhood Task Force developed a comprehensive set of proposals for the Governor and General Assembly. It should be noted that early childhood development had been identified as one of Governor Patton's major initiatives for the 2000 session and that strong gubernatorial interest gave that Task Force momentum in fully developing recommendations for consideration by the Governor and General Assembly.

In contrast to the administrations of Governor Wilkinson and Governor Jones, the Patton administration maintained good relations with the General Assembly during its first term. Governor Patton regularly held meetings with the legislative leadership and individual members of both parties in efforts to acquire the legislative support he needed to insure legislative approval of his policy initiatives and budget recommendations.

Governor Patton was reelected for a second 4-year term in November 1999 and began preparing for the 2000 session. Two factors significantly altered executive and legislative relationships and Governor Patton's legislative and program initiative success in 2000: one factor being political; the other factor being economic. The political factor involved the change in party control of the Senate and the associated leadership change. The loss of his party's control of the Senate impacted how the Governor worked with the legislature and his ability to influence budget and revenue policy, while the economic factor (the 2001 recession and subsequent economic impacting events) impacted state revenues. The economic slowdown that began in 2000 reduced anticipated state revenues, forced changes in the execution of the FY 2001 budget, and changed budget planning and decision making for the last "budget" session of Governor Patton's second term.

The Republican-controlled Senate could not mandate their budget priorities in the 2000 budget session, but they were in a position to stop or significantly alter executive branch budgetary and revenue initiatives that were proposed by the Governor and supported by the Democratically controlled House. For example, in his 2000 session budget recommendations (for FY 2002 and FY 2003), Governor Patton proposed a series of tax reform measures that would enhance the elasticity and improve the "fairness" of the state's tax structure, while producing additional revenue (tax increases) for education. After enactment of a scaled-down version of the Governor's tax-reform proposal by the Democratically controlled House of Representatives, the Senate rejected the package. The Senate did agree to a limited revenue-raising measure that maintained the state's commitment to education, but tax reform failed due to disagreements between the Democratically controlled House and Republican controlled Senate.

As a consequence of the economic slowdown, Kentucky's General Fund revenues began to underperform and budget shortfalls resulted. The budget shortfall in FY 2001 was approximately $185 million, while the shortfall in FY 2002 increased to approximately $680 million. In fact, the receipts for FY 2002 fell below actual collections in FY 2001, the first time this had occurred in Kentucky in over 40 years. Such shortfalls were principally due to job losses that, in turn, reduced individual income and sales taxes (the state's two major General Fund revenue sources). In addition, the combined effects of the national recession of January 2001 through September 2001, the aftermath of the September 11 tragedy in New York City, and the impact of corporate scandals led to a dramatic drop in the financial markets that negatively impacted state capital gains and corporate income tax payments.

Kentucky's General Assembly has a history of including in its appropriation bill special language granting the executive branch special authority to deal with budget shortfalls. The appropriation bill language (referred to as the "Budget Reduction Plan") lays out actions, in priority order, that the executive branch must take to prevent a budget deficit in the event that a budget shortfall is anticipated as a result of the Consensus Forecasting Group "officially" reducing the states revenue estimate. The plan provides guidance when the Legislature is not in session and a special session of the General Assembly is not called to deal with the shortfall. Consequently, the primary policy decision facing the Governor was whether to balance the budget pursuant to the Budget Reduction Plan enacted by the General Assembly, or to "call" the General Assembly into a special session forcing the legislature to deal with cuts. Governor Patton elected to use the executive powers granted by the General Assembly via the Budget Reduction Plan to manage the cuts in FY 2001 and FY 2002.

The Governor adopted a budget balancing policy designed to minimize programmatic impact and to exempt, to the maximum degree possible, education from budget cuts. To do so, the Governor executed a series of cutback orders that relied heavily on one-time funds and limited continuing program reductions. Included in the budget balancing plan were: (1) the use of budget reserve trust fund moneys or "rainy day funds" of approximately $280 million, which depleted the rainy day fund; (2) fund transfers from nongeneral fund and offbudget accounts to the General Fund; (3) refinancing of outstanding debt to realize debt service savings; (4) implementation of efficiency measures such as reduced overtime, reduction of state motor pool vehicles, reduction in state employee travel, and the like; and (5) actual cuts in selected lower priority programs.

The budget balancing policy pursued by Governor Patton produced a "financially" balanced budget as constitutionally required but created a "structural imbalance" as one-time revenues were principally utilized to mange the budget shortfall. The executive branch did perform an analysis that showed the resumption of "normal" or historic revenue growth levels in the FY 2003 and FY 2004 biennium would restore structural balance by FY 2005. That is, the expectation that 2 years of reduced economic and revenue growth in FY 2001 and FY 2002, followed by a pattern of more normal revenue growth, in combination with managed and constrained expenditure growth, would permit the realization of a structurally balanced budget by FY 2005.

In 2002, the executive branch budget contained only minimal revenue growth to utilize in dealing with the continuing budget shortfall, so Governor Patton recommended a "flat" budget (i.e., most agencies would receive funding in FY 2003 and FY 2004 equal to their FY 2002 funding level with no adjustments for inflation or service demand growth). The Governor described his proposed budget as a "bad" budget, but the best that could be produced in a weak economic environment. The House of Representatives enacted the Governor's recommendation, essentially, as presented. However, the House did identify additional fund transfers of one-time money that, in the short term, would continue to benefit K-12 education, but in the long term would add to the state's structural budget imbalance that had already emerged due to the executive branch's cutback and budget balancing policies taken to balance the FY 2001 and FY 2002 budgets.

The Republican-controlled Senate approved an appropriation bill that was similar in funding and language to that recommended by the Governor and approved by the House, with one major exception. For over 10 years, Kentucky law provided for public funding of gubernatorial elections. The Republican-controlled Senate deleted the campaign funding recommended by the Governor and approved by the House from the Senate's version of the budget. The total funding for the biennium for public campaign financing was approximately $7 million (out of a combined biennial General Fund budget of $14 billion). However, in Conference Committee, the policy of public financing of gubernatorial elections was the focus of the debate and the budget became the vehicle for this policy discussion. The Budget Conference Committee could not agree on the issue of campaign financing and the General Assembly adjourned without adopting a budget. The Governor immediately called the General Assembly into Special Session to deal with the issue, but the budget again became the vehicle for the debate of public financing of gubernatorial elections, and again the General Assembly concluded their Special Session without resolution of this issue or the enactment of a state budget.

The inability of the Kentucky General Assembly to pass a biennial budget marked the first time in Kentucky history that the legislative body failed to pass an appropriation bill for financing state government as required by the state's Constitution. This dilemma presented the Governor with several options: (1) continue to call the General Assembly into Special Session in the hope that they would adopt a budget; (2) identify "essential" government services and provide funding for those services at the start of the new fiscal year; (3) create a "continuing resolution" type of budget as has occurred when the federal government has been unable to approve appropriation bills for a new fiscal year; or (4) operate state government agencies and programs at levels reflecting the Governor's original recommendations to the General Assembly, which had been, essentially, adopted separately by the House and Senate in a form similar to that recommended by the Governor, except for the funding of gubernatorial campaign financing.

Because the Kentucky Constitution and Kentucky statutes do not indicate what the executive branch can or should do when an appropriation bill is not passed by the General Assembly, the Governor had no legal basis or "precedent" to follow in deciding the course of action that he should pursue under this unique set of circumstances.

The Governor chose the last option (continue government operations and expenditures at levels adopted "independently" by the House and Senate but not approved by both due to the conflict over gubernatorial election financing). Consequently, on July 1, Kentucky's state government agencies and programs were operated as they would have been had the General Assembly adopted a budget. The Governor's expenditure plan was, essentially, a "business as usual" approach to governmental operations. Immediately, lawsuits were filed to challenge the Governor's authority to expend state funds without a legislative appropriation. This intriguing constitutional legal challenge to Governor Patton's "business as usual" expenditure plan remained unresolved in the courts when the General Assembly completed action on the FY 2003 and FY 2004 budgets during the 2003 legislative session—9 months after the start of the FY 2003 fiscal year.

The major Patton administration Federal policy challenge occurred during the administration's transition into office. Patton's first biennial budget had to be produced at a time when there was no Federal budget and a Federal government "shut down" had just occurred, a result of major policy differences between the Clinton White house and the Republican Congress. As a result, the state's 2-year budget was developed without knowledge of federal funding levels and program specifics in areas such as Medicaid, welfare, and the like. The Medicaid program was subsequently modified but other human service programs, such as Aid to Families with Dependent Children (AFDC), were replaced with programs such as Temporary Assistance for Needy Families (TANF). As a result of the Federal budget and policy uncertainty, Kentucky had to develop its budget with limited federal policy information and guidance.

The Patton administration played an active role in public policy discussions regarding the above proposed Federal program changes. In addition, working through the National Governors Association (Governor Patton served in several NGA roles, including Chair), Governor Patton pursued an active role on behalf of the states in program and appropriation debates regarding a number of programs including those associated with the Federal Highway Trust Fund.

# BUDGET PROCESS AND POLICY CHANGES IN THE 1990s

As suggested, Kentucky's budget process and policy changes in the "1990s" reflect the state's budgetary and financial conditions as well as its changing political environment. Such change drivers were noted in a previous era.[9] In the 1980s, Kentucky as well as other states went through a period characterized by economic and financial instability. During that period, Kentucky and other states had to manage their finances during a period of double-digit inflation, and two recessions. Those conditions fostered revenue shortfalls and budget cuts. In fact, in Kentucky, fourteen "within fiscal year" budget reductions were made during the 12 fiscal years (from 1981 to 1993) to insure that the constitutional balanced budget requirement was met. The budget adjustments produced program reductions and generated concerns and frustrations for the executive and legislative branches as well the public.

As indicated earlier, the Kentucky Supreme Court Case of 1989 that declared Kentucky's system of public education unconstitutional, the changing federal policies that impacted federal/state fiscal relations, and other circumstances created an environment that encouraged Kentucky's Governors and legislators to work together to stabilize Kentucky's financial condition in the 1990s. Among the initiatives were the following:

- Governor Wilkinson's Revenue Revitalization Program, a program of tax increases that, through a series of tax code changes, raised approximately 18 percent more state tax revenues to finance education and other programs and increase the progressivity and growth potential of Kentucky's tax structure.

- Establishment of the Consensus Forecasting Group by Executive Order by Governor Jones in 1993 to increase confidence in and accuracy of state revenue forecasts by involving both executive and legislative branches in developing the official state's revenue forecasts.

- Establishment of a Budget Reserve Trust Fund or "rainy day fund" (with a policy of funding the trust fund at a level of 5 percent of the General Fund) by the Jones administration in the 1995 Special Session.

- Codification of the consensus forecasting initiative during the first term of the Patton administration.

- Establishment of a policy of maintaining a "structurally balanced budget" by Governor Patton in 1996. The policy included a provision for multiyear projections (4 years forward) of continuing expenditures and revenues.

- Establishment of a "surplus expenditure plan" as a means of financing capital expenditures with cash during periods of budget surpluses so as to reduce the incentive to commit one-time dollars for continuing expenditures by Governor Patton in 1996.

This series of budget related process adjustments reflected efforts to enhance Kentucky's financial stability by more effective short (next budget period) and long-term revenue and expenditure forecasting. In addition, Kentucky's financial stability was strengthened by creating the Budget Reserve Trust Fund (rainy day fund) and the surplus expenditure plan to mitigate unanticipated fluctuations in state revenues. The forecasting and other financial management initiatives received support and participation of both branches and tended to reduce interbranch tensions of the budgetary process.

## LEGISLATIVE/EXECUTIVE BUDGET POLICY ROLE CHANGES

As indicated in an earlier paper,[10] the executive and legislative branch roles in the Kentucky budgetary process underwent significant and continuous change during the decades of the 1970s and 1980s. The enhanced role of the legislative branch, during the period, was influenced by a number of factors. Among the factors were: (1) court decisions that further defined the legislature's role in Kentucky budgeting;[11] (2) legislative actions including House Bill 649 in 1982 that altered budget preparation processes;[12] (3) enhanced legislative staff capability and professionalism; and (4) adjustments to capital budgeting procedures that reduced executive branch budgeting flexibility.

By the end of the 1980s, the executive and legislative branches had adjusted to the new "legislative independence" and the legislature's new equivalent status in the budget process. In a sense, a new "equilibrium" was achieved relative to policy and budgetary authority and power that would influence executive/legislative relationships in the 1990s. As the review of the gubernatorial terms of Governors Wilkinson, Jones, and Patton suggest, the new parity of the two branches was further solidified by a series of circumstances in the 1990s and "early 2000s." Among these were the following:

• The 1989 Kentucky Supreme Court decision declaring Kentucky's system of public schools unconstitutional and directing the Kentucky General Assembly to develop a new system that met its requirements for efficiency and adequacy. This event thrust the General Assembly into an unaccustomed policy role and enhanced its confidence in dealing with broad-based complex public policy issues. It also set in motion a new cooperative relationship between the executive and legislative branches with the establishment of the joint executive/legislative Task Force to develop recommendations and legislation for consideration by the 1990 session of the Kentucky General Assembly.

• The enhanced reliance on joint executive/legislative Committees or Task Forces to consider major policy issues during the legislative interim including: (1) the Tax Policy Commission appointed by Governor Jones; (2) the Higher Education Reform Task Force appointed by Governor Patton; (3) the Electricity Restructuring Task Force established by the 1998 session of the Kentucky General Assembly; (4) the Utility Tax Task Force established by the 1998 session of the Kentucky General Assembly; (5) the Early Childhood Task Force established by the 1998 session of the Kentucky General Assembly; and (6) the Phase II Kentucky Tobacco Settlement Task Force appointed by Governor Patton to consider alternative ways of distributing

Phase II tobacco settlement funds to Kentucky tobacco farmers. This pattern of establishing work groups with representatives from both branches has become the pattern for dealing with long-term broad-based pubic policy issues and has been an effective means of increasing information and support for policy initiatives in the 1990s.

- The shift in legislative political power from the Democratic to the Republican Party during the decade has influenced the executive/legislative policy process as well. The growing strength of the Republicans, particularly in the Senate, led to greater pre-release and "during session" consultation and bargaining in 1996 and 1998 between Governor Patton and the Republican leadership regarding budgetary policy and recommendations than had been previously experienced. Such consultation translated into budget policy influence and resulted in a further adjustment to traditional budget policy practices in the commonwealth. The "take-over" of the Senate in 2000 by the Republican Party and its ability to enhance its margin of control in the 2002 election further solidified its role as a strong partner in the budget process.

- The 2002 budget stalemate over campaign financing witnessed a new role for the budget—relegislating state policy through the state budget. Time will tell if this is the birth of a new trend or, simply, another chapter on executive/legislative budgetary relations as those relations adjust to changing executive/legislative branch roles and political party power shifts.

## SUMMARY

The role of the legislative and executive branches in the budgetary process underwent significant change during the decades of the 1970s and 1980s. By the end of the 1980s, the transition process had achieved an equilibrium of sorts as both branches adjusted to their new roles and activities in the budget development and approval process. The transition from a strong executive process to a balanced process continued in the 1990s, although at a slower pace. Buoyed by a major Supreme Court decision in 1989, the Kentucky legislature began taking a more proactive role in budget policy development.

The changing environment also encouraged the use of joint legislative/executive Task Forces and special committees to develop policy and legislative options in several major policy areas such as higher education, early childhood education, and energy deregulation. In all of these cases, the closer working relationships that the Task Forces engendered appear to have enhanced the legislative and policy process. Finally, the policy role of the legislature during the 1990s changed as the relative power of the two political parties in the General Assembly followed regional trends and the Republican Party gained strength, particularly in the Senate. That change resulted in more intensive presubmission and during session consultation between the executive and legislative branches.

The roles of the two branches in the budget process continue to change over time in Kentucky. The courts, legislation, party changes, and the like have been major factors influencing such change. As a result of the transition, the Kentucky legislature has gained budget preparation and execution authority and responsibility, while the executive branch has become more open and willing to seek legislative input into its budget policy, preparation, and execution processes in the new executive/legislative environment.

## REFERENCES

Carson, Ronald, "The 1984–86 Kentucky State Budget," *Kentucky Economy: Review & Perspective*, 8(2) (1984), 3–7.

Clynch, Edward, and Thomas Lauth, *Governors, Legislatures, and Budgets*. New York: Greenwood Press, 1991.

Hackbart, Merl, "Kentucky: Transitions, Adjustments, and Innovations," in Clynch and Lauth, Eds. *Governors, Legislatures, and Budgets*, New York: Greenwood Press, 1991, pp. 83–92.

Hackbart, Merl, and Ron Carson, "Budget Theory and State Budget Practice: Analysis and Perspective, *Public Budgeting and Financial Management*, 5(1) (1993).

Jordan, Meagan, and Merl Hackbart, "The Status of Performance Budgeting Among the States," *Public Budgeting and Finance*, 19(1) (Spring, 1999).

Kentucky Commission on Tax Policy, *Kentucky Commission on Tax Policy: A Blueprint for Comprehensive Reform* (November, 1995).

Patton, Governor Paul, Jim Ramsey and Merl Hackbart, *Strengthening the Financial Condition of Kentucky State Government: The Patton Plan*, Frankfort, KY: Governor's Office, 1998.

Shick, Allen, "The Road to PPB: The Stages of Budget Reform," *Public Administration Review*, 26 (December, 1966).

Shick, Allen, "The Road from ZBB," *Public Administration Review*, 38 (March/April, 1978).

Snyder, Sheryl G., and Robert M. Ireland, "The Separation of Governmental Powers under the Constitution of Kentucky: A Legal and Historical Analysis of L.R.C. v. Brown," *Kentucky Law Journal* (1984–1985), 165.

## NOTES

1. Clynch and Lauth, 1991.
2. Shick, 1966; Shick, 1978; Jordan and Hackbart, 1999.
3. Hackbart, 1991.
4. 88 S. C. 804 TG (KY, 1989).
5. 664 S. W. 2d 907 (KY 1984).
6. Snyder and Ireland, 1984–1985.
7. Kentucky Commission on Tax Policy, 1995.
8. Governor Paul Patton et al., 1998.
9. Hackbart and Carson, 1993.
10. Hackbart, 1991.
11. *L. R. C. v. Brown*, 664 S. W. 2d 907 (KY 1984), and *Armstrong v. Collins* 709, S.W. 2nd 437 (KY 1986).
12. Carson, 1984.

# CHAPTER 10

# Nevada: Budgeting at the Crossroads[1]

*Paula D. Yeary*

As a state that includes "sin city" and the "Biggest Little City,"[2] Nevada is a land of contrasts and quirky trivia stemming largely from its history, tourism-driven economy, and geography, which is nearly completely desert. The population is urban, with over 75 percent living within metropolitan statistical areas and yet it contains vast stretches of undeveloped areas, having 85 percent of its land being federally owned. Founded by rugged miners and individuals and with a state motto of "Battle Born" the state's culture, though evolving, has kept true to its beginnings.

The state's history and economy have helped shape the almost libertarian attitude of many Nevadans who prefer less government and are willing to forego high levels of government services in return for lower taxes. Governors, Democrat and Republican, traditionally adhere to this perspective and follow fiscally conservative budgetary practices. In keeping with this libertarian philosophy, the public has been, in general, socially liberal as well, as reflected by approving through referenda a "pro-choice" stance on abortion and still permitting legalized prostitution in rural counties.[3] Even with the huge influx of new residents over the last decade, this mentality has, by and large, not changed.

Between 1990 and 2000, Nevada's population grew by 66 percent, from 1,201,675 to 1,998,257, garnering the status of fastest growing state in the nation. The vast majority of the population resides in Southern Nevada (1.4 million). The result of this huge influx has been a financially strained education system that must accommodate new students faster than schools can be built. The state continues to search for new means of acquiring water rights for its ever-growing desert cities, and, unless successful, Southern Nevada will likely face stymied growth in the future. Adding further stress, the economic and tax systems have not adapted to these new population levels. The state continues to rely on gaming and tourism as its economic base and as its primary sources of tax revenue.

In the past, the state has staved off severe fiscal crises by limiting government expenditures and maintaining a well financed rainy day fund. Through the 1990s, the state was able to meet the increasing service costs caused by population growth due to the concomitant boom in gaming and tourism. However, the strain of growth eventually resulted in real fiscal stress and necessitated a search for new tax alternatives. In real, per capita dollars, General Fund revenues were projected to drop to $594 in FY 2005, down from $667 in FY 1995.

Although the immediate curtailment of tourism after the September 11 terrorist attacks and the subsequent economic recession certainly hurt the state's economy, Nevada's tourism numbers have rebounded; however, tourists now typically spend less than previously.[4] The effects of these events on the state's revenues have been dramatic, resulting in unprecedented shortfalls over the last biennium (Nevada's legislative sessions and budgets are biennial). In FY 2002, General Fund revenue collections grew by a meager 1 percent and were $68.2 million below the official forecast of $1.82 billion. For the following fiscal year, revenue growth expanded somewhat, with a 3.8 percent increase, but still left a shortfall exceeding $80 million.[5]

Because of its traditionally conservative spending patterns, the state government did not have significant levels of excess service or personnel capacity, making the fiscal crisis, which began in 2001, particularly difficult. In order to end the biennium in balance, the Governor adopted several standard cost-saving measures. The largest of these was a 3 percent across-the-board reduction in state spending with the agencies maintaining the flexibility to choose how those cuts would be made.[6] However, primary and secondary education funds were protected from rescission, and because this expenditure category constitutes over 25 percent of the entire budget, a large portion of the budget was unaffected, necessitating larger cuts in other departments. Furthermore, the state removed $47 million in funding for one-time equipment purchases and maintenance projects and imposed a hiring freeze over the biennium (total of 1,500 positions).[7] Finally, the state decimated its rainy day fund in the last biennium, leaving only one million of the original $135 million.

A more systemic concern for the state has been the establishment of Indian gaming in California, Nevada's largest source of tourists. Companies managing these casinos in California are the industry's leaders, with plans to create high-grade establishments that can effectively compete with Nevada. Although most agree that Las Vegas would not be dramatically affected, the real concern is that Indian gaming will drastically hurt tourism in Reno and Lake Tahoe.[8]

Due to the confluence of these serious fiscal impacts—continued population growth, economic recession, curtailed tourism due to threats of terrorism, and Indian gaming in California—the state's political leadership was forced to finally evaluate whether the government could continue to survive on tourism-based taxes and to search for a stable, general tax source. Many government officials knew the state needed to raise taxes and create a more stable tax base, but they also realized that to do so would (1) require a political crisis, and (2) risk reelection. The current governor, in his second term, was in a position to advocate such a long-term philosophical change in the tax system through the 2003–2005 Executive Budget.

In order to close the projected $700 million revenue shortfall for the 2003–2005 biennium, Governor Guinn proposed a myriad of tax changes in his Executive Budget. Several of these recommendations came from the legislatively authorized Task Force on Tax Policy, which had conducted a year of study and hearings on the state's future financial outlook. After a lengthy special session and a decision from the State Supreme Court, the legislature finally approved the necessary tax increases with the required two-thirds majority, an extraordinary delay of 3 weeks after the beginning of the fiscal year.[9]

## BUDGET PROCESS

The state's budget process over the last two decades can be characterized as pragmatic, with a strong attention to detail. This generalization stems from several important causes including the personnel in both executive and legislative budget offices, the budget format, and the size of the state government. The budget process and format are legally defined through state statute (NRS chapter 353); however, the process and final decisions are strongly influenced by the attention to cost details by long-serving legislators as well as the inclinations of budget staff.

The state's budget format is very important because it frames the questions for the budget as well as the relations between the executive and legislative branches. The Executive Budget document is a compilation of many individual budget accounts, each of which are divided into three main components: an adjusted base budget, a maintenance budget, and the enhancement budget, creating an incremental budgeting system. The base budget reflects actual expenditures from the prior fiscal year (work program year is not used) and is the overwhelming portion of the entire budget. For the 2003–2005 biennium, the base budget constituted 80 percent of the entire General Fund appropriation.[10] Maintenance decision items include additional funding for demographic/caseload changes (i.e., prisoners, school children, or environmental permits), inflation, fringe benefit rate adjustments, federal mandates, and court orders while enhancements include all other requests for additional spending such as new programs, program expansion, or new delivery mechanisms. One-time equipment purchases for existing programs are listed as enhancement items as well. Within the maintenance and enhancement budgets, new spending is separated by decision unit. For example, additional spending for mandates would be one decision unit, while spending for inflation would be another, and both would be placed within the maintenance section of the budget. By explicitly dividing the budget in this manner, the budget document becomes very lengthy and cumbersome, but also focuses agency directors', the governor's, and the legislators' attention on new spending rather than debating current expenditures for agencies.

To the extent that legislators focus on enhancements and the policy questions the decision units encompass, the budget and legislative fiscal staff maintain high levels of discretion on determining spending in other parts of the budget. However, Budget Office staff and their legislative counterparts must expend considerable time deciding what spending goes where, resulting in less attention on evaluating the merits of the budget request. Within that setting, agency directors and their financial staff work to keep as many items as possible in the base budget and to classify new spending as maintenance rather than as enhancement items due to the belief that maintenance requests will be approved more readily than enhancements.

For the last several decades, the Executive Budget has had a line-item format, which is then divided into spending categories such as personnel, operating, equipment, etc. The line-item format suits the culture of the state legislature, which has historically preferred to keep spending down and ensure "one shot" expenditures such as equipment are removed from the base budget. At times though, this format distracts legislators and their fiscal staff from evaluating the merits of new spending. Until the mid-1980s, the state government was small enough so that legislators had the time to evaluate the budget in such detail; however, with the biennial budget having exceeded $15 billion, high levels of attention by legislators to line-item expenditures may be distracting.[11]

The budget management cycle officially begins with the submission of agency requests on or before August 15, preceding the upcoming legislative session. Agencies develop their requests from a detailed set of instructions issued by the Budget Office. To avoid conflict over format decisions during the legislative session, the Budget Office works closely with the legislative fiscal office in developing the budget instructions.

The Budget Office has traditionally maintained high levels of expertise and longevity of its staff for two key reasons. First, the Budget Office is a division within the Department of Administration and not within the Governor's Office, and, more importantly, all but three positions within the budget office are classified. Two of the unclassified positions are the Budget Director (who also serves as the Director of Administration) and Deputy Budget Director. Although turnover is inevitable due to retirement, promotions, and transfers, some of which are more frequent after particularly stressful legislative sessions, staff have very high levels of expertise concerning their assigned agencies and the process itself. Secondly, budget analysts generally have worked several years for the state in financial positions prior to reaching the division and are promoted more for their technical skills and common sense rather than their political associations.

With only three appointed positions, the Budget Office staff could be considered nonpartisan, although they submit an executive budget. The budget director works with the governor on policy decisions, which are transmitted to the analysts for inclusion into the budget. Analysts are expected to make decisions concerning technical or maintenance changes to the budget, such as requests for new equipment, as well as offer recommendations on budget enhancements. The generally apolitical nature of the technical and maintenance decisions encourages staff to take long-term views of their agencies' budgetary and personnel needs as well as the overall managerial success of the agency. Furthermore, the budget director tends to regularly reassign analysts to particular agencies, increasing each analyst's knowledge about his or her agencies, its success in meeting program goals, and leadership effectiveness. With this background knowledge, analysts usually use common sense and their trust in an agency's leadership in making budget recommendations. Agencies with strong leadership, competent financial personnel, and a history of programmatic achievement are more likely to have a successful and smoother budget process. Due to the individual nature of the budget review process, technical decisions among the budget analysts have not always been consistent. To alleviate that problem, the office recently established two supervisory positions who are responsible for reviewing analysts' technical decisions to ensure consistency across departments.[12]

The legislative counterpart to the Budget Office is the nonpartisan Legislative Counsel Bureau (LCB). Created in 1963, the LCB fiscal division serves both the Senate and Assembly by reviewing the Executive Budget, providing revenue and expenditure projections, analyzing proposed legislation for fiscal impact, and staffing the legislature's Interim Finance Committee.[13] Like the Budget Office, LCB analysts typically have several years of prior state experience and hiring requirements include technical expertise and not political affiliation. Over the years, LCB has been very successful at retaining their fiscal analysts, which has improved the office's overall expertise and knowledge of agency performance and, in turn, led to high levels of trust between LCB staff and the legislators sitting on the appropriation committees. LCB also tries to maintain continuity between legislative sessions by reassigning analysts to particular agencies. Along with a higher knowledge base, reassignments offer LCB and Budget Office analysts an opportunity to develop stronger working relationships.

The legislature expects LCB staff to review the Executive Budget for (1) technical merit, and (2) to highlight policy issues and make recommendations on those policies. Due to state statute as well as informal agreements between the Budget Director and LCB leadership, LCB fiscal analysts have tremendous access to information while the Executive Budget is being prepared, including a copy of the agency request and attendance at agency budget hearings during executive preparation phase of the budget.

This formal access to information is supplemented with informal discussions among LCB analysts, agencies' executives and fiscal staff, and Budget Office analysts. Due to the charge of LCB fiscal staff and their access to information, the Budget Office analysts often find it worthwhile to work with the LCB on many of the technical aspects of the budget, such as determining whether an item should be considered as maintenance or enhancement or calculating the per capita costs for case load increases. To the extent that individual LCB and the Budget Office personnel can reach an agreement before presenting the Executive Budget to the legislature, the legislative budget phase proceeds much more smoothly, allowing more attention to be focused on policy issues and less on format concerns. When such agreement is not reached though, LCB analysts have been known to highlight technical errors in the Executive Budget and require extensive information from agencies on enhancement items. By highlighting technical errors and rigorously questioning enhancement items, an analyst may improve his or her standing with legislators, and more importantly, provide political ammunition to legislators on the appropriations committees. However, the degree to which LCB acts politically is determined foremost by its chief administrators and their perspectives for guiding the culture of the agency.

The Economic Forum, established by the Legislature in 1983 in response to previous revenue shortfalls and political arguments over revenue forecasts, provides significant assistance in focusing attention to spending decisions by determining the official revenue forecast.[14] The Forum is composed of five appointed members, none of whom can be employees of the state government and who serve for 2-year terms. The Governor appoints three members, and the Senate Majority Leader and the Speaker of the Assembly each appoint one member. Using forecasts provided by various public agencies including the Budget Office, LCB, the State Demographer, and the Gaming Commission, the Forum selects the General Fund revenue estimates for the upcoming biennium. Both the governor for the Executive Budget and the legislature for the final appropriations act are bound by those estimates. The first forecast is made on December 1, which the Governor uses to submit the Executive Budget and the second forecast is made on May 1, from which the Legislature approves a final appropriations act. During times of fiscal stress, such as that experienced for the 2003 Legislative Session, the Economic Forum removes a key source of political gamesmanship in the budgeting process. The trend has been for the Forum to set a more conservative December 1 forecast and slightly higher numbers for the second. This practice is largely due to the fact that May 1 is simply closer to the beginning of the upcoming fiscal year and more accurate numbers are available. Furthermore, the higher revenue level in the second forecast provides legislators opportunities to add new spending for their favored projects and still pass a balanced budget as required by law.

Even with the high level of review the Executive Budget undergoes in the legislature, changes tend to be relatively small, and the state's governors have historically been successful in ensuring that the legislature approves their budget priorities. In contrast to the federal budget process, even when the government is split (i.e., the governor and assembly/senate majority are of different parties), the Executive Budget is the main working document. In other words, LCB has never developed a second, or replacement budget for the legislature. This phenomenon is perhaps due to the LCB–Budget Office consensus on technical issues, but also as likely a result of the historically limited revenues available for discretionary spending. The low tax revenues and high population growth over the last two decades has limited the chief executives' abilities to propose expansive new programs and services.[15] In essence, after funding the base and maintenance budgets, little revenue is left to fund enhancements; therefore, the legislature has little opportunity to cut spending or propose new projects themselves.

The Budget Office, LCB, and the executive agencies' fiscal personnel work closely together not only during the budget preparation but also during legislative review and budget execution. After the legislature has approved the budget and passed the appropriations act, any budget adjustments, grant or gift acceptance, or reclassification of state merit positions during the biennium must first be approved by the Budget Office and, if thresholds are met, approved by the Interim Finance Committee (IFC).[16] Established in 1969 to function on behalf of the Legislature between sessions, the IFC is composed of members of both the Senate Finance and the Assembly's Ways and Means committees. Furthermore, the State Board of Examiners and the IFC approve all agency requests for revenues from the state contingency fund. The need for IFC review in budget amendments ensures that the LCB and the legislature maintain awareness of agency activities during the biennium. Since the IFC only includes members from two committees, the majority of the legislature is not involved in significant budgetary and finance decisions throughout the biennium. However, as yet, the legality of the IFC to make legislative decisions has not been questioned. Furthermore, in keeping with the state's culture, there appears to be little to no strong political impetus to change the legislature from part-time (biennial) to full-time (annual), leaving the necessity for IFC intact.

## BUDGET REFORM

By the mid-1990s, the Budget Office and State Legislature had officially required agencies to develop performance measures as part of the budget process. Agency executives and fiscal personnel received training on how to develop measures from the Budget Office and received assistance from their assigned analyst. The results of the reform have been mixed, with the primary obstacles being the inherent political nature of the budgeting process and the format of the budget document.

Being part of the budget process, politics have pervaded performance measurement. Some agency executives with troubled programs resist providing effectiveness measures using standard excuses such as outside factors influencing goal achievement, the costs and difficulty in collecting data, or the mismatch of program timelines with the funding cycle. The resistance is not unreasonable because there is no agreement between the executive and legislative branches on responding to agency performance. If agencies provide damaging information in the hope of receiving additional resources and thereby overcome program problems, the Budget Office cannot offer any protection from the Legislature's response to that information. The fear of the unknown promotes conservativeness and to the extent that agencies control performance information and develop the measures, the ability of LCB or the Budget Office to delve into specific programmatic achievement is limited. For agencies with successful programs, the measures simply highlight their achievements and the reform's purpose, improving agency performance, is not fulfilled. Furthermore, agencies that have recently acquired unsuccessful programs are usually more than willing to document that trouble as protection and justification in future budget cycles. Overall, legislators support having measures in the budget as a form of accountability, although the measures are often used as after-the-fact justifications rather than as tools in decision making. In addition, legislators are free to require an agency to develop new measures for the upcoming biennium, which can lead to continually changing measures, which in turn impedes consistent measurement of activities over time as well as increasing record keeping costs.

The budget document itself also prohibits an effective connection between agency performance and appropriations. By dividing the budget accounts into expenditure categories rather than programs, linking costs to program results is difficult. Due to space limitations, only a handful of measures can be included in the document as well, which limits a complete and consistent use of measurement for all programs. By limiting how many measures can be used, agencies are implicitly encouraged to "cherry pick" their best programs or include measures with the most favorable numbers.

Although not a panacea for all budget allocations, there exist a few important and useful aspects of the reform. First, the use of efficiency measures in determining caseload costs (maintenance budget) is extremely important for all the analysts working on budget development. For example, the Department of Prisons, the Budget Office, and LCB will work together to determine a cost per prisoner for the upcoming biennium. The efficiency measures complement the state's cost-saving mentality, while also being easily understood by the legislators. The Budget Office and the Legislature often use these measures in deciding whether to approve maintenance decision units. Second, the Budget Office has found that a top-down approach to measuring performance does not work and now encourages agency acceptance of performance measurement by promoting the reform as a management tool. Some agency executives have made positive use of the tool and have incorporated measures into their internal reviews.

In contrast to budget theory, it is technology that has led to the most successful improvements in the budget process in recent years. In the 2000–2002 biennium, the Budget Office installed a new computerized budget system that has greatly improved budget operations by reducing the manual input of figures by the budget analyst.[17] The new system has (1) resulted in far fewer opportunities for calculation errors by analysts, and (2) enabled analysts to focus substantially more time on analysis and less on data entry. The system also permits the legislative staff and the agencies to view the budget electronically, although they can be kept from making adjustments to the document during different phases of the budget cycle. By permitting this access, the various budget stakeholders in executive agencies and the LCB can review changes to the budget and, therefore, reduce questions about budget status.

## REVENUES[18]

The State of Nevada has historically kept tax burdens low for its citizens by relying on revenues from tourism, and in particular from gaming. Gaming and sales taxes have been so successful that the state does not impose an income tax and the maximum state-local sales tax rate is just 7.5 percent.[19] The primary drawback of relying on tourism taxes is the state's vulnerability to economic downturns, as was evidenced by the shortfall during the 2001–2003 biennium. In FY 2002, the tax on gaming win fell by 2.8 percent, taxable sales declined by 0.1 percent, and job growth was meager at less than 2 percent.[20]

The state's largest revenue, the general sales and use tax, remained unchanged during the turbulent 2003 Legislative Session. Sales taxes comprise the largest portion of the state's General Fund, generating $655 million in FY 2002 (approximately one-third of the General Fund).[21] Tax revenue depends greatly upon the state's level of economic growth. During the late 1990s, Las Vegas/Clark County experienced a construction boom, with several new casinos and thousands of homes being built, resulting in an average annual growth rate of 6.3 percent between FY 1997 and FY 2001.[22] With the number of casinos and the number of tourists per casino having stabilized, the state expects the rate of increase in sales tax revenues to fall somewhat as well (5.3% per year between FY 2002 to FY 2005).[23] The state's portion of the general sales and use tax equals 2 percent and exempts food purchased for home consumption as well as medical prescriptions. With these exemptions, the sales tax imposes a proportional effective tax rate on consumers (i.e., an individual's average tax rate is the same at each level of income).[24] However, because food purchased for home consumption, which is exempt from the tax, is primarily purchased by residents, nonresidents pay a relatively larger portion of the tax.

The state levies an additional 2.25 percent for local school support, 0.5 percent for basic city-county support, and 1.75 percent for supplemental city-county tax relief for a minimum sales tax rate of 6.5 percent. For these first two local taxes, the state distributes tax revenues to either the school district or the county based upon the point of sale. For the supplemental city-county tax, the Department of Taxation distributes revenues based on statutory formula. The state authorizes counties several other local option sales taxes for items such as flood control, infrastructure, tourism promotion, or open space. Several of these local sales taxes are county-specific, and all must be passed by local referenda for enactment.

While the vast majority of states consider gaming revenues only a minor portion of their budget, in Nevada gaming taxes constitute approximately one-third of the state's General Fund. In FY 2002, gaming taxes raised $590 of the $1,752 million General Fund.[25] The tax is on gaming win, which means that the tax applies when casinos receive the winnings from their customers rather than when that money is owed to the casino. In the FY 2003 the Legislature raised the rate by 0.5 percent for all casinos, which had been safe from tax increases for the last several years. The tax rate is graduated based on casino size, with the largest businesses now paying a maximum rate of 6.75 percent. Casinos can pass the tax forward to gamblers by changing the odds of winning. By being embedded in the overall operation costs of the casino, out-of-state customers are typically unaware that they are paying the tax. Furthermore, as a recreational activity, most in-state gamblers do not object to paying it either. However, as a recreational activity, to the extent that discretionary income falls, such as in a recession, so will casino activity (the amount people are willing to bet) and, subsequently, tax revenues.

As mentioned earlier, Governor Guinn proposed several expansions to existing taxes, the creation of small excise taxes, and one major new tax as part of the 2003–2005 Executive Budget. The most significant change he proposed was institution of a gross receipts tax on all businesses. It was this proposal, as well as the need to raise hundreds of millions of dollars of additional tax revenues that resulted in two special sessions of the Legislature after the conclusion of the 120-day regular session. Ultimately, the Governor only partially succeeded in achieving his tax reform goals. Several existing excise taxes were broadened as recommended in the Executive Budget, but the gross receipts tax was not approved, and in its place the Legislature created a gross payroll tax entitled the Modified Business Tax.

Although not openly debated during the legislative session, the business tax on gross payroll will likely have the effect of depressing wages in a service economy that relies heavily on low-wage jobs such as housekeepers and waitresses in the casinos. The tax rate equals 0.7 percent of gross payroll after deductions for health benefits paid by the employer for employees.[26] By creating a strong incentive for businesses to offer health insurance to workers, the Democrats in the Legislature hoped to reduce the negative effects of the tax on workers. While businesses will likely either begin offering or expand their health benefits to employees due to the deduction, the tax will undoubtedly suppress wages.[27] The Legislature approved a similar tax on financial institutions only at a higher rate of 2 percent. With the passage of the payroll tax, the state also eliminated its original business tax, which was a head tax that charged businesses with over twenty-five employees $100 annually per full-time equivalent employee. As a comparison, in FY 2002, the original business tax raised just $78.4 million; however, the new tax increased the General Fund by approximately $161.6 million in FY 2004.

The primary objectives of the payroll tax are to broaden and stabilize the tax base. Generally, payroll taxes, such as Social Security, are relatively stable simply because individuals must earn wages to support themselves. For Nevada, the payroll tax will likely provide a steadier source of revenue as compared to their existing taxes; however, the state continues to depend upon a service industry (i.e., gaming), which in turn relies upon outside economic conditions.[28] In essence, moderate fluctuations in employment and payroll tax revenues are to be expected.

In addition to the sales, gaming, and modified business taxes, Nevada relies on a myriad of lesser taxes and fees and user charges. Sin taxes on alcohol and cigarettes raise a substantial amount of revenue for the state's general fund at 1.3 percent and 4.1 percent for the 2005—2007 biennium, respectively. Again, because of the nature of the state's economy, the majority of these taxpayers are tourists. Another tourist-oriented tax is the tax on live entertainment that contributes about 4.5 percent of the revenue for the General Fund. Like many other states, Nevada continues to collect taxes related to property such as those on real property transfers. Other major General Fund revenue sources are the insurance premium tax (8.5%), corporate filing fees for the Secretary of State (3.2%), and the tax on receipts from mining precious minerals, primarily gold (0.6%).[29] Although dedicated to the State Highway Fund, the Motor Fuel Tax raises significant revenues for the state's transportation system ($399 million in FY 2004). The state rate equals 18.455 cents per gallon with an additional county share of 6.35 cents per gallon.[30]

In terms of the complete budget, revenues are distributed among several funds. The General Fund comprises just 36 percent of all revenue sources for the Executive Budget. The other major funds are federal funds (23.6%), the highway fund (4.6%), and an "other" category (26.4%).[31] Federal funds include an assortment of grants for programs such as for highway construction, Medicaid, and environmental protection. The "other" category includes funds such as the pension fund, enterprise funds, and the state's smaller trust funds. The distribution reflects (1) the importance of federal funds to the state's budget, and (2) the diversity of revenues the state relies upon.

For last several decades, Nevada has successfully exported a large portion of its tax burden to nonresidents by relying on tourism-related taxes, particularly gaming win and sales and use taxes. However, there have been serious consequences to this strategy. Firstly, these taxes are highly elastic to income, meaning that as incomes fall, such as in a recession, so do tax revenues. Secondly, by relying heavily on general sales and excise taxes to fund services, the state has likely created an overall tax system that is slightly regressive to proportional at best for its residents. Attempting to deal with the inherent problems associated with their traditional tax base, the Governor and the Legislature adopted a new gross payroll tax. Unfortunately, the tax's structure and unpredictability may continue to leave the state vulnerable to revenue shortfalls in the upcoming years. In the long run, if the state is going to successfully generate tax revenues and provide services sufficient for its growing population, it will have to evolve from its "company town" economy to one that is diverse enough to cope with external forces such as business competition and population expansion.

## FISCAL FEDERALISM

For the last several years, public school districts in Nevada have been financially strained to sufficiently accommodate the tremendous increases in the number of students attending elementary and secondary schools. Of the state's seventeen school districts, the largest by far is Clark County, with approximately 70 percent of all students (K-12).[32] The strain has been felt not only in school districts' ability to hire a sufficient number of teachers but also in their ability to build an adequate number of schools. The state government has traditionally played a strong role in both funding and oversight of the elementary and secondary education system; however, that funding has typically only included instructional support, leaving responsibilities for infrastructure improvements to the local districts.

The state determines funding for elementary and secondary education based on a statewide minimum or guaranteed level of support for each full-time pupil referred to in statute as the "Nevada Plan." The state determines the level of per-pupil funding for each school district through a formula that considers economic, demographic, and wealth characteristics of the community in order to adjust for cost-of-living variances between urban and rural school districts.[33] In other words, wealthier areas will have a lower "guarantee" than a poorer community, reflecting the latter's more limited ability to raise revenues for education. For FY 2004, the average per-pupil funding equaled $4,245. To generate revenue for this basic level of support, each school district receives revenues from a state-mandated 2.25 percent general sales and use tax plus revenues from a property tax equaling $0.25 per $100 of assessed value. If revenues from these two sources are insufficient to meet the support guarantee, the state's Distributive School Account, funded primarily through the General Fund, the out-of-state use tax, and a slot machine tax, compensates for the difference. The amount of state support varies annually by school district.

In poorer, rural areas, state funding is much higher. For example, in FY 2004 Lincoln County (1,012 students enrolled in 2003-2004) received 93 percent of its funding from the state, while Clark County's (270,529 students enrolled in 2003–2004) guaranteed funding was only 39 percent of state revenue. Essentially, the degree to which each community generates sales tax revenue will determine the amount of additional state funding it receives.

Governors and the Legislature may add to the basic support amount with other special programs. For example, the state also provides revenues to support a class-size reduction program for grades first through third. Under this program, the state pays the salaries and benefits of teachers to ensure these elementary grades have student-teacher ratios of not larger than 16:1 for first and second grade and 19:1 for third grade. The state gives additional funds for special education, remediation programs for low performing schools, and for at-risk youth. For the last couple of bienniums, the state has offered additional funds for textbooks and supplies on a per-pupil basis. The state portion of these programs plus the basic support exceeded $900 million for FY 2004 alone.[34] In addition, school districts may levy additional property taxes to pay for school infrastructure and operating expenditures.

Although the federal "No Child Left Behind" legislation has received substantial attention in newspaper headlines across the country, Nevada, like other states had previously implemented academic standards. The initial legislation mandating standards passed in 1997 (commonly referred to as the Nevada Education Reform Act) with subsequent legislation in the following legislative sessions. Under these statutes, the state established an academic council to develop measurable standards for grades K-12 in not only core curriculum courses such as English language arts, mathematics, and science, but also for social studies, computer technology, physical education, and the arts. Standards also exist for teacher qualifications. Rather than being punitive, the state has used the results of the standards and testing to provide additional funds for low-performing schools, students at risk of failing the standardized proficiency exams, and education technology.

The 1997 act also created a legislative bureau for educational accountability and evaluation.[35] The purpose of this small bureau housed within LCB is to review and report to the Legislature the progress public schools have made in achieving the state's academic standards. Through the bureau, an important source of independent review can be achieved for the Legislature.

Nevada's funding and performance standards resemble the general trend across the country in regard to fiscal federalism. States are finding they must provide more and more support to lower levels of government in order to ensure adequate service levels. However, these funds are not given carte blanche. Rather, state governments want to know in measurable terms how well their funds are being spent. Fortunately for Nevada schools, the state has opted to use this information not as means to intimidate them but instead to seek out problem areas and focus greater attention on alleviating them.

The "Nevada Plan" for state-supported education reflects the long-standing power of northern and rural legislators in a state whose population overwhelmingly resides in the Las Vegas metropolitan area. For example, the current Senate Majority Leader, William Raggio (R-Washoe), has held either that position or that of minority floor leader for over 20 years. Because the state's primary revenues derive from sales and gaming, the state transfers tax revenues from urban tourist counties such as Clark to rural counties under the per-pupil funding guarantee. Conversely, as a population-based program, class-size reduction provides the greatest financial benefits to Clark and Washoe Counties (Reno/Sparks). Support for class-size reduction has generally been based on party affiliation rather than benefits toward a legislator's district with Democrats favoring the program and Republicans less so, although there has been substantial movement across party lines in support and opposition to it since its inception in the mid-1990s. With two-thirds of the members, if the Clark County delegation ever chooses to work as a unified force (and therefore cross party lines), the remaining Legislature would have a difficult time stopping them. Because of this disparity in geographic representation, fiscal federalism has the power to be a divisive issue in the future.

## CONCLUSION

Nevada's fiscal culture of conservativeness and pragmatism has served its population relatively well for the last several decades. These attributes can be seen in the line-item budget format, the cooperation between the LCB and Budget Office in developing the budget, and most significantly in the revenue choices made by politicians and the public. The central issue for Nevada's future is whether that pragmatism will permit its political culture to adapt to the forces changing the state. With an ever-expanding population, competition from Indian gaming, and concerns over homeland security, the traditional means of conducting business may no longer be appropriate. The State had the opportunity to significantly reform its tax structure in 2003, but chose only to tweak the system rather than implement comprehensive change. Nevada gambled its future on maintaining the status quo, and now the citizens must wait to see whether that bet will pay off or break the house.

## NOTES

1. The phrase was taken from Governor Kenny Guinn's *State of the State Address*, January 20, 2003.

2. The City of Reno's long-standing motto.

3. Nevada Revised Statute 244.345.

4. From an interview with John P. Comeaux, State of Nevada, Director of the Department of Administration, July 31, 2003.

5. Nevada Budget Division, *State of Nevada 2003–2005 Executive Budget in Brief*, Carson City, NV: January, 2003.

6. Interview with John. P. Comeaux, July 31, 2003.

7. The Director of Administration is also the Director of the Budget Office.

8. Interview with John. P. Comeaux, July 31, 2003.

9. Governor Guinn petitioned the Nevada Supreme Court to order the State Legislature to pass an appropriations bill. The Court ruled that the constitution's substantial mandate to fund education superseded the procedural constitutional provision that the Legislature can only approve tax increases with a two-thirds majority of both the Senate and the Assembly.

10. Nevada Budget Division, *State of Nevada 2003–2005 Executive Budget in Brief*.

11. Budget figures are taken from Nevada Budget Division's *State of Nevada 2005–2007 Executive Budget in Brief*.

12. Interview with John. P. Comeaux, July 31, 2003.

13. State of Nevada Legislative Counsel Bureau. See http://leg.state.nv.us/lcb/morelcb.cfm and http://leg.state.nv.us/lcb/fiscal/fiscal.cfm. Note: The Legislative Counsel Bureau was originally created in 1945. The Fiscal Division was created in 1963 as part of a reorganization of LCB.

14. Nevada Revised Statutes 353.226–229.

15. Of course, one exception would be a major reorganization of state government, which occurred in 1993 as part of Governor Bob Miller's 1993–2005 Executive Budget.

16. Nevada Legislative Counsel Bureau, http://lg.state.nv.us/lcb/interim.cfm.

17. Interview with John P. Comeaux, July 31, 2003.

18. For a comprehensive list of all of Nevada's taxes as well as the recent tax changes, see the Nevada Department of Taxation's Web site, http://tax.state.nv.us.

19. The Nevada State Constitution prohibits an income tax, although the constitution can be amended by electoral approval in two consecutive general elections. Clark County, which includes the City of Las Vegas, raised its sales tax rate to 7.5 percent, effective October, 2003.

20. Nevada Budget Division, *State of Nevada 2003–2005 Executive Budget in Brief*.

21. Ibid.

22. Ibid.

23. Ibid.

24. Harvey S. Rosen, *Public Finance*, 4th edition. Chicago, IL: Irwin, 1995, p. 581.

25. Nevada Budget Division, *State of Nevada 2003–2005 Executive Budget in Brief*.

26. Nevada Department of Taxation Web site, http://tax.state.nv.us/taxnew/news_legislative_update.htm.

27. Figures for the revenues estimates, *Reno Gazette-Journal*, "Breakdown of Taxes," at http://www.rgj.com/news/stories/html (July 23, 2003).

28. The Nevada gaming industry is primarily affected not only by California's economy, but also the U.S. national economy, as well as the conditions in foreign countries such as Japan and those in Western Europe.

29. Nevada Budget Division, *State of Nevada 2005–2007 Executive Budget*.

30. Nevada Department of Transportation, State of Nevada Transportation Facts and Figures, Carson City, NV: August 2005.

31. Nevada Budget Division, *State of Nevada 2005–2007 Executive Budget in Brief*.

32. Nevada Office of the Controller, State of Nevada Comprehensive Annual Report for June 30, 2002, Carson City, NV: 2003, p. 171. Note: numbers represent full-time equivalent pupil (Fall enrollment). Nevada also supports charter schools organized under statutory authority.

33. Nevada Budget Division, *State of Nevada 2003–2005 Executive Budget*, Carson City, January 2003, K12 ED-7–K12 ED-11.

34. Nevada Budget Division, *State of Nevada 2003–2005 Executive Budget*, K12 ED-11.

35. See the Web site for the Legislative Counsel Bureau's Fiscal Division, http//www.leg.state.nv.us/lcb/fiscal/LeBeape.

# CHAPTER 11

# South Carolina: Executive Budgeting Brings a Stronger Gubernatorial Voice to the Table

*Cole Blease Graham, Jr.*

## OVERVIEW

Like other states and the national government, South Carolina's constitutional framework creates legislative, executive, and judicial branches. The constitution distributes power among these branches as a means to "check and balance" their relative influence. But, the exercise of constitutional and political power in South Carolina, built on longstanding traditions established in colonial arrangements, has been historically centered in the legislature. The result has been a weak executive branch divided among many publicly elected offices and many governing boards and commissions.

In recent decades, however, the expansion of civil rights, the development of suburbs, the impact of population-based redistricting on elections, and the emergence of party competition have increased pressures on South Carolina for changes in its political institutions. Among these changes has been a growth in the formal and informal powers of the governor. The governor is now eligible to run for a second 4-year term, directly manages thirteen cabinet agencies, and prepares the budget for the legislature.

### Executive–Legislative Relations

A political structure in which the governor plays a key role in decision making is relatively new in South Carolina. "There is nothing to it except the honor" is how V. O. Key, Jr., described South Carolina's governor in 1949.[1] But, half-a-century after Key's writing, things have changed. Today, the South Carolina governor has a stronger voice in state government generally and more specifically in the budgeting process.

A longstanding model for assessing a governor's formal, institutional strength defines the office with respect to five major powers: tenure potential, appointment making, budget-making, organization authority, and veto. An institutionally strong governor has significant control over these powers. A weak governor is part of a "plural executive." That is, there are many and varied structural or political arrangements for allocating or exercising major executive powers.

Schlesinger[2] and Beyle[3] have assessed the formal powers of governors at different times in the past. Table 11.1 reports their ratings of the South Carolina governor. The third column in Table 11.1 is an estimate of these formal powers today. The underlying rationale for the current ratings is presented in the following brief discussion of each formal power. The discussion emphasizes how the increasing formal powers of the governor challenge the tradition of legislative dominance. Central is the development of an executive budget process beginning in the 1990s.

### Factor 1: Tenure Potential

Tenure potential defines how long a governor can serve and whether a sitting governor can run for reelection. Gubernatorial influence over the legislature and the administrative bureaucracy is weakened by one term or a short term.

A governor rated as having a "very strong" tenure potential has a 4-year term with no limit on eligibility for reelection. The most common type among the American states today is a "strong" governor with a 4-year term who may be reelected while in office. A "moderately powerful" tenure is a single 4-year term, and "weak" tenure means a 2-year term regardless of limits on reelection.[4]

South Carolina's Constitution of 1790 followed the practice of the time by creating a 2-year term for the governor, but asserted legislative control by requiring that the legislature elect the governor.[5] When popular election of the governor began with the new state constitution in 1865, the term was extended to 4 years, then reduced to 2 years in the new 1868 state constitution and back to a single 4-year term beginning with the 1926 election.

Generally, tenure potential for governors has increased since the mid-twentieth century, with many states adopting the presidential succession model of two 4-year terms. Many southern states adopted the two-term governor in the 1970s–1980s, perhaps to give incumbent Democratic governors an advantage in their efforts to fend off increasingly potent Republican challengers. Expansion of the governor's tenure potential in South Carolina to a second consecutive 4-year term was recommended in 1969 by a legislative commission created to study improvements in the Constitution of 1895.[6]

South Carolina made the change in 1981. The state's first governor to serve eight consecutive years, Richard W. Riley (D-Greenville), was elected in 1979

**Table 11.1**
**South Carolina Governor: Comparative Measures of Power**

| Factors: | Schlesinger (1965) | Beyle (1981) | 2004 Estimate |
|---|---|---|---|
| Tenure | Moderate (3) | Strong (4) | Strong (4) |
| Appointment | Very Weak (1) | Very Weak (1) | Moderate (3) |
| Budget | Very Weak (1) | Very Weak (1) | Strong (4) |
| Organization | Very Weak (1) | Very Weak (1) | Very Weak (1) |
| Veto | Moderate (3) | Moderate (3) | Strong (4) |
| Total | 9 | 10 | 16 |
| Average | 1.8 | 2.0 | 3.1 |

Scale: Very Strong = 5; Strong = 4; Moderate = 3; Weak = 2; Very Weak = 1. Maximum Score = 25

*Note:* Professor Thad Beyle updates his ranking of the governors in all the states in "The Governors" in Virginia Gray and Russell L. Hanson (Eds.), *Politics in the American States: A Comparative Analysis*, 8th edition. Washington, DC: CQ Press, 2004, pp. 194–231. Using a 5-point scale over six individual indicators of institutional powers, Beyle ranks the South Carolina governor in 2002 as follows:

1. number of separately elected executive officials (1.0);
2. tenure potential (4.0);
3. appointment powers in six program areas (2.5);
4. budget power (2.0);
5. veto power (5);
6. gubernatorial party control (4.0).

Dividing the total (18.5) by 6 gives an average score of 3.1.
*Sources:* J. A. Schlesinger, "The Politics of the Executive," in H. Jacob and K. Vines (Eds.), *Politics in the American States*, 1st edition. Boston: Little, Brown, 1965, pp. 207–237; and Thad A. Beyle, "Governors," in Virginia Gray, Herbert Jacob, and Kenneth Vines, *Politics in the American States*, 4th edition. Boston: Little, Brown, 1983, pp. 180–221.

and 1982. A Republican governor, Carroll A. Campbell, Jr. (R-Greenville), was elected in 1986 and 1990. The Republican governor elected in 1994, David Beasley (R-Darlington), served only one term and lost in 1998 to a one-term Democrat, Jim Hodges (D-Lancaster). A Republican, Mark Sanford (R-Charleston), recaptured the governor's office in 2002.

The possibility of a second consecutive term is a very important formal increase of power. It has enhanced the influence of the governor over the budgetary process as well as in legislative decisions and indicates a "strong" rating for the South Carolina governor today. Even without the formal executive budget or the modified cabinet system added in the early 1990s, a second term boosts appointment power and potentially diminishes legislative control over boards and commissions. No state agency board or commission member serves as long as 8 years. Thus, where possible, an 8-year governor could participate in appointments to all the seats on an agency board or commission.[7]

A dominant legislator—long-time House Speaker Sol Blatt (D-Barnwell)—opposed the two terms for a governor on these grounds:

The Governor who is in there and is allowed to succeed himself doesn't do as good a job as Governor if he wasn't allowed to succeed himself. It takes the first year of his term to get acquainted with the Governor's office, how many people he's got to appoint, who to appoint, how much money he has to spend; Federal funds flow through his office down there in the millions. Well, he spends it – that's one year. The second year he does the job that's supposed to be done by him by arranging for the distribution of those Federal funds and where they should go, he makes his appointments, and then he starts running for re-election, if you let him run for re-election, and he doesn't confine his efforts to serving the people as it was intended for him to do. Now, in the second term, he's not eligible to run for re-election as Governor, but he does have an open eye looking toward Washington. And, therefore, he starts playing politics in order to get elected to the United States Senate.[8]

Since then, South Carolina's two 8-year chief executives have gone to Washington, but not as senators. Riley was education secretary in the Clinton administration and Campbell was a lobbyist for the American Council of Life Insurers.

Blatt's general criticism is especially appropriate for the last 2 years of a governor's term of any length. By the third or seventh year of a governor's term, every legislator has stood for reelection and a new legislative session has begun, new candidates for governor are emerging, and the governor's original plans have been acted on by the legislature in some way. New executive policy proposals may be rejected simply because the sitting governor will not be around to implement them. A governor may easily become a "lame duck" for the last half year of a 4 or 8-year term.[9]

### Factor 2: Appointment Power

A governor with unilateral power of appointment over cabinet-type agencies rates as more powerful than one who must have legislative confirmation of an appointment by either or both houses. Governors who only approve appointments rather than initiate them have even less power. The weakest governors neither appoint nor approve recommended appointments, but have a separate body do so. In some states, there are separately elected officials who head state departments.[10]

Today, South Carolina's governor seems a "moderate" power in this category. The General Assembly still controls the selection of judges, public service commissioners—the utility regulators, and six out of seven department of transportation members. Eight executive officials other than the governor are popularly elected, including lieutenant governor, secretary of state, attorney general, state treasurer, comptroller general, adjutant general, and heads of the departments of education and agriculture—so the plural executive persists. When creating new agencies in the past, the General Assembly has typically allocated governing power to a board or commission, not the governor. Many of these decisions have not been changed. For example, a recent *Legislative Manual*[11] includes 178 statutory state agencies in executive and legislative branches with more than a dozen means of appointment for board members.

Reliance on a board or commission rather than a more unified executive has raised questions of accountability. There have been revelations that many appointed members seemed encumbered by conflicts or potential conflicts of interest.[12] Boards were increasingly criticized as unrepresentative whether by demographic characteristics such as gender or by proportion of population. A February 1991 review of 313 positions on thirty-six selected boards showed that only twenty seats (6%) were held by women.[13] Furthermore, judicial circuits, which ranged in size at the time from 105,000 people to 408,000 people, were, and still are, the basis for choosing some boards and commissions.

Beginning in 1991, *The State* newspaper ran about 150 articles in seventeen installments to tell the story of "power failure" in South Carolina. The articles described the members of the state's 133 executive boards and commissions as "Our 1,200 Barons" in a system of government not really answerable to any one, perhaps not even the General Assembly that created it. The varying methods of appointment made it especially difficult for observers to determine accountability for agency performance. Boards appeared as autonomous bodies, working independently of the others in shaping public policy in narrow areas of authority.

In an outcome startling to many, the General Assembly in its 1993 session significantly revised the appointment arrangements for many state agencies through major restructuring legislation linked to the state appropriations bill. The result of restructuring was an increase in the formal, statutory powers of the governor over the governance and operations of many agencies.

The 1993 legislation created thirteen cabinet-type departments.[14] The governor hires and fires the agency director in eleven of them, including Alcohol and Other Drug Abuse Services, Commerce, and Revenue and Taxation. The chief executive recommends the directors of the departments of public safety and law enforcement to the legislature and can remove them only for cause.

Other departments reflect varying control of the governor over the agency head. For example, the governor names the board members for the department for disabilities and special needs as well as the department for natural resources, but the board members hire the agency director. In the transportation department (the old highway department less the highway patrol and the division of motor vehicles), the governor appoints the board chair with advice and consent of the senate, the legislature appoints the board members, and the board names the agency head.

Another reality confounding to reformers is that the General Assembly retains control or significant influence over appointments to the most important state agencies and the ones that spend the most money, such as the elected heads of agriculture and public education, the trustees of higher education institutions, and transportation board members. But, even where there are not significant appointment powers, the governor may be around long enough to make a difference over 8 years in office by hammering away with persuasive arguments at policy decisions by legislatively run boards and commissions or independently elected executives.

## Factor 3: The Budgetary Power

Control over the budgetary process is another method by which an executive can set policy priorities and control and manage administrative agencies. In a 1981 survey conducted by Glen Abney and Thomas Lauth, state agency heads were asked to rank the budgetary influence of the governor on administrative departments in their states. At least 25 percent of agency heads ranked the governor as most influential in all but seven states. South Carolina and Colorado were the only two states where not a single agency head cited the governor as the most influential actor in the budgetary process.[15] Beyle's 1981 analysis of the budget-making powers of the governor placed South Carolina, along with Mississippi and Texas, in the weakest category.[16]

South Carolina's chief executive has traditionally ranked very weak because it shared budgetary powers with several other independent sources of executive and legislative strength on a separate budgeting board, the State Budget and Control Board (SBCB). Even in the face of a stronger governor, it is easy to assert that the most powerful agency in South Carolina government is the SBCB. It is certainly the most comprehensive. Its form today results from a long line of shared budgetary responsibility between the legislature and executives.

Legislatively appointed local commissions to manage taxing and spending existed during South Carolina's colonial period. They were replaced by elected or legislatively appointed local commissions for important fiscal matters, such as care for the poor and management of roads.[17] Use of a commission method at the state level occurred as early as 1870 when a body called the Sinking Fund Commission was established to manage repayment of the state debt and interest. Members of the Sinking Fund Commission were the Governor, the Attorney General, and the chairs of the Senate Finance Committee and the House Ways and Means Committee. In 1883, the State Treasurer was added as a member.

A major reform of state budgeting in 1916 created a separate state tax commission to oversee the collection of state revenues. The push for the state commission came from the unequal assessment ratios for the state property tax used by county auditors. The legislature wanted a central tax commission to ensure equalization of assessments in response to taxpayer protests.

Establishment of a budget commission in 1919 was a more direct effort to involve executive participation in state agency revenue and expenditures. The commission brought legislative and executive leaders together in a formal process to propose a state budget. This commission, composed of the governor and the chairs of the Senate Finance Committee and the House Ways and Means Committee, was required to meet each year after November 1. They were to hold hearings of all parties interested in the new budget and then report to the General Assembly in January. The broad purpose of the budget commission was to take the pressure for budget preparation off the legislative committees and to give a publicized, focused, starting point for budget deliberations.[18]

The state budget commission functioned as the starting point for each annual appropriation for the next 30 years. In general, it tended to be more tentative and advisory than actually to direct the budget process as had been hoped. It neither exercised the degree of influence that advocates had envisioned for it, nor did it end the legislative budget logjam during the adoption phase.

The next major change in the budget commission occurred in 1950. The remodeled commission emerged as a compromise between executive reformers and legislative traditionalists who fought over control of the budget power. Following several studies, the state budget commission was enlarged and reorganized. This new five-member body, called the State Budget and Control Board (SBCB), included two new popularly elected executive members, the State Treasurer and the Comptroller General. The Governor remained as chair of the body and the two legislative positions remained. Several separate boards were abolished by the creation of the new board and became part of its operation.[19] The state highway commission continued to operate independently of the new board.

Creation of the SBCB did not immediately change the state's method of budgeting. It continued to rely on a detailed, line-item, and expenditure-oriented budgeting format rather than on program budgeting. In fact, the first budget submitted by the SBCB for the FY 1952–1953 was almost 500 pages long and included information on only sixty-three state agencies.[20]

During this time, SBCB staff members frequently were recruited from the state's public education department as a source of expertise. Because public education was the single largest state expenditure, financial experts from that department moved over to the SBCB to run the board and ensure that basic education financing policies could be maintained. This became especially important in the 1960s during a time of racial integration and major changes in public school curricula.

With the arrangement of the SBCB, any gubernatorial budgeting success depended on credibility with legislators. A governor's credibility was typically measured by effectiveness in previous legislative service. For example, Ernest F. Hollings (D-Charleston, 1959–1963) had been elected to the legislature for 10 years and as Lieutenant Governor. Along with other legislators, he was able to persuade State Senator Edgar Brown (D-Barnwell), chair of the Senate Finance Committee, to support the financing of a system of technical education colleges.[21]

Another example is Robert McNair (D-Allendale, 1965–1971), who served in the legislature for 12 years and as Lieutenant Governor, before becoming governor with the resignation of Governor Donald Russell (D-Spartanburg, 1963–1965). He was elected governor in 1966 and had the advantage of 6 years in office. In addition to his legislative experience, McNair was relatively successful in policymaking because of his persuasive style and his political friendship with legislative leaders such as the aging Senator Brown and Speaker Blatt. McNair led major drives for tourism development, education reform, and industrial recruitment. He also led the state through school desegregation and broad civil unrest during the late 1960s. He created an Office of Administration to manage federal funds and used the governor's power to designate a state agency for specific categories of funds as a way to leverage executive direction over agencies often more loyal to a board or commission. The budget in his first year was passed without the need for a conference committee, a rarity in state politics.

Governor John West (D-Kershaw, 1971–1975) had served 13 years in the Senate and had been Lieutenant Governor for 4 years. He was able to work effectively with House Speakers Sol Blatt and Rex Carter (D-Greenville) along with his political associates Senators Edgar Brown, Marion Gressette (D-Calhoun), and Rembert Dennis (D-Berkeley). To head off controversies, West often conferred directly with legislators as they introduced bills or items in the appropriations bill.[22]

In West's administration, a major review of state budgeting and management was conducted in 1972 by the Governor's Management Review Commission, composed of executives from private corporations in South Carolina. It was critical of the state's reliance on an incremental approach to budgeting. It also recommended consolidation of the SBCB's divisions and the development of the office of executive director to oversee the entire operation. The executive director position was passed into law in 1978. Deputy executive directors were appointed after an internal reorganization in 1986. Subsequent adjustments to the alignment of divisions in the internal organization of the board have often been made.

The addition of new functions to the board and the reflection of board decisions in state policies are a convenient barometer with which to measure the growing presence of a more unified executive structure, albeit not directly under the governor's formal control. For example, the SBCB has absorbed the revenue estimating responsibilities from the tax commission through a board of economic advisors. Two other units that began in the governor's office of administration on the basis of executive orders by Governor Robert McNair—the state personnel department and the state planning office—are now divisions of the board established by permanent legislation.[23]

The Office of State Budget (OSB) was established in the SBCB in 1984 when the finance division was split into the OSB and the State Auditor. The OSB plays a dual role in the budget process today. It assists the governor's executive budget hearings in the summer and fall by coordinating agency requests for funds according to the priorities in the executive budget. After the executive budget is proposed, OSB is extensively involved in the adoption phase through its numerous services to the legislative branch. It works with the Senate Finance Committee and the House Ways and Means Committee by maintaining the official database for the varying versions of the appropriations bill and any provisos[24] and it conducts various studies on demand.

The General Assembly begins work on the appropriations bill in January. State agencies testify first before subcommittees of the House where they seek to change the governor's recommendations and add or amend provisos. The House version is final usually in February for submission to the Senate. A similar process creates a Senate version by late April and a conference committee develops a common version that is typically adopted before the start of the fiscal year on July 1. As the General Assembly is considering the budget, OSB staff members work directly with the committees and individual legislators to provide information on any matter affecting expenditures or revenue. These considerations may contradict the original priorities of the governor.

The governor's influence over capital projects is filtered through a legislative Joint Bond Review Committee, composed of five legislators from each house. The joint committee, with the assistance of the OSB, studies and monitors policies and procedures for approving permanent improvement projects and issuing state general obligation and institutional bonds. It also evaluates the effect of current and past policies on the bond credit rating of the state and provides advisory assistance in establishing future capital management projects.

The most significant change, discussed later in this chapter, is legislative authorization for the governor to submit an independent, executive budget, done for the first time for the FY 1993–1994 budget. The potential for direct gubernatorial influence on policy priorities is greatly enhanced by this increase in institutional capacity.

## Factor 4: Organizational Power

Since 1920, at least eight studies of the administrative structure in South Carolina have recommended a stronger chief executive with increased formal powers to organize and manage state agencies.[25] The underlying assumption of these studies is the Wilsonian[26] view that governmental agencies should be unified under the authority of a single, chief executive. Returning military veterans led by J. Strom Thurmond (D-Edgefield, 1947–1951) as governor used one of the structural studies, the Preparedness for Peace Commission Report in 1945, as a platform to address changes. In response, the legislature created a state reorganization commission to study and recommend how to reduce duplication and fill gaps in state agencies.

However, the state reorganization commission became more of an intermediary for the legislature's interest in administrative changes than an advocate for a strong executive. Consequently, the commission functioned irregularly and largely passively, until it was discontinued in the 1990s. Some significant recommendations were made: for example, the merger of the health and pollution agencies in the early 1970s, and the consolidation of alcohol and drug abuse programs for more efficient administration. The commission conducted various studies of state government structures and operations, including a county-based demonstration of state agency local service coordination.[27]

Within the executive branch, governors and agency heads have occasionally worked out new operating arrangements for more consistent state policy. For example, interagency councils were initiated by Governor Robert McNair and were used extensively in the 1960s for informal coordination of agency operations.

The current governor, Mark Sanford (R-Charleston, 2001–PRESENT) established a Governor's Commission on Management, Accountability, and Performance (MAP), modeled after President Ronald Reagan's Grace Commission. At its meeting, on June 17, 2003, the MAP members heard from the president of Citizens Against Government Waste about ways to reduce the size of government. The MAP especially focused on the SBCB with the aim of consolidating some SBCB functions in a division of administration directly under the governor's supervision and allocating some of its other activities to "enterprise agencies" not directly supported by tax revenue. Its September 2003 report is a virtual catalog of recommendations around themes of executive consolidation and privatization.[28]

Through its 2006 session, the legislature stalled enactment of significant MAP recommendations. Concerns about agency performance evaluation and accountability may spur legislation enabling the governor to supervise state administrative functions directly as a complement to the governor's established authority to propose the state's budget. For example, the SBCB general services division came under scrutiny in early summer 2004 when the Governor's Mansion was invaded by mold and slime in the air system of the newly remodeled building. The governor's wife and children resettled in their private home and the governor lived in the Mansion's swimming pool house until the problem was fixed. Implications are that the SBCB did not do an appropriate job of contract management and that its current organization may be cumbersome enough to be a part of the problem.

### Factor 5: Veto Power

The final factor is the governor's veto power. The type of veto power varies by state and may include total bill veto, amendatory veto, item veto, or item reduction veto. Use of the veto authority by a governor is usually rare because it may simply invite retaliation by the legislature.[29] South Carolina governors have a general veto, but have used it sparingly. The governor has an item veto on the appropriations bill and recent governors have increased their item veto of provisos.[30] For example, over 250 single items were struck by Governor Campbell from the 1988 appropriations bill and none were overridden. Successful vetoes may measure the potency of informal gubernatorial power as much as formal powers.

As frequently discussed in the state, the executive budget seems to require the principle that if the governor has the veto on the end, then the governor should reveal preferences first. The governor and the executive branch have to be involved from start to finish if the legislative process is to be relevant to more organized budgeting. The 170 legislators individually and collectively lament that it is very difficult for them to plan. There is nothing to reward a legislator for a long-term plan. House members serve for 2 years and, from the viewpoint of reelection, are not really interested in a project that promises a return 5 years in the future. Senators tend to be more patient since they serve 4 years, but their program performance horizon is similarly limited. Through the submission of an executive budget, Governor Campbell began to tell the legislature upfront what he wanted so that gubernatorial vetoes were no longer a surprise after the legislature acted.

Of course, vetoes may also reflect a budgetary game known to all the players. Many items are often put on the budget bill as provisos, sometimes called "bobtails," which, when struck, give the legislator a bargaining chip with the governor in the future. "Since the governor struck the item, the governor owes the legislator and the legislator's constituents a favor." The favor might be to let it pass in a future bill or to give in on some other project that the governor may be delaying. The vetoes also give the legislator a convenient opportunity to explain to voters that "I tried so hard, but those big interests in Columbia (or the governor's office) beat me down." In this respect, the SBCB is helpful in sharing executive responsibility with the Governor, because it often issues the background studies or impact statements that justify the vetoes and thereby shoulders some of the blame.

The veto and its use may become more significant if partisan interests develop to prevent legislative overrides. Because it takes a two-thirds vote to override a veto, members of a political party, tightly organized and voting with discipline, could block an override by the opposing party if it had more than one-third membership in either house. Of course, the veto is still a negative, blocking tactic, and the incentives for partisan cohesion are reduced because of local pressures on legislators.

Currently, the South Carolina legislature has majority Republican control in the House and Senate. Although a party with majorities in both houses is not likely to override the veto of a governor in the same party, 2004 was an exception. Governor Sanford made 106 vetoes to close a $16 million deficit in the legislature's 2004–2005 state budget. His concern was that a balanced budget is a constitutional requirement that could not be ignored. He chided the legislature by carrying two live, squealing piglets into the statehouse main lobby to emphasize the "pork" in the vetoed measures. The stunt made national news, but did not convince legislators who overrode 105 of the vetoes. In the aftermath, Sanford's approval ratings topped 70 percent.

### Revenue

General Fund revenue estimates are provided through the SBCB by the board of economic advisors in consultation with the state economist. The first forecast for an upcoming fiscal year (FY) is made by November 10, and a final forecast is made on February 15. Forecasts are also made by fiscal year quarters. If General Fund revenues lag 4 percent or more behind expected revenue collections for the first or second quarter, SBCB has to implement an across-the-board budget cut to avoid a year-end deficit.

For FY 2005–2006, the total state budget was approximately $18 billion. Of this, approximately one-third, about $5.6 billion, was in the general fund. About $6.2 billion were federal funds and the remaining, or "other," funds of more than $6 billion represented revenues received by agencies through grants, contracts, or payment for services. Education Improvement Act (EIA) funds, lottery funds, highway funds, and Health Care Trust Funds (the tobacco securitization interest revenue) were also included in "other" funds.

From the beginning of FY 1993 through FY 1998, South Carolina's general fund revenues increased an average of 6.5 percent annually. In FY 1999 the rate of increase was only 1.75 percent and in FY 2002, revenues shrank by almost 3 percent.[31] In FY 2003, general fund revenues are composed of approximately 39.5 percent sales tax, 42.1 percent individual income tax, 3.1 percent corporate income tax, and 15.3 percent from other sources. The major declines have centered on the individual income tax and on decreased sales tax revenue from the tourism industry.

To balance the state's budget in FY 2001, $87.4 million had to be withdrawn from the state reserve fund[32] and another $62.8 million from the reserve fund to balance in FY 2002. Under its authority, the SBCB took an additional $48 million across-the-board from agencies in June 2001 to prevent a deficit.

The executive budget for FY 2002, proposed by Governor Hodges in December 2000, recommended an increase of $132 million for K-12 education including $68 million for a $2,000 increase for each school teacher's salary and $54 million for the Education Accountability Act for at-risk schools. He also advocated borrowing $40 million to buy new school buses and $102 million for public school buildings. The proposed budget included about $481 million in tax cuts including $25 million in food sales tax exemption and $55 million to maintain the property tax exemption for senior homesteads. To reduce ongoing dependency on one-time money from about $700 million to $250 million,

Governor Hodges proposed a 15 percent cut in state agencies, including $127 million from higher education, $50 million for Corrections, $34 million for Medicaid, and $36 million in state aid to local governments.

In December 2001, Governor Hodges' budget emphasized education, health care, and security. But to balance it he proposed borrowing $212 from agency trust funds and reserve accounts and delaying state agency bill payments by one month in June 2003. Immediately the House Ways and Means chair expressed the opinion that the OSB would not approve the governor's borrowing and delaying approach. The chair of Senate Finance said that the governor placed too much emphasis on the SBCB, perhaps laying the groundwork for Governor Sanford's aim to place more of the SBCB functions under the governor's office.

Revenue scarcity and the continuing threats of new cuts have dominated recent budget discussions. And, they were a central theme in the 2002 election battle between Hodges and Sanford. After his defeat, Hodges refused to convene the SBCB to deal with upcoming budget cuts. He left them for Sanford, advising that agencies set aside 5 percent for shortfalls through June 2003. Governor Sanford has continued to hack away at a budget that he claims supports a state government that costs 130 percent of the national average. His 2004–2005 budget increased state spending by 1 percent and included $53 million in tax relief. The centerpiece of Sanford's revenue plan is to reduce state income tax rates from 7 to 4.5 percent and reduce state spending to balance with available revenue. He has the attention and support of limited government groups in the state and across the nation.

### Fiscal Federalism

The modernization of the budgetary process in South Carolina was stimulated by external initiatives, especially the enormous infusion of federal funds beginning during the 1960s administration of Governor Robert McNair. Often, federal funds were managed and controlled directly through the governor's office, especially for social and human services and housing. A special office was created in the governor's division of administration to coordinate federal funding with local governments through a federally mandated review process. Another unit was created specifically as a reward for the support of municipal councils in 1966 McNair's election. Headed by a former mayor, it helped local governments find discretionary federal dollars and made sure that every federal dollar went to the political loyalists.

The Great Society and New Federalism made governors a stronger *de facto* budget actor in South Carolina. Their administrative staff grew[33] to accommodate the responsibilities of managing the new federal resources. Having staff expertise in planning gave governors an important ability to integrate planning into the management of agencies using federal funds. Although somewhat diminished today by the increased role of state agencies and the governor's cabinet officers in federal funds management, the division of administration has continued its important influence on state agencies and local governments, despite changing types and amounts of funds.

General revenue sharing ended in the mid-eighties. Since the nineteen eighties, many categorical grants have been consolidated into block grants to give the state and local governments more latitude in spending decisions. Medicaid funding has increased while the more traditional education and community development grants have decreased. For example, health and human services funds make up about 60 percent of the federal aid to South Carolina today. The majority of these funds go to Medicaid. Funds for education equal about 9 percent and housing is almost 8 percent of total federal funds. About 10 percent is devoted to transportation. The state transportation department gets virtually all of its money from the state fuel tax and the federal government. It has not been axed in recent state budget cuts, but it has been chronically underfunded, maintained by some to be the lowest per mile in the country.

## Rational Budget Reform

Within its annual budget process, South Carolina decision makers increase or decrease the base from the previous fiscal year using a line item format. Although there were separate bills introduced in the 2003–2004 legislative session to adopt a biennial budget, use a program budget format, and implement a zero-based appropriations system, none passed.

Although more political than rational, the state's most significant budgetary modernization reform has been the gubernatorially based, executive budget. It was not a planned change. Changing the governor's tenure potential to two terms may have been a driving force. Since the governor inherits the budget proposed by his predecessor in the first year and is a "lame duck" in his last year, at best, there are perhaps 2 years in a 4-year term in which to influence the budget. Given the timing of elections, the 2 years are not even in the same legislative session, making it even harder to work in a consistent political environment. With the possibility for 8 years in office, governors began to understand and leverage their fiscal influence more widely.

The real changes in the state budgetary process that led to the formal executive budget began with Governor Riley and continued under Campbell. Informally, Riley began to call for budgetary decisions in the State of the State address. It was actually not a budget message. Riley said here is what he would like to accomplish, here is what the revenue stream is, and here is what it would cost. He was able to win support for an education improvement act in 1984, including a 1 percent increase in the sales tax to fund it. Riley was focused on education reform and committed himself and his office to its passage.[34] Riley skillfully used mass media, political and party influence along with task forces, public forums, and his State of the State address to push the program. In all these efforts lie the antecedents of an executive budget.

Riley viewed his impact on the budgetary process as simple hard work. He cultivated all the agency boards and commissions for their support. He held with them what he referred to as "tent meetings"[35] to sell his budget priorities. He also visited with legislators and held receptions for them. Riley believed he got the legislature to frame the budget nearly like he requested it because he worked at it day and night.

Governor Campbell did not have as much personal contact with legislators as Riley. He was generally seen more like the "chairman of the board." During his 1986 gubernatorial campaign, Campbell advocated a need for a change in the budgetary process. Campbell, who had served on the Ways and Means Committee in the United States Congress, pointed out the difficulty in planning without an executive budget and noted that the process used in South Carolina was incremental and disjointed. Following his election, Campbell designated two staff positions, one for finance and administration, the other for budget and policy.

In 1987, Governor Campbell took the executive budget one more step forward by presenting his proposals for FY 1988–1989 officially to the SBCB. This really let the governor "sit at the head of the SBCB table." Although there was resistance to the executive budget, his budget proposals were generally adopted by the board without changes. Thus, the precedent of an executive budget presentation to the SBCB was established informally. Governor Campbell continued with a proposed executive budget in subsequent fiscal years, thereby enhancing the governor's role as a policy actor with substantive input to back up his leadership of the board.[36]

Now, the executive budget is institutionalized. South Carolina Code, section 11-11-15, and provides that the governor submit the proposed annual state budget to the General Assembly. It was done for the first time under this authority for FY 1993–1994. So far, there have been twelve executive budgets in South Carolina.[37]

The formal executive budget has been helped and hurt by ongoing changes in budgetary practices. For example, the SBCB no longer holds budget hearings, deferring to the Governor's requests for information directly from agencies. To give executive authority more latitude in meeting new goals and objectives, after 1993–1995, agency regulations were changed to allow agencies to promote staff from within without a position search. By allowing a 10 percent carryforward at the end of the fiscal year, agencies could better motivate staff through internal pay for performance. Some agencies stashed the carryforward or used it to fund activities not always congruent with the governor's plan or the legislature's knowledge. As a reaction to slow the agencies, 1996–1997 saw increased emphasis on accountability reports. These reports fueled the increased ability of the House Ways and Means staff and the OSB staff to articulate budgetary goals/objectives and to quantify management indicators to help legislators evaluate new agency requests.

In his December 1995 executive budget message, Governor David Beasley initiated a new format to make the budget more taxpayer friendly. The new format included priority ranked programs for agencies to fully disclose programs and their costs, identification of new expenditures on separate lines to readily identify increases, separation of the sources of funds as state-federal-other, and disclosure of major components of operations such as travel by "unrolling" these operational lines in the budget.

Much of the executive power of the governor, formal and informal, budgetary and otherwise, lingers within the SBCB. Although the governor is now empowered by statute to recommend the budget to the General Assembly, the SBCB controls every phase of the budget process except the governor's recommendations and its adoption by the General Assembly. Even so, the Office of State Budget within the SBCB helps staff the governor's proposals and it is still a source of considerable influence over state agencies by providing staff assistance for the work of the House Ways and Means Committee and the Senate Finance Committee.

## Court Decisions

Article IV, section 21 of the South Carolina Constitution requires the General Assembly to appropriate money in "distinct items and sections" and authorizes the governor to veto "items or sections" in appropriations bills. The state constitution does not define an "item" thereby leaving it to the courts to fashion some standard for interpretation. Generally the courts have said that the legislature must itemize appropriations since lump-sum funding would negate the governor's veto powers. In Governor Sanford's first veto message, he objected to the way the legislature "rolled up" multiple items into single lines or provisos in an apparent effort to thwart veto action.

In *Drummond v. Beasley* (331 S. C. 559, 503 S.E.2nd 455 (1998)), the South Carolina Supreme Court considered article IV, section 21 and concluded the Governor can veto only "those parts labeled by the legislature as items or sections" in an appropriations bill. It ruled that the governor cannot excise or alter language in a bill. Rather, a "common sense construction" should be used that requires the governor to strike whole items distinctly labeled by the legislature. Otherwise, by selectively striking a "word, phrase, clause, or sentence, the Governor creates legislation inconsistent with that enacted by the General Assembly" (*Drummond v. Beasley*, 331 S. C. 559 at 563, 1998).

In a related question, the court considered whether the governor could combine several distinct items, sections, or subsections into a single veto message to the General Assembly. The Court asserted there was no requirement in the constitution or by the legislature to prohibit the governor from returning a veto message with multiple items or subitems in it. The Court avoided deciding whether the governor could redirect funds appropriated by the General Assembly through the veto message.

A parallel debate about the line-item veto is whether the governor can veto legislative measures passed at the end of the legislative session when the legislature will not be returning to vote on the veto. Such "post adjournment" vetoes have been sustained by custom in South Carolina unless the governor calls a special legislative session.

Another controversy addressed recently by Governor Sanford is "wish list" funding, that is the appropriation of general fund revenue in excess of amounts officially recognized by the Board of Economic Advisors. The governor expressed that such a practice created unrealistic expectations and avoided priorities or needed thrift in hard budget times.

In *Condon v. Hodges* (Opinion no. 25451, April 19, 2002), under its original jurisdiction, the State Supreme Court considered three questions: (1) whether the Attorney General has the authority to bring a legal action against the governor; (2) if so, whether a separation of powers violation had occurred; and (3) whether the governor is required to return a balanced budget to the General Assembly.

In the FY 2002 state budget, the General Assembly reduced the recurring budgets of the state's colleges and universities and ordered the state treasurer to transfer $38.5 million from the Barnwell Fund to the higher education institutions. The Barnwell Fund is an escrow fund to care perpetually for control or closure of the Barnwell nuclear site. In his veto message, on June 27, 2001, Governor Hodges vetoed these reductions, resulting in increased expenditures of $88 million and a budget $23 million out of balance. As a remedy, some of the colleges and universities agreed to return more than $28 million, which, in this legal action, was sought to be returned to the Barnwell Fund.

The court found that indeed the attorney general could and should have the authority to bring such an action because the office has the dual role of acting as attorney for the governor and as attorney for the collective citizens of the state to vindicate wrongs. The governor's request for return of the funds and the attempts of the various executive branch officers to set up an account to do so violate the constitution. Not only is there no code or constitutional provision allowing the governor to make a transfer, but there is also clear, express language in the code (sec. 11–9-10, 1986) that only the legislature can make a transfer as provided in the annual appropriations act. On the third point, the court could find no provision requiring the governor to arrive at a balanced budget when exercising vetoes. The responsibility for a balanced budget lies with the legislature.

Equity in public school funding is another major area of legal activity. In 1999 in *Abbeville County School District et al. v. The State of South Carolina* (April 22, 1999, Opinion Number 24939), the state Supreme Court ruled that the state was only required to fund a minimally adequate education. Minimally adequate meant the ability to read, write, and speak the English language and to have knowledge of mathematics and physical sciences. The problem is that students in areas of poverty or where schools have little money have difficulty in meeting the state's educational standards. This is a problem with respect to national legislation requiring every student to be proficient in schoolwork by 2013–2014.

In its 1999 decision, the Supreme Court noted that it cannot set school policy as a "super-legislature" and referred the matter to a state district court for additional hearings. The hearings began on July 28, 2003, and continued into 2004, with large implications for state funding priorities in the pending decision.

## CONCLUSION

Past observers have pointed out that the quasiparliamentary merger of executive and legislative leadership in South Carolina's traditional budgetary practices, especially in the SBCB, may actually serve the public interest of the state better in the days of tight budgets than would be possible given strict adherence to the doctrines of separation of powers and executive direction of the budget.[38] In fact, Bernard Pitsvada claimed that the hybrid budget preparation process involving the SBCB demonstrates a rather ingenious method of defusing budgetary conflict before it begins.[39]

These assertions are being constantly challenged in South Carolina today. Increasing demands for executive leadership have advanced the governor's budgetary responsibilities and supported the need for an executive budget proposed by the governor. The SBCB no longer holds traditional budget hearings, thereby putting more emphasis on the governor's role in the budget process. The recognition of a direct role for the governor in the budget represents a continuing evolution of stronger executive powers in South Carolina. Past reorganizing efforts and the 1993 restructuring legislation have enhanced executive appointment and removal powers and also are a big boost to the executive branch.

Current conditions of static or declining revenue and increased demand for state expenditures increase pressures on budget makers. From the executive perspective, these demands lead to pressures to make government more rational, to justify specific programs and processes, and to reduce government's scope by making it more politically accountable to fiscal conservatives. From the legislative view, new pressures demand more oversight and, in a changing party structure, more partisan oversight. Sharply defined party lines have often limited the executive impulse to reposition state agencies, to streamline, rationalize, or reorganize them. Even though the Republican Party is now the majority, personality and ideological splits within the party have emerged that constrain the governor's impulse to reorganize and reduce state government.

It is the budgetary arena in which many of these tensions are acted out. The move to the executive budget means that the allocation of resources depends on analysis as well as politics. The hope is for increased rational control as the budget is "integrated" under the authority of an elected chief executive. Through various means, such as, productivity analysis, increasing use of private providers for traditional state services, or the hierarchical structure of administrative departments under the governor for unity of command, the hope is that decisions may be directed toward the best interest of all citizens, while agency accountability is enhanced.

## NOTES

1. V. O. Key, Jr., *Southern Politics in State and Nation.* New York: Vintage, 1949, p. 150. At the time of Key's writing, the formal powers of chief executives in the other Southern states were also typically weak, both institutionally and politically. Governors in the region had little or no direct role over state administration. South Carolina was often cited by scholars and other observers as the best example of a formally weak southern governor in a legislatively dominated state. See Robert B. Highsaw, "The Southern Governor—Challenge to the Strong Executive Theme," *Public Administration Review* 19 (1959), 7–11.

2. J. A. Schlesinger, "The Politics of the Executive," in H. Jacob and K. Vines, Eds., *Politics in the American States*, 1st edition. Boston, MA: Little, Brown, 1965, pp. 207–237.

3. Thad A. Beyle, "Governors," in Virginia Gray, Herbert Jacob, and Kenneth Vines, *Politics in the American States*, 4th edition. Boston, MA: Little, Brown, 1983, pp. 180–221; and Beyle, "Governors," in Virginia Gray, Herbert Jacob, and Robert B. Albritton, *Politics in the American States*, 5th edition. Glenview, IL: Scott, Foresman, 1990, pp. 201–251.

The most recent update is in Beyle, "The Governors" in Virginia Gray and Russell Hanson (Eds.), *Politics in the American States: A Comparative Analysis*, 8th edition. Washington, DC: CQ Press, 2004, pp. 194–231.

4. Thad A. Beyle, "Appendix, Formal Powers of the Governor," 1990, p. 568.

5. Ten of the governors of the thirteen original states had 1-year terms, another had a 2-year term, and two had 3-year terms. Beyle, "Governors," 1983, p. 194.

6. Ten years total tenure was possible if the governor's office became vacant just after a general election and the lieutenant governor became governor and then was elected twice as governor.

7. Cole Blease Graham, Jr., "The Evolving Executive in South Carolina," in Charlie B. Tyer and S. Jane Massey, Eds., *Government in the Palmetto State: Perspectives and Issues.* Columbia, SC: University of South Carolina Bureau of Governmental Research and Service, 1988, p. 180.

8. David S. Mann, "Mr. Solomon Blatt: Fifty Years in the South Carolina State Legislature (An Oral History)." A paper presented at the University of South Carolina Symposium on South Carolina, Aiken, SC, March 1–2, 1985, p. 33.

9. In a newly published, parallel index, Beyle has developed a measure of a governor's personal powers. He connects a governor's electoral mandate, how far the governor has come on a political ambition ladder, the tenure potential interpreted as

how long the governor has been in a term, and the governor's performance rating in public opinion polls on a 5-point scale in which each indicator is weighted equally. In 2003, the South Carolina governor (Mark Sanford) rated a 4.0, placing the governor personally on a par with the governor in Arkansas, Georgia, Maine, Ohio, and Vermont and stronger than the 50-state average of 3.7. See Beyle, "The Governors" in Virginia Gray and Russell Hanson (Eds.), *Politics in the American States: A Comparative Analysis*, 8th edition. Washington, DC: CQ Press, 2004, pp. 207–208.

10. Beyle, "Governors," 1983, p. 197.

11. South Carolina General Assembly, *Legislative Manual*, Columbia, SC: 2003.

12. For example, in 1988, the chair of the Manufactured Housing Board, which regulates mobile home sales, was employed by the vice-chair as a mobile home sales person. In 1990, the daughter of a member of the Professional Counselor's Examining Board was paid $1,700 to write a code of ethics for the board. Members of the Tax Commission, which audits tax returns, have been partners in accounting firms that file tax returns for citizens and corporations. In the same year, of the eighteen members of the State Board of Education, one was a superintendent, two were principals, one was married to a principal, and one was director of a consortium that lobbies for twenty school districts. And, for 2 years, the chair of the Alcoholic Beverage Control Commission was a lobbyist for resort businesses that were licensed by the commission. Jobs on five of the state's commissions were considered political plums because they paid salaries ranging from $64,900 to $73,600 for what was usually part-time employment. Of these twenty-three positions, eleven were held by former legislators in July 1991.

13. South Carolina General Assembly, *Legislative Manual*, Columbia, SC: 1991.

14. There are thirteen Cabinet agencies:

Department of Alcohol and other Drug Abuse Services

Department of Commerce

Department of Corrections

Department of Health and Human Services

Department of Insurance

Department of Juvenile Justice

Department of Labor, Licensing, and Regulation

Department of Parks, Recreation, and Tourism

Department of Probation, Parole, and Pardon Services

Department of Public Safety

Department of Revenue and Taxation

Department of Social Services

State Law Enforcement Division

15. Glenn Abney and Thomas P. Lauth, *The Politics of State and City Administration*. Albany, NY: State University of New York Press, 1986, pp. 42–43.

16. Beyle, "Governors," 1983, p. 456. In the assessment of gubernatorial powers in 1989, Beyle breaks the index into two parts, the budget-making power of the governor and the legislative budget-changing authority. Under this scheme, South Carolina's

governor scores a 4 on the 5-point scale, but only five other states score as low. The 4 points mean that the governor shares the responsibility with others. On the legislative budget changing authority, South Carolina scores 1 point along with forty-six other states. See Beyle, "Governors, Appendix B," 1990, pp. 570–571.

17. James L. Underwood, *The Constitution of South Carolina*, vol. II, "The Journey Toward Local Government." Columbia, SC: University of South Carolina Press, 1989), pp. 18–19.

18. Graham, "The Evolving Executive in South Carolina," 1988, p. 172.

19. They were the old State Budget Commission, the State Finance Committee, the Board of Claims, the Commission on the State House and State House Grounds, the Joint Committee on Printing, and the South Carolina Retirement System. All of them were absorbed at the time into the operations of three Budget and Control Board divisions: finance, purchasing and property, and personnel administration. See South Carolina, *Journal of the Senate* (January 10, 1950), Columbia, SC: South Carolina Senate.

20. South Carolina Reorganization Commission, *The Budget Process in South Carolina: A Management Study*. Columbia, SC: State Reorganization Commission, 1985, p. A-47.

21. A popular story has it that this was done one evening over a fifth of bourbon. By the end of the evening, the bottle was empty and the agreement was sealed in a handwritten paragraph that omitted any term expiration dates for the appointed commissioners. Subsequent legislation was required to define the terms of the commissioners. Governor John C. West, personal interview by the author, Hilton Head, SC: July 17, 2003.

22. Governor West describes that he would invite legislators to his office or to a meeting in the Governor's Mansion to sit down with them and discuss the pending bill. He would say, "Fellows, don't bring me anything like that; let's think about this." Often, a compromise would be worked out and the bill would then be introduced. Governor John C. West, personal interview by the author, Hilton Head: SC, July 17, 2003.

23. The SBCB is composed of five members who serve based on the position or office they hold. The Board is chaired by the governor and includes the state treasurer, the comptroller general, the chair of the senate finance committee, and the chair of the house Ways and Means committee.

The members of the SBCB also constitute the State Education Assistance-Educational Facilities Authority, the South Carolina Resources Authority, the South Carolina Water Quality Revolving Fund Authority, the South Carolina Infrastructure Facilities Authority, and the Tobacco Settlement Revenue Management Authority Board. The Board is the trustee for the South Carolina Retirement Systems. Since 1999, it has responsibility to approve pension fund investments in the stock market as recommended by the Retirement Systems Investment Panel, a body of investment professionals.

The Board meets about ten times annually. As the central administrative agency for South Carolina state government, the SBCB manages the state budget, the state workforce, state buildings, the state public employee pension and health insurance systems, procurement, information technology, research, motor vehicles, and property-casualty-liability insurance for public employees and facilities. The Board approves the sale, purchase, and lease of all land and buildings by state agencies, new state government construction projects, bond issues, and salaries for state agency heads. It approves policies and guidelines governing the recruitment, retention, and development of state employees. There are eight internal SBCB divisions to manage these administrative activities. The State Auditor reports directly to the Board but is independent of the Board's other operations.

The Board can also act on statewide fiscal matters, particularly when the General Assembly is not in session. It may enact across-the-board cuts for state agencies if state revenues do not meet estimates. The Board may not exempt any agencies or programs from such cuts. It may also act if an individual agency is close to running a deficit.

The Office of State Budget is within the SBCB's Division of Budget and Analysis. The office is responsible for development and oversight of the preparation of the annual state budget. Also within the Division is: (1) the Human Resources Office, which guides policy, support, and administrative functions for state personnel statewide, including classification and pay, employee relations, grievance administration, training, recruitment, and interagency merit system; and (2) Research and Statistical Services, which is responsible for various information and research services involving state revenues and expenditures, information relating to economy, health, geography, geodesy, and geology, as well as the coordination of statistical services and information technology planning generally; and (3) the Board of Economic Advisors headed by a chief economic advisor, which provides general economic advice for the state and provides revenue forecasting for the Board.

24. A proviso is a temporary qualification, condition, or restriction that is effective for 1 year.

25. Among them are the Coleman Report (1936), the Preparedness for Peace Report (1945), and the Governor's Commission on Restructuring (1991).

26. Woodrow Wilson wrote that government operations would work best if it worked more like a business. Wilson worked during the 1880s, a time during which American corporations were rapidly developing new approaches to management. He advocated the concentration of power in a single authority at the top of a hierarchical structure. Woodrow Wilson, "The Study of Administration," *Political Science Quarterly* 2 (June 1887), 197–222. The highly integrated and centralized administrative structure required a strong chief executive. Reform studies have generally recommended more integration and coordination of South Carolina's divided administrative structure with the governor as the centerpiece.

27. South Carolina State Reorganization Commission, Overview, South Carolina Human Services Demonstration Project (1978), and South Carolina Human Services Demonstration Project: A Report on the Final Conference (1983). See also, Charlie B. Tyer and Joyce F. Prokop, *A Framework and Policy Options for State Government Modernization*, prepared for the Governor and the State Reorganization Commission (1977).

28. Governor's Commission on Management, Accountability, and Performance, Kenneth B. Wingate, Chair, Charting a Course for South Carolina's Future. Columbia, SC: The Commission, September 30, 2003.

29. Thomas R. Dye, *Politics in States and Communities*, 4th edition. Englewood Cliffs, NJ: Prentice-Hall, 1981, p. 161.

30. For a comprehensive study of the dynamics of the item veto in the fifty states, see Glenn Abney and Thomas P. Lauth, "The Item Veto and Fiscal Responsibility," *The Journal of Politics*, 57(August, 1997), 882–892.

31. South Carolina State Budget and Control Board, *Historical Analysis Through September 25, 2002*, p. 8.

32. There is a constitutional and statutory requirement that the General Assembly provide for a general reserve fund of 3 percent of the general fund revenue of the latest completed fiscal year. There is also a constitutional and statutory requirement that the General Assembly provide for a capital reserve fund of 2 percent of the general fund revenue of the latest completed fiscal year.

33. Governor Robert McNair (1965–1971) had an administrative staff of approximately sixty to seventy personnel. Governor John West's staff (1971–1975) totaled 480. The state's first Republican governor, James Edwards (1975–1979) reduced the staff size somewhat, but during Governor Richard Riley's term (1979–1987), the governor's staff grew to approximately 550. Governor Carroll Campbell (1987–1955) had over 800 staff personnel.

34. It was even mentioned among political insiders that when Riley delivered a eulogy for a legislator who died during the EIA campaign, he recalled how strongly the deceased had supported education reform.

35. "Tent meetings" refers to the practice of itinerant evangelists who pitch a tent in an open lot or field in order to hold a religious revival.

36. Campbell's executive budget initiative preceded restructuring. In 1992, a restructuring plan to reduce 133 statewide agencies governed by boards and commissions to fifteen cabinet-type agencies passed the house but failed the senate by just a few votes. In the next year two Democratic legislators who were House committee chairs developed a plan that introduced a restructuring act to the judiciary committee and linked it to the appropriations bill in the Ways and Means committee. If the restructuring bill failed, appropriations could go forward by categories of agencies and coordinate a functional allocation of resources, even if the formal agency structure was not in place. Under these pressures, the 133 executive agencies were reduced to sixty-nine and the thirteen cabinet agencies mentioned earlier were created under the direct or significant control of the governor.

37. Governor Campbell proposed three different executive budgets (1993–1996), Governors Beasley (1996–2000) and Hodges (2001–2004) four each, and Governor Sanford (2005). In late summer 2004, Governor Sanford began preparation of the 2005–2006 executive budget.

38. John Dempsey and Samuel M. Hines, Jr., "Management and Administration in South Carolina State Government," in Luther F. Carter and David S. Mann, Eds., *Government in the Palmetto State*. Columbia, SC: University of South Carolina Bureau of Governmental Research and Service, 1983, p. 150.

39. Bernard T. Pitsvada, "The Executive Budget—An Idea Whose Time Has Passed," *Public Budgeting and Finance* 8 (Spring 1988), 90.

## CHAPTER 12

# Virginia: Expenditure Increases, Tax Cuts, and Budget Deficits

*James K. Conant*

A Senate Finance Committee analysis found [governor elect] Gilmore's (car tax repeal) plan would cost as much as $531 million in the next two years—more than twice the $260 million price tag cited by Gilmore . . . the total cost of cutting the tax is predicted to be as high as $2.8 billion—which would be 75 percent more than the $1.6 billion estimated by Gilmore. The analysts predicted that strong growth in Virginia's revenue would provide enough money to cover the costs of Gilmore's promise in the first two years—even at the higher estimates—but they warned there was no guarantee that such surpluses would continue after that.[1]
                                              —*The Washington Post*, November 1997

Virginia's fiscal status could be described as a car crash—both literally and figuratively.
                                              —*Governing Magazine*, February 2003

This chapter on budgeting in Virginia is focused on the state's projected budget deficits for Fiscal Years 2002, 2003, and 2004. The state's fiscal problems are examined within the context of the national recession that officially began in March 2001. As the recession took hold, state lawmakers were faced with projected budget deficits running in the range of 10–15 percent of General Fund Revenues. The large size of Virginia's fiscal problems was the result of both cyclical (economic) and structural (policy) causes.

This chapter begins with a brief overview of Virginia's fiscal problems in FY 2002, FY 2003, and FY 2004. Then, background is provided on Virginia's pre-recession economic growth, revenue growth, revenue structure, and expenditure patterns. The 1998–2001 policy decisions that opened up the big gap between recurring revenues and expenditures are described in the next section, followed by an extensive description of the various elements of the FY 2000–2002 biennial budget process and the revenue and expenditure decisions made as part of that process. Then, a brief description is provided of the revenue and expenditure decisions made during the FY 2002–2004 budgetary process. The chapter ends with some reflections on both the causes of Virginia's budget problems and elected officials' responses to those deficits.

A brief description of Virginia's budgetary process is provided here to facilitate reading the chapter. Virginia's governor must present a proposed budget to the General Assembly, Virginia's legislature, by December 20, each year. The legislature convenes on the second Wednesday of January to review and act on the governor's budget bill; the legislature adjourns on the first Wednesday of March. The governor has 30 days to sign, veto the entire appropriation bill, veto items in the bill, or recommend amendments to it. The legislature reconvenes in mid-April to sustain or override vetoes or to consider proposed amendments. The new budget becomes effective on July 1.

## OVERVIEW: THE FY 2002, AND FY 2003–2004 BUDGET DEFICITS

In March 2001, Virginia's projected deficit for FY 2002 was $1.3 billion; later estimates put the figure at $1.5 billion.[2] Thus, the projected deficit was between 12 percent and 14 percent of General Fund Revenues. In March 2002, the projected budget gap for the FY 2003–2004 biennium was approximately $2.5 billion.[3] Thus, the 3-year budget gap (FY 2002, 2003, and 2004) totaled approximately $3.8 to $4.0 billion.

The most visible effect of the 2001 economic recession, the cyclical cause of Virginia's fiscal problems, was on the revenue side of the budget. For example, state general fund tax collections were actually 3.8 percent lower in FY 2002 than they were in FY 2001. The gap between early estimates of state tax revenues for FY 2002 and actual revenues was even larger, consisting of approximately $1 billion or 7.5 percent.[4]

The structural component of the state's budget problems, which consisted of a gap between recurring expenditures and recurring revenue, was mostly created by policy decisions made between 1998 and 2001. During these 4 years, Virginia's elected officials cut state taxes and fees and, at the same time, substantially increased state General Fund expenditures. Specifically, General Fund expenditures grew from $8.1 billion in FY 1997 to $12.3 billion in FY 2001, an increase of more than $4.2 billion, or 51 percent.[5] The largest expenditure increases occurred in the areas of K-12 education, higher education, mental health, prisons, and Medicaid.

On the revenue side of the budget, sixteen taxes were reduced or eliminated.[6] The largest reduction involved the car tax. Specifically, the tax on vehicles with a value of $20,000 or less was to be eliminated over a 5-year period of time. The cost of the car tax was a matter of heated debate from the summer of 1997, when gubernatorial candidate James Gilmore made his "no more car tax" pledge, all the way through 2001, when the governor and the Senate clashed over ways to balance the budget. Estimates developed in 1999, however, indicated that the car tax cut would cost the state about $1.1 billion a year by 2002, when it was fully phased in.[7]

It is worth noting, however, that, in budgetary terms, the car tax cut had to be "booked" on the expenditure side of the state budget. Revenue generated by the car tax flowed to local governments, and it made up 20–30 percent of most local governments' revenue stream. The elimination of the car tax revenues could have been catastrophic for local governments in Virginia if the state had not replaced the "lost" revenue.

Fee cuts also reduced General Fund Revenue between 1998 and 2001. The most important of these cuts occurred in the area of university tuition for in-state undergraduates. Specifically, tuition was cut by 20 percent.[8] Like the car tax, however, the reduction in university tuition costs showed up as additional state expenditures. State officials attempted to compensate universities for lost tuition by expanding state support for them.

In short, state expenditures rose at a very rapid rate during the period between 1998 and 2001. Ironically, the rapid, but artificially high, revenue growth of 1998, 1999, and 2000, masked the underlying structural imbalance between recurring revenues and expenditures that had already been created. Indeed, this artificial economic/revenue boom undoubtedly contributed to the mistaken belief apparently held by the governor and some legislators that the extraordinary tax cuts and spending increases they put in place between 1998 and 2001 was affordable.

## Responses to the Projected Deficits

State policymakers' responses to the projected FY 2002 and FY 2003 budget shortfalls or deficits could largely be described as short-term responses aimed primarily at addressing the cyclical dimensions of the current budget problems. One-time revenues were generated for both years, and the state's Budget Stabilization Fund was tapped. The fund was used in FY 2004, as well. Modest cuts in state spending were made in 2001, and substantial cuts were made in various state programs and activities during FY 2002 and FY 2003. As a result of these cuts, General Fund Appropriations for FY 2002 and FY 2003 were less than they were for FY 2001, and the FY 2004 figure was only .7 percent higher than FY 2001. The spending cuts adversely affected many citizens, resulted in layoffs of state employees, and meant no raises for state employees and K-12 teachers.

Despite the actions taken by Virginia's elected officials in 2001, 2002, and 2003, however, the underlying structural problem (the gap between recurring revenues and expenditures) remained unresolved in the spring of 2003. Thus, additional tough choices would have to be made to balance the 2004–2006 budget.[9]

In short, the Virginia case underscores the fiscal pain that can be caused by cyclical fluctuations in the economy. It also highlights the risks that governors and legislators run when they create an imbalance between recurring revenues and recurring expenditures. Finally, the Virginia case highlights the difficulty governors and legislators have in addressing a structural deficit once it has been created.

## VIRGINIA'S ECONOMY AND REVENUE PATTERNS: 1990–2001

### Economic Indicators

Virginia's annual unemployment rate was below the average rate for the United States during the period from 1990 to 2001. The national average for the period was 5.55 percent. In comparison, Virginia's average unemployment rate was 4.38 percent for the years from 1990 to 1997 and 3.98 percent from 1998 to 2002.[10] The two periods are identified separately because Virginia changed its unemployment benchmark in 1998. This change may have contributed to the increase in the (positive) difference between Virginia's unemployment rate and the national unemployment rate.

Between 1990 and 2001, Virginia's employment grew at an average rate of 1.78 percent a year, compared to the national average annual rate of 1.696 percent for the same period.[11] Virginia's employment, as a share of U.S. employment, increased slightly, from 2.65 percent in 1990 to 2.68 percent in 2001.[12]

Virginia's per capita personal income exceeded the personal per capita income for the United States as a whole by 4.7 percent in 1990; in 2001 Virginia's per capita income exceeded U.S. per capita income by 6.9 percent. Virginia's per capita income rose a total of 37 percent from 1990 to 2001. Virginia's growth rate was slightly larger than the growth in U.S. per capita income, which rose by just under 36 percent.

The per capita income for the United States as a whole grew at an average rate of 3.9 percent annually, while Virginia's per capita income increased at an average annual rate of 4.1 percent.[13] During this period, Virginia's per capita income grew at a steady annual rate, increasing from $20,527 in 1990 to $32,431 in 2001. For every year of this period Virginia maintained a higher per capita income than the United States as a whole, by an average of $1,159.[14]

**Table 12.1**
**Virginia Revenue Patterns: Growth in Total General Fund Tax Revenues,
Fiscal Years 1990–2002 ($ in millions)**

| Fiscal Year | Total G.F. Tax Revenue | Percent Growth |
|---|---|---|
| 1990 | 5,945 | 3.0 |
| 1991 | 5,472 | 4.0 |
| 1992 | 5,623 | 2.8 |
| 1993 | 6,134 | 9.1 |
| 1994 | 6,503 | 6.0 |
| 1995 | 6,881 | 5.8 |
| 1996 | 7,356 | 6.9 |
| 1997 | 7,949 | 8.1 |
| 1998 | 8,774 | 10.4 |
| 1999 | 9,703 | 10.6 |
| 2000 | 10,722 | 10.5 |
| 2001 | 11,054 | 3.1 |
| 2002 | 10,619 | −3.9 |

*Source:* John M. Bennett, "Actual General Fund Revenues for FY 2002; Revised Economic Outlook and Revenue Forecast for FY 2003 and 2004," Appendix, August 19, 2002.

### Revenue Patterns

During the 1990s, General Fund Tax Revenue growth in Virginia averaged 6.0 percent. At the beginning of the decade, tax revenue growth was modest. Indeed, due to an emerging recession, negative growth of −0.5 percent was recorded in FY 1991. This figure is important not only because it was negative but also because it was the first time in over 30 years the state did not have tax revenue growth. In contrast, General Fund Tax Revenue growth was particularly strong at the end of the decade. Growth rates of more than 10 percent were recorded in both FY 1998 and FY 1999.

General Fund Tax Revenue growth also exceeded 10 percent in FY 2000. However, General Fund Tax Revenue growth fell sharply in FY 2001 to only 3.1 percent. Then, in FY 2002, the growth figure moved into negative territory at −3.9 percent. The −3.9 percent was the worst tax revenue performance on record for the state.[15] The General Fund Tax Revenue growth is displayed in Table 12.1.

## VIRGINIA: REVENUE STRUCTURE

In FY 2002, Virginia's Total General Fund Revenue was $10.679 billion. Of this total, $ 9.8 billion was generated from the state's major taxes. Virginia has a relatively low rank in taxes raised per capita. In 2001, the state ranked 29th on that scale.[16]

## Taxes

The principal sources of tax revenue for Virginia are the Individual Income and the Sales and Use Tax. In FY 2002, the Individual Income Tax generated $6.7 billion of the $10.7 billion General Fund Revenues, or 62.8 percent.[17] Income tax rates range from a minimum of 2.0 percent, for incomes under $3,000, to a maximum of 5.75 percent, for incomes over $17,000.[18]

In FY 2002, the Sales and Use Tax generated more than $2.4 billion, or 22.8 percent of General Fund Revenue.[19] The Sales and Use Tax is 4.5 percent of retail purchases.[20] There is a wide range of exemptions from the sales tax, and many services are not subject to the sales tax.[21] Prescription drugs were exempted from the tax in 1998, and a plan to phase out the sales tax on food was passed in the same year. The effort stalled, however, with the onset of recent budget problems.

Other state taxes include the Corporate Income Tax, Insurance Premiums Tax, and Public Service Tax. Collectively, these taxes accounted for $660 million in FY 2002, or 6.2 percent of General Fund Revenue.[22] All other state taxes and fees defined as General Fund Revenues totaled $878 million, or 8.2 percent of all General Fund Revenue.[23] Among these taxes and fees is the tobacco tax. It is worth noting that Virginia's tobacco tax in FY 2002 was the lowest in the country, at 2.5 cents per pack.[24]

## Revenue Estimation

Revenue estimates in Virginia are developed under the auspices of the governor. The process of producing the estimates involves a multi-step process.[25] The Department of Taxation, which is headed by a gubernatorial appointee, is the lead agency in the initial development of General Fund Revenues. The process begins with a forecast of the economy and general fund revenues. Two consulting firms generate these forecasts. The Department of Taxation uses these economic forecasts to develop its forecast of General Fund Revenues.

The Department of Taxation's forecast must, according to statutory requirement, provide a 6-year forecast. The Department's "draft" revenue forecast is released during the summer or early fall. The Governor's Advisory Board of Economists and the Governor's Advisory Council on Revenue Estimates then review it in October and November, respectively. The first "official forecast" is provided by the governor in December. A "mid-session update" is produced during the General Assembly session (January/February), and a "post-session" forecast, which incorporates law changes, is released sometime between March and May.[26]

It is noteworthy that the legislature's role in revenue forecasting is limited. Some members of the legislative leadership may serve on the Governor's Advisory Council on Revenue Estimates. However, the legislature does not have independent revenue estimating capacity. This limitation can sometimes be a source of frustration for members of the legislature, and, in institutional terms, it serves as an important constraint on legislative independence and decision-making.

### Rainy Day Fund

The requirements for Virginia's Budget Stabilization Fund are provided in Article X, section 8 of the Constitution of Virginia.[27] The impetus for the establishment of this constitutional provision was the 1990–1991 recession. Although the Revenue Stabilization Fund is "routinely segregated from the General Fund," Virginia law requires "that the Revenue Stabilization fund be included as a component of the General Fund for accounting purposes."[28] Thus, it is included as a "cash asset and as a reserved component of fund balance."[29]

The constitutional provisions for the Budget Stabilization Fund also place limits on the amount of money that can be put into the fund. Specifically, the amount cannot exceed 10 percent of Virginia's average annual revenues generated from taxes on income and retail sales for the preceding 3 fiscal years. In any given year, the amount estimated as required for deposit in the Budget Stabilization Fund must be appropriated by the General Assembly.[30]

The Budget Stabilization Fund can be used if "revenue collections fall significantly and unexpectedly from the amount in an enacted budget."[31] Transfers from the Budget Stabilization Fund are limited to the lesser of either one-half the balance in the fund or one-half the amount by which appropriated revenue (appropriations) exceeds the revised revenue forecast.[32]

The maximum amount that could have been in the Budget Stabilization Fund in FY 2002 was $934.5.[33] At the end of FY 2002, however, there was only $472.4 million in the fund.[34] During that fiscal year, $467.7 million was drawn down into general appropriations, while $187.1 million was deposited in the fund.[35]

## VIRGINIA: EXPENDITURE PATTERNS

Virginia had ongoing expenditure growth during the decade of the 1990s, but the growth during the period from 1997–2001 was truly remarkable. It was during the latter period of time that the new commitments made by elected officials pushed General Fund budget appropriations up from $8.1 billion in FY 1997 to $12.3 billion in FY 2001, an increase of 51 percent.[36] A portrait of both the decade-long expenditure growth and growth in the period from 1998 to 2001 is provided in this section.

**Table 12.2**
**Virginia Expenditure Patterns: General Fund Expenditures, Fiscal Years 1990–2001 ($ in Millions)**

| Fiscal Year | General Fund Expenditures | $ Change | Percent Change |
|---|---|---|---|
| 1990 | 5,893 | | |
| 1991 | 6,331 | 438 | 7.4 |
| 1992 | 6,144 | 187 | 3.0 |
| 1993 | 6,436 | 292 | 4.8 |
| 1994 | 6,742 | 306 | 4.8 |
| 1995 | 7,490 | 748 | 11.1 |
| 1996 | 7,655 | 165 | 2.2 |
| 1997 | 8,183 | 528 | 6.9 |
| 1998 | 8,335 | 152 | 1.9 |
| 1999 | 10,194 | 1859 | 22.3 |
| 2000 | 11,282 | 1088 | 10.7 |
| 2001 | 12,339 | 1057 | 9.4 |

*Source:* U.S. Census Bureau, *Statistical Abstract of the United States: 2001*, "State Resources, Expenditures, and Balances, 1999–2000," and Statistical Abstract volumes from 1990–2000.

## Expenditure Growth: 1990–1999

In 1990, Virginia's General Fund expenditures were nearly $5.9 billion. In 1999, General Fund expenditures were almost $10.2 billion. Over the course of the decade, spending rose by $4.3 billion, or almost 73 percent. These data are shown in Table 12.2.

Why did state General Fund expenditures grow so rapidly? The simple explanation is that the state's elected officials made policy decisions that expanded spending commitments. In its study of state expenditure growth from FY 1981 to FY 2002, however, the Joint Legislative and Audit Review Committee of the Virginia General Assembly attempted to identify other, deeper causes. The Committee noted that "Virginia became a more populous and richer State" during the 1980s and 1990s. The Committee also reported that, "State spending grew in response to substantial growth in almost every category of persons served by State programs, whether Medicaid recipients, child support recipients, college students, State park visitors, or prison inmates."[37]

## Major Expenditure Initiatives: 1998–2001

Between 1998 and 2001, General Fund expenditures in Virginia grew by 43 percent, "the fourth-biggest jump over that period, after California, Colorado, and Idaho."[38] Ironically, the increase in expenditures occurred during the term of Republican Governor James Gilmore, whose "fiscal conservatism" was considered a "hallmark of his career."[39] Of course, the governor did not act alone. During this period of time, biennial budgets for 1998–2000 and 2000–2002 were reviewed by two different legislatures.

Republicans controlled the Senate in the 1998–1999 legislature, but the number of seats controlled by Democrats and Republicans was evenly divided in the House of Delegates. This circumstance resulted in a power sharing arrangement. During the 2000–2001 legislature, Republicans held a majority in both the Senate and the House of Delegates.

As already noted, the governor and the legislature made K-12 education and higher education the principal areas of expenditure growth. The governor and the General Assembly increased spending on K-12 education by $1.1 billion, and they increased higher education spending by $500 million. In percentage terms, the increase for K-12 education was 36 percent and the increase for higher education was 48 percent.[40] A substantial part of the increase in K-12 education funding was designed to hire new teachers, improve teacher pay, and provide support for Standards of Learning testing.

Mental health was a third area where elected officials substantially increased expenditures. Between 1997 and 2001, Governor Gilmore and the General Assembly increased "spending on mental health services" by $213 million, or 49 percent.[41] The principal objective for these funds was to reduce waiting lists for mental retardation services.[42]

## THE FY 2000–2002 BIENNIAL BUDGET

### The 2000–2002 Executive Budget

December of 1999 was a key month in the 2000–2002 biennial budget process. It was the month the governor was supposed to release the state's official 6-year revenue forecast, and it was the month the FY 2000–2002 executive budget document was supposed to be submitted to the General Assembly. Prior to their release, there was a good deal of speculation and concern about what they would contain.

The official revenue estimates showed relatively "bullish" assumptions about economic growth and revenue growth. For example, Secretary of Finance, Ronald L. Tillett, reported that "ideal conditions prevailed" in Virginia, and "that money will continue to flow rapidly into the state."[43] Revenue growth of 3.8 percent was forecast for FY 2001, and growth of 7 percent was forecast for FY 2002.[44]

This rosy revenue forecast for the biennium, combined with a $509 million balance carried forward from FY 2000 and Transfers of $705 million generated General Fund "Total Resources" of $24.7 billion. Governor Gilmore's proposed budget included expenditures of all but a small fraction, $5.1 million, of the "Total Resources." In short, the governor proposed to expand spending for the 2000–2002 biennium by $3.25 billion over the base budget or "current services" budget.[45]

The single largest proposed spending increase was $878 million for car tax relief. An increase of $656 million was proposed for K-12 education, and $410 million was proposed for transportation. Other notable spending increases included $275 million for human resources, $250 million for public safety, $200 million for capital outlay, $128 million for employee compensation and benefits, and $108 million for higher education. Additionally, $200 million was slated for the Revenue Stabilization Fund.[46]

In addition to the spending increases for the 2000–2002 biennium, which included FY 2001 and FY 2002, Governor Gilmore also proposed amendments to the FY 2000 budget. These amendments included additional spending of $176 million. The single largest expenditure increase was $67 million for car tax relief, followed by $58.2 million for human resources, and $18.7 million for K-12 education.

### Legislative Response

Although the legislature modified some of the governor's proposals, the biennial budget that emerged from the legislature contained most of what Governor Gilmore proposed. The spending increases proposed for the FY 2000 budget were largely approved, and the principal spending increases for the FY 2000–2002 biennial budget won legislative support. Among the reasons the governor's proposals received such a positive response from the legislature was that the governor's party controlled both houses of the General Assembly, and many Republicans were willing to accede to the wishes and demands of their party's leader.

### The Governor's Budget Amendments for the FY 2000–2002 Budget and Concerns About the Cost of the Car Tax Repeal

On December 20 of 2000, only several months after the FY 2000–2002 budget was approved by the legislature and signed by the chief executive, Governor Gilmore submitted his proposed FY 2000–2002 budget amendments to the legislature. In the budget amendment briefing document given to the Senate Finance Committee, the House Appropriations Committee, and the House Finance Committee on December 20, 2000, the first item listed under "Highlights of the Governor's amendments to the 2000–2002 budget" was the continuation of "the car tax repeal phase-in as originally planned . . . (70 % for tax year 2001 and 100% for tax year 2002)."[47]

Other "highlights" included a repeat of the governor's priorities as articulated in the 2000–2002 executive budget document. The governor also reiterated his determination to preserve "our Revenue Stabilization Fund for a severe economic downturn (deposits are continued with no withdrawal of funds)."

There were, however, some hints that all was not right in the FY 2000–2002 budget. For example, the briefing document contained a reference to the need to set "tough spending priorities" and the need to reduce employer contributions for teacher retirement benefits by $70 million. Perhaps most important, however, was the governor's proposal to sell "Virginia's allocation for future years under the Master Settlement Agreement with tobacco manufacturers" in order to add "another $460 million to general fund revenue during the 2000–2002 biennium."[48]

Last, but not least, the briefing document reported that the governor's budget amendments also included $206 million in "executive management savings." In short, these expenditure cuts, as well as the infusion of what turned out to be a proposed $483 million (not $460 million) from the tobacco settlement, were to be used to fund the next installment of the car tax repeal, "fulfilling," as the governor put it, "a 'sacred' promise to voters."[49]

### The 2001 Legislative Session on the Governor's 2000–2002 Budget Amendments

When the legislature met in January, 2001, it was clear that some members, particularly in the State Senate, were concerned about the validity of the economic assumptions and revenue estimates on which the 2000–2002 biennial budget and Governor Gilmore's proposed budget amendments were built. Among those expressing concern were members of the governor's own party, who warned that, "Virginia's cooling economy cannot support the $1 billion price tag," which was the estimated annual cost of fully phasing out the car tax.[50]

Gilmore firmly asserted, however, that the state had the money needed to fund the next installment of the car-tax repeal.[51] Yet, on the basis of the budget amendments the governor had proposed, it was also clear to some legislators that the governor was relying "on state spending cuts and an infusion of $483 million from a federal tobacco settlement to help fund the next installment of the car-tax repeal."[52] The governor's cutback strategy included reducing some state agency budgets by 3 percent in 2001 and by 6 percent in 2002, the year after he left office.[53]

While the expenditure cuts may have been an essential element of paying for the car tax repeal and balancing the budget, it was the revenue component of Gilmore's plan that mattered most. Specifically, Gilmore maintained that the infusion of the tobacco settlement money "would allow the state to meet the revenue targets established in the 1998 car-tax law, so that the cut can continue in 2001."[54] The 1998 law stipulated that the tax cut could not go forward in any year if the cost exceeded 8 percent of the state's general fund, or if revenue estimates for the year fell one-half percent below forecast.[55]

As the 60-day legislative session wore on, the conflict over the car tax continued between the governor and the Senate. The House of Delegates, however, lined-up with the governor. A committee consisting of representatives from the two houses was formed, and an attempt was made to work out the differences. The gap between the two houses was too large, however, and a compromise solution proved elusive.

The impasse left the FY 2002 "budget in limbo," which meant that the governor might have to rely on the FY 2002 budget passed in 2000 to fund state government agencies and programs. Although the 2000–2002 biennial budget included a 70 percent car-tax cut in FY 2001, Gilmore wanted a new spending plan that would pay for the full cost of the car-tax cut and new initiatives.[56]

## The Governor's Actions to Balance the State Budget

On March 12, 2001, the "Governor issued Executive Order 74 (2001) to fulfill his Constitutional duty to balance the state's budget."[57] Gilmore had to address a projected $421 million shortfall in the FY 2002 budget, and he proposed to do so with $274.5 million of revenue from delayed capital projects, $85.3 million of additional revenue from a variety of sources, and budget cutbacks totaling $146.2 million.[58] By taking these actions, the governor believed he had found a way to balance the budget and to preserve his top priority: the continued phase out of the car tax.

## Special Session of the General Assembly

On April 25, 2001, members of the General Assembly returned to Richmond to meet in a special session. The main task of the session was to determine whether the stalled budget negotiations could be restarted. From the outset, however, many were pessimistic about the prospects for success. Some members of the Senate, including the Finance Chair, Republican John Chichester, made it clear that they would continue to resist the governor's plan to complete the car tax repeal. The governor's plan, Chichester argued, could "jeopardize the financial stability of state government."[59] Others inside and outside state government voiced similar sentiments.

During the special session, Chichester and the Senate offered a compromise budget plan that would have increased the car tax cut from 47.5 percent to 55 percent in FY 2002, rather than the 70 percent Governor Gilmore wanted. Chichester had the backing of all eighteen of the Senate's Democrats and most of the Senate's Republicans.[60] Although it seemed a sensible plan, particularly given the formal announcement in March 2001 that the national economy was in recession, Chichester did not win the support of either the governor or the House of Delegates.

Thus, on May 9, 2001, the special General Assembly session on the budget adjourned without the passage of a new budget. Among the consequences of ending the special legislative session without a revised 2002 budget was that a pay raise of $125 million for the state's 200,000 state government workers and teachers was frozen.[61]

The failure to break the budget stalemate, however, gave Gilmore the opportunity to save his car tax by reworking the budget for FY 2002. With the departure of the legislature from the state capital, Gilmore also regained control of the public podium, and he used it actively to campaign for the budget he wanted.

### The August 2001 Financial Report and the Aftermath

In mid-August 2001, only a few months after the special session of the General Assembly dissolved on May 9 without a revised 2002 budget, key information was published that gave additional ammunition to legislators who were concerned about the state's financial circumstances. The information was presented in a table titled "Fiscal Year 2001 General Fund Collections: Actual and Forecast," and the table was part of a report submitted to the General Assembly by the Finance Secretary, John W. Forbes.[62]

Data in the report showed that the revenue from major tax sources was $155 million below the amount forecast for FY 2001, and it showed that total FY 2001 General Fund Revenues were below predictions by $73 million. In other words, revenues grew only 2.9 percent, rather than the 3.6 percent that had been forecast.[63] Finally, the report showed a General Fund "shortfall of $52 million in fiscal 2001, which ended in June."[64]

On August 20, during the traditional summer visit to the assembly's money committee, Gilmore "offered an optimistic picture of the state's economy."[65] He stuck by his 7 percent revenue growth forecast for FY 2002.[66] He also "skirted the most troubling aspects of the budget picture" by asserting that "modest revenue growth and solid financial stewardship" had kept the state's FY 2001 budget in balance.[67]

Senior members of both parties of the legislature, however, found the financial news and Gilmore's comments very troubling, and they rebutted his "rosy accounting."[68] "I've heard of rosy-colored glasses," one delegate said, but "this is more like a rosy-colored fog that's been rolled out for us, telling us how lovely everything is."[69] Leaders of both parties warned that the budget problem for FY 2002 could be ten times bigger than the $52 million revenue shortfall reported by Gilmore.[70]

The concerns legislators expressed about the state's fiscal condition, however, seemed to energize Gilmore. On August 21, 2001, he used an "appearance at George Mason University to shoot back at Republican and Democratic lawmakers."[71] Gilmore "criticized lawmakers for a 'premature' assessment of the state's budget" situation, and he repeated his "upbeat portrayal."[72] He also used the occasion to announce that he was restoring to the University $15 million of capital funding for new buildings that had been cut out as part of his efforts to find capital savings to balance the FY 2002 budget.

The symbolic nature of this gesture was unmistakable. Gilmore was reassuring the public and telling legislators that he had the money to do what he wanted to do.[73] What the governor was not reporting, however, was that his ability to distribute funds to George Mason University and other state agencies and constituencies depended in part on his decision to use $467.7 million from the Budget Stabilization Fund to balance the FY 2002 General Fund budget.

## THE FY 2002–2004 BUDGET

### The Executive Budget Document

On December 20, 2001, Governor Gilmore presented his 2002–2004 Executive Budget to the General Assembly. Given the national recession that was underway, the economic assumptions that were used to develop the revenue forecast for FY 2002 and FY 2003 may have seemed a bit optimistic. The governor's operating presumption was that: "National economic growth" would "rebound after three slow quarters."[74] Consequently, General Fund tax revenues were expected to "increase by 4.1 and 5.5 percent in FY 2003 and FY 2004," respectively.[75]

Using this optimistic forecast, Gilmore proposed a net increase in General Fund Expenditures of more than $800 million.[76] The spending increases he proposed actually totaled nearly $2.1 billion, but they were offset in part by almost $1.3 billion in proposed spending reductions. Legislative budget documents show that the governor proposed to spend an additional $75.2 million to complete the phase out of the car tax in FY 2004, $288.6 million for a 2 percent salary increase for state employees and public school teachers in FY 2003, $66.6 million for higher education, $459.7 million for K-12 education, and $892.9 million for human resources.[77]

The $1.2 billion in spending reductions proposed by the governor were secured by "making tough choices" required to balance the budget.[78] The savings were to be achieved through cost containment actions, targeted reductions, and across-the-board reductions. Specifically, Gilmore expected to save $631.7 million in FY 2003 and $593.7 million in FY 2004.[79]

Gilmore's Executive Budget also included an announcement that there would be no tax increase for the FY 2002–2004 biennium. A related note, however, was that the governor planned to transfer $467 million from the Budget Stabilization Fund to the general fund in 2002.[80]

### Legislative Response

The legislative session to review the governor's 2002–2004 budget proposal and his amendments for FY 2002 began in January 2002. Although some lawmakers continued to express doubts about whether the state could afford the cost of the car tax repeal, Gilmore got what he wanted. The FY 2002 budget was amended to include an additional $127.6 million to pay for the additional costs of the car tax. Among the factors that contributed to the governor's "success" on this issue was the new, enlarged Republican majority that was in place in both the House of Delegates and Senate.

The legislature did, however, make some important modifications in the governor's 2002 spending increases and expenditure reductions. Total spending increases were expanded by $140 million, while cutbacks were more than $400 million higher than the governor recommended. The net increase in spending for 2002–2004 was $551 million, rather than the $830 million Gilmore proposed.[81]

### Governor Warner's Proposed Amendments to the FY 2002–2004 Budget

In November of 2001, Democrat Mark Warner was elected governor. There was little time for him to celebrate the election victory, however. A few weeks before the election, "Warner and his new budget team were shocked to learn that the fiscal calamity awaiting them was much worse" than the "$1 billion shortfall (in the FY 2002–2004 budget) that even Gilmore was acknowledging by the end of 2001."[82]

On December 20, 2001, Warner put forward proposed amendments to the FY 2002–2004 budget passed in the spring of 2002. In the briefing document that accompanied his budget amendments, Warner said that he had to address a budget shortfall of nearly $1 billion for FY 2003, the fiscal year that was already nearly half over. In addition, he said the projected shortfall for FY 2004 would exceed $1 billion.[83]

The $2.1 billion budget shortfall he faced for the 2002–2004 biennium consisted of $1.5 million attributed to "revenue shortfall" and $600 million from "spending requirements." His proposed amendments included using $246 million from the Budget Stabilization Fund for FY 2003 and $129 million for FY 2004. He also proposed some fee increases.

Most of the projected deficit was to be closed, however, through spending cuts totaling $725 million for the biennium. Warner also anticipated that at least 1,837 state employees would be laid off, with another 4,570 layoffs possible in state institutions of higher education.

An important, additional part of the fiscal medicine Warner proposed was a (temporary) freeze on the full phase out of the car tax. Specifically, Warner proposed holding the car tax repeal at 70 percent, rather than moving to a 100 percent repeal of the tax on cars with a value of less than $20,000.

## REFLECTIONS

The Virginia case not only illustrates the powerful effects that an economic recession can have on a state budget but also what happens when elected officials pass large tax cuts and, at the same time, rapidly increase spending. The Virginia case also shows the way in which the nexus between the anti-tax ideology articulated Governor Gilmore and House Republicans, election results that seemed to favor those who held the anti-tax ideology, a booming economy, and new spending commitments led to huge budget deficits.

The dominant player in the Virginia budget drama from 1998 to 2002 was the Republican Governor, James Gilmore. He narrowly defeated incumbent Lt. Governor Don Beyer in the 1997 general election, and his narrow victory margin is often attributed to his "no more car tax" pledge. Having made the election promise to "eliminate" the car tax, Gilmore clung doggedly to this decision. Despite the onset of the recession in March 2001, Gilmore insisted that the state had the money to pay for the car tax. His economic forecasts and revenue projections growth seemed to provide support for this claim, but they proved to be overly optimistic.

The car tax repeal, with an ongoing, annual cost of nearly $1 billion, was a key causal factor in the state's FY 2002 budget deficit. It was also a key factor in the projected deficit for the FY 2002–2004 biennium. The car tax cut's price tag also crowded out other needs, priorities, and programs that might have been funded with "one-time" allocations when the state was awash in new money in 1999, 2000, and 2001.

For example, the state's enormous backlog in school construction and school renovation might have been reduced dramatically if the funds used for the car tax repeal had been allocated for this purpose in 1999, 2000, and 2001. Like-wise, Virginia's transportation needs/problems might have been addressed more rapidly and effectively had money used on the car tax been put into road, bus, and rail enhancements during 1999, 2000, and 2001. Furthermore, there was also a high cost to maintaining the car tax cut once the economic and revenue boom was over. Specifically, using state revenues to sustain the car tax meant that other worthwhile state services had to be cut in order to balance the budget.

The fact that tax cuts have significant "costs" provides a basis for raising an important question about the Virginia case. Specifically, it is interesting to ask what might have happened if Governor Gilmore had been elected on the basis of a "no more car tax" pledge but had only a modest amount of new revenue growth (say 2 or 3%) to work with in 1998, 1999, and 2000.

Given the extraordinary costs of the car tax cut initiative, legislative passage of the cut would have crowded out almost all other new spending and it might have required immediate cuts in existing state programs. If the tradeoffs be-tween the car tax cut and other public services such as K-12 education had been visible from the outset, one wonders whether the governor's initiative would have been adopted by the legislature in the first place. In short, tax cuts do have high costs, and an honest presentation of the consequences associated with a tax cut would include the public services that will have to be cut if the tax cut is enacted.

Finally, one other element of the Virginia case stands out: the impasse between Governor Gilmore and the leaders and members of the State Senate. Immediately after the election results were known in 1997, members of the Senate challenged the unrealistically low estimates the governor was using for the financial costs of the car tax cut. The Senate's independent analysis and its steadfastness in the face of Gilmore's harsh criticism ultimately led to an acknowledgement by the governor that the costs of his proposal would be nearly double his estimates.

On other occasions, particularly in 2001, the Senate also had the courage to challenge the governor's rosy economic forecast and revenue prediction. At stake was not only the question of whether the final phases of the car tax were affordable but also whether the costs would push the budget out of balance. Again, despite withering criticism from the governor, the Senate's perspective on the condition of the economy and the state's financial circumstances turned out to be much closer to the mark than the governor's. Indeed, one of the most remarkable aspects of this study of budgeting in Virginia is the courage and skill demonstrated by Republican Senator John Chichester, Finance Committee Chair, in the extended budget battle with Governor Gilmore and House Republicans. The other members of the Senate's Republican majority, as well as their Democratic colleagues, also deserve praise for their bipartisan spirit and their unwavering commitment to sound financial management.

## ACKNOWLEDGMENTS

An earlier version of this chapter was presented as a paper at the 2003 WSSA Annual Conference. The paper was produced for the section on Public Finance and Budgeting, administered by Bill Simonsen and Mark Robbins. Jennifer Teal began the assembly of materials for this study; Hilary Kennedy served as research assistant through the completion of the conference paper and its revision for this book. Susan Conant made editorial recommendations on a draft version of this manuscript. Financial support for this research was provided by the College of Arts and Sciences at George Mason University. Thanks to all who contributed and to Edward Clynch and Tom Lauth for including Virginia in this book.

## NOTES

1. The words bracketed by parentheses have been added to the quotation to provide the context included in the full text of the article by Ellen Nakashima titled "Cost of Cutting Car Tax in Va. Could Double: Gilmore's Estimates Challenged by Report," *The Washington Post* (November 21, 1997), A 1.

2. The $1.3 billion figure is found in Michael D. Shear, "In Va. Budget, No Accounting for Change," *The Washington Post* (March 3, 2002), C-1, C-4. The $1.5 billion

deficit figure is found in Paul Goldman, "Behind Virginia's Budget Woes, A Deficit of Candor," *The Washington Post* (December 16, 2001), B-2.

3. Michael D. Shear, "In Va. Budget, No Accounting for Change," *The Washington Post* (March 3, 2002), C-1, C-4.

4. Virginia Department of Planning and Budget, *The 2002–2004 Executive Budget Document* (December 19, 2001), A-5.

5. U.S. Census Bureau, *Statistical Abstract of the United States: 2001*, "State Resources, Expenditures and Balances, 1999–2000," and *Statistical Abstract* volumes for 1998–2000.

6. Department of Planning and Budget, *The 2002–2004 Executive Budget Document*, p. A-2.

7. Craig Timberg, "Cost of Tax Cut: Traffic; Funds Could Aid Roads, Some Say," *The Washington Post* (August 28, 1999), B-1.

8. Department of Planning and Budget, *The 2002–2004 Executive Budget Document*, p. A-2.

9. For a case study of the 2004–2006 budgetary process in Virginia, see James K. Conant, "Virginia Budgeting in the Post-Recessionary Period," presented for the Public Finance and Budgeting Section, at the Western Social Science Annual Meeting, April 15, 2005, Albequerque, NM.

10. U.S. Department of Labor, Bureau of Labor Statistics, "Local Area Unemployment Statistics;" and U.S. Department of Labor, Bureau of Labor Statistics, "Labor Force Statistics From the Current Population Survey."

11. U.S. Department of Labor, Bureau of Labor Statistics, "State and Area Employment, Hours, and Earnings—Virginia;" and U.S. Department of Labor, Bureau of Labor Statistics, "National Employment, Hours, and Earnings."

12. Ibid.

13. U.S. Department of Commerce, Bureau of Economic Analysis, "Regional Accounts Data, Annual State Personal Income."

14. Ibid.

15. John M. Bennett, "Actual General Fund Revenues for FY 2002: Revised Economic Outlook for Revenue Forecast for FY 2003 and 2004," August 19, 2002, 4.

16. "Governance Performance Project 2003 Report Card: Virginia," http://governing.com/gpp/2003/gp3va.htm, 2.

17. John M. Bennett, "Actual General Fund Revenues for FY 2002: Revised Economic Outlook for Revenue Forecast for FY 2003 and 2004," August 19, 2002, 4.

18. http://www. taxadmin.org//fta/rate/ind_inc.html.

19. John M. Bennett, "Actual General Fund Revenues for FY 2002: Revised Economic Outlook for Revenue Forecast for FY 2003 and 2004," 4.

20. Virginia Department of Taxation, "Sales and Use Tax," 1–2, http://www.tax.state.va.us/site.cfm?alias=SalesUseTax.

21. "Governance Performance Project 2003 Report card: Virginia," http://governing.com/gpp/2003/gp3va.htm, 2.

22. John M. Bennett, "Actual General Fund Revenues for FY 2002: Revised Economic Outlook for Revenue Forecast for FY 2003 and 2004," 4.

23. Ibid.

24. "Governance Performance Project 2003 Report Card: Virginia," http://governing.com/gpp/2003/gp3va.htm, 2.

25. Joint Legislative Audit and Review Commission of the Virginia General Assembly, "Spending in State Government: Revenue Forecasting Process," October 9, 2001.

26. Ibid., 10.

27. David A. Von Moll, Comptroller, "Preliminary Annual Report on the Financial Condition of the General Fund for FY 2002," August 15, 2002, 16.

28. Ibid., iii.

29. Ibid.

30. Ibid., 16.

31. Department of Planning and Budget, *The 2002–2004 Executive Budget Document* (December 19, 2001), A-3.

32. Ibid., A-7.

33. David A. Von Moll, Comptroller, "Preliminary Annual Report on the Financial Condition of the General Fund for FY 2002," 16.

34. Ibid.

35. Ibid.

36. Department of Planning and Budget, "State-Wide Summary 1996–1998 Operating/Dollars—(chapter 899, 1998 Acts of Assembly)," and Department of Planning and Budget, "State-Wide Summary 2000–2002 Operating/Dollars—(chapter 814, 2002 Acts of Assembly)."

37. Joint Legislative and Audit Committee, (No. 276). Interim Report: Review of State Spending, January 2002, 1.

38. Craig Timberg, "Gilmore's Successor Faces Mounting Budget Shortfall," *The Washington Post* (September 11, 2001), A1.

39. R. H. Melton, "Va. Legislators Fume at Car-Tax Plan; Bipartisan Opposition Greets Proposal to Use Tobacco Fund to Balance Budgets," *The Washington Post* (December 21, 2000), B 1.

40. Department of Planning and Budget, *The 2002–2004 Executive Budget Document*, A-2.

41. Ibid.

42. Ibid.

43. Michael D. Shear, "In Va. Budget, No Accounting for Change," *The Washington Post* (March 3, 2002), C-4.

44. Ibid., C-4.

45. Scott D. Pattison, "Governor Gilmore's Proposed Executive Budget for the 2000–02 Biennium: A Briefing for the Senate Finance Committee, the House Appropriations Committee, and the House Finance Committee," December 17, 1999, 1.

46. Ibid.

47. Scott D. Pattison, "Governor Gilmore's Proposed Amendments to the 2000–02 Biennial Budget: A Briefing for the Senate Finance Committee, the House Appropriations Committee, and the House Finance Committee," December 20, 2000, 1.

48. Ibid., 12.

49. R. H. Melton, "Gilmore Adds Tobacco Funds to Car-Tax Mix: Settlement Money and Cuts Would Help Finance Repeal," *The Washington Post* (December 19, 2000), B 1.

50. R. H. Melton, "New Math Revives Car-Tax Repeal; Republicans among Critic of Gilmore Plan," *The Washington Post* (December 17, 2000), C1.

51. Ibid.

52. R. H. Melton, "Gilmore Adds Tobacco Fund to Car-Tax Mix: Settlement Money and Cuts Would Help Finance Repeal," *The Washington Post* (December 19, 2000), B1.

53. R. H. Melton, "VA Legislators Fume at Car-Tax Plan; Bipartisan Opposition Greets Proposal to Use Tobacco Funds to Balance Budgets," *The Washington Post* (December 21, 2000), B 1.

54. Ibid.

55. Spencer S. Hsu and R. H. Melton, "Va.'s Car-Tax Cut Is Ready to Roll," *The Washington Post* (April 25, 1998), A1.

56. R. H. Melton, "Senator Stands Firm on Car Tax; Finance Chairman Vows to Keep Fighting Gilmore on Budget," *The Washington Post* (March 1, 2001), B 9.

57. Department of Planning and Budget, "Governor's Actions to Balance the State Budget," March 12, 2001, 1.

58. Ibid., 3.

59. R. H. Melton, "Key Senator Rejects Proposal for Raises; Plan Would Pay for Salaries and Fund 70% Car-Tax Cut This Year and Next," *The Washington Post* (April 6, 2001), B 7.

60. Ibid.

61. R. H. Melton, "Virginia Budget Session Collapses; Car-Tax Dispute's Political Price Looms for GOP," *The Washington Post* (May 10, 2001), A 1.

62. John W. Forbes, "Actual Fiscal Year 2001 Revenues and the State of the Virginia Economy: A Presentation to the Senate Finance, House Finance, and House Appropriations Committees," August 21, 2001.

63. Ibid., 13.

64. Craig Timberg and William Branigin, "Gilmore Returns Fire in Budget Clash: Governor Call Legislators' Assessment 'Premature,' Revives GMU Project," *The Washington Post* (August 22, 2001), B-1.

65. Ibid.

66. Michael D. Shear, "In Va. Budget, No Accounting for Change," *The Washington Post* (March 3, 2002), C-4.

67. R. H. Melton, "Virginia Leaders Warn of Shortfall," *The Washington Post* (August 21, 2001), A1.

68. Ibid.

69. Ibid., A7.

70. Ibid., A1.

71. Craig Timberg and William Branigin, "Gilmore Returns Fire in Budget Clash," *The Washington Post* (August 22, 2001), B1.

72. Ibid.

73. A marvelous discussion of the use of symbols to threaten or reassure can be found in Murray Edelman's books, *Politics as Symbolic Action*, and *The Symbolic Uses of Politics*.

74. John W. Forbes, "Actual Fiscal Year 2001 Revenues and the State of the Virginia Economy," August 20, 2001, 10.

75. Department of Budget and Planning, *The 2002–2004 Executive Budget Document*, A-25.

76. Legislative Information System, "2002–2004 Budget Process," at http://leg2.state.va.us/MoneyWeb.NSF/sb2002.

77. Ibid. It is important to note that there appear to be important differences between these figures and data contained in *The 2002–2004 Executive Budget Document*.

78. Department of Budget and Planning, *The 2002–2004 Executive Budget Document*, A-8.

79. Ibid.

80. Ibid., A-7.

81. Legislative Information System, "2002–04 Budget Process."

82. R. H. Melton, "State's Newest Budget Crisis Promises a Defining Moment for Warner," *The Washington Post* (September 19, 2002), T2.

83. Richard D. Brown, "Governor Warner's Proposed Amendments to the 2002–2004 Biennial Budget," December 20, 2002.

# CHAPTER 13

# Wisconsin: Institutions, Processes, and Policies

*James K. Conant*

Among the areas of state government budgeting that have been of interest to scholars are the way in which the institutional (formal) powers of governors and legislatures are distributed, the process through which budget decisions are made, the systems that support budgetary decision-making, intergovernmental relationships and fund transfers, the structure of state revenues and state expenditures, and the fiscal climate in which budget deliberations take place.[1] In this study of Wisconsin budgeting, each of these areas is examined. The principal objectives of this chapter are to highlight some of the distinctive features of Wisconsin budgeting, identify ways in which these features can create an interesting dynamic in the budgetary process, and describe and analyze some of the consequences these distinctive features have on budgetary outcomes.

## EXECUTIVE–LEGISLATIVE RELATIONS

The relative degree of influence exercised by a governor or legislature in the state budgetary process depends on a number of factors, including formal powers, the party line-up in the legislature, the fiscal climate of the times, the influence of various interest groups, journalistic coverage of the budget process, and public opinion. Of these factors, formal power is often the most important. The formal powers that governors and legislatures can employ in the budgetary process are established in state constitutions and state statutes. Because the distribution of these powers varies from state to state, states can be placed along a continuum that has a dominant governor at one end and a dominant legislature at the other end. In the middle of this continuum are the states that have a relatively even balance in the distribution of formal powers.

**Figure 13.1**
**Formal Institutional Power in the State Budgetary Process**

Governor Dominant                                                                 Legislature Dominant
|-----**---------------------------------------------------|---------------------------------------------------|
            Wisconsin


In this classification scheme, Wisconsin must be placed close to one end of the continuum, among the states where the governor has dominant formal power in the budgetary process.[2] An illustration of the separation of power continuum, and Wisconsin's location on that continuum is provided in Figure 13.1.

## Formal Powers and Executive Dominance

The key to the Wisconsin governor's formal power is the partial veto. The partial veto is a more powerful and flexible tool than the item veto, which is available to governors in approximately forty states.[3] The partial veto gives the Wisconsin governor the power to cross out or veto: (1) any part of a line in the state budget bill; (2) a whole line in the budget bill; or (3) a series of lines that are related to appropriations. For example, the partial veto can be used to reduce a $100,000,000 appropriation in the budget bill to a $1 appropriation by striking out all of the zeros. Thus, the program for which the appropriation was intended can be left on the books, but the money needed to run the program is deleted.

The partial veto was added to the Wisconsin's Constitution in 1930 through the amendment process.[4] During the 1920s, efforts were made at both the national and state levels to improve budgetary processes. A key thrust of these "reform" efforts was to give the chief executive more formal power and thus a more important role in the budgetary process. In Wisconsin, supporters of the partial veto amendment argued that this tool was essential for controlling wasteful pork barrel spending by the state legislature.

It is worth noting that the eventual winner of the 1930 gubernatorial election, Philip La Follette, opposed the partial veto amendment on the grounds that it would give the governor too much power. Despite the favorable public vote on the amendment during the 1930 election, La Follette remained true to his original position on the partial veto and used the new power sparingly. Equally important, he set a precedent that most governors followed for the next 50 years, that is, the partial veto was used in a conservative manner.

In the early 1970s, however, Governor Patrick J. Lucey (Democrat) broke with tradition and began to employ the partial veto with greater frequency. Generally speaking, Lucey justified his use of the item veto on economic or fiscal grounds (saving money). Members of the opposition party in the legislature, however, were quick to complain that the governor was using the partial veto for partisan purposes. In retrospect, it does appear that, at least some of the time, Lucey used the partial veto in a manner that fell outside the boundaries of restraining "legislative pork."

Lucey's successors in the governorship, Democrat Martin Schreiber, Republican Lee Dreyfus, and Democrat Tony Earl, incrementally expanded the use of the partial veto. Then, in the late 1980s, Republican Governor Tommy Thompson dramatically expanded the use of this tool. During the 1980s, it was the Democrats in the state legislature, rather than the Republicans, who complained that the governor was using the partial veto as a partisan tool.

One of the key questions budgetary scholars asked about the item veto during the 1970s and the 1980s was whether it was used primarily as a tool of fiscal restraint or as a tool of partisanship.[5] A third question worthy of consideration is whether governors used the item veto as a policymaking tool. A formal study of the use of the partial veto in Wisconsin was conducted by examining the budgetary process during the 10-year period from 1975 through 1985.[6]

The author of the Wisconsin study concluded that governors had used the partial veto "primarily as a tool for policymaking and partisan advantage rather than of fiscal restraint."[7] The author also noted, however, that the partial veto had been used as a tool of fiscal restraint, saving "the state treasury from a low of $493,000 ... in 1983–1985 to a high of nearly $200 million ... in 1981–1983."[8]

Some of the ways in which Wisconsin's governors have used the partial veto for policy-making and partisan purposes are worth noting. During modern times, for example, Wisconsin governors have used the partial veto to delete specific words, phrases, or even sections of legislative provisions attached to an appropriation. By doing so, governors may have changed the scope or the direction of the governmental activity intended by the legislature. Governors have also used the partial veto to create governmental activity not supported by the legislature, to expand the scope of existing governmental activity, and to redirect governmental action.

Recent governors, particularly Tommy Thompson, have also used the partial veto to create public law without legislative activity or intent; they have done so by selectively deleting words and letters on consecutive pages of the budget bill. The remaining letters and words then form new sentences that may have meaning neither intended nor imagined by the legislature. Unless the item veto is overridden, the governor has essentially written new law and assumed the powers of both the legislature and the executive.

### Legislative Response: Frustration, Acquiescence, and Reaction

While such use (or abuse) of the partial veto power has sparked intense disputes between Wisconsin governors and the legislature, governors usually win the battle and the war. In order to overturn a partial veto, two-thirds of both legislative houses must vote for an override. As a practical matter, it is not particularly difficult for governors to find a sufficient number of elected officials from their own party to secure the one-third minority needed in each house to block an override attempt. By casting their lot with the governor on these matters, however, legislators may weaken the institution of which they are members. As members of the legislature themselves sometimes acknowledge, the institutional power game is a zero-sum game. When governors gain power, legislators lose power.[9]

Moreover, the Wisconsin Supreme Court has been very reluctant to intervene in these legislative/executive disputes, even when it was asked to do so by a group of legislators. For example, in 1986, a bipartisan group of legislators challenged Governor Tommy Thompson's use of the partial veto to create new legislation. In 1988, the Court decided, by a vote of 4 to 3, against the legislators.[10]

Frustrated by the court decision, some of these same legislators decided to take an alternative approach to contain gubernatorial power in the budgetary process. They sponsored an amendment to the State Constitution. The amendment was commonly known as the "Vanna White" amendment. It was named after the female celebrity in the television show called *Wheel of Fortune*, who turns the squares on a game board to display individual letters in a word. It is, of course, up to the contestants to figure out what word can be made out of the individual letters.

The Vanna White amendment explicitly prohibited the governor from creating new legislation by selectively striking out existing words or letters in the budget bill. Both houses of the legislature passed the amendment in 1987. It passed both houses of the legislature a second time in 1989, and in 1990 it was formally adopted by a popular vote of 387,068 to 252,481.[11]

Nine years after this amendment was approved, the State Supreme Court made a decision that further circumscribed the chief executive's use of the partial veto. In *Risser v. Klauser (1997)*,[12] the court decided that the governor could not use the partial veto on revenue items that were contained in the budget bill. In its decision, the court agreed with the plaintiffs, and it told Governor Thompson that the partial veto could only be applied to appropriations. Consequently, the governor had to restore revenues that he had stricken from the budget with the partial veto.

## BUDGETARY PROCESS

Just as states can be placed along a continuum when attempts are made to define the ways in which formal powers are divided between governors and legislatures, states can also be classified with respect to the requirements and/or limitations they have for the budgetary process. The key to this continuum is the extent to which a state separates or segregates appropriations from policy development.

**Figure 13.2**
**Type of Budgetary Process**

Appropriations Only                                                  Policy and Appropriations
|----------------------------------------------------|----------------------------------------------------**-|
                                                                                        Wisconsin

At one end of the continuum are the states in which the budgetary process is limited to appropriations for existing legislation. Existing scholarship shows that states such as Colorado and Pennsylvania can be placed in this category.[13] At the other end of the continuum are the states that fold appropriations and policy development into the same (budgetary) process. New York, Ohio, California, and Oregon can be placed near this end of the continuum.[14] In the middle of the continuum are the states that permit some policy amendment or development within the appropriations process.

Wisconsin has to be placed at one end of this continuum, as illustrated in Figure 13.2. Specifically, in Wisconsin, appropriations and policy development are folded into the budgetary process. The Wisconsin budgetary process operates under a statutory requirement that all legislation with a cost in excess of $100,000 must be included in the budget bill.[15] Furthermore, this statute determines the legislative session clock itself. The legislative session begins with the introduction of the budget bill, and it ends with the passage of the bill.

A related feature that makes budget decision-making in Wisconsin different from budgeting in some other states is the way in which tax policy decision-making is handled. For the most part, amendments to existing tax policy and the development of new tax policy are included in the budget bill. Thus the budgetary process brings together decisionmaking about both revenues and expenditures and, at least in theory, provides a clear-cut mechanism for elected officials to ensure that expected revenues equal anticipated expenditures.

Several other features of the budgetary process are noteworthy in Wisconsin. First, Wisconsin's budget is a biennial budget. In contrast, some states, like the national government, have annual appropriations processes. Second, Wisconsin's biennial budget process is supplemented, by statutory requirement, with an "annual review" or "budget adjustment" bill.[16] The original premise of the annual review bill was that it would be limited to technical corrections in the biennial budget bill. As a matter of practice, however, both governors and legislatures have found this restriction too constraining, and they are now making substantive changes to existing law and adopting new legislation during this session. Thus, the current product of the review process is called the budget adjustment bill.

A fourth feature of the Wisconsin budgetary process worthy of attention is the way in which the legislature makes its decisions. The key decision-making body in the Wisconsin Legislature is the Joint Finance Committee.

This committee consists of nine members of the State Assembly and nine members of the State Senate. The Legislative Fiscal Bureau, a nonpartisan entity, provides staff support for the Joint Finance Committee. The bureau's staff members not only review and critique the governor's budget bill but also identify ways in which legislative preferences might be incorporated into the bill.

After the Joint Finance Committee has completed its work on the budget bill, both houses of the legislature vote on its contents. It is quite common for each house to pass its own version of the budget. A conference committee then crafts a compromise version.

## RATIONAL BUDGETING: SYSTEMS, TOOLS, AND METHODS

Because the demand for state expenditures almost always exceeds the supply of revenue available, budgeting can be viewed as a process of rationing new money in times of economic growth and rationing cuts in times of recession. Thus, the outputs of the budgetary process are often described as incremental increases (or decreases) in programs and agencies budgets.[17] Political factors, including which party holds the governorship, whether the same party controls the legislature, and the relative influence of various interest groups are likely to be the dominant variables shaping the way this rationing takes place in the states at any given time.

Attempts to "reform" budgeting, or to make it a more rational and comprehensive enterprise, have bloomed and faded a number of times at the national and state levels over the past 40 years. Perhaps the most visible and effectively documented of these budget reform efforts was the attempt to install the Planning-Programming Budgeting System (PPBS) at the national level in the 1960s.[18] Among the key presumptions of this system was that budgets would be program-based, rather than agency-based, they would be connected to long-term goals, and individual budgetary decisions would be made on the basis of cost-benefit calculations, rather than political considerations.

In the early 1960s, Wisconsin was among the pioneers of budget reform in the states, as Wisconsin legislators and members of the executive branch attempted to move in the direction of a PPB type system.[19] In 1963, the Legislature's Joint Finance Committee asked the Office of Management, in the Department of Administration, to put the line-item budget they had just approved into a program format.[20] Committee members were so delighted with the new document that they instructed the Office of Management to put all future budgets into a program format.[21]

These actions gave Wisconsin nation-wide visibility, and Wisconsin was one of five states invited to participate in a special initiative directed by Selma J. Mushkin, an economist in the U.S. Bureau of the Budget. Mushkin's mission was to move the PPBS concepts from the Office of Management and Budget (national government) to state and local governments. Thus, the lead figures in Wisconsin's budget reform initiative had the benefit of pooling information with other national, state, and local budget officials.[22]

By 1965, a program structure for Wisconsin's state budget was established, and the focus of the budget deliberations moved from "items 'bought' (input orientation) to the goals, objectives, and accomplishments to be attained (output orientation) as a result of a given expenditure level."[23] Additionally, a Legislative Audit Bureau was established to conduct financial and performance audits.[24]

During the later part of the 1960s and the early 1970s, an effort was made to connect statewide, long-term goals (planning) to budget decision-making. Governor Warren Knowles moved the statewide planning unit from the Department of Development to the Department of Administration, which provided proximity to the Wisconsin's Office of Management and budget preparation. Additionally, an attempt was made to create, in the Office of Management, the technical and analytic capability required to make a program or planning-program approach to budgeting work.

By the mid-1970s, however, key officials in Wisconsin's executive branch concluded that statewide planning could not be effectively integrated into the budgetary process, and the value attached to planning declined. Nevertheless, the program structure and the use of program budgeting were sustained. One noteworthy result of the budget reform initiatives was the increased influence the chief executive gained over the executive branch agencies and in the budgetary process.[25] A second result was that the legislative branch gained an important new tool to affect budget decision making via the performance audits conducted by the Legislative Audit Bureau.

During the late 1970s and 1980s, additional efforts were made to strengthen the legislative branch's ability to make rational budget decisions. Specifically, efforts were made to strengthen the Legislative Fiscal Bureau, the legislature's budget office. Additional staff was hired, improved information systems were created, and the Bureau developed the capability to generate its own revenue estimates. All these initiatives yielded substantial dividends as work products became more sophisticated and the Bureau's reputation steadily improved. The growing strength of the Legislative Fiscal Bureau helped the legislature recover some of its currency in the budgetary process, and the Bureau's ability to generate its own revenue estimates gave the legislature the capacity to operate with greater independence from the executive branch.

## Macro Budgeting

Another tool or method for rationalizing budget decision-making that has evolved in Wisconsin over the past 35 years is "macro" budgeting. Macro budgeting involves setting the overall parameters, assumptions, or framework within which all other budget decisions are made. Among other things, this framework may include a definition of how much the state will spend, how the revenues to support that spending will be raised, what the policy priorities will be, and what share of state expenditures each program, agency, or function will be assigned.

The Thompson Administration (1987–2000) was both adept at and aggressive in its use of macro budgeting. One illustration is the way in which the administration decided to allocate shares of the budget to each of the three major functional areas: State Operations, Local Assistance (money for local governments and K-12 schools), and Aids to Individuals and Organizations. In formulating his first biennial budget (1987–1989), Governor Thompson decided to increase the amount of money allocated for Local Assistance (primarily for additional K-12 school aid). He also decided to fund part of this increase by reducing the money allocated to state agencies (State Operations).

In his autobiographical book about his time as governor, Thompson describes the process he used to fund his priorities, "I asked my newly appointed cabinet secretaries to submit a budget spending only 95 percent of what their agency spent the year before . . . I gave each agency a choice: if you don't make the cuts, I'll make them for you."[26]

The 1987–1989 budget was just the opening gambit in Governor Thompson's efforts to define the way in which budget shares were allocated. For example, in the 1995–1997 budget, the governor decided to cover the state's expanded commitment for K-12 schools without a tax increase. The first year (1996) cost of this commitment was an estimated $1.2 billion. Once again, the budget share allocated to State Operations was reduced while the share going to Local Assistance was increased. Thus, in the 1995–1997 budget, Governor Thompson told the state agencies to reduce their expenditures by 5 percent in the first year and 10 percent in the second year of the biennium.[27] Thompson also used $400 million of new state revenue to help cover the costs of the expanded school aids commitment.[28]

### Performance Budgeting

The most recent effort at budget "reform" in Wisconsin was initiated in the legislative branch, but the responsibility for implementation was assigned to the executive branch, particularly the Department of Administration. In the 1999–2001 budget, funding was added to set up a performance measurement budgeting system. Like PPBS, performance budgeting is designed to break the cycle of incremental adjustments by shifting the focus away from incremental increases to weeding out expenditures and programs that do not get "results." Additionally, like zero-base budgeting (ZBB), the base allocation given to an agency or program is neither protected nor secure in performance budgeting.

Although Wisconsin was following, rather than leading, other states in this latest budget "reform" initiative, the system put in place in 2001 highlights the strong institutional capacity that exists in the executive branch agencies in

**Figure 13.3**
**Federal Aid as Percent of State Revenue**

```
Low                                                                    High
|--------------**-------------------------------------|------------------------------------------------|
            Wisconsin
```

general and the Department of Administration in particular. Beginning with the 2001–2003 Executive Budget, an impressive range of performance data and measurements was incorporated into the state's budget documents. These data and measurements can be used by elected officials, administrators, citizens, and the press as a basis for a more informed debate about the results the state is getting for its "investments." The data and measurement also provide a means to have a more rational debate about state priorities.

Whether the promise of the performance measurement system will be realized, however, remains an open question. Like PPBS, a vulnerability of performance measurement budgeting system is its high overhead costs. The performance measurement system will have to penetrate the "bureaucratic routines" of the executive branch agencies and the political routines of top executive branch and legislative decision makers if it is to be sustained. As the academic literature on PPBS showed, it failed in part because it did not penetrate those core decision-making routines.[29] Some members of Wisconsin's executive and legislative branch seem optimistic that this latest budget reform will be successfully implemented. Others, particularly those who are familiar with past reform initiatives like PPBS, seem less optimistic.

## FISCAL FEDERALISM

As the "middleman" in the U.S. intergovernmental system, states look (up) to the national government for financial assistance. In the same way, local governments look (up) to state governments for financial aid. Of course the degree of financial aid that flows from the national government to states varies, just as the amount of financial support that states give to local governments varies. Thus, here again, a continuum can be established for the share of state revenues that come from the national government. At one end are the state's that receive a relatively small share of total revenues from the national government; at the other end are states that receive a relatively large share. The continuum listing Wisconsin's position with respect to aid from the national government is shown in Figure 13.3.

On the continuum, Wisconsin falls among the states whose share of revenue from the national government is comparatively low. For example, in FY 1999, only 19 percent of Wisconsin's revenue came from the national government.[30] In contrast, the average figure for the states in 1999 was more than several percentage points higher, with some states getting considerably more than

25 percent. The fact that Wisconsin's share is comparatively low among the states does not mean that the revenue from the national government is unimportant. Indeed, this revenue serves a variety of purposes in Wisconsin that otherwise might not be served in the same manner or same degree.

From an evaluative point of view, however, the state's fiscal position vis-à-vis the national government could be regarded in at least two different ways. On the negative side, the relatively low level of federal support means that Wisconsin has to raise a higher share of what it spends in a number of key functional areas than many other states. In turn, this means that Wisconsin has to tax its citizens at higher rates, charge more for services delivered, or both. On the positive side, however, one might conclude that Wisconsin is less dependent on the national government's generosity than other states. Less dependency may leave the state freer to pursue its own objectives, and it may reduce the state's risk of large losses of national government funds if national policy changes.

For the most part, the comparatively low portion of revenue provided to Wisconsin by the national government has been an ongoing source of frustration for Wisconsin's governors, legislators, and congressional delegation. In short the state's elected officials have usually focused on the costs, rather than the benefits of the situation. This is not surprising, because elected officials tend to prefer lower taxes for citizens to higher taxes.

During the 1970s, 1980s, and 1990s, a focal point for the frustration of elected officials in Wisconsin was the relatively low share the state receives of federal gasoline tax money collected in the state. Specifically, Wisconsin received only 85 to 88 cents for every dollar of federal gasoline tax collected and sent to Washington DC, while some states received more than one dollar for each dollar they collected. Wisconsin's small return on its collection of federal gasoline taxes has commonly been viewed as a powerful constraint on the state's ability to develop and maintain its interstate highways.

It is worth noting, however, that Wisconsin's position did improve in the most recent version of the surface transportation act. It now appears that the state will be getting 92 or 93 cents for every dollar of federal gasoline tax collected. A coalition of states that had previously been losers under the older versions of this act had to work together to bring about the change. During his tenure as governor of Wisconsin, Tommy Thompson not only focused the attention of Wisconsin's congressional delegation on this task but also worked with the governors of other disadvantaged states to build the coalition.

Other areas in which the flow of federal funds into Wisconsin is comparatively low include expenditures for national forests and parks, farm price support, and defense funding. It is important to note, however, that national government expenditures in these areas do not flow from the national budget into the state budget. Rather, the flow of money is from the U.S. government into the state's economy in the form of employment or subsidies. For example, Wisconsin does not have a single military base for active duty personnel, thus

**Figure 13.4**
**Percentage of Wisconsin State Expenditures Going to School Districts and Local Governments**

```
Low                                                                        High
|----------------------------------------------|---------------------------------------------**-|
                                                                    Wisconsin
```

Wisconsin's share of defense spending is very small. Additionally, because less than 4 percent of Wisconsin's land is owned by the national government,[31] very little of the money the national government spends for national parks or forests flows into Wisconsin. Finally, Wisconsin has been severely disadvantaged in the milk price support system for the past 50 years, because the subsidy rate is calculated on the basis of the distance a dairy farm is from Eau Claire Wisconsin. The greater the distance from Eau Claire, the greater the amount of subsidy. In sum, all of these factors add to the frustration felt in Wisconsin over the state's relatively poor position in the flow of national government funds to the fifty states.

## The State and Local Government Relationship

Despite the fact that the state of Wisconsin has not fared particularly well in the distribution of national government revenues, the state has been very generous in the way it shares with local governments the revenues it raises through state taxes. Less than 30 years after Wisconsin achieved statehood in 1848, it began to share state raised revenues with local schools. That sharing of revenues was expanded to municipalities and counties in 1911, when state voters adopted a constitutional amendment that provided for an income tax. Another benchmark was established in the early 1960s, when the state adopted a sales tax. Revenues from this source were also shared with local governments.

Wisconsin currently shares more of the general revenue it raises with schools and local governments than any state except Michigan.[32] In the FY 2002 budget, 60.2 percent of the state's General Purpose Revenue was distributed to local governments.[33] Twenty-three percent of the state's General Purpose Revenue was spent on state operations (state agencies and state programs), while 16.8 percent was distributed to individuals and organizations.[34]

A continuum can be established for the percentage of local government revenues that flow from a state government to its local governments. Once again, the continuum can run from a smaller share to a larger share. The continuum for state aid to local governments is shown as Figure 13.4, and Wisconsin's place on that continuum is clearly marked at the high end.

Simply on the basis of the way state funds are allocated, one might conclude that the state's elected officials decided some time in the past that their principal function was to raise revenues for local governments. The presumption here is that state officials must make it possible for local governments to deliver services and function effectively without placing a heavy tax burden on local property owners.

Given this presumption, it is probably no surprise that the single largest allocation of the state's General Purpose Revenue in the state's FY 2002 budget was school aids. The second largest allocation of General Purpose Revenue went to municipalities and counties through the shared revenue fund.[35] Other funds, such as the General Property Tax Relief Fund also provided support for local governments. Still other state revenue was dedicated to local vocational technical school districts.

An alternative causal explanation for the state's generosity to local governments might be built upon an interest group approach to policymaking. In the halls of the State Capitol, one can find active and effective lobbies for local governments in the form of teachers unions, municipal associations, and a county association. Additionally, the teachers unions in particular make an effort to turn out the vote at election time.

Undoubtedly, these public sector lobbies have contributed to the decisions made repeatedly by the state's governor and legislatures to give top priority to local governments. Yet, the state's generosity to local governments preceded these modern day lobbies, and the commitment itself seems to be deeply rooted in Wisconsin's progressive tradition.

It is also important to note, however, that there are critics of the state's approach to local governments both within and outside the state. Perhaps the most common reason for the criticism is that state tax burdens must be relatively high to sustain the enormous amount of revenue required to maintain state commitments to local governments. This situation is demonstrated in part by the fact that Wisconsin's tax burdens have been among the top ten states for most of the past 30 years.

Second, the strong commitment to local governments means that the state may have difficulty supporting its own programs. The greater the share of state revenues that goes to local governments, the smaller the share that is available for state programs. Thus, even the state's large and politically powerful university system may not get the level of state funding it wants because it must compete with other state programs for funds after most of the state's general revenues are distributed to local governments.[36]

A third potential problem with the extraordinary commitment the state makes to local governments is that state lawmakers can lose control of state expenditures. For example, if the state guarantees funding for 66 percent of K-12 school costs, the amount of new money the state must raise each year to sustain that percentage can crowd out all other programs or even require tax increases. This vulnerability is particularly apparent during times of economic recession.

Fourth, the state's generosity may generate some unintended consequences, including higher levels of local spending than would otherwise be the case. This is not difficult to understand, because local government officials might tend to see state money as free money. The same phenomena may be present at the state level at least some of the time, when money flows from the national government to the states.

Finally, a fifth problem that may result from the state's generosity to its local governments is that state officials may decide to control state expenditures by limiting local spending and local revenue raising. Indeed, this scenario has played out multiple times over the past 30 years or so, as the governor and legislature have imposed expenditure controls on schools and levy (or revenue) limits on municipal and county governments.

While levy limits and expenditure controls may constrain state costs somewhat, they also take away the local discretion that presumably state programs were designed to enhance in the first place. This Catch-22 type situation is a source of frustration for both state and local officials, and it creates extraordinary pressures for "exception" decisions to these controls. Some local officials also maintain that these controls lead to highly irrational decisions by local governments.

## REVENUES, EXPENDITURES, AND ECONOMIC CYCLES

Wisconsin's budgetary expenditures are supported by state revenues from both tax and nontax sources. State tax collections in FY 2002 totaled just over $10 billion, and they made up approximately 90 percent of total General Purpose Revenues ($11.1 billion).[37] For some important budgeting purposes, General Purpose Revenues (GPR) are referred to as General Fund Revenues; thus the term General Fund appears to be interchangeable with the GPR budget.[38] In fact, however, for accounting purposes, the General Fund Revenues totaled $20.9 billion, and they included GPR, Federal Revenues, Program Revenues (mostly user fees), and other Transfer Funds.

In FY 2002, state taxes made up more than 48.1 percent of the FY 2002 General Fund Revenues, Federal Revenues made up 34 percent, and Program Revenues made up approximately 17.9 percent.[39] In addition to the General Fund, total state revenues included Transportation Funds, Conservation Funds, and other funds. The revenues in these funds totaled almost $ 6 billion in FY 2002.[40]

The primary sources of state tax revenue in Wisconsin are the Personal Income Tax, the Sales and Use Tax, and the Corporate Income and Franchise Tax. Utility Taxes and Inheritance Taxes also contribute to the state's tax revenue. Wisconsin was the first state to establish a progressive income tax (1911), and this tax source generated almost 50 percent of state tax revenue in FY 2002. The Sales and Use Tax and the Corporate Income Tax generated approximately 37 percent and 5 percent, respectively.

The fact that Wisconsin has relied on a variety of state taxes for most of the twentieth century, rather than a single tax or a couple of the major taxes, makes it different from some states. For example, some states have relied heavily on a single general tax, such as Florida with the sales tax, or other specialized taxes, such as Texas with taxes on oil production. The emphasis on tax diversity in Wisconsin is partly a matter of policy choice and partly a function of Wisconsin's economy. For example, Wisconsin does not have a Disney World, so it could not generate the level of sales tax that Florida can. Furthermore, the state has a long-standing commitment to progressive taxation, and reliance on the sales tax as the primary or even single tax source would run counter to the state's political heritage.

The extent to which the state's tax structure and tax revenue is adequate, more than adequate (the state runs surpluses), or inadequate (the state runs deficits), however, depends on two key factors: (1) tax and expenditure policy decisions Wisconsin officials make as part of each biennial budget; and (2) the fluctuations of the economic (business) cycle.

As noted earlier in this chapter, Wisconsin's elected officials have made an extraordinary financial commitment to local governments and to K-12 schools. Wisconsin's governors and legislators have also generously supported the University of Wisconsin System, natural resource protection and management, health care and social services, and highways. Among the reasons for this strong support is that state citizens tend to demand and expect a high level of service.

When the state's expenditure commitments are added together, a substantial revenue stream is required to support and sustain those commitments. Indeed, because elected officials enacted a series of new spending commitments during the 1990s that totaled nearly $2 billion, a steadily growing revenue stream was required. In 1997 and 1999, however, state officials made cuts in state tax revenues that totaled $2.6 billion.[41] The net result was the creation of a permanent imbalance between expenditures and revenues. This type of imbalance is often referred to as a structural deficit. The scope and scale of this structural deficit is outlined in a 2002 paper published by a scholar at the University of Wisconsin-Madison.[42]

### Economic Cycles, Policy Decisions, Budget Surpluses, and Budget Deficits

In Wisconsin, as in all other states, the fiscal climate can have a big impact on the state budget and budget decision-making. In turn, the factor that usually has the biggest impact on the state's fiscal climate is the national economy. When the economy is growing, the state's revenue stream is likely to expand as personal income, corporate income, and sales tax collections grow. Rapid growth of state tax revenues can create a budgetary surplus.

On the other hand, when there is little economic growth (and little inflation) revenue growth tends to stall, and when recessions occur state tax collections may actually decline. Depending on the length and severity of the recession, the state is likely to face a budgetary deficit, the size of which may vary from small to very large. Deficits that emerge from a recessionary phase of the business cycle are often called "cyclical deficits."

The fiscal stress Wisconsin experienced during the national recession of the early 1990s was cyclical. That is to say, Wisconsin had to deal with a potential cyclical deficit, as revenue growth slowed and expenditure requirements rose. The scale of the fiscal stress Wisconsin experienced during that recession, however, was relatively mild in comparison to other states.[43]

The relationship between the national and state economies has been the subject of research by economists at the University of Wisconsin-Madison. Among the important findings from these studies is that Wisconsin's economy tends to slide into recession 3 to 6 months after the national economy is in recession, but the recovery cycle also tends to lag behind by approximately the same time frame.

The relationship between national economic growth, state economic growth, and state revenues has also been studied. Among the findings of such studies is that relatively modest changes in economic activity can have a surprisingly large impact on state revenues. For example, one study showed that the estimated cost of recession in the 1991–1993 budget was approximately $400 million in revenue, when compared to what would have been generated if state employment had grown by only 2 percent.[44] If the assumption of more rapid growth (comparable to the pre-recession period) was used, the recessionary price tag grew to almost $900 million of lost revenue.

Ironically, periods of economic growth can also lead to fiscal stress in state budgeting. For example, good economic times and the revenue growth that usually accompanies them can lead to spending levels that might not otherwise have occurred. Although program expansion may seem relatively painless in good economic times, the use of what might be considered "short-term surplus" revenues to permanently expand state expenditures can add to a state's fiscal stress during periods of slow economic growth or recession.

Likewise, good economic times can stimulate pressure for tax cuts, and short-term decision-making on taxes can have significant long-term effects. For example, the permanent loss of state revenue from a tax cut may create a significant hole in a state's revenues during less favorable economic times. Additionally, even in times of moderate growth, revenue reduction may mean that a state cannot deliver services that state lawmakers would like to deliver without raising taxes or cutting other expenditures.

In short, economic cycles consisting of rapid economic growth followed by economic recession can, all by themselves, create a boom and bust cycle in a state. The effects of these economic cycles are often made worse by decisions that exacerbate or exaggerate those cycles. Nevertheless, lawmakers in the states have often been unable to resist the "opportunity" to cut taxes or substantially increase spending during good times. Unfortunately, the longer-term structural imbalance these decisions create between ongoing revenues

**Figure 13.5**
**Economic (Business) Cycle and the Wisconsin Budget Boom and Bust Cycle**

```
Economic (Business) and
Budget
Boom                           ******              *********************
|------------|--------------------------------|-----------------------------------------------|
Bust     1983-1985                     1991-1993                          2001-2003
         (Severe)                      (Moderate)                         (Severe)
```

and ongoing expenditures may not be visible until an economic downturn occurs.

In the 20 years between 1970 and 1990, Wisconsin's elected officials fell into the jaws of the economic boom and bust trap several times. The effects of this trap were felt during the 1975–1977 budget process, the 4-year period that included the 1981–1983 and 1983–1985 budget processes, and the 1991–1993 budget process. The points of time at which each of the three most recent "trap doors" opened are shown in Figure 13.5.

In each of these cases, decisions made during good economic times to increase spending levels, cut taxes, or both, had significant consequences during the recessions that followed. In each of these cases, the state faced current year fiscal deficits. The state also had to go through biennial decision-making processes in which program reductions were required and new or expanded activity had to be postponed. Of these three "trap door" situations, the 1981–1985 case was the most severe, because the fiscal crisis had both cyclical and structural components.

## The 2001–2003 Budget Deficit

The most recent opening of the boom and bust "trap door" was visible in 2001, as state lawmakers struggled to balance the FY 2001–2003 budget. In January of that year, the budget deficit for the 2001–2003 biennium was estimated to be $2.4 billion. Of this total, $1.1 billion was described in state budget documents as a structural deficit carried over from the 1999–2001 budget, and $1.3 billion was defined as revenue shortfall.[45]

It is worth noting that extraordinary tactics were required to secure passage of the FY 2001–2003 biennial budget bill in August of 2001. In order to bring estimated spending into balance with estimated revenues, state lawmakers had cut expenditures, and, because there was no money in the state's Rainy-Day-Fund, they chose to use $450 million of the tobacco settlement money to supplement state revenues.[46] There were some who argued that these funds should be used over the 25 years of the tobacco settlement to pay for smoking-related medical care and to fund a campaign to prevent children and teens from smoking, but these purposes gave way to political expediency.

Although the governor and state legislators apparently believed that they had fixed the 2001–2003 budget problem with the passage of the biennial budget bill, more trouble lay just ahead. Less than 6 months after the 2001–2003 budget bill was passed, Governor McCallum announced in January 2002, that the state was facing an additional $1.1 billion deficit in the 2001–2003 budget. When this new figure was added to the budget shortfall projected in January 2001, the biennial problem totaled $3.5 billion.

In order to address this new $1.1 billion fiscal problem, the governor put forward a "Budget Reform Bill." The governor's recommendations for addressing the additional red ink now projected included more spending cuts and more use of the Tobacco Settlement Funds. As the contents of the final 2002 budget adjustment bill show, many legislators decided that the size of the new budget gap left them with no other viable option for balancing the budget than using up the tobacco settlement funds. Raising taxes was viewed politically as a poison pill, and there was a limit to the expenditure reductions they were willing to make. Having used the tobacco funds in this manner, however, lawmakers were reducing their options for the future.[47]

## The 2003–2005 Budget Deficit

In November 2002, Democrat Jim Doyle defeated incumbent Scott McCallum (Republican) for the governorship. In February 2003, Doyle reported that the size of the projected budget deficit for the 2003–2005 biennium was $3.2 billion.[48] During the 2002 election campaign, Doyle promised not to increase taxes as a means to address the state's budget woes. This pledge, along with the fact that the state's tobacco settlement funds were largely used up, meant that Doyle's February 2002 budget recommendations had to include a wide range of deep budget cuts and fee increases.

In the *Budget in Brief* for 2003–2005, Governor Doyle included a stinging criticism of the state's fiscal management by the previous administrations and legislatures. Specifically, in a section titled "Restoring Fiscal Discipline," Doyle says:

For over 20 years, Wisconsin has had a significant gap between ongoing expenditures and revenues. That gap is manifest in the perennial deficit that we must disclose under generally accepted accounting principles (GAAP). These principles represent "truth-in-budgeting." They also shine a bright light on the many tricks used to portray a "balanced" state budget over the past 20 years. These tricks ran from shifting the entire shared revenue payment from one fiscal year to the next in the early 1980s to the school aid payment shifts made in the mid-1990s in order to fund two-thirds school costs.

Wisconsin has also had a Budget Stabilization ("rainy day") Fund on the books since the last series of budget crises in the mid-1980s. Building such a fund requires strong financial discipline. Unfortunately, no legislative action has ever been taken to divert monies into that fund.

The economic boom of the 1990s masked these underlying structural problems in the state's budget. Decisions on addressing these problems were deferred as decision-makers became convinced that the economic cycle only pointed up. Ironically, the surpluses created during the boom years could have been used to shore up these weaknesses in the state budget. By the time the boom became a bust, the surpluses had been spent and the structural weaknesses remained.[49]

## CONCLUSION

Wisconsin's budget and budgetary process have a number of characteristics that are unusual or even distinctive among the states, and the interaction among these characteristics creates some interesting dynamics and yields some interesting outcomes. For example, the governor's formal powers give the head of the executive branch a dominant position in the budgetary process, and that position is reinforced by a budgetary process that incorporates all significant tax and expenditure policy decision-making.

The chief executive's dominance gives the occupants of this office unusual opportunities to shape state tax and expenditure policy. This remarkable power, however, also places an unusually high level of responsibility upon Wisconsin's governor. Perhaps the most important elements of this responsibility are: (1) the need to avoid actions that relegate the state legislature to a nominal role in budget and policy decision-making, and (2) the need to ensure that the state's short-term and long-term fiscal condition is sound. Among recent governors, Governor Anthony Earl (1983–87) seems to stand out as a chief executive who took great care with both elements of his responsibility. In contrast, Governor Tommy Thompson (1988-2001) rejected the first and fell short in the second.

Indeed, the best grade that can be given for the record of fiscal management during the 1990s is "poor." as shown by the budget crisis that began in Wisconsin in 2001 and continued beyond 2003. The structural dimension of the FY 2001–2003 and 2003–2005 budget problems was largely the result of gubernatorial and the legislative policy decisions made during the 1990s that added more than $2 billion worth of expenditure increases to the base budget and cut taxes by almost $2.6 billion. If the structural dimension of this crisis had been avoided, both the severity and duration of fiscal stress the state began encountering in 2001 would have been substantially reduced.

Furthermore, the cyclical dimension of the recent budget crisis could have been substantially blunted if the state had put money into its Rainy Day Fund during the late 1980s and 1990s. Governor Earl and the state legislature established a Rainy Day Fund in 1986, when the severe fiscal problems they had to confront in the 1983–1985 and 1985–1987 budgets had been fully addressed. Yet, over the next 14 years, no money was allocated for the fund.

Consequently, when the sharp cyclical downturn began in 2001, a key tool that could have been used to reduce its effects was not available.

Wisconsin's tardiness in establishing a Rainy Day Fund and, even worse, its failure to place money in the fund after it was established, seem rather surprising in a state known for both its progressive approaches to governance and marvelous institutional capacity. Likewise, the huge structural deficit that resulted from an overly aggressive drive to cut taxes and expand spending seems odd for the same reasons. Unfortunately, these dual failures in basic fiscal discipline resulted in a 2001–2005 budget crisis that will have significant, adverse effects on the state's institutions, processes, policies, and, most importantly, its people, for many years to come.

## NOTES

1. These topics are covered in a number of books and articles on state budgeting. A convenient source for an examination of several of these topics in eight states is: Edward J. Clynch and Thomas P. Lauth (Eds.), *Governors, Legislatures, and Budgets: Diversity Across the American States* (New York: Greenwood Press, 1991).

2. In some studies of governors' formal powers, Wisconsin's governor has been placed closer to the middle of the continuum than the (dominant power) end of the continuum. As shown in this paper, however, there are good reasons to place the governor near the dominant pole when it comes to formal power in the budgetary process.

3. Glenn Abney and Thomas P. Lauth, "The Line-Item Veto in the State: An Instrument for Fiscal Restraint or Partisanship?" *Public Administration Review*, 45(3) (May/June 1985), 372–377.

4. Wisconsin's constitutional amendment process requires that both houses of the legislature pass a proposed amendment in two consecutive sessions before it goes to a vote of the people. Both houses of the legislative approved the proposed amendment in 1927 and again in 1929. In the 1930 popular vote 255,622 favored the amendment and 153,703 opposed it. See *Wisconsin Blue Book*, 1999–2000 (Madison, WI: Joint Committee on Legislative Organization, 1999), p. 193.

5. Glenn Abney and Thomas P. Lauth, "The Line-Item Veto in the State: An Instrument for Fiscal Restraint or Partisanship?" *Public Administration Review*, 45(3) (May/June 1985), 372–377.

6. James J. Gosling, "Wisconsin Item-Veto Lessons," *Public Administration Review*, 46(4) (July/August 1986), 292–300.

7. Ibid., 297.

8. Ibid.

9. For a (former) legislators view on this topic, see Tom Loftus, *The Art of Legislative Politics*. (Washington, DC: CQ Press, 1991).

10. *State Ex. Rel. State Senate v. Thompson*, 144 Wis.2d. 429 (Wis. 1988).

11. *Wisconsin Blue Book*, 1999–2000 (Madison, WI: Joint Committee on Legislative Organization, 1999), p. 196.

12. *Risser v. Klauser*, 207 Wis.2d. 674 (1996).

13. James G. Gosling, *Budgetary Politics in American Governments* (White Plains, NY: Longman Publishing Group, 1992), pp. 103–104.

14. Ibid.

15. John Torphy, "Wisconsin's Budget," in James K. Conant, Robert H. Haveman, and Jack Huddleston (Eds.), *Dollars and Sense: Policy Choices and the Wisconsin Budget*, vol. 2 (Madison, WI: The Robert La Follette Institute of Public Affairs, 1991).

16. The original title was *Annual Review Session*, but the current title is *Budget Adjustment*.

17. This view has been regularly articulated in the academic literature, particularly since the publication of Aaron Wildavsky's, *The Politics of the Budgetary Process* (Boston, MA: Little Brown, 1964).

18. For an excellent listing of academic works on PPBS, see George J. Gordon, *Public Administration in America*, 4th edition (New York: St. Martin's Press, 1992), p. 383, endnote 25.

19. Information about budget reform initiatives in other states can be found in a number of sources, including: Alan Schick, *Budget Innovation in the States* (Washington, DC: Brookings, 1977), and Robert D. Lee, Jr., and Ronald W. Johnson, *Public Budgeting Systems*, 4th edition (Rockville, MD: Aspen Publishing, 1989).

20. Interview with Wayne McGown, Director of Wisconsin's Office of Management from 1963 to 1967, and Secretary of the Department of Administration from 1967 to 1971.

21. At approximately the same time, the Kellett Commission, a Blue Ribbon Commission charged with developing recommendations for improving government performance, also recommended that the state move to a program or planning-program type budget.

22. Interview with Wayne McGown.

23. Dale Cattanach and Terry A. Rhodes, "The Budget-State Fiscal Policy Document," *Wisconsin Blue Book 1970* (Madison, WI: Wisconsin Legislative Reference Bureau, 1970), p. 270.

24. Ibid., 271.

25. Specifically, the state's chief executive not only had more information about programs and agency budgets flowing in but also had much greater capacity to analyze agency and program budget requests. Most of that capacity was located in the state budget office.

26. Tommy G. Thompson, *Power to the People: An American State at Work* (New York: Harper Collins Publishers, 1966), p. 128.

27. Ibid., 140–141.

28. Ibid., 143.

29. Perhaps the best known of the academic articles containing this argument is: Alan Schick's, "A Death in the Bureaucracy: The Demise of Federal PPB," *Public Administration Review*, 33 (March/April 1973), 146–156.

30. Wisconsin Department of Administration, *FY 1999 Annual Fiscal Report: Budgetary Basis*, 7.

31. In some states, the national government owns 35 percent to 50 percent of the land. Thus national government activity and expenditures in those states is likely to be much higher than it is in Wisconsin.

32. Wisconsin Taxpayers Alliance, "An Unusual Approach to State-Local Finance," *The Wisconsin Taxpayer*, September 1998, 66(9), 1, 3.

33. Wisconsin Department of Administration, *FY 2002 Annual Fiscal Report: Budgetary Basis*, 8.

34. Ibid.

35. Ibid., 9.

36. For a fascinating discussion of the University of Wisconsin's budget see W. Lee Hansen and Kathryn Sell, "The UW System Budget," in James K. Conant, Robert H. Haveman, and Jack Huddleston (Eds.), *Dollars and Sense: Policy Choices and the Wisconsin Budget*, 2 (Madison, WI: The Robert La Follette Institute of Public Affairs, 1991).

37. Department of Administration, *FY 2002 Annual Fiscal Report: Budgetary Basis* (October 2002).

38. For example, the General Fund Condition Statement prepared by the Legislative Fiscal Bureau uses only GPR revenues as its Total Revenues. See p. 12, Department of Administration, FY 2002 *Annual Fiscal Report: Budgetary Basis* (October 2002). Also, compare p. 12 to p. 19.

39. Department of Administration, *FY 2002 Annual Fiscal Report: Budgetary Basis* (October 2002), 19.

40. Ibid.

41. Legislative Fiscal Bureau, "Tax Law Changes Beginning in 1995," November 2002.

42. Andy Rechovsky, "Wisconsin's Structural Deficit: Our Fiscal Future at the Crossroads," La Follette Institute of Public Affairs, University of Wisconsin-Madison (May 2002).

43. Russell S. Sobell and Randall G. Holcombe, "The Impact of State Rainy Day Funds in Easing State Fiscal Crises during the 1990–91 Recession," *Public Budgeting and Finance* (Fall 1999), 28–48.

44. Donald A. Nichols, "The Effect of the Economic Recession on the Budget," in James K. Conant, Robert H. Haveman, and Jack Huddleston (Eds.), *Dollars and Sense: Policy Choices and the Wisconsin Budget*, 2 (Madison, WI: The Robert La Follette Institute of Public Affairs, 1991), p. 71.

45. Scott McCallum, Governor, "Budget Reform Bill Summary," Division of Executive Budget and Finance, Department of Administration ( January 2002), 1.

46. For more background on Wisconsin's failure to fund its Rainy Day Fund, see James K. Conant, "Wisconsin's Budget Deficit: Size, Causes, Remedies, and Consequences," *Public Budgeting and Finance* (Summer 2003), 5–25.

47. A comparison of the scale, causes, and responses to the FY 2002 fiscal problems in Wisconsin and Georgia can be found in a mini symposium in *Public Budgeting and Finance*, (Summer 2003), 1–38. The Georgia article, by Thomas P. Lauth is titled: "Budgeting During a Recession Phase of the Business Cycle in Georgia."

48. Division of Executive Budget and Finance, Department of Administration, *Budget in Brief* (February 2003), 18.

49. Ibid., 36.

# CHAPTER 14

# Mississippi: Changing Gubernatorial–Legislative Dynamics in Budget Decision Making

*Edward J. Clynch*

State budget decisions determine how much a state spends and whose social values prevail. States make these decisions through a complicated and continually changing interplay between governors and legislators. Governors gain influence through formal executive powers such as reviewing agency budgets, making a unified budget proposal to the legislature, and line-item vetoes. Chief executives also draw upon informal tools like mobilizing public opinion and party discipline. At the same time, independently elected legislators must approve revenue enhancements and spending. Since neither the governor nor the legislature can completely eclipse the other, decisions usually emerge as compromises. Gubernatorial influence over budget outcomes may differ in periods of revenue scarcity from cycles of robust revenue growth. In bad times, many governors possess the power to reduce budgets unilaterally in order to bring expenditures in line with revenue shortfalls. In bad times, legislators are more likely to let the governor take the lead in proposing new taxes or fees. Economic downturns often disrupt normal incremental and conflict-avoidance budget patterns.[1] During Mississippi's economic downturn in the mid-1980s, incremental cuts were not compatible with fiscal austerity. Political fallout from not funding promised improvements in education was greater than problems caused by budget reductions in other areas.[2]

After a brief description of the Mississippi budget process, this chapter outlines and analyzes gubernatorial and legislative impact on taxing and spending policies during the last three administrations. Mississippi experienced healthy revenue growth during the Kirk Fordice era (1992–2000). Conversely both Ronnie Musgrove (2000–2004) and Haley Barbour (2004–) served during a period of revenue scarcity. Formal gubernatorial powers did not change since 1992, but the influence of these governors over budget decisions varied due to revenue accessibility, the successful use of the bully pulpit, and party discipline.

## MISSISSIPPI'S BUDGET PROCESS

Mississippi governors lack the institutional powers of presidents and chief executives in many other states. In Mississippi, the chief executive lacks will and pleasure appointments that provide many state chief executives with back door leverage over budget proposals. Like most states, Mississippi elects a plethora of statewide officials. Unlike many states, independent boards and commissions oversee major service delivery agencies such as health and mental health. Unlike most states, independent boards oversee major internal service agencies such as civil service, data processing, and revenue collection.

Another institutional shortcoming results from the statutory existence of the fourteen-member Joint Legislative Budget Committee (JLBC), a joint senate and house committee under the leadership of the Lieutenant Governor and the Speaker of the House, which prepares the unified budget used in the legislative session as the working document. The governor and the JLBC set the initial revenue estimate in a joint meeting in October, but the legislature may change the estimate during the session and this body sets the sine die figure.[3]

To avoid confusion and duplication, the governor and the JLBC jointly develop the budget guidelines that agencies use to prepare budget proposals.[4] Instructions provide no dollar ceiling guidelines, not even in regard to inflationary pressures on major contractual and commodity expenses such as utilities. The only spending instructions concern new programs or program modifications mandated in previous legislative sessions, court decisions, or changing federal requirements.[5] Mississippi law requires agencies to place performance measures in their budget proposals and the legislature to include these indicators in agency appropriation bills.[6] Evidence suggests that their inclusion is symbolic however, because the numbers do not effect the allocation of resources.[7]

The Legislative Budget Office, the staff arm of the JLBC, makes a detailed review of budget requests, the JLBC then holds budget hearings, marks up the budget, and submits a budget proposal to the full legislature. Analysts in the Governor's Budget Office also review agency proposals and help the governor assemble a budget proposal for the legislature. The governor's budget proposal outlines suggested divisions among agencies, but it does not contain the detail of the JLBC proposal. Historically, the JLBC recommendation serves as the starting point of appropriation subcommittee deliberations, and legislators ignore the governor's proposal.[8]

Like many other governors, Mississippi's chief executive may veto any bill and line-item veto appropriation bills, and the legislature may override gubernatorial objections with a 2/3 vote in each chamber.[9] But Mississippi agencies receive lump sum appropriations or line-item appropriations for each object classification, such as salaries and equipment. Using the item veto would mean striking out all of an agency's equipment, etc. Between 1973 and 1992 Mississippi Governors used the line-item veto eleven times, six to reduce spending and five to cut out language. Vetoes reduced general fund spending by only 0.02 percent.[10]

The responsibility to keep revenues in line with expenditures falls to the governor. The law allows chief executives to reduce and revise general fund agency estimates up to 5 percent of the agency's budget. Once the governor reduces all general fund agencies by 5 percent, any additional cuts must be uniform and include all general fund agencies.[11] Recently Mississippi set up "Rainy Day Funds" to minimize midyear cuts. Mississippi holds back 2 percent of each year's revenue estimate to cushion current year revenue short falls.[12] The state also keeps an amount equal to 7.5 percent of general fund expenditures as rainy day money in the Working Cash-Stabilization Reserve Fund. Except for $50 million set aside to cover within year cash flow problems, the remaining money may be used to cover revenue shortfalls and court decisions. The Governor may transfer up to $50 million each year to cover projected spending year deficits.[13]

## GOVERNOR FORDICE – CONSERVATIVE OUTSIDER

Reagan conservative and building contractor Kirk Fordice, in his first bid for public office, unseated Democrat Ray Mabus and became the first Republican governor since reconstruction in January 1992. In the 1991 and 1995 statewide elections, Governor Fordice was elected along with a substantial majority of Democrats in both legislative chambers. In 1991, Democrats elected 94 of 122 members (77%) and thirty-nine of fifty-two senate members (75%). In 1995, Democrats won 72 percent of the house seats, a figure that dropped to 69 percent with party switchers after the election.

Fordice took office during a recession, but state revenues quickly picked up and robust growth occurred during his tenure. General fund revenues increased 73.3 percent with an average yearly growth of 9.16 percent.[14] Mississippi's economic growth was boosted by the emergence of gaming revenue. By the mid-1990s, about 10 percent of general fund revenue came from gaming taxes and gaming-related increases in sales and income taxes.[15]

Fordice brought a conservative low-tax, low-spending agenda to office and focused his energies on curbing spending, limiting the growth in government, and returning money to the taxpayers. He did not change his message or priorities despite robust revenue growth. In his FY 1994 budget message delivered in January 1993, he stated ". . . the responsibility that the voters expect of us demands that we restrain ourselves from spending every dollar that comes through the State Treasury."[16.]

Governor Fordice's taxing and spending philosophy ran counter to the perspectives of legislators. As one person involved in the budget process put it, "legislators believe that Mississippi agencies are under funded. New money needs to support increased services. Many legislators sense that citizens desire the expansion of services, particularly when dollars are available without increasing taxes."

Fordice's "construction boss" approach to interpersonal relations limited his ability to influence both Democratic and Republican legislators. As governor, he often remained aloof from the legislative process. He did not make major efforts to influence bills and surprised many legislators with his after the fact vetoes. The strained relationship was evident when several of Fordice's State-of-the-State addresses were not *once* interrupted by applause. Traditionally the outgoing governor addresses the legislature a few days before leaving office. In January 2000, the House of Representatives did not issue an invitation to Fordice to deliver an address.[17]

During his 8 years in office Fordice strongly objected to tax increases and wanted tax cuts from the state's fiscal dividend. While always reluctant to raise taxes, the legislature in 1992, under the leadership of pro-education Lieutenant Governor Democrat Ronnie Musgrove, the state increased the sales tax from 6 to 7 cents on the dollar to help education. Money raised with the additional 1 cent went to all levels of education with the exception of $25 million sent to the state's "Rainy Day Fund." The governor strongly objected to raising taxes and vetoed the bill. In his veto message he stated:

This bill has been touted by the special interests as "a one-penny tax for education." In truth, however, this bill is a 16 2/3 percent tax increase for more government. Should this bill become law, every checkout slip at the grocery store, hardware store, appliance store, furniture store and bookstore would reflect a tax hike of nearly 17%. [Quotes and underlining in the original][18]

Many Democrats and a few Republicans voted to override the veto and the Educational Enhancement Fund became a key part of education financing. This fund grew during Fordice's tenure from $141 million in the first year to $405 million in 1999.[19]

Fordice made several proposals to cut taxes, particularly changes that reduce the tax liability of more affluent citizens. Overall his efforts to cut taxes produced only limited success. During his terms in office, the legislature only made two small cuts in revenues, the elimination of capital gains tax on Mississippi investments in 1992 and the elimination of the marriage penalty in 1996.[20]

Governor Fordice's term also included several attempts to control spending particularly by using the veto. From 1992 through 1999 he vetoed thirty-three bills, including eight line-item vetoes. About 65 percent of his vetoes were efforts to control spending through eliminating bond debt bills, stopping tax increases on spending, and the use of public money to benefit private groups.[21]

A major policy controversy between the governor and legislature revolved around borrowing money through the sale of bonds, particularly general obligation bonds. The 1992 legislative session produced fireworks between the governor and the legislature over a $98,000,000 "bond bill" for FY 1993. This legislation authorized the borrowing of money to pay for repairs and renovation of existing facilities, as well as the construction of several new buildings. The governor in his veto message suggested "the bill was put together like a quilting bee created by patchwork in order to draw support for it and for some other issues."[22] The legislature ignored his advice and overrode this veto.

For FY 1994 Governor Fordice "line-item vetoed" a bond bill in an unsuccessful attempt to expand gubernatorial veto authority. A general obligation bond bill started as a $2,000,000 request to repair storm damage on the Mississippi University for Women campus in Columbus. By the time the bill reached the governor's desk, the bill totaled $65,900,000. Fordice took the position that bond bills authorize spending, and thus they are subject to a line-item veto. He line-itemed all projects except the repairs at MUW and construction at Alcorn State University in Lorman. Legislative leaders and Attorney General Mike Moore challenged Fordice's actions in the state court system, contending that bond bills are primarily revenue raising measures not subject to line-item vetoes. The Mississippi Constitution only allows governors to strike out portions of an appropriation bill. For other types of legislation, the governor must accept or veto the entire bill. The Mississippi State Supreme Court affirmed a lower court decision that the line item veto does not apply to bond bills.[23]

Fordice continued to veto various bond bills throughout his terms. Other vetoes included bonds for a university system communications network, refurbishing historic sites, a small business assistance revolving fund, and refurbishing the Farish Street area in the heart of the Jackson African American community. Overall, his selective bond vetoes assumed the appearance of the boy with a finger in the dike. During his 8 years, Mississippi's general obligation bonded indebtedness grew from 448.1 million in FY 1992 to $1,951.7 billion in FY 2000. General fund principal and interest payments increased from 1.1 percent of the general fund expenditures to 4.6 percent.[24]

Fordice and the legislature also sparred additional times over the breadth of the gubernatorial veto power. Fordice objected to the number of positions authorized for state agencies in FY 1994 appropriations bills. He maintained that a statute requiring a 2 percent reduction in agency positions mandated the legislature to lower the number of authorized positions by 2 percent. The governor drew a line through the number of authorized positions and inserted a figure 2 percent lower than the FY 1993 total. An attorney general's opinion ruled the governor's action as null and void. The opinion stated that governors may delete parts of appropriate bills but may not amend them. In essence, governors could eliminate all 100 positions but not to strike out 100 and write in 98.[25]

For FY 1995, the governor decided to eliminate all directives in the Department of Human Services appropriation bill that set conditions on how this agency spent its money. Fordice argued that governors possess the authority to eliminate legislative spending instructions while leaving the amount appropriated intact. He made the case that the Human Services appropriation bill exceeded his request by $8,000,000. Fordice argued that the director, a gubernatorial appointee, would not spend the $8,000,000 if given flexibility on how to spend the appropriated money. An attorney general's opinion disagreed with this line of reasoning and held that spending directives are integral parts of appropriation bills. If a governor strikes out dollars, the conditions are void. In addition a governor cannot strike out conditions and leave the money appropriated.[26]

Another major confrontation between Governor Fordice and the legislature involved his veto of the Mississippi Adequate Education Act in FY 1998. This law gave teachers a pay raise over 3 years, authorized a limited number of charter schools, provided supplemental grants to poor school districts, and gave all school districts the opportunity to finance capital improvements that are paid for with state-backed bonds. Many school districts find it difficult to pass local bond issues for capital improvements since passage requires a 60 percent "yes" vote. The governor objected mostly to the bonding provision. In his veto message he stated ". . . when it is considered that no local referendum is needed to issue these bonds, and the state will be forced to 'take all action necessary' to guarantee their payoff, I believe that is cause for concern."[27] The governor was convinced that he could make his case to legislators and work out a compromise. He placed this veto on his call for a special session on April 23, 1997, but the proponents held their ground, and the veto was overridden. By the end of the submission and approval period, local school districts received approval for more than $400,000,000 in projects backed by Mississippi's bonding authority.[28]

The legislature emerged the clear winner in taxing and spending struggles with Governor Fordice. While the governor achieved two minor tax cuts the legislature overrode his veto of a major sales tax increase. On the spending side, Fordice was unable to stop legislative efforts to channel money into K-12 education and other agencies. Between FY 1992 and FY 2000, general fund spending grew from 1.994 billion to 3.457 billion, an increase of 79 percent. Both exploding revenues and Fordice's interpersonal style limited his success. The public liked his "tell it like it is" rhetoric, but he was unable to influence legislators by mobilizing public opinion. Senators and Representatives used fiscal dividend to satisfy constituent desires with more services.

## RONNIE MUSGROVE—FISCAL LIBERAL

Democratic Governor Ronnie Musgrove assumed office in January 2000, with a very limited mandate. In 1999 only about 8,000 votes separated first place finisher Musgrove and Republican Mike Parker. Nevertheless, Democrats won 89 of 122 house contests (73%) and thirty-four of fifty-two senate campaigns (65%). Governor Musgrove assumed office as an experienced Mississippi budgeter since he served as Lieutenant Governor from 1996 to 2000 and as a state senator from 1988 to 1996. Other political actors view Musgrove as an idea person who works to sell his thoughts to others. As Lieutenant Governor, Musgrove successfully lead pro-education efforts over the opposition of conservative Republican Governor Kirk Fordice. Musgrove engineered the passage of the Educational Enhancement Fund and the 1-cent sales tax increase to fund it. In 1997, he spearheaded a successful legislative effort to pass the Mississippi Adequate Education Act.[29] This section discusses Musgrove's efforts to increase spending for K-12 education and Medicaid, to settle the Ayers court case dealing with university funding disparities, to keep revenue estimates in line with economic conditions, to plug budget holes with one-time money, and to keep spending from exceeding collected revenues through fiscal midyear budget cuts.

Musgrove took office with big spending plans and little new money. The recession of 2001 hit Mississippi like other states. From FY 2001 through FY 2004, general fund revenues grew by a yearly average of 1.4 percent. During the recessionary dip revenues actually declined 1.2 percent from FY 2001 to FY 2002.[30] Despite his desire to expand spending, particularly for K-12 education and Medicaid, Musgrove took a no tax increase position. The governor realized that any attempt to raise taxes could not succeed in the legislature and would damage his reelection chances in 2003. The Mississippi Constitution requires that any *changes* in laws affecting revenue must pass by a super majority of 60 percent in each legislative chamber.[31] During his term, despite revenue problems, the state's Medicaid match money increased 53.7 percent and K-12 education support 11.6 percent.[32]

### K-12 Education

Musgrove persuaded the legislature to increase Mississippi K-12 teacher pay to the Southeastern average over a 5-year period. No money was required during FY 2001, but the legislative needed to make a substantial financial commitment in FY 2002 through FY 2006. The teacher pay raise was backloaded with each teacher receiving an $8,000 raise during both FY 2005 and FY 2006.[33]

Musgrove sold the teacher pay raise to the legislature as he had done with other educational programs in past years. He even testified personally before the House Appropriations Committee and took questions like any other witness. Many legislators recognized that a teacher pay increase commitment could mean limited new money for other programs or even result in other program cuts. Consequently the legislature, with Lieutenant Governor Amy Tuck taking the lead, added a provision that teacher pay increases would not occur in any fiscal year in which general fund revenue did not grow by at least 5 percent. Musgrove endorsed Tuck's action because the "trigger" was necessary to secure legislative passage, but after the legislature adjourned he criticized the trigger publicly on numerous occasions.

Legislators responded to the public pressure created by the governor and teacher organizations and included the first year pay increase of 2 percent, costing $22 million in the FY 2002 budget. But the legislature did not create a permanent salary increase since the 2 percent pay raise was added to the Department of Education appropriation bill without accompanying legislation that adjusted teacher pay scales. After the session ended, the Department of Education informed school districts that the increase represented a one-time supplement.[34]

Shortly after the session ended, Governor Musgrove embarked on a public campaign to remove the trigger requirement. In a news conference the governor made this statement: "That means because of the legislators' actions our teachers are not guaranteed a pay raise in the future. The Legislature has played games with our teachers. They played games with our children's education. They played games with all of us."[35] After a public campaign by the governor and teacher organizations, Lieutenant Governor Amy Tuck and House Speaker Tim Ford held a news conference to announce their support for removal of the 5 percent trigger. Governor Musgrove wasted no time calling a special session devoted exclusively to removing the pay raise trigger. The repeal passed overwhelmingly with a House vote of 112–3 and a Senate vote of 45–3. The new law placed the teacher pay raise in stone because the legislature removed the trigger and amended the teacher pay scale through fiscal year 2006 to incorporate yearly increases.[36]

During his State of the State address in January 2003, Musgrove urged the legislature "to put education first" and pass FY 2004 funding for "pre-kindergarten through higher education at 62 percent of the general fund budget" by the end of January 2003, before other appropriations bills were finalized. The governor repeated his call during several meetings throughout the state, and the legislature approved education funding by February 1, 2003, including the third year of the teacher pay raise.[37]

### Medicaid and CHIP

A second priority spending area for Governor Musgrove involved increased Medicaid spending, particularly for the Children's Health Insurance Program (CHIP). By 2004 CHIP recipients grew to 62,000 compared to 542 in 2000. Mississippi covers the state CHIP match of 17 percent through the Medicaid budget. The Governor's office publicized CHIP with flyers passed out in shopping centers and meetings around the state. CHIP added costs to Medicaid, but the CHIP publicity campaign also attracted applicants who met the stricter requirement for Medicaid benefits. Over 66,000 children who applied for

CHIP benefits were ruled eligible for Medicaid along with adult members of their families. As a result, state resources to match increased Medicaid costs grew dramatically. Due to escalating costs, many legislators proposed cuts in Medicaid benefits during the FY 2003 budget consideration. To counter this move, Governor Musgrove made publicized visits to nursing homes and assured Medicaid supported residents that he would fight for them so they could stay in these facilities.[38]

## The Ayers Case

The Ayers court case was already 25 years old when Governor Musgrove assumed office in January 2000. In 1992, the United States Supreme Court agreed with the plaintiffs that Mississippi continues to discriminate against African Americans because historically black universities and historically white universities differ in the range of academic programs and level of financial support.[39] The parties negotiated over a settlement without success until African American Congressman Bennie Thompson assumed the role of lead plaintiff and chief negotiator, and Musgrove appointed a bargaining team that included a former African American Mississippi Supreme Court Justice. After a settlement was reached in 2002, a group of plaintiffs appealed in federal court for further action. In 2004, the Fifth District Court of Appeals upheld the settlement, and the case ended later that year when the U.S. Supreme Court refused to consider an appeal.[40] Mississippi agreed to provide $503 million to the three historically black universities in increments between FY 2002 and FY 2019. The total settlement included special appropriations received by these three universities in FY 2002 and FY 2003. The major components included $246 million for new and expanded academic programs, $75 million in capital improvements, and $110 million for endowments. Despite tight money, Mississippi has met appropriated money as required by the Ayers settlement.

## Plugging the Revenue Gap—Manipulating the Revenue Estimate

Many governors cope with declining revenues by advocating conservative revenue estimates that force legislators to limit spending. According to Mississippi law, "The General Fund revenue estimate shall be the estimate jointly adopted by the Governor and the LBC, but no legal remedy applies when the two parties fail to adopt a joint estimate."[41] During Musgrove's years in office he sparred with the legislative leadership over the amount of money available for appropriations.

In September 2000, Musgrove proposed a FY 2002 budget based on a 5.3 percent increase in revenues, but he accepted the official joint 3.7 percent growth estimate in October. By February 2001, the Governor concluded that the 3.7 percent official revenue growth estimate for upcoming FY 2002 was too high, and he wrote a budget based on a 1 percent growth rate.[42] The Governor threatened to veto appropriation bills if legislature did not pass appropriations bills reflecting his lower revenue estimate. The legislature refused to take his advice, and the governor responded with forty-two appropriation bill vetoes in March. The Legislature's override votes occurred with House and Senate considering bills as a group. The House voted 111–9 on House originated bills and 117–5 on bills starting in the senate. The Senate voted 39–12 on Senate bills and 41–10 on House bills.[43]

Governor Musgrove and legislators placed different interpretations on this very public confrontation. Musgrove suggested that appropriations could only be fully funded by spending the $70 million set aside to cover current fiscal year revenue shortfalls, and by tapping $50 million that governors can withdraw each fiscal year from the Cash Stabilization "Rainy Day Fund." He suggested "that is irresponsible not to mention the fact that it is a violation of the law."[44] Legislators justified 3.7 percent growth because the figure represents the amount agreed upon by experts who assisted setting the joint estimate in October 2000. Nevertheless, in October 2001, during the spending year, the JLBC revised the FY 2002 revenue growth estimate downward to 0.7 percent. Even with the revised computation the state spent the $70 million set aside for revenue shortfalls, forced the governor to take $50 million from the Cash Stabilization "Rainy Day Fund," and required him to cut agency budgets by $51 million.[45]

The battle over competing revenue estimates continued when the Governor and JLBC met to set the revenue estimate for FY 2003 on November 14, 2001. The LBC accepted the 4.3 percent growth projection of the professional estimators who made a recommendation to policymakers. The Governor balked and suggested a 1 percent growth rate was more appropriate given the state's sluggish economy. After the meeting progressed, he agreed to accept 2.6 percent growth projection, but the LBC remained firm and raised the growth estimate to 4.3 percent before the start of the legislative session. The JLBC wrote a FY 2003 budget recommendation based on a 4.3 percent revenue growth, but the Governor refused to prepare a budget recommendation without an estimate. Musgrove recognized that budget proposals for the JLBC and the Governor's office were no longer influential since both proposals are based on revenue from ongoing taxes and fees. During Musgrove's term, the legislature added substantial one-time money to cover spending needs. In March 2002, the legislature lowered the sine die estimate for FY 2003 to 3.3 percent, and in October 2002, during the spending year, the JLBC lowered the FY 2003 estimate to 1.6 percent.

A similar war did not materialize when the governor and legislative leadership set the FY 2004 revenue estimate. Both sides agreed on a 2.6 increase over the lowered FY 2003 estimate set in October 2002. The legislature dropped the requirement for setting aside 2 percent of the revenue estimate for fiscal year shortfalls, thus allowing appropriations based on 100 percent of estimated revenue.[46]

**Table 14.1**
**Revenue Supporting General Fund Spending FY 2001–FY 2004 ($ in Millions)**

| | FY 2001 | FY 2002 | FY 2003 | FY 2004 | TOTALS |
|---|---|---|---|---|---|
| General Fund Sources | 3,443.9 | 3,398.9 | 3,461.3 | 3,601.6 | |
| Rainy Day Funds | 85 | 96.2 | 98.7 | 20.0 | 299.9 |
| Diverted Taxes | 18.8 | 23.6 | 30.7 | 36.5 | 109.6 |
| Tobacco Settlement | 66.1 | 177.6 | 178.9 | 103.5 | 526.1 |
| Contingency Funds | 0 | 82.1 | 105.7 | 290.2 | 478.0 |
| Total Revenues Supporting General Expenditures | 3,613.8 | 3,778.4 | 3,875.3 | 4,051.8 | 1,413.6 |
| Percent One-Time Money Used to Cover GF Expenditure | 4.7 | 10.0 | 10.7 | 11.1 | 100.0 |

*Source:* The data for Table 14.1 was provided by the Mississippi Department of Finance and Administration.

## Plugging the Revenue Gaps—The Use of One-Time Money

In addition to appropriating the 2 percent set aside for current year short-falls and making mid-fiscal year spending cuts, Mississippi also plugged budget holes with one-time revenue. Table 14.1 shows the one-time revenue sources diverted to cover general fund spending. Overall, Mississippi used $1.4 billion to cover ongoing general fund expenditures. Musgrove and the legislature depleted the "Rainy Day" portion of the Cash Stabilization Fund by the Governor transferring $50 million each fiscal year and the legislature authorizing additional withdrawals. Other sources of stopgap revenue included diverting gas and oil severance revenue to the general fund from a special education trust fund for FY 2001 through FY 2006. Previously, interest from the trust had supported a variety of projects such as the creation of a math and science high school, the purchase of textbooks, and the buying of vocational education equipment.[47] Tobacco money also served as a major source to one-time money. Mississippi deposited yearly payments into a tobacco trust fund with each year's interest covering general fund expenditures. For FY 2001, only the interest was spent. For fiscal years 2002–2004, Governor Musgrove and the legislature spent the interest and the diverted yearly payments to cover general fund expenditures.[48]

The legislature also diverted special fund balances into a "contingency fund" and listed the contingency fund as a source of revenue for higher education and other agencies. Some transfers tapped accumulated balances, such as money in the unclaimed property fund managed by the treasurer's office, but some transfers cut services. Money taken from the School Building Fund reduced state support for construction, and funds removed from the Education Ad Valorum Property Tax Reduction Fund forced local districts to raise taxes or cut services.[49]

### Midyear Budget Cuts

Mississippi law requires governors to cut spending if the revenue estimate is below 98 percent of the projection after November 1.[50] State law allows governors to cut budgets selectively as long as no budget is reduced more than 5 percent. Once every agency is cut 5 percent, any additional cuts must be across the board. In October 2000, Governor Musgrove cut $50 million from budgets he viewed as low priority. He made no reductions in education at any level or in public safety. Nevertheless, in February 2001, the Governor also reduced budgets by another $56 million including education and public safety. With the February cut, all general fund budgets were reduced by 5 percent with the exception of K-12 education spending. These budgets were reduced only 3 percent. General fund budgets were spared further reductions since, as allowed by law some special funds were cut by $12.9 million with the proceeds transferred to the general fund. Education also suffered cuts at all levels since sales tax revenue fell below estimates and this tax supports the Educational Enhancement Fund. For K-12 total reductions equated to $63 million or 3.8 percent of total spending, for community colleges $12.5 million or 6.9 percent, and for universities $38 million or 6.0 percent.

Unlike previous governors, Musgrove "reserved" rather than cut budgets. By using this option reductions could be restored later if money became available. On the last business day of the FY 2001, Musgrove restored $13.5 million to the Department of Education, including $10 million for the minimum foundation program that was passed through to school districts. Although the fiscal year was over, most school districts replaced money taken from their reserve funds used to cover costs during the FY 2001.

At the beginning of FY 2002 and FY 2003 Governor Musgrove asked agencies to spend only 45 percent of their first 6-month allotment. While voluntary, the governor's request suggested that agencies plan on cuts during the fiscal year and make the necessary adjustments at the beginning of the fiscal year rather than later. If cuts proved unnecessary, the money would be available during the second allotment period that begins January 1. Unfortunately money was not restored for either fiscal year.[51]

## BARBOUR—EXPERIENCED FISCAL CONSERVATIVE INSIDER

Former Republican National Committee Chairman Haley Barbour defeated incumbent Democrat Ronnie Musgrove with 53 percent of the vote.

The 2003 election also tilted the legislature toward the Republicans who captured twenty-two of fifty-two senate contests (42%) and 46 of 122 house seats (38%). Lieutenant Governor Amy Tuck switched from the Democratic to the Republican Party before the 2003 election and was reelected as a Republican. Thus Barbour took office with a powerful ally and *de facto* Republican control of the state senate. The majority of state senators followed the lead of the lieutenant governor since the person holding this office appoints committee members and chairs. At the same time, Democratic Speaker Billy McCoy maintained control of the house despite efforts of Republicans to pick up votes from fiscally conservative Democrats on crucial budgeting issues.

### Barbour's Policy Initiatives

Barbour's budget policy initiatives reflected his conservative political view that Mississippi must cut services to bring expenditures into line with the revenue stream. As was true in Musgrove's last few years, the JLBC document no longer served as the working document for the legislative consideration since the committee based its general fund spending proposal on continuing taxes and fees. For FY 2005, the JLBC budget proposed appropriating 100 percent of estimated revenues from general fund ongoing sources, instead of setting aside 2 percent to cover potential revenue shortfalls. The JLBC also made an exception to its revenue rule and proposed using the FY 2005 tobacco payment to cover general fund expenditures. Since the JLBC budget proposal did not include any special fund transfers into a contingency fund many programs faced cuts in base budgets, including K-12 and higher education. The JLBC did recommend level funding for Medicaid.[52]

Barbour, as required by law, introduced his first budget on January 28, 2004, within a month of assuming office.[53] The governor recommended that K-12 receive the cuts proposed by the JLBC, a step that would make it impossible to fund the mandated 8 percent pay raise without dismissing teachers and making massive cuts in other education programs. The governor favored higher education and recommended the same funding as the previous year. Barbour also recommended a 32 percent increase in Medicaid funding over FY 2004. Despite Barbour's substantial proposed increase, Medicaid and CHIP programs required a 55 percent funding increase to provide current services. Barbour recommended selected increases in spending, cuts in various agency budgets, and the use of one-time money from various special fund balances. He also proposed a 1-year removal of civil service protection for persons in the thirteen agencies that report to the governor. Thus, agency heads could restructure agencies and save money by dismissing current employees. Overall, Barbour suggested spending only 1.3 percent more in FY 2005 compared to FY 2004.[54]

The Republican lead senate endorsed his proposal with twenty-eight of the fifty-two senators signing on as cosponsors, but Democrats in the house expressed concern, particularly about lack of funding for K-12 education. Speaker Billy McCoy introduced a counter budget proposal that recommended K-12 funding increase 10 percent over FY 2004 levels. As a result, teachers could receive their 8 percent raise and school districts would not need to cut services or raise local property taxes. McCoy's proposal accepted Barbour's suggestions of level funding for higher education and of limiting Medicaid to a 32 percent increase. Overall, McCoy proposed increasing FY 2005 spending almost 5 percent over FY 2004, with the additional spending paid for by cuts in some agency budgets, more special fund fee and taxes diverted to the general fund, and increasing the revenue estimate by almost 2 percent.[55]

A conference committee composed of house and senate leaders reached final budget decisions, but Barbour maintained a strong hand in the negotiations through the senate leaders. At the insistence of the governor, senate leaders scuttled some house-senate agreements and forced renegotiation. Many house members objected to under-funding Medicaid, but the governor would not budge from his initial plan. The house leadership agreed to Medicaid cuts to avoid a stalemate that could prevent budgets from passing on time.[56] The final FY 2005 Medicaid budget allocated 38 percent more than FY 2004 and mandated the removal of 65,000 poverty-level aged and disabled (PLAD) citizens with yearly incomes over $9,300. Their sole medical coverage would come from Medicare after July 1, a date pushed back to October 1 by the governor. The lack of Medicare prescription drug coverage created a major problem for many removed recipients until federal coverage begins in 2006.[57]

The Medicaid appropriation bill required Barbour to seek Medicaid waivers from the U.S. Department of Health and Human Services for 17,000 young disabled recipients not covered by Medicare and for persons with costly drug bills to cover antirejection drugs, chemotherapy, kidney dialysis, and antipsychotic drugs.[58] In late September 2004, a group of PLAD recipients sued the Barbour administration in federal court. The Plaintiffs argued that letters sent by Medicaid were confusing and contradictory.[59] Just before the hearing Democratic Attorney General Jim Hood intervened on behalf of the plaintiffs with a brief that supported the contention that PLAD recipients were not properly notified of changes in Medicaid law.[60] The Barbour administration agreed to a consent degree that postponed legal action until January 31, 2005. The governor said that the legislature must find money to cover the $100 million FY 2005 Medicaid shortfall created by keeping PLAD recipients on Medicaid roles.[61]

Final appropriations for FY 2005 demonstrate that both gubernatorial and house budget proposals influenced spending decisions. K-12 education received 3.3 percent increase over FY 2004. The compromise bill provided money for teacher pay raises, but the state underfunded the K-12 education formula by 2.5 percent. Thus local districts were forced to cut programs, spend reserve funds, and/or raise property taxes. Higher education received 3.7 percent less money in FY 2005 with the unspoken understanding that

**Table 14.2**
**Revenue Supporting General Fund Spending FY 2005 ($ in Millions)**

| General Fund Sources | Rainy Day Funds | Diverted Taxes | Tobacco Settlement | Contingency Funds | Total Revenues Supporting General Expenditures | Percent One-Time Money Used to Cover GF Expenditures |
|---|---|---|---|---|---|---|
| 3,596.00 | 8.0 | 72.0 | 215.9 | 217.0 | 4,108.9 | 12.6 |

*Source:* The Author compiled Table 14.2 from data provided by the Mississippi Department of Finance and Administration.

universities and community colleges would raise tuition once the session adjourned. Barbour's request for a 1-year free hand to restructure agencies and reduce staff was only approved for the Department of Corrections.[62]

### Plugging Revenue Holes

The FY 2005 revenue picture proved as bleak as during Musgrove's term. Both Governor Barbour and legislators agreed to plug revenue deficiencies with one-time money. Barbour's budget proposal advocated reducing the general fund's dependence on one time money by 50 percent in FY 2005 and then to zero in FY 2006. As a fiscal conservative, the governor publicly indicated that he would veto any tax or fee increase, and none passed. Table 14.2 displays diversions for FY 2005.[63]

Unfortunately, transfers in previous years depleted both the rainy day and Cash Stabilization portions set aside for cash flow purposes. For FY 2005, the State Treasurer will manage fiscal year cash flow general fund needs with special fund balances. To reduce dependence on one time contingency money and to replace Cash Stabilization "Rainy Day" money, the governor and the legislature created new ongoing general fund revenue sources. A change in law diverted gaming tax money set aside in a special fund for roads near casinos. The general fund will also receive money from the tobacco trust fund corpus in addition to yearly payments through FY 2009. For FY 2005, $216 million was moved to the general fund, an amount far in excess of the current payment and accrued interest. In fact, current law diverts a decreasing amount from the corpus through FY 2009.[64] At the same time the Governor refused to support any tax or fee increases.

### CONCLUSION

Several factors shape the influence of Mississippi's governors and the state legislature over budget outcomes including the mix of formal and informal powers, revenue bounty or revenue scarcity, dependence on federal money, and occasional court decisions. The revenue picture during this decade suggests that the state faces a structural deficit in which the current tax base is static and spending demands keep escalating. Data compiled for Representative Cecil Brown raises doubts that the state can grow out of its "revenue problem."[65] The current and future governors and legislators face the prospect of tax increases or holding budget growth at a minimal level.

The struggle between governors and the legislature evolved during the terms of the state's last three governors. Fiscal conservative Kirk Fordice faced a legislature with powerful formal powers and a desire to spend a ballooning fiscal dividend. Given his inability to mobilize public opinion and the limited number of Republican legislators, he lost an 8-year battle with the legislature over using the fiscal dividend for tax relief. As a poor state, Mississippi relies heavily on federal money, and legislators took advantage of a favorable Medicaid match to expand the number of recipients. Fiscal liberal Ronnie Musgrove took office as revenues declined, but he used the bully pulpit to secure approval of a multiyear teaching pay raise and to expand the number of Medicaid and CHIP recipients. Musgrove also pushed settlement of the Ayers Higher Education case, and the result was a noticeable long-term state fiscal commitment. During his first year in office, fiscal conservative Haley Barbour found it difficult to control spending given the public support for the teacher pay raise and the public outcry created by efforts to trim Medicaid roles. At the same time, the election of Haley Barbour appears to signal the arrival of two party politics in Mississippi. Barbour and Republican state senate leaders used party discipline to gain leverage over budget decisions.

Budgeting during the last decade shows the importance of governors enhancing limited formal powers with the informal powers of the bully pulpit and party discipline. The emergence of two party politics may leave a lasting impact on budget decisions. Battles between political parties are replacing conflicts between executive and legislative institutions. Party discipline is providing the current Mississippi governor with the ability to overcome a very institutionally junior role in the budget process.

## NOTES

1. Kurt Thurmaier and James J. Gosling, "The Shifting Roles State Budget Offices in the Midwest: Gosling Revisited," *Public Budgeting and Finance* 17(3) (Fall 1997), 48–70.

2. *Mississippi Code Annotated*, section 27-103-101, available at http://www.mississippi.gov.

3. Edward J. Clynch, "Budgeting in Mississippi: Are Two Budgets Better Than One?" *State and Local Government Review* 18, (2), 49–55.

4. Edward J. Clynch, "Government and Money in Mississippi," in *Politics in Mississippi*, 2nd edition, Ed. Joseph Parker (Salem, WI: Sheffield Publishing, 2001), pp. 189–213.

5. *Mississippi Code Annotated*, section 27–103–153, available at http://www. Mississippi.gov.

6. Edward J. Clynch, "Changes During the Past Decade: A Push Toward Program Budgeting," in *Case Studies in Public Budgeting and Financial Management*, Eds. Aman Khan and W. Bartley Hildreth (New York: Marcel Decker, 2003), pp. 93–114.

7. Parker, *Politics in Mississippi*.

8. Mississippi Constitution of 1890, Article 4, Sections 72 and 73, available at http:/www.mississippi.gov.

9. Catherine C. Reece, "The Line-Item Veto in Ten Southern States," *Public Administration Review* 57(6) (November/December 1997), 510–516.

10. *Mississippi Code Annotated*, section 27-104-13, available at http://www. Mississippi.gov.

11. *Mississippi Code Annotated*, section 27-103-211, available at http://www. Mississippi.gov.

12. *Mississippi Code Annotated*, section 27-103-203, available at http://www. Mississippi.gov.

13. Mississippi Department of Finance and Administration, *Mississippi Comprehensive Annual Financial Report for the Fiscal Year Ended June 30, 2000* (2000), 156–157.

14. John Lee, "Economic Impacts of Casino Gaming" (Jackson, MS: Mississippi Center for Policy Research and Planning, July 1994), pp. 1–2.

15. Governor Kirk Fordice, *Governor's Budget Recommendation for Fiscal Year 1993* (Jackson, MS: Governor's Office), January 31, 1992.

16. "Fordice Won't Address the Legislature" (Jackson, MS: *The Clarion Ledger*), January 6, 2000.

17. Governor Kirk Fordice, Veto Message for Senate Bill No. 3057 (Jackson, MS: Governor's Office), May 6 1992.

18. Mississippi Department of Finance and Administration, *Mississippi Comprehensive Annual Financial Report for the Fiscal Year Ended June 30, 1999* (1999).

19. *Mississippi Code Annotated*, section 27-7-17, available at http://www.Mississippi. gov.

20. The author analyzed and classified the Fordice vetoes.

21. Governor Kirk Fordice, "Veto Message of Senate Bill 3120" (Jackson, MS: Governor's Office), May 3, 1992.

22. *Fordice v. Bryan et al.* 94-CA-00031 (Jackson, MS: Mississippi Supreme Court), January 12, 1995.

23. Mississippi Department of Finance and Administration, *Mississippi Comprehensive Annual Financial Report for the Fiscal Year Ended June 30, 2000* (2000), p. 158.

24. Document 000006763 (Jackson, MS: Office of the Mississippi Attorney General), May 5, 1993.

25. Document 199470701 (Jackson, MS: Office of the Mississippi Attorney General), July 1, 1994.

26. Governor Kirk Fordice, "Veto Message of Senate House Bill 1162" (Jackson, MS: Governor's Office), April 10, 1997.

27. Unlike most other revenue sources yearly gaming tax revenue increased during the last 4 years.

28. *Constitution of the State of Mississippi*, Article 4, Section 70, 1890.

29. Edward, J. Clynch, "Government and Money in Mississippi," in Joseph Parker, Ed., Salem, WI: Sheffield Publishing Company, 2001.

30. Marianne Hill, "Easing the Budget Squeeze," *Mississippi Economic Review and Outlook* (Jackson, MS: Center for Policy Research and Planning, Mississippi Institutions of Higher Learning), June 2003.

31. Cecil Brown, "Revenue vs. Expenditures." Report provided to the author by Representative Cecil Brown, June 2003.

32. Mississippi Department of Finance and Administration, *Mississippi Comprehensive Annual Financial Report for The Fiscal Year Ended June 30, 2003* (2003).

33. *Mississippi Code Annotated*, section 37-19-7, available at http://www.Mississippi.gov.

34. Interview with Judy Rhoades, Department of Education, June 2001.

35. Speaker Tim Ford in an interview with *The Clarion Ledger* (Jackson, MS), May 11, 2001.

36. *Mississippi Code Annotated*, section 37-19-7, available at http://www.Mississippi.gov.

37. Mississippi Legislature, House Bill 1033, and Senate Bill 2876, 2003 regular legislative session, http://www.Mississippi.gov.

38. Sid Salter, "Medicaid: The Wedge Issue," *The Clarion Ledger* (April, 27, 2003).

39. *United States v. Fordice*, 505 U.S. 717 (1992).

40. *Jake Ayers et al. v. Bennie G. Thompson and Haley Barbour*, U.S. 02-60493, (2004).

41. *Mississippi Code Annotated*, section 27-103-139, available at http://www.Mississippi.gov.

42. State of Mississippi Governor's Office, *Executive Budget Recommendation*, February 18, 2001.

43. Governor's Veto Messages and Legislative Overrides, March 30, 2001, available at http://www.Mississippi.gov.

44. Governor Ronnie Musgrove, quoted in *The Clarion Ledger* (Jackson, MS), March 31, 2001.

45. Joint Legislative Budget Committee, November 15, 2001.

46. *Mississippi Code Annotated*, section 27-103-125, available at http://www.Mississippi.gov.

47. *Mississippi Code Annotated*, section 27-25-506, available at http://www.Mississippi.gov.

48. *Mississippi Code Annotated*, section 43-13-407, available at http://www.Mississippi.gov.

49. *Mississippi Code Annotated*, sections 27-103-301 and 37-151-7, available at http://www.Mississippi.gov.

50. *Mississippi Code Annotated*, section 27-104-13, available at http:/www.Mississippi.gov.

51. Information about Governor Musgrove's midyear cuts was obtained from the Mississippi Department of Finance and Administration.

52. "Proposed Budget for Fiscal Year 2005," prepared by the Joint Legislative Budget Committee (Jackson, MS), December 1, 2003.

53. *Mississippi Code Annotated*, section 27-106-139, available at http://www.Mississippi.gov.

54. "Operation Streamline," prepared by the Office of the Governor (Jackson, MS), January 28, 2004.

55. "House Bill 1279," Mississippi House of Representatives, February 24, 2004.

56. The information in this section was gathered from personal interviews with legislators and other state officials.

57. *Mississippi Code Annotated*, section 43-13-107, available at http://www. Mississippi.gov.

58. State of Mississippi, Office of the Governor, statement issued on September 9, 2004,

59. *Aldora Vinson et al. v. Barbour*, Civil Action No. 3.04-CV-784 WSU, United States Court for the Southern District of Mississippi, November 4, 2004.

60. State of Mississippi, Office of the Attorney General (Jackson, MS), September 29, 2004.

61. State of Mississippi, Office of the Governor, statement issued October 14, 2004.

62. "State Budget Bulletin," Joint Legislative Budget Committee, June 15, 2004 and House Bill 1279, section 13, regular session of the 2004 Legislature.

63. The author compiled Table 2 from data provided by the Mississippi Department of Finance and Administration.

64. House Bill 1279, sections 1 and 12, regular session of the 2004 Legislature.

65. Information provided by Representative Cecil Brown, July 24, 2004.

# CHAPTER 15

# Texas: The Use of Performance Data in Budgeting and Management

*Robert L. (Bob) Bland and Wes Clarke*

## INTRODUCTION

In 1991, the Texas Legislature adopted a performance budgeting system to re-place what was essentially a program budget. Under the old budgeting system, agency appropriations were divided among line-items that described individ-ual programs within each agency. Fiscal stress and instability in the 1980s and increasing frustration on the part of legislators over a lack of accountability led to the adoption of the current system designed to meet the informational needs of legislators in the budget process and to increase the accountability of agency officials for their agency's performance. After 12 years the system has matured to the point that officials in both the executive and legislative branches value it as a management tool even if its usefulness to inform bud-get choices in the heat of a legislative session is not universally felt. It is a widely held proposition that the format and amount of information do not influence budgetary decisions,[1] but the Texas system is making a difference in the behavior of officials in the legislature and executive agencies.

Budgeting in Texas is not typical of state processes. In most states and general-purpose local governments, the executive budget process typically in-volves the executive (governor, mayor, or city manager) proposing a budget to the legislature for consideration. The legislature, working from the executive proposal as a starting point, produces an appropriation bill or bills. At the state level, the governor then signs or vetoes the bill, or in some cases line-item ve-toes the legislation. At the local level, the passage of the budget by ordinance is the legal requirement for adoption of the budget.

The budget presented to the Texas Legislature is a product of the Legisla-tive Budget Board (LBB), a legislative staff unit coheaded by the lieutenant governor and speaker of the house plus eight other members of the legislature. While the governor produces an executive budget proposal in the form of broad policy statements, the LBB budget document is actually the starting point for legislative consideration of the budget. The governor's vision statement informs the LBB proposal but the Texas governor actually has little formal budget power, except at the conclusion of the process through line-item veto power, and relies on avenues of indirect influence to shape budget outcomes. It may be the lack of input early in the process that forces the governor to use the line-item veto. In other cases the governor may be reacting to the harsh realities of governmental budgeting. For example, when the Comptroller of Public Accounts threatened to withhold certification of the budget in 2003 as passed by the legislature, Governor Rick Perry used the line-item veto to cut $500 million in new spending. Increased political use of the line-item veto in Texas usually results in the bundling of items in appropriations bills by future legislatures. A good example is passage of lump sum appropriations for higher education beginning in 1987 to curtail tinkering by Governor Bill Clements as he began his second term.[2] The practice of bundling appropriations into a single line in Texas passed legal muster early in the twentieth century when the legislature summed eighteen lines of committee detail for the budget of the Attorney General and included it in the appropriations measure as a single item. The Court reasoned that the language of appropriations bills, or any other bills, is the prerogative of the legislature.[3]

One of the primary means of influence for the governor is the budget instructions sent to agencies from both the Governor's Office of Budget and Planning (GOBP) and the LBB. The instructions are produced by both offices jointly but include a copy of the governor's vision statement. The fact that the vision statement and the technical instructions for preparing agency budgets are linked is indicative of the union between budgeting and planning in Texas.

## THE IMPETUS FOR PLANNING

In the 1980s Texas went through turbulent economic times with the oil bust and a quantum political shift from a strong one-party state government controlled by the Democrats to one dominated by Republicans. By 2002, every statewide elected office was held by a Republican. The oil bust of the middle years of the 1980s, coupled with depressed prices for Texas' agricultural output, left state officials convinced that Texas could no longer rely on the petroleum industry to provide both jobs and resources for state coffers. In an effort to diversify the state's economic base, local governments—those in the Dallas/Fort Worth, Austin, San Antonio, and Houston areas particularly— attempted to attract businesses unrelated to the petroleum industry that would reduce the shock of another downcycle in oil. To a great extent these areas were successful in attracting companies in telecommunications, computer software, and related fields.

**Table 15.1**
**The Texas State Revenue Structure, 1980–2002**

|  | FY 1980 | | FY 1990 | | FY 2000 | | FY 2002 | |
|---|---|---|---|---|---|---|---|---|
|  | $ in Billions | % of Total | $ in Billions | % of Total | $ in Billions | % of Total | $ in Billions | % of Total |
| Total Taxes | 6.34 | 59.5 | 13.63 | 58.5 | 25.28 | 50.7 | 26.28 | 47.6 |
| General Sales | 2.52 | 23.7 | 7.59 | 32.6 | 13.98 | 28.0 | 14.52 | 26.3 |
| Excise | 1.79 | 16.8 | 4.21 | 18.1 | 7.81 | 15.7 | 8.47 | 15.3 |
| Severance | 1.52 | 14.3 | 1.08 | 4.6 | 1.11 | 2.2 | 0.97 | 1.7 |
| Total Non-Taxes | 4.32 | 40.5 | 9.66 | 41.5 | 24.56 | 49.3 | 28.94 | 52.4 |
| Federal Aid | 2.61 | 24.5 | 5.93 | 25.5 | 14.80 | 29.7 | 18.17 | 32.9 |
| Lottery* | – | | – | | 1.30 | 2.6 | 1.39 | 2.5 |
| Total State Revenue | 10.66 | | 23.29 | | 49.85 | | 55.22 | |
| State Population (000s) | 14,229 | | 16,986 | | 20,852 | | 21,780 | |
| Per Capita State Revenue | 749 | | 1,371 | | 2,391 | | 2,535 | |

*The Texas lottery was not implemented until 1992. At its peak in 1997, the lottery yielded $1.86 billion in revenue or 4.4 percent of total state revenue.
*Source:* Texas State Comptroller of Public Accounts, *Window on State Government*, "Texas Revenue History by Source, 1978–2002," http://www.cpa.state.tx.us/taxbud/revenue.html.

## State Revenue

Texas is one of seven states that does not levy a personal income tax, a fact Texans proudly point to as explaining the state's continued appeal to business investment and households. However, that distinction comes at a heavy price as noted in *Governing's* rating of state revenue structures,[4] which in 2003 ranked the state's tax structure as 50th in fairness to taxpayers and 49th in its adequacy to support state services.

Table 15.1 illustrates several significant trends in the state's revenue structure that have shaped budget deliberations and decisions over the past two decades. First, severance taxes on oil and natural gas have declined from 14.3 percent of state revenues in 1980 to a meager 1.7 percent in FY 2002. Several factors account for this trend, but most notably the declining role of Texas oil in the national market that followed the rise of OPEC. It also has meant that the state is less able to export its tax burden to the extent it did previously.

Second, the state has countered the national trend toward less dependence on federal aid, increasing from 24.5 percent of state revenues in 1980 to nearly one-third of state funds in 2002. During roughly the same period, the average state reliance on federal aid decreased from 24.5 percent in 1980 to 21.3 percent in 1999.[5] The trend in Texas is driven, in part, by the state's growth in population relative to the nation and possibly by the increasing political power of the state's congressional delegation and White House connections.

Third, the state relies heavily on general and excise sales taxes. In 1980, 40.5 percent of the state's revenue came from these sources. Following two general sales tax rate increases in the 1980s and 1990s to the current state rate of 6.25 percent, these sources now represent 41.6 percent of state funding. In fact, this understates the true magnitude of the role of consumption-based taxes in the state. Cities, public transit authorities, and nonurban counties levy an additional general sales tax of up to 2 percent, making the combined 8.25 percent rate one of the higher rates in the nation.

Finally, the Texas lottery mirrors the nearly universal experience among the states: a relatively small and volatile source of revenue that has had a negligible impact on state budgets. At its peak in 1997, the lottery yielded $1.86 billion in revenue, or 4.4 percent of the state's revenue, but it has steadily declined in importance. Part of the recent decline in lottery revenue may be due to the slumping economy and the availability of casino gambling in locations such as Shreveport, Louisiana, and Biloxi, Mississippi, that are within a few hours' drive of the major population centers of Dallas/Fort Worth, and Houston. As a means of countering this loss, the Texas Lottery Commission in 2003 modified its primary numbers game to reduce the odds of winning in hopes that larger jackpots would produce more ticket purchases.[6] The Commission is also considering partnering with one or more states in a multistate game that would likely produce larger jackpots.[7]

### Economic Change

Diversification bolstered Texas' economy during the 1990s causing it to grow faster than the surging national economy.[8] Houston and the Gulf Coast led the way assisted by the Interstate 35 corridor that runs from Laredo, on the border with Mexico, through San Antonio, Austin, and the Dallas/Forth Worth Metroplex. The 1993 North American Free Trade Agreement increased the economic activity of this central Texas route immensely. By the late 1990s, oil and gas production, which had been a little more than a fourth of the state's economy, was less than 7 percent of gross state product.

Governor Ann Richards, the last Democrat to hold the governor's office in Texas, reasoned that if long-range planning was good for the Texas economy, it would also be good for state government. In 1991, Governor Richards discussed the idea of mandating strategic planning in Texas government by requiring agencies to submit 5-year plans to the Governor's Office of Budget and Planning. Executive branch career bureaucrats and legislative leaders told the governor that the only way to ensure that agency heads took the process seriously would be to link it to their budgets. Otherwise, they predicted, the plans would be meaningless; reports would be produced and presented to the

GOBP, but little would change in the way agencies went about their business. This prediction was borne out in some measure in the legislative budget hearings, discussed later.

Once all parties were convinced that strategic planning and budgeting could be (and should be) linked, State Comptroller John Sharp and other executive and legislative branch officials designed a system of budget planning and performance reporting that came to be known as the Texas Performance Review, or TPR.[9] The system called for development of strategic plans in the even-numbered years and development of the budget in the odd-numbered years. Governor Richards delivered her first vision statement, *Texas Tomorrow—A Statewide Strategic Plan*, in 1992.

George W. Bush defeated Ann Richards in the 1994 governor's race, making the change to a Republican-controlled state government entrenched, if not complete. Still, the new governor believed in the process that his predecessor had put in place, later calling the document simply *Vision Texas*.

## SYSTEM IMPLEMENTATION AND DESCRIPTION

### Strategic Plans

The 2-year cycle of the Texas budget process consists of three main elements: planning, budgeting, and monitoring. The strategic planning process provides the foundation for the state's budget by identifying the major goals and objectives of the state and each state agency; developing strategies to achieve those goals; and establishing targets in the form of quantitative and qualitative measures for performance. Agencies are tasked with developing a new strategic plan each biennium. In January of even-numbered years (a year prior to the legislative session), the LBB and GOBP begin the process by sending strategic planning instructions to agencies along with statewide goals set forth in the governor's vision document. The primary purpose of strategic planning is "to anticipate and accommodate the future by identifying issues, opportunities, and problems."[10]

There are nine tiers to the planning template in the system (see Table 15.2). The governor and the LBB develop the first two in the statewide vision with the agency filling in the remaining seven for each program or service it produces. For purposes here, we focus on tiers seven and eight, those involving the objective measures of performance, outcomes, and efficiency, but a critical component of the process is for the agency to convince the GOBP and the LBB that its programs or services advance a stated goal in the vision statement.

The instructions state that the plan "serves as the basis for an agency's appropriation request (and) as a general rule, only approved goals, objectives, strategies, and measures may be included and carried forward to the [request]."[11] In other words, once a strategic plan is set and performance

**Table 15.2**
**Strategic Planning Tiers**

---

1. Statewide Vision, Mission, and Philosophy
   - Vision—the preferred future
   - Mission—a statement of a basic governmental purpose
   - Philosophy—a core value underlying the program or service
2. Statewide Goals and Benchmarks
   - Statewide goals—general ends toward which the state directs its efforts
   - Statewide benchmarks—specific performance indicators and targets used to assess progress
3. Agency Mission
   - The reason for an agency's existence
4. Agency Philosophy
   - The expression of core values and principles for the conduct of the mission
5. External/Internal Assessment
   - An evaluation of key factors that influence the success of an agency
6. Agency Goals
   - General ends toward which an agency directs its effort
7. Objectives and Outcome Measures
   - Clear targets for specific action and the quantified results or impacts of that action
8. Strategies and Output, Efficiency, and Explanatory Measures
   - Methods to achieve goals and objectives and the quantified end products proficiencies, and descriptive indicators of the agency's effort
9. Action Plans
   - Detailed methods that implement the strategies

---

*Source:* State of Texas.

measures established, any change to the performance measures must be approved through the system. In March of even-numbered years, agencies may request changes to the set of performance measures set for a program. Those are reviewed jointly by the GOBP and the LBB and, if approved, reported to the agency in June. Since the agency strategic plans are also due in June, the GOBP and LBB are not disposed to approve requested changes except for good reason in order to avoid delay. John Barton, Manager of the Fiscal Analysis and Reporting Group at LBB, notes that his staff works closely with agencies so that approved changes do not cause undue delay in submitting strategic plans.

Agencies submit their strategic plans by June 1. The LBB reviews literally thousands of targets and measures, sometimes rewriting agency goals and strategies. Performance measures are divided into four groups: output, efficiency, outcome, and explanatory. As an example, the Commission for the

**Table 15.3**
**Example of an Objective, Strategy, and Related Measures**

An example of an objective, strategy, and related measures is presented below to
illustrate the distinction between these measure classifications
Objective
    By fiscal year [20XX], increase library use by Texans with disabilities to
    12 percent of the eligible population
Strategy
    Provide direct library service by mail to Texas citizens with disabilities from a
    centralized collection of large print, Braille, and recorded books
Outcome Measures
    Percent of eligible population registered for Talking Book Program Services
Outcome Measures
    Number of persons served
    Number of volumes circulated
    Number of institutions served
Efficiency Measure
    Cost per person/institution served
    Cost per volume circulated
    Average time (in days) for requests
Explanatory Measure
    Number of Texans eligible for the Talking Book program
As part of the process of defining measures used in strategic planning, the two
budget offices will assist agencies in classifying measures into the categories used
in the budget request

*Source:* State of Texas.

Blind developed an objective to increase library use by citizens with disabilities to 12 percent of the eligible population (see Table 15.3). The strategy to
accomplish this objective was to provide direct mail availability of library materials called the Talking Book Program. Output measures include the number
of persons served and the number of volumes circulated. Efficiency measures
focus on the cost per person or unit. The outcome measure is the percent of
the eligible population using the service, and the explanatory measure is the
number of Texans eligible to use the service. Explanatory measures provide
legislators a context or indication of need.

## Appropriations Requests

In April of even-numbered years, instructions for the submissions of Legislative Appropriations Requests (LARS) are distributed to state agencies by the
GOBP and LBB, with the completed requests due in July or August. The performance budgeting system uses the goals and strategies as the major budget

elements with the legislature appropriating funds for each goal or strategy. Each of the 250 state agencies and institutions of higher education is required to have at least one goal and at least one strategy for each goal. Agency appropriations requests are organized around the performance measures used to indicate accomplishment of the larger strategy and goal.

The LBB collects the budget requests in July and August in preparation for joint budget hearings held by the LBB and GOBP. These hearings, held in August and September prior to the start of the legislative session in January of the odd-numbered years, gives the LBB and GOBP a first chance to ask questions of administrators about their agency's performance indicators. From October to December, the LBB and GOBP develop the budget proposal that will be presented to the state legislature. It will not be lost on students of government budgeting that budget hearings held by two staff agencies, even if one is legislative staff, is a bit unusual. Of perhaps more influence is the role of the LBB in producing *Budget Performance Assessments: State Agencies and Institutions*, the document used by legislators during the legislative session.

During the joint budget hearings, the LBB and GOBP staffs reach an agreement with each agency regarding the items to be included in the LAR, including the performance indicators. A small agency may compile data on dozens of indicators, large agencies hundreds. The book presented to legislators contains typically only four or five indicators for even the largest agencies. Since the document is prepared by the LBB, legislative staff has the final say on what is included. Of course, the indicators included must be those that present a full picture of the agency's purpose.

As an example, the performance measures for the Texas Education Agency (TEA) included in the book used by the 77th Texas Legislature in January 2001 were the percent of students passing the state standardized test, dropout rate, the retained in grade rate, and the percent of equalized revenue in the Foundation School Program, the state's education grant program designed to equalize education funding across districts. The program funding the TEA receives is divided among various efforts to improve the schools' (and thus the agency's) performance. Programs designed to reduce the dropout rate among Texas high school students are justified by the strategies put forward if the proposals are new and by the outcome performance indicators once the program is up and running.

Higher education performance measures are standardized across the state. Faculty at state institutions receive regular reports on their institution's performance on the indicators and are given information to be used for improving performance. For example, one indicator for all higher education institutions is the retention rate of all first time, full time, degree-seeking students beyond the first year. The legislator's book shows an overall statistic for the state along with statistics for each institution. Faculty at state institutions receive class rolls that identify students who are in this group, enabling them to focus special attention where it will most likely have an impact on the institution's retention rate.

## Performance Monitoring

Performance monitoring is the responsibility jointly of the LBB and the State Auditor's Office (SAO). The actual fieldwork is performed by the SAO and presented to the LBB in the form of a Measure Certification Audit. For example, an agency might report thirty performance measures in its appropriations request and have five of them audited by the SAO. Bringing to bear the audit skills of the SAO on the reporting process has forced agencies to take greater care in compiling and reporting performance data to ensure their accuracy and completeness. Hildreth[12] argues that the disclosure and audit standards of relevance, materiality, reliability, and neutrality commonly applied to financial reporting should be applied to productivity analyses. Brown and Pyers[13] pessimistically predict that the lack of an auditor's mindset in determining the accuracy of reported performance data is "tantamount to requiring the reporting of misleading data." The SAO brings the auditor's mindset to the Texas performance monitoring system.

Agencies are required to submit quarterly reports on their performance for each measure included in their budget. Agencies submit their actual performance electronically through the Automated Budget and Evaluation System of Texas (ABEST). This information can be accessed by the SAO, LBB, GOBP, and by members of the legislature although legislators typically use the system to inquire about agencies of particular interest, relying on the book that LBB produces for most of their information.

The LBB, GOBP, and SAO jointly produce a document called *Guide to Performance Measure Management* that is distributed to agencies. The stated purpose of the fifty-page document is to inform agencies about the state's performance measurement system and to identify the governor and legislature's expectations for agency involvement with the system. It also explains how changes can be made to the system (see the planning items in Figure 15.1), and the state auditor's role to ensure compliance and make information available.

At the end of each quarter, agencies have 1 month to enter information into ABEST with an explanation for any variation from any target of more than 5 percent. In December, the LBB produces the assessments report for the fiscal year that ended on August 30. Legislators use the report in budget deliberations during the legislative session; in even-numbered years, interim legislative committees study the assessment report. The interim committees, comprised of members from both the policy and funding committees, recognize good performance and expect explanations for poor performance.

John Barton of the LBB maintains that the interim years have become much more productive from a management and oversight perspective. This is made

Figure 15.1
Example of an Objective, Strategy, and Related Measures

# Texas' Strategic Planning, Performance Budgeting, and Performance Monitoring System

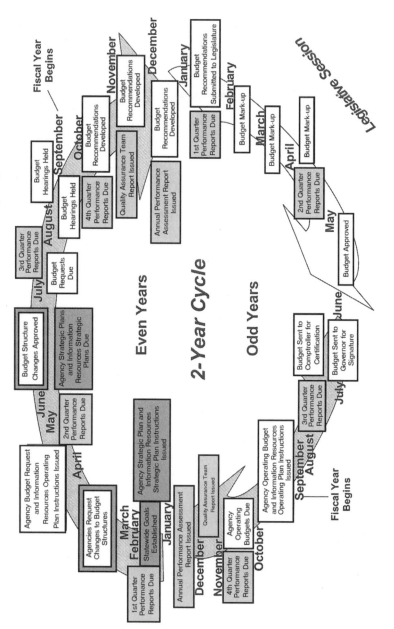

possible by the biennial budget format. Legislators in most states must produce a budget every year, often under severe time constraints that limit the attention given to oversight of agency performance in terms of both budget compliance and program results. The interim in the 2-year cycle provides an opportunity not only for that work to take place, but also for the policy and funding committees to work together. Cooperation between these committees has given legislators an understanding of both committees' perspectives.

In 1998 the House Appropriations Subcommittee on Performance Based Budgeting asked the LBB to produce a list of agencies that did a good job using the system and a list of those that were not doing a good job and to schedule hearings with those agency heads. The list, which came to be known as the "Good, the Bad, and the Ugly" is now institutionalized and agency heads seek to be included on the list of good performers and, once included among the bad or ugly, do what it takes to stay off the list in subsequent compilations. Former Representative Henry Cuellar, who holds both a law degree and Ph.D. in government from the University of Texas and later served as Texas Secretary of State, chaired the subcommittee during the first round of interim hearings in 1994 and grilled agency heads from the bad and ugly list. Having been a proponent of the system from the start, Cuellar made sure that agency heads understood legislative oversight in Austin was changing.

Oversight agencies also use the reports made available through ABEST. The Comptroller of Public Accounts uses the data in performance audits conducted under the state program evaluation effort, Texas Performance Review. The Texas Sunset Review Commission uses information in its evaluation of state agencies. The sunset review operates on a 12-year cycle to provide information on most state agencies.

## THE EFFECTS OF PERFORMANCE BUDGETING

### Budget Hearings

Budget hearings provide a forum for agency heads to make their case for appropriations requests and for members of the legislature to obtain information. Prior to the 1991 reforms, hearings conducted by the Texas Legislature were like hearings elsewhere, with agency heads talking about needs and members focusing on dollar amounts. Now there is as much, if not more, interest in performance. Agencies talk about the impact of budget increases in terms of agency effectiveness and accomplishments, and members ask pointed questions about failure to meet performance targets.

Members of the legislature receive the LBB and SAO reports prior to the hearings. At first, agency heads were caught off guard, not being prepared to answer questions about their agency's performance. According to John Barton, by the time hearings were held in February and March of 1995 for the 1996–1997 biennia it was apparent that agency heads understood that the hearings had changed in a fundamental way. Hearing preparation became very important for agency heads. Barton says that while it might be difficult to make the case that there is a more efficient allocation of resources, the process gives legislators more tools and has made agency heads more aware of their agency's performance. David Ammons[14] argues that progress in the use of performance information stems from agency heads' resignation to its use. In the Texas legislature, its use means that members have more knowledge and ask better questions than before, making the hearings more productive. Agencies have a powerful tool as well. They often make the claim that performance costs money and that legislators must put the state's money where their mouths are if they want targets met.

### LBB Workload

Analysts at the LBB must now understand agency activities to a greater degree than in the past. The real difficulty is developing a set of measures that reflect the economic value of an activity. One of the primary reasons for the failure of PPBS's rollout in the federal government during the Johnson administration was a feeling on the part of agency administrators that the value of their services simply could not be measured. They assumed that they would not be successful in the budget process or at least not as successful as agencies that were able to quantify their programs and services.[15]

To some degree agency heads in Texas have experienced this same feeling of helplessness from a lack of control. When asked about the failure to meet a target, agency heads are likely to respond, "Yes, but ..." hedging their discussions of performance. The task for the analyst is to determine whether a performance level as reported is reasonable. If the analyst is convinced that the agency's performance is acceptable, even commendable, but did not meet the target as set by the appropriations legislation, the expectations for the indicator may be adjusted in the interim cycle. John Barton reports that, early in the process, his office handled a large number of revisions to expected performance targets when there was no history. Even after a decade of development, LBB analysts spend a great amount of their time working with agencies on their strategic plans and performance indicators. The result of this has been to increase both the management function of the LBB and its expertise about agency operations.

Another cause of budget reform failure in governments has been the lack of technical capacity within agencies to track and produce new information and to organize their budget requests in new ways. PPBS was successful initially at the Department of Defense because consultants familiar with the techniques of operations research assisted in its implementation at DOD. In the early stages of the ABEST system, consultants were brought in to help in its implementation at the agency level. There was a steep learning curve and the LBB had to walk agencies through the process. Agency personnel were made to feel a part of the design team (their knowledge was critical because they know their agencies and programs best) along with the consultants retained to assist agencies. This reduced the feeling that a new process was being forced on them. Agency officials were assured that no one expected the system to be perfect immediately and that it would take time to develop a set of performance indicators that would ultimately represent the accomplishments of their agencies.

The number of measures reported to the LBB was reduced by 25 percent from 1998 to 2001 and the goal is to reduce this further in order to streamline the system. The major purpose of this effort has been to eliminate measures deemed invalid or that lack reliability, key characteristics of useful performance measures.[16] The LBB and GOBP want to develop better measures, not more. LBB's John Barton suggests that the performance reporting could be more closely linked with budget decisions, but for now the LBB and Texas Legislature are content with improvements in the performance indicators.

## LBB Influence

The Legislative Budget Board has tremendous influence in the budget preparation process. First, it has a great deal of power to determine the list of performance indicators included in the performance assessment documents used by legislators during the regular legislative session and in the interim. Representative Cuellar requested that the LBB produce the good, bad, and ugly list. This list now consists of ten agencies that did a good job during the previous cycle, ten that improved, and ten that need to improve. Media coverage of the list ensures that agency heads seek to be included among the good and find inclusion among the bad and ugly uncomfortable. This latter group of agencies works with the LBB staff to improve their performance.

In 1993 the LBB was given power to penalize agencies as they saw fit for poor performance. The LBB was reluctant to impose harsh penalties, preferring instead to focus on positive incentives. In an unprecedented move, the legislature agreed to allow the LBB to bestow employee pay bonuses to agencies that performed well both in terms of process and outcomes. In 1999 five agencies were given this reward. When legislators discovered that the bonuses were concentrated in those agencies' top management, the program was modified to ensure that all employees responsible for excellent performance share in the benefit. The next year about 40 agencies qualified for bonus compensation. The system is now institutionalized as the Enhanced Compensation Awards program. An agency or institution that meets or exceeds the performance targets included in the appropriations bill is authorized to provide compensation for employees who directly contributed to such improvements needed to reach those goals. The awards are only available to classified employees and may not exceed 6.8 percent of the employee's annual base pay.

## CONCLUSION

The Texas performance budget system, in place for more than a decade, has become an institutionalized part of budget preparation and adoption. Its ability to last so long stems from the importance placed on its use by key officials in both the executive and legislative branches of Texas state government. The longevity of this type of budget reform is often hindered by the difficulty of establishing performance measures suited to the needs of legislators and agency officials, the perception by key actors in the process that nothing has changed as a result of its implementation.[17] In Texas the establishment of performance measures has taken a decade but the impact on agency behavior was apparent in the second budget cycle.

When budget scholars discuss the use of performance or outcome budgeting, scholar X invariably poses the question whether an agency's failure to meet a target should result in a budget increase, under the assumption that more resources will produce greater performance, or a budget cut as punishment. Scholar Y's response is almost as predictable as the question: "It depends." In fact, neither is the case. The most dramatic changes produced by this budget reform in Texas have not been in budget outcomes. No one points to budget changes, either incremental or otherwise, and attributes them to the performance data. Rather, the Texas system has changed the interaction between legislators and agency officials in the hearing process and in how agency heads manage the performance of their programs. Executive branch officials appear before legislative committees better prepared to answer questions about the performance of their agencies and return to the trenches to focus agency effort toward meeting the targets.

A few political leaders have resisted development of performance indicators because of the potential fallout from failure to meet those targets. For instance, the Texas Education Agency (TEA) has resisted using the percent of students who pass the state's standardized academic test, the Texas Assessment of Knowledge and Skills (TAKS), as a performance indicator that would affect the agency's budget. But the TEA has little hope of convincing legislators, the state auditor, GOBP, and LBB that this indicator does not meet the characteristics of validity and reliability. Moreover, these data are easily reported and any resistance to their use is likely to raise questions about the agency's motive.

It is much more likely that the legislature would question the agency as to the cause for the failure rather than use some predetermined rubric for calculating a new budget. If the agency can demonstrate the relationship between a known problem and its lagging performance, it could well receive greater resources to address the issue. For example, if the TEA could show a causal relationship between truancy and performance on TAKS, it might receive greater funds for programs that address that problem. If the agency cannot offer a reasonable explanation for its failure or demonstrate that the target was unrealistic, the legislative response is likely to be greater oversight rather than a change to the budget. Unfortunately this may require evaluative expertise the agency lacks.

There is no denying that the use of performance indicators in Texas has changed the way executive branch officials manage. The common complaint for years about standardized tests in public schools, such as the TAKS, is that they force teachers to teach to the test. For better or worse, all state agencies in Texas now have performance indicators for each and every state program. Developing indicators that are valid and reliable is the primary concern for both agencies and the legislature. The consensus from the LBB and GOBP is that the new system is helping state government in Texas achieve greater performance.

## REFERENCES

Ammons, David N., "A Proper Mentality for Benchmarking," *PAR* (March/April, 1999), 105–109.

Barrett, Katherine, Richard Greene, Michele Mariani, and Anya Sostek, "The Way We Tax," *Governing* (February 2003), 20–97.

Barton, John, *Personal interview* (April 6, 2001).

Brown, Richard E., and James B. Pyers, "Service Efforts and Accomplishments Reporting: Has Its Time Really Come," *Public Budgeting & Finance* (Winter 1998), 101–113.

Cothran, Dan A., "Entrepreneurial Budgeting: An Emerging Reform?" *PAR* (September/October, 1993), 445–454.

Governor's Office of Budget and Planning, and Legislative Budget Board, *Instructions for Preparing and Submitting Agency Strategic Plans, Fiscal Years 2001–2005*. Austin, TX: State of Texas, 2000.

Grizzle, Gloria, "Performance Measures for Budget Justification: Developing a Selection Strategy," *Public Productivity and Performance Review* (Winter 1985), 328–341.

———, "Does Budget Format Really Govern the Actions of Budget-makers?" *Public Budgeting & Finance* (Spring 1986), 60–70.

Herman, Ken, "Will Lotto Get Harder to Win? Bet on It," *Austin American Statesman* (January 31, 2003a), B1.

———, "Texas May Join Both Big Lotteries," *Austin American Statesman* (July 1, 2003b), B1.

Hildreth, W. Bartley, Applying Professional Disclosure Standards to Productivity Financial Analyses, *Public Productivity and Management Review* (September 1983), 269–287.

Kraemer, Richard H., Charldean Newell, and David F. Prindle, *Texas Politics*, 8th edition. Belmont, CA: Wadsworth, 2002.

Lauth, Thomas P., "Performance Budgeting in the Georgia Budgetary Process," *Public Budgeting & Finance* (Spring 1985), 67–82.

———, "Budget and Productivity in State Government: Not Integrated but Friendly," *Public Productivity and Management Review* (Spring 1987), 21–32.

Legislative Budget Board, *Budget and Performance Assessments: State Agencies and Institutions*. Austin, TX: State of Texas, 2000.

Legislative Budget Board, Governor's Office of Budget and Planning, and State Auditor's Office, *Guide to Performance Measure Management*, 2000 edition. Austin, TX: State of Texas. Allen Schick, "The Road to PPB," *PAR* (December 1966), 243–258.

———, "Budgeting for Results: Recent Developments in Five Industrialized Countries," *PAR* (January/February 1990), 26–34.

Wildavsky, Aaron, "Rescuing Policy Analysis from PPBS," *PAR*, (March/April, 1969), 189.

## NOTES

1. Schick, 1966, 1990; Lauth, 1985, 1987; Grizzle, 1986.
2. Kraemer and Newell, 2002, 280.
3. See *Fulmore v. Lane*, 140 S.W. 405, 421 (Texas 1911).
4. Barrett et al. 2003, 88.
5. Figures calculated from data in *The Book of the States* (2003) and *Statistical Abstract of the United States* (2003).
6. Herman, 2003a.
7. Herman, 2003b.
8. Kraemer, Newell, and Prindle, 2002, 127.
9. Kraemer, Newell, and Prindle, 2002, 220.
10. GOBP, LBB, 2000.
11. GOBP, LBB, 2000, 12.
12. Hildreth, 1983.
13. Brown and Pyers, 1998.
14. Ammons, 1999.
15. Schick, 1966; Wildavsky, 1969.
16. Grizzle, 1985.
17. Cothran, 1993.

# CHAPTER 16

# Utah: Economics, Political Culture, and Priority Setting

*James J. Gosling*

Policymakers in Utah, together with those in most other states, were forced to confront major revenue shortfalls in the early years of the twenty-first century. A national recession followed by a less-than-robust recovery dropped revenues well below what was required to continue spending at current levels, let alone pay for recession-sensitive spending increases. In that regard, Utah fared pretty much like the rest of the states. Yet Utah's predicament, and its response to it, bore a certain distinctiveness, which Utah's political culture and demography help us to understand.

## UTAH'S POLITICAL CULTURE

Unlike the rest of the West, Utah was settled by a community rather than by individuals seeking their economic fortune. Driven successively from New York, Ohio, Illinois, and Missouri, the early Mormon pioneers sought refuge in what is today the state of Utah. With their leader Brigham Young, the majority of settlers made their homes in the valley of the northern Wasatch Mountains, east of the Great Salt Lake. Other pioneers branched out into central and southern Utah, while still others migrated to parts of what is now southern Idaho and southern Nevada. But the Salt Lake valley soon became the religious, economic, and cultural center of this new land of Zion.

Today about 70 percent of Utahns are members of the Church of Jesus Christ of Latter Day Saints (or the LDS Church, as it is called), or at least their names appear on the church's rolls, whether they remain active or not. All members of Utah's congressional delegation are Mormon, as are its governor, attorney general, and 90 percent of state legislators.[1] This heavily dispropor-tionate religious affiliation gives Utah's political culture a decidedly moralistic character, in which both residents and policymakers look to government to advance and protect widely held conceptions of the common good. The LDS Church's religious teachings and moral principles clearly influence popular conceptions of what constitutes the public interest in Utah. At the same time, however, Utahans are not immune from the West's ideological attraction to individualism, which values personal liberty, entrepreneurship, and governmental restraint. A tension thus exists between the pulls of moralism and individualism—one that is typically resolved in favor of individualism, with its classical liberal roots, unless, that is, it runs up against the moral teachings or interests of the dominant religion. Issues of abortion, alcohol sales, legalized gambling, or same-sex marriage especially resonate with LDS Church members and evoke the active interest and, when deemed necessary, the political intervention of church leaders. On these select matters, religious and moral considerations trump individualism's tenets. Otherwise, Utahans, like their neighbors in surrounding states, prize individual effort, personal responsibility, market-based outcomes, and limited government.

Despite its religious dominance, the LDS Church operates no parochial elementary or secondary schools.[2] The Utah Constitution, ratified in 1895, specifies that "the legislature shall make laws for the establishment and maintenance of a system of public schools, which shall be open to all the children of the state and be free from sectarian control."[3] This provision, along with two other events, helped pave the way to statehood. Five years earlier, Church President Wilford Woodruff proscribed the practice of plural marriage (polygamy) and cohabitation, and made it grounds for excommunication. In the following year, 1891, leaders dissolved the People's Party, a political party that had functioned as the political arm of the LDS Church, and Mormon authorities urged members to affiliate with one of the two major national political parties, the Republicans or the Democrats.[4] After six unsuccessful petitions for statehood, Utah's founding fathers were determined to send a message to the nation's capital that Utah's political leaders had taken important steps toward formally separating civil and religious affairs. With these actions as assurance, President Grover Cleveland, on January 4, 1896, gave final approval to Utah's addition as the forty-fifth state in the Union, following the tenets of the Enabling Act passed by Congress.

## UTAH'S DISTINCTIVE DEMOGRAPHY AND ITS BUDGETARY IMPLICATIONS

The choice of LDS Church leaders not to establish a parochial school system has had important implications for public education in Utah, and for state budgetary support for it. With the highest percentage of school-age children of any state, reflecting the value placed by the LDS Church on large families, Utah educates one and a half children for every child educated on the national average. Since Utah has a comparatively low percentage of students attending private schools, the financial burden of meeting this demographic challenge falls largely to state taxpayers.

Elementary and secondary education account for 47 percent of Utah's combined general fund and uniform school fund expenditures. (Together, they are comparable to most states' general fund.) Higher Education gets another 19 percent, bringing education's share of state spending to about two-thirds.[5] This high claim on state resources taxes the ability-to-pay of a working population that earns only 83 percent of the national average annual salary.[6] Among the states, Utah ranks tenth in state spending on public education per $1,000 of personal income.[7] But given the large number of students to be educated, Utah ranks dead last in per pupil spending. It would take an additional $1 billion in state funding to put Utah's per pupil spending at the national average, an amount equal to about 50 percent more than state and local governments currently spend on K-12 education.[8]

In addition to having the highest birthrate in the nation, Utah has experienced the fastest rate of growth in minority student population in the nation since 1998, adding to the enrollment pressure placed on its schools. Hispanic students constitute the vast majority of that growth.[9]

## UTAH'S ECONOMY

Between 1992 and 2000, America's record period of economic growth, Utah's economy performed better than the national average on all significant indicators, including population, employment, average annual pay, and personal income.[10] Among the states, Utah was the nation's third fastest job creator during the 1990s. A favorable business climate, a well-diversified economy, and an educated workforce promoted economic growth. The Corporation for Enterprise Development has consistently given Utah a grade of A for economic development and performance, placing it among the top states nationally.[11] Utah's economy is highly diversified, led by the service, high technology, biomedical, health, and defense-related sectors. The LDS Church's national headquarters and the state's universities and colleges add prominent major employers. Utah offers its employers a highly educated workforce, ranking second among the states in the percentage of the population with a high school diploma and eleventh in the percent of residents over the age of 25 years who hold bachelor's degrees, and leading the nation in the percentage of homes with personal computers.[12]

Like most of the nation, however, Utah has fallen on hard economic times. It has especially felt the effects of a national economic downturn in the high technology and biomedical industries. Although Utah fared better than most states in population growth and unemployment rate in 2001 and 2002, it fell below the national average in the growth of employment, taxable retail sales, and personal income.[13] Between December 2000 and December 2002, nonfarm employment in Utah fell by 2.3 percent, compared to a national average of 1.3 percent. It should not be a surprise that as the economy softened, state government revenues fell short of projections.

## FACING REVENUE SHORTFALLS

In Utah, revenue estimates are made by a committee composed of executive and legislative branch staff members, together with university and private sector economists. The Revenue Assumptions Committee, as the body is called, includes representatives from the Governor's Office of Planning and Budget, the Tax Commission, the Department of Workforce Services, the Energy Office, the Office of the Legislative Fiscal Analyst, the University of Utah and Brigham Young University, Salt Lake City, and economists from the financial services and industrial sectors.

A comparative review of revenue estimating among the states suggests that the traditional major institutional players in revenue estimating—the governor's participants, including the state budget office and executive revenue agency, and the legislative fiscal office—should be expected to play highly influential roles in projecting revenues even within a broadly representative committee structure. And that is clearly the case in Utah. The Governor's Office of Planning and Budget assumes the lead role as the Committee prepares revenue estimates that accompany the governor's executive budget recommendations. Later, when the budgetary process moves into the legislative review phase, the Office of the Legislative Fiscal Analyst takes the lead. The legislature's Executive Appropriations Committee (about which more will be said later) is not legally bound to adopt the Revenue Assumptions Committee's estimates, but it usually does, or it makes only modest departures from them.

Confronted with sagging economic indicators, revenue estimates made in October 2001 put the projected FY 2002 revenue shortfall at $177 million. The Revenue Assumptions Committee raised the projected shortfall to $203 million just 2 months later, as the economic effects of the September 11 terrorist attacks became clearer. With budgetary action shifting to the legislature, and with the advantage of another quarter of tax collections and more recent data on leading economic indicators, the Committee in February revised the December revenue estimates downward again, pointing to a $257 million revenue shortfall. The legislature completed action in early March (the details of which are recounted below), to eliminate the shortfall for FY 2002 and pass what legislators and fiscal analysts believed to be a balanced budget for FY 2003.

Just a month later, the Revenue Assumption Committee revised revenues down again for 2002, this time by an additional $138 million, even though only a little more than 2 months remained in the fiscal year. The Committee also projected a $173 million revenue shortfall for the coming 2003 fiscal year. To address the FY 2002 shortfall, Governor Michael Leavitt responded by calling the legislature into a May special session to eliminate the gap between expected revenues and budgeted expenditures. He also gave notice that he would later work with the legislature to create a plan to address the expected shortfall in FY 2003. After identifying priorities and working with his budget staff to develop gubernatorial recommendations, Governor Leavitt called the legislature into another special session on June 26, and brought them back on July 8 and 9. Then, 6 months later, a declining stock market, reinforced by growing fears of a U.S. war in Iraq, undermined consumer confidence and depressed revenues further, resulting in a newly projected revenue shortfall of $117 million for the 6-plus months remaining in FY 2003.

Although this chapter focuses on the fiscal challenges and difficult politics associated with economic downturn, it should be noted that Utah, like other western states, found its economic fortunes much improved by mid-decade. In near rags-to-riches fashion, strongly accelerating economic growth added over $1 billion to state tax coffers for the 2006 and 2007 fiscal years alone. Instead of worrying about how to eliminate a revenue shortfall, budget makers' attention turned to what to do with sizable projected budget surpluses.

## TAKING ACTION TO BALANCE THE BUDGET

For both FY 2002 and FY 2003, Utah's budget makers had to plug a combined revenue shortfall of $685 million. To put that level in perspective, Utah's approved annual general fund and school fund budgets averaged about $3.6 billion for FY 2002 and FY 2003.[14] Thus Utah's governor and legislature faced no trifling task in bringing the state budget into balance.

To erase a combined $395 million revenue shortfall in FY 2002, the legislature tapped the state's "rainy day" fund for $113 million. Although that looks like an easy part of the budget balancing equation, it engendered a heated political discussion in both legislative chambers. Some conservative Republicans objected to drawing that much from the contingency fund, despite their Republican governor's support, and favored deeper spending cuts to reduce the amount taken. They also took umbrage at the governor's call to use bonding to finance capital spending that the legislature had previously funded out of the operating budget. The programmatically painless expediency of the substitution proved compelling to a legislative majority, as the legislature acted to replace $70 million of operating funds with bond revenue. To fill the rest of the gap, the legislature turned to budget reductions in all major budget categories. (See Table 16.1 for a categorical breakdown of the actions taken to eliminate the FY 2002 shortfall.)

Facing a combined revenue shortfall of $290 million in FY 2003, and with a nearly depleted "rainy day" fund, legislators searched for ways to balance expenditures and revenues short of major cuts in state programs. Among the most significant actions, the legislature shifted $66 million from Utah's Centennial Highway Fund to cover general fund expenditures.[15] It also replaced

**Table 16.1**
**Accommodating Revenue Shortfalls**

| | |
|---|---|
| **FY 2002** | |
| *General Session* | |
| Revenue Shortfall | ($256.9 million) |
| Budget Reductions | $144.1 million |
| Transfer from Rainy Day Fund | $45.4 million |
| Other Sources | $67.4 million |
| *May Special Session* | |
| Revenue Shortfall | ($137.9 million) |
| Transfer from Rainy Day Fund | $67.9 million |
| Replace Cash with Bond Revenue | $70.0 million |
| **FY 2003** | |
| *June/July Special Session* | |
| Revenue Shortfall | ($173.1 million) |
| Budget Reductions | $69.2 million |
| Replace Cash with Bond Revenue | $15.8 million |
| Transfer from Centennial Highway Fund | $66.4 million |
| Transfer from Tobacco Settlement Fund | $17.8 million |
| Miscellaneous Revenue | $3.9 million |
| *December Special Session* | |
| Revenue Shortfall | ($117.3 million) |
| Operating Budget Reductions | $21.5 million |
| Cash-Funded Capital Reductions | $24.3 million |
| Replace Cash with Bond Revenue | $35.0 million |
| Transfer from Tobacco Settlement Fund | $21.1 million |
| Designated Sales Tax | $4.5 million |
| Other Sources | $10.9 million |
| Total Shortfall, FY 2002 and FY 2003 | ($685.2 million) |

*Source:* Office of the Utah Legislative Fiscal Analyst, *2003–2004 Appropriations Report.*

$51 million of cash-funded capital projects with bond revenues, and drew $39 million in one-time revenues from the Tobacco Permanent Trust Fund to further close the state-funded revenue shortfall. Budget reductions added another $118 million in savings.

Again, conservative Republicans argued that budget reductions failed to go deep enough, preferring steeper cuts instead of increased reliance on bonding and a slowdown in state highway construction. Conservatives worried that the legislature's reliance on fund transfers and bonding would make general tax increases necessary if the revenue situation worsened.

As Table 16.1 illustrates, of the total $685 million in revenue shortfall to be dealt with in the 2002 and 2003 fiscal years, the legislature used budget reductions to eliminate $259 million, or 38 percent of the total. The rest was accommodated using fund transfers, substituting bonding for cash, and drawing upon one-time revenues. Both Governor Leavitt and the legislative leaders made good on their commitment to avoid a general tax increase.

This is not to suggest that coming up with $259 million in budget cuts is easily done. Experience shows that to get that level of reduction, budget cutters must turn to the state's biggest ticket items—elementary and secondary education, higher education, corrections, and health (primarily Medicaid). With elementary and secondary education claiming nearly half of state-funded expenditures in Utah, public education is a logical place to turn for budget savings. Yet there is no question that education is the most politically sensitive policy area in the budget. In addition to the pressures imposed by Utah's demography, the Utah Education Association is one of the most visible and effective lobby groups in a state in which organized labor is otherwise politically weak. Teachers waged a statewide campaign aimed at convincing the legislature to limit cuts to education by using bonding and fund transfers to bear the bulk of shortfall reduction. Governor Leavitt embraced the teachers' message, urging the legislature to protect education.

Public education took a hit of $25 million, or 17 percent of the $144 million in budget reductions, to eliminate the revenue shortfall in FY 2002, but it amounted to only about 1.5 percent of appropriated funding.[16] In the special sessions to deal with the FY 2003 revenue shortfall, education escaped essentially unscathed, as the legislature substituted bonding authority in place of lost operating funding for school facilities—a substitution that would not have likely happened a few years earlier.[17] Over the 2 years, corrections, public safety, health, human services, and commerce bore the largest share of shortfall reduction.

Public education went on to receive an additional $29 million in state funds for FY 2004.[18] Governor Leavitt complimented the legislature for passing "a lean, responsible and balanced budget and carefully prioritized complex policy decisions. The budget was balanced without raising general taxes—an important priority to the governor during these difficult economic times—or dipping into the rainy day fund."[19] He saw the budget as reflecting the priorities he communicated to the legislature. In his budget recommendations, the governor challenged the legislature not to raise general taxes or further draw down an already eviscerated rainy day fund. He also set education and health care for the needy as his top policy priorities.

Although public education received $13 million less in state funds than the governor requested, the legislature approved the governor's requested $30 million increase for health.[20] Among the most costly areas of the budget, Medicaid received the highest percentage increase in state funds, at 13 percent, restoring part of the reductions made in prior budget-balancing actions. Major shares of that increase went to restore eligibility for the medically needy to 100 percent of the federal poverty level and to meet caseload growth.

To accommodate spending increases, the legislature made significant reductions in the budgets for natural resources and economic development, and increased state funds for higher education by only three-tenths of 1 percent, though it allowed the state's colleges and universities to increase tuition by $27 million. To bring in new revenues without a general tax increase, the legislature eliminated the sales tax exemptions for cable and satellite services (+$14 million), increased taxes and fees on waste (+$2.3 million), raised fees and markups in state liquor stores (+1.7 million), and modified sales tax definitions (+$1.4 million). The legislature also dipped into $9.1 million of one-time tobacco settlement revenues.

## GUBERNATORIAL–LEGISLATIVE POLITICAL RELATIONSHIPS

The recent period of revenue shortfalls has brought with it more cooperative relations between the legislature and the governor. In a time of fiscal need, when expenditures must be brought into line with available revenues, perhaps the governor's recommendations give the legislature a certain political cover. Legislators can deflect some of the criticism over budget cuts to the governor. Yet the governor's lead can also put legislators in a political box. A governor who publicly urges the legislature to eliminate shortfalls without a general tax increase puts that body in a tenuous political position. A legislature that does not want to be seen by voters as raising taxes against the governor's wishes (usually an unpopular thing to do, whether the governor supports it or not) must either find alternative sources of revenue or come up with corresponding budget reductions. Following the governor's roadmap for cuts, with perhaps some fine-tuning to reflect legislative interests, is often the comparatively safest political course for the legislature during difficult economic times.

In times of strong economic growth and revenue expansion, however, the legislature has a freer political hand to go its own way. The prospect of a large revenue surplus gives the legislature (as well as the governor) greater latitude to push for increased spending for projects of importance to them and their political supporters, and it invites debate about how much of the anticipated surplus should be returned to taxpayers in the form of tax cuts. Not only can that debate divide the legislature; it can also drive a wedge between the legislature and the governor, even when the legislative majority and the governor are of the same political party. That appears to be what happened in Utah during the economic good times of the last half of the 1990s.

Utah is the second most Republican state in the nation, right behind Idaho. The Republican Party in Utah holds nearly all of the major elected offices in the state, including the governorship, both U.S. Senate seats, two of the three U.S. House seats, and the attorney general's office. Within the legislature, Republicans hold "veto-proof" majorities, outnumbering Democrats in the

Senate by a margin of 22–7, and by 52–23 in the House. But that does not mean that relations within the majority party in the legislature, or between the majority party and the governor, have been smooth.

Within the legislature, internal Republican Party divisions have both normative and geographic roots. Normative differences center on questions about what should be government's appropriate role in society; the extent to which government should seek to control growth; the degree to which public policy decisions should be made locally; and how much government should tax and spend, and for what purposes. Geographic divisions align the interests of rural legislators against urban legislators.

These strains of difference overlap. Rural legislators on the whole are more politically conservative than their urban colleagues, tending to be fiscally conservative and to take an individualistic perspective on matters of public policy that do not involve matters of morality. Rural legislators are also better organized and more cohesive than their urban counterparts. Rural influence in Utah politics peaked during House Speaker Mel Brown's tenure (1995–1998). Brown was elected speaker with the unified support of rural legislators representing districts outside of the populous northern Wasatch Front, who comprised the legislature's so-called cowboy caucus. Although a representative from Midvale within the highly urbanized Salt Lake County, Brown owned a 285-acre dairy farm in rural Coalville, located about 50 miles northeast of Salt Lake City, and he shared his rural colleagues' ideology and interests. He, like them, set out to shift political influence away from what they perceived as the moderate, even liberal, contingent within the party, into which they readily lumped Governor Leavitt. Having a friendly House Speaker for leverage, rural conservatives looked to win support from sympathetic conservative suburban legislators.

For rural conservatives, the contest was not about ideology and interests alone; it was also about wielding political power. Not surprisingly, that concern spilled over into gubernatorial–legislative relations. Utah's award of the 2002 Winter Olympics crystallized ideological and fiscal differences between the governor and rural conservatives, especially those pertaining to growth and transportation. Suspicious of state-led planning efforts, rural legislators also worried about the high cost of making Olympics-related, or at least Olympics-justified, transportation improvements that would benefit the urban northern part of the state, where the Olympic venues would be located.

Realizing that the governor is best positioned to set the state's policy and budgetary agenda, Speaker Brown led an effort within the legislature to make inroads into gubernatorial leadership. With the support, or at least acquiescence, of the Senate leadership, Speaker Brown instructed the Legislative Fiscal Analyst in 1997 to no longer include the governor's budget recommendations in legislative budget documents. The Office of the Legislative Fiscal Analyst had traditionally used the governor's recommendations as the starting point in the appropriations process, offering alternatives where deemed appropriated. Making no mention of the governor's recommendation, the change substituted last year's appropriation as the starting point, a practice that continues to this day.[21]

Relations between the legislature and the governor improved toward the end of the decade for two reasons: the creation and ascendancy of a countervailing caucus of moderate Republicans, and the election of a new House speaker who showed greater willingness to work cooperatively with the governor. The new speaker, Marty Stephens, came to power amidst ethics violations that forced former Speaker Brown's resignation. Stephens, a banking executive from suburban Ogden, shared the individualistic and conservative fiscal values of rural legislators, but proved more attentive to the concerns of the party's more moderate, urban legislators. Those issues included educational finance and accountability, economic development, and deregulation. With the economic downturn of the early 2000s and the successive revenue shortfalls that accompanied it, Stephens' attention, and that of his counterpart, Senate President Al Mansell, necessarily turned to budget balancing and its fiscal and policy implications.

There exists no systematic, empirical study of institutional influence on budgetary outcomes in Utah. Nevertheless, one comparative study of executive–legislative power struggles over the budgetary process in western states explored attributed influence. The author asked executive and legislative budget analysts in thirteen states whether they had observed a shift in executive–legislative influence in state budgeting. Those responding "yes" were then asked whether the shift favored the governor or the legislature. A majority of the Utah respondents saw a shift that favored the legislature in the 1990s.[22]

## LEGISLATIVE BUDGETING IN AN EXECUTIVE BUDGET STATE[23]

Utah is an executive budget state. Assisted by the Office of Planning and Budget (OPB), administratively part of the Governor's Office, the governor begins the executive phase of the budgetary process in June by issuing instructions and guidelines to state agencies on budget preparation. Agencies prepare their budget requests during the summer, and typically submit them to the OPB in September. From September through November, executive budget analysts review the requests, and the governor, budget director, and key budget staff members hold executive budget hearings. The OPB then prepares budget recommendations and briefs the governor on them. The budget must be wrapped up before Christmas, to meet the statutory requirement that the Legislative Fiscal Analyst receive a draft copy of the executive budget, "on a confidential basis," 30 days before it is due for presentation to the legislature."[24]

Legislative fiscal analysts do not wait for the governor's executive budget recommendations before they begin their review of agency requests. They are able to get a head start because the OPB, as a matter of established practice, sends copies of agency requests to the Office of the Legislative Fiscal Analyst shortly after it receives them. This allows legislative analysts to review agency requests and develop recommendations on a timeline that roughly parallels that followed by the governor's budget analysts.

Utah's legislative process of budgetary review and decision making has several distinctive features. First, all 104 legislators are members of the Joint Appropriations Committee and are assigned to one or more of its nine subcommittees. That gives each member a tangible role and active involvement in the committee phase of the budgetary process. It also creates the potential for unwieldy proceedings. Imagine requiring the subcommittees to report to the Joint Appropriations Committee, which in Utah's case, is the entire legislative body.

To bring order and coherence to the process of legislative budgeting, the legislature makes use of a unique institutional adaptation: the 20-member Executive Appropriations Committee. It is composed of the cochairs of the Joint Appropriations Committee (drawn from the majority party), who also chair the Executive Appropriations Committee; five majority-party leaders and four minority-party leaders from both the House and the Senate; and two other majority-party members, who serve as covice chairs but may only vote when representing an absent cochair. Thus, the Executive Appropriations Committee has eighteen voting members—ten from the majority party, and eight from the minority party, giving the majority party only a two-seat margin.

The structure of the Executive Appropriations Committee institutionalizes the legislative leadership's role in the process of budgetary review and decision making. Committee membership includes the House Speaker and the Senate President, together with the majority leaders, majority whips, and assistant majority whips of the two chambers. Minority-party membership includes *both* chambers' minority leaders, whips and assistant whips, and caucus managers.

The Executive Appropriations Committee's influence is felt most at the beginning and toward the end of the legislative budgetary process. At the beginning, the Executive Appropriations Committee (not the Joint Appropriations Committee) parcels out appropriations targets to each of the appropriations subcommittees based on revenue projections, normally holding some funding leeway in reserve. The subcommittees are then expected to set spending priorities and make associated appropriations decisions within the targets. However, by allocating targets to subcommittees, the Executive Appropriations Committee establishes policy priorities even before the subcommittees arrive at their spending choices. Toward the end of the budgetary process, the Committee can approve the subcommittees' actions, revise them up or down, reallocate among appropriations, and decide what to do with the fiscal resources held in reserve.

The short, 45-day legislative session, which puts the Executive Appropriations Committee at the center of legislative budgeting, usually affords little time for floor debate on the budget. With the partisan imbalance that exists in

Utah's legislature, the vote on the floor becomes routinely predictable. In the contemporary setting, the Republicans can do just about whatever they want. The major compromises and concessions that Republicans make to Democrats typically come out of the Executive Appropriations process, fashioned by negotiations between the two parties' legislative leaders. The Republicans' intraparty accommodations are frequently the product of negotiations between urban and rural legislative leaders within the Executive Appropriations Committee. It is no coincidence that, at the time of this writing, one of the Executive Appropriations Committee cochairs represents a rural legislative district, while the other represents an urban district.

## THE ROLE AND INFLUENCE OF THE LEGISLATIVE FISCAL ANALYST

The Office of the Legislative Fiscal Analyst plays an important role in the legislative phase of the budgetary process. The Legislative Fiscal Analyst assigns analysts to support each of the appropriations subcommittees. Using last year's appropriations as the base, analysts review agency requests, consider the governor's recommendations without including them in the documents the office produces, staff subcommittee hearings, and make budgetary recommendations to their assigned subcommittees.

Since senators and representatives in Utah are part-time legislators deliberating in a short legislative session, they appear to rely heavily on the fiscal analysts' counsel. Although legislative leaders have acquired reasonable legislative tenure and familiarity with budget issues, higher turnover among the rank and file accentuates their dependence on the expertise of fiscal analysts. It is not uncommon to find appropriations subcommittees making only marginal changes to their analysts' recommendations (although no empirical study of that relationship exists).

In addition to the considerable situational dependence of legislators on fiscal analysts, the influence of the Office has been heightened by the personal credibility attained by its director. Appointed the founding Legislative Fiscal Analyst in 1966, Leo Memmott served in that capacity until his retirement in 1998. The Office grew from three to fourteen analysts over those years. Memmott established the trust and confidence of legislative leaders, whose advice they sought in setting budgetary priorities and crafting compromises. He paved the way for the continued close involvement and influence of his successors.

## CONCLUSION

The debate over educational finance continues to take center stage in Utah state budgeting and enrollment projections provide no reason to expect that to change. In fact, demographers estimate that by 2011 elementary and secondary schools will have added over 100,000 students from their 2001 enrollment level, an increase of 22 percent. Compare that to a growth rate of 7 percent over the previous 10 years.[25] With nearly half of state spending already going to elementary and secondary education, the fiscal implications of such marked growth are evident. Public education can be expected to squeeze the rest of state spending and intensify its claim on tax revenues. As state spending on education rises, so will legislative calls for increased accountability of results, highlighting education's political profile even more.

In addition to education, Medicaid will likely exert increased pressure on state fiscal resources. Fueled by projected double-digit inflation in health care services and prescription drugs, and by expected increases in Utah's immigrant population, the governor and legislature could face difficult policy choices in the coming years, including reducing optional medical services for adults, lowering payments to service providers, or increasing co-payments borne by recipients. The legislature was forced to institute Medicaid cost controls in the 2002 and 2003 fiscal years as part of its effort to eliminate revenue shortfalls, though it restored some of the cuts in the approved FY 2004 budget.

Although it is true that significant improvement in the state's economy would help ease enrollment pressure on the program, Medicaid's share of state spending still rose between 1997 and 2000, years of strong economic growth.[26]

The future performance of the economy will provide an important context for the budgetary choices that governors and legislators will make in the coming years. Just as strong economic growth in the mid-2000s followed recession and slow economic recovery earlier in the decade, the historical lesson of the business cycle is that strong economic growth is not sustainable.

Politically, it appears likely that the Republicans will continue to enjoy strong majorities in both legislative chambers. It also looks as if legislative power will continue its rural to urban shift, producing a modest moderating influence politically. And with Utah's current Republican governor, John Hunstman, Jr., enjoying high approval ratings, it appears that Republicans will control both policymaking branches of government for the foreseeable future. A pressing question is whether legislative Republicans will view Governor Huntsman as they did Governor Leavitt before him, as being too politically moderate for their tastes. The politics of policymaking will continue to center within the Republican Party, not between Republicans and Democrats. Yet an even more interesting question is whether the change in gubernatorial leadership will itself make much of a difference in budgetary outcomes. At the heart of this query lies a central debate within the discipline of political science itself: whether economics or politics most influences policy choice. There can be no doubt that economic conditions constrain or enable fiscal choices. At the same time, political leadership influences how policymakers respond to those conditions and make discrete choices within them, as this chapter's discussion of the politics of revenue shortfall suggests.

## NOTES

1. Julie Cart, "Olympics Balancing Act for LDS," *Salt Lake Tribune* (January 17, 2002).

2. The LDS Church does operate religious institutes for high-school age church members, which are typically located a short walking distance from Utah's public high schools.

3. Articles X.

4. *State and Local Government in Utah*. Salt Lake City, UT: Utah Foundation, 1992, pp. 4–5.

5. Michael O. Leavitt, *FY 2004 Budget Recommendations*. Salt Lake City, UT: Office of Planning and Budget, 2003, p. 6.

6. *Utah at the Crossroads: Challenges for K-12 Education in the Coming Ten Years*. Research Report No. 653, Salt Lake City, UT: Utah Foundation, September 2002, p. 7.

7. *Public Education Data Book*. Salt Lake City, UT: Office of the Legislative Fiscal Analyst, 2002, p. 36.

8. *Utah at the Crossroads: Challenges for K-12 Education in the Coming Ten Years*, p. 4.

9. *Public Education Data Book*, pp. 16, 20.

10. *Utah at the Crossroads: Challenges for K-12 Education in the Coming Ten Years*, p. 11.

11. *Development Report Card for States*. Washington, DC: The Corporation for Enterprise Development, 2002, http://drc.cfed.org/grades/utah.html.

12. *1999 Economic Report to the Governor: Executive Summary*. Salt Lake City, UT: Utah Foundation, 1999, p. 4; *Utah at the Crossroads: Challenges for K-12 Education in the Coming Ten Years*, p. 1.

13. *The National Recession: Its Impacts on Utah and the Mountain West*. Research Report No. 656, Salt Lake City, UT: Utah Foundation, February 2003; Governor Michael O. Leavitt, *FY 2004 Budget Overview*. Salt Lake City, UT: Office of the Governor, December 16, 2002.

14. *Appropriations Report*, 2002–2003. Salt Lake City, UT: Office of the Legislative Fiscal Analyst, August 2002, pp. 13–14; *Appropriations Report*, 2003–2004, p. 13.

15. The legislature had previously set aside general fund revenues to finance a level of highway projects beyond what could be accomplished using segregated highway funds. This action transfers them back to the state's general fund, making them available to pay for a range of unfunded operating costs.

16. *Appropriations Report*, 2002–2003, p. 14.

17. *Appropriations Report*, 2003–2004, p. 14.

18. *Appropriations Summary: Fiscal Years 2003 & 2004*. Salt Lake City, UT: Office of the Legislative Fiscal Analyst, March 2003.

19. *2003 Legislative Highlights*. Salt Lake City, UT: Office of the Governor, March 5, 2003.

20. *Appropriations Summary: Fiscal Years 2003 & 2004*; *FY 2004 Budget Overview: Budget Recommendations FY 2004, Supplementals FY 2003*. Salt Lake City, UT: Office of the Governor, December 16, 2002.

21. Robert P. Huefner and Carl Mott, "Utah," in *Roundtable: State Budgeting in the 13 Western States*, Eds. Robert Huefner, F. Ted Hebert, and Carl Mott. Salt Lake City, UT: Center for Public Policy and Administration, December 1998, p. 146.

22. Doug Goodman, *Executive–Legislative Power Struggles over the Budgetary Process: Budgetary Orientations and Decision Making in Thirteen Western States*. Ph.D. Dissertation, University of Utah, August 2002, p. 94.

23. This is the title of the chapter on Utah budgeting that appeared in Edward J. Clynch and Tom Lauth's 1991 comparative study of state budgeting. See F. Ted Hebert, "Utah: Legislative Budgeting in an Executive Budget State," in *Governors, Legislatures, and Budgets*, Eds. Edward J. Clynch and Thomas P. Lauth. New York: Greenwood Press, 1991, pp. 103–114. The following discussion selectively draws from this earlier work.

24. *Utah Code Annotated* 63–38–2.

25. *Utah at the Crossroads: Challenges for K-12 Education in the Coming Ten Years*, pp. 13–14.

26. *Medicaid Spending: Controlling Costs*. Salt Lake City, UT: Office of Legislative Research and General Counsel, November 2002, p. 1.

# Conclusion—Budgeting in the States: Innovations and Implications

*Edward J. Clynch, Thomas P. Lauth, and Barbara A. Patrick*

Over the last 25 years states experienced many political, demographic, and economic changes. Florida, Georgia, and Mississippi elected their first Republican Governors since Reconstruction. Elected officials in Kentucky were ridiculed for the "Boptrot" corruption scandal. Members of the South Carolina State Legislature made national headlines for overriding 105 of the governor's 106 vetoes. Virginia made major budgetary changes as a result of the reduction of the state's dreaded car tax. Wisconsin gained attention when voters passed the "Vanna White" amendment to the state constitution. California, Florida, and Nevada saw drastic population increases. An oil bust occurred in Texas in the 1980s; Utah won the bid for the 2002 Winter Olympics. And the State of New York suffered through the tragic events of September 11 that left imprints on the budgeting system of all fifty states.

These events were recorded in many places, but no document captures these changes better than the state budget. It highlights which state policies are the most important. In our examination of the budgeting institutions, processes, and practices of fifteen states we capture the uniqueness of each state's struggle between governors and legislators by exploring the institutional powers of each branch, by assessing the impact of court decisions on the division of institutional powers, by reviewing the role of political parties as a way for governors to gain or lose influence over budget outcomes, by analyzing the extent to which rational budget reforms alter the leverage of the executive and legislative branches, and by investigating the impact of citizens through voter initiatives. We also examine gubernatorial and legislative responses to own source revenue abundance and scarcity, and the use of federal dollars for state services.

## EXECUTIVE–LEGISLATIVE INSTITUTIONAL POWERS: THE STARTING POINT

State constitutions and statutes establish gubernatorial and legislative institutional powers. Some of the institutional tools that enhance the governor's power include executive control of the revenue estimating process, the legislature's use of the gubernatorial budget proposal as its working document, and a strong line item veto that provides leverage over the content of appropriation bills. Often, the threat of a veto forces the legislature to adopt executive policy preferences. State constitutions and statutes in California, Georgia, and New York give these tools to governors and make the chief executive a powerful player in the budgetary process. In other states such as Connecticut, Illinois, and Oregon governors maintain strong influence through their budget proposal and veto powers. Governors and legislatures share power more equally in Florida, Kentucky, Nevada, South Carolina, Virginia, and Wisconsin. Finally, Mississippi, Texas, and Utah delegate budgetary powers to the state legislature and leave the governor with few formal tools to influence the budget.

### Courts Arbitrate Division of Institutional Power

From time to time, governors and legislators have relied on the courts to settle disputes about the distribution of institutional power. In Wisconsin, former Governor Tommy Thompson's frequent use of the line item veto to change words and letters sparked a court challenge by legislators. The court ruled in favor of the governor, but the citizens and state legislature passed the "Vanna White" amendment to the Wisconsin state constitution, curbing the line item veto power of the governor. In South Carolina the state Supreme Court took the same position as its Wisconsin counterpart. Its ruling also limited the South Carolina governor's line item veto powers by restricting the altering of words, phases, clauses, or sentences. The Texas Supreme Court ruled that the state legislature could bundle dollars for various functions in order to weaken the governor's line item veto power. In Florida the courts also restricted the veto power by ruling that governors cannot strike qualifications and restrictions in appropriations bills without also cutting out the money. In contrast, Georgia governors regularly exercise narrative vetoes without cutting money. In Mississippi and Wisconsin the state courts ruled that revenue bills are not subject to line item vetoes.

Courts also deal with conflicts over other institutional powers. In Florida the court stopped governors from cutting budgets to cover revenue shortfalls, saying this power rests with the legislature. In New York the court upheld limits on legislative power. The legislature may reduce spending items in the governor's budget, but it cannot add items not in the governor's proposal. In Kentucky when the state legislature adjourned without passing the 2003–2004 budget because of conflict between the governor and state legislature, the governor took charge and instructed the state to continue with business as usual without a legislative passed budget. Several members of the state legislature legally challenged the governor's authority to expend state funds without legislative approval. The lawsuit became moot when the 2003–2004 budget was passed later by the legislature.

## BUDGET REFORMS: POTENTIAL SHAPERS OF INSTITUTIONAL POWER

For over a century advocates of budget reform have proposed changes in budget processes as a way to give executives the tools needed to shape budget outcomes. Some budget reforms are more symbolic than meaningful, but successful budget transformations could increase governor and legislator leverage over budget decisions. Several states have altered budget processes to increase agency accountability to governors and legislators by linking spending with programs and priorities and by expanding staff capabilities. Nevertheless, evidence is sketchy about whether or how these rationalizing reforms penetrated budget processes and changed budget outcomes. One state noted for its budget reforms is Georgia. Over the last 30 years it has adopted zero-based budgeting, redirection, results-based budgeting, and prioritized budgeting. Redirection increased gubernatorial influence for a few years with the governor shifting money to education and redirecting other agency funds to higher priority agency programs. Results-based budgeting experienced limited success because the governor failed to support it, and prioritized budgeting remains in its early stages of development. It is too soon tell whether or not it will be successful.

In 1991 the Texas legislature introduced an elaborate planning and benchmark system intended to highlight budget output and outcome successes. It later added performance measures to its budgeting process and currently allows agencies to submit their performance measures electronically. The state also rewards agencies that have performed well by listing them among the five "good agencies" on the states "The good, the bad, and the ugly list." Agencies listed among the bad and the ugly are quizzed during budget hearings and publicly humiliated.

Florida implemented performance-based budgeting in 1994 in an effort to make agencies more accountable to governors and legislators. In 2001 the state moved to enhance accountability by implementing activity-based planning and budgeting that linked cost with performance. All funds were appropriated as specific activity rather than object classifications such as personnel or equipment. In 1995 South Carolina's governor reformed budgeting practices by prioritizing and ranking programs for agencies and requiring agencies to fully disclose program and cost. In 1999 Wisconsin established performance measurement budgeting with the goal of improving agency performance. The change sought to improve performance by not guaranteeing agencies the same funds that they received in the previous years.

Other states have made less sweeping reforms that also could enhance the decision-making capabilities of elected officials. California recently adopted an automated budgeting system that allows departments and agencies to view a current services budget base that builds in cost increases for additional required ongoing activities and adds money needed to cover program changes mandated by legislative action. Nevada installed a new computerized budgeting system that reduces manual input of figures by budget analysts, cuts down on errors, and allows agency and legislative staff to view the budget electronically. New York has implemented automated budgeting along with multiyear planning and consensus forecasting. Kentucky and other states briefly implemented tax amnesty programs to allow delinquent taxpayers to voluntarily pay taxes without penalty as a means of increasing revenue during times of fiscal stress.

## Political Parties: An Informal Source of Leverage over Budget Outcomes

Political parties both reduce and enhance gubernatorial influence over budget outcomes. Generally when the governor's party controls both chambers of the legislature, his or her policy preferences are successfully implemented. Governor Jeb Bush in Florida opened lines of communication with the Republican controlled state legislature and achieved results. Statutes passed that granted the governor a more active role in budget preparation and execution, including the elimination of the requirement that agencies submit preliminary budget requests to legislators for comment before making a formal submission to the governor. In Mississippi a Republican dominated state senate helped Republican Governor Haley Barbour gain leverage over tax policy and spending for education and Medicaid.

When the party opposing the governor controls one or both legislative chambers conflict, negotiation, and compromise result. Prior to Bush's election, Florida's budgetary decisions were plagued with conflicts and battles between the Republican legislature and Democratic governors. In Kentucky, Democratic Governor Patton's budget proposals were passed by the state legislature until the Republicans gained control of the senate in 2000. The Republican controlled senate rejected his plan to increase taxes to raise money for education and fought with him over funding for gubernatorial elections. Battles between the executive and legislature resulted in the legislature adjourning without passing a budget for the FY 2003–2004, leaving state agencies in limbo. Illinois and New York experienced several budget cycles with the opposing party controlling one chamber. As a result, a pattern of party negotiation and compromise became the operational norm.

Party unity between the governor and members of the state legislature does not always lead to policy victory for the governor. State government in Utah is dominated by the Republican Party, with Republicans holding a veto proof majority in both chambers of the state legislature. However, conflict between the rural and urban Republicans ensued when rural House Speaker Mel Brown instructed the Legislative Fiscal Analyst Office to break from tradition and not accept the governor's budget recommendations. Although Republicans controlled both chambers of the Virginia legislature in 2001, conflict between the governor and the legislature led to the legislature adjourning without passing a budgeting for the next fiscal year. The Republican Chairperson of the Finance Committee also enlisted and gained the support of Democrats and Republicans in an effort to hinder the governor's car tax repeal. Democrats controlled both chambers of the Georgia General Assembly and the office of the governor from the end of Reconstruction until 2002. Republicans now control both chambers and the governor's office. Budget battles in Georgia historically were interbranch rather than interparty; now they are mostly interbranch but with a partisan flavor reflecting the presence of a significant Democratic minority in the legislature.

While party unity limited institutional conflict in several states, other entities experienced open warfare between the governor and legislature. In Mississippi, prior to Governor Barbour's term Democratic Governor Musgrove vetoed most appropriation bills and the Democratic legislature promptly overrode his actions. Governor Sanford of South Carolina received similar treatment. The state legislature, dominated by members of his Republican party, overrode all but one of his 106 appropriation vetoes. In Wisconsin, Republicans in the state legislature joined Democrats in a bipartisan effort to limit the line item veto power of Republican Governor Tommy Thompson. In New York the Republican controlled Senate teamed up with the Democratic controlled Assembly and gave New York Governor Pataki a major defeat by overriding all of his appropriation vetoes.

### Voter Initiatives: Citizens Shape the Budget Process and Budget Outcomes

Voters in California, Florida, and Oregon affect budget processes and outcomes through initiatives. Many residents of these states believe that the initiative process is a better policymaking tool than relying on their governor and state legislature. All three states have increased the governor's leverage over budget outcomes by creating legislative term limits that lead to constant turnover in leadership and limits institutional memory. In addition, voters have bypassed the budget process and used initiatives to limit taxes and to mandate spending for education and other programs. Elected officials find budget and taxing decisions constrained by these voter mandates.

### Revenues: Division among Budget Outcomes Creates Conflict

Large revenue increases often bury spending conflicts. At the same time, declining revenues often lead to conflict. The way governors and legislators distribute budget outcomes depends on their policy differences and the array of formal and informal power available to both sides.

Since 1990, state revenues experienced a decade of substantial growth followed by a period of stagnant and declining revenues. During this time several states increased revenue by turning to lotteries and gaming. Others have relied on the use of rainy day funds to offset declines in revenue experienced as a result of the economic downturn of 2000. After the deep recession in the early 1980s, states saved for a rainy day by setting aside a small percentage of the general funds, usually 3 to 5 percent, for use during economic downturn. Mississippi, Nevada, Kentucky, Georgia, South Carolina, Utah, Virginia, and other states all used rainy day funds to help address budgetary shortfalls during economic recessions. Given slow growth in state revenues since the recession, many states did not and have not deposited monies into the accounts for future emergencies. Other states, such as Wisconsin, have also established rainy day funds but never deposited monies into the accounts. In addition, several states tapped tobacco settlement money to cover shortfalls. With the antitax temper of the times, states did not raise taxes as several had during the recession in the early 1980s.

Federal money gives states the opportunity to offer more services to citizens. Federal money supports health, social programs, education, and capital grants for infrastructure and highways. Several states improved the quality of health of thousands of children with the help of federal funds for the Children's Health Insurance Program. Federal Medicaid money led many states to expand health services to the poor in the 1990s only to face problems paying the state match after revenues declined at a time when health costs soared. As a result several states reduced or eliminated optional benefits.

### Governors, Legislatures, and Budgets: Concluding Thoughts

Gubernatorial and legislative impact on budget outcomes stems from an array of factors, and influence of each branch evolves over time. Power over revenue and spending decisions starts with institutional powers resting in each unit. Courts often arbitrate heated disputes about institutional rules because both realize that the formal rules of the game affect budget outcomes. Often executives push the envelope to expand their line item veto power because an enhanced veto expands gubernatorial institutional leverage over budget outcomes, and legislators fight back in court. Often, legislators of both political parties work in tandem when legislative institutional prerogatives are at stake.

Political parties serve as a way for weak governors to gain strength and for strong governors to find themselves forced to compromise with the opposition party. Legislative institutional powers melt away if a majority of the governor's party controls one or both chambers, and if this majority is willing to follow the governor's policy lead. At the same time, an institutionally weak but resistant legislature dominated by the other party can delay action and force even strong governors to negotiate and work out deals before budgets can pass.

Budget reform advocates view most suggested changes as ways of enhancing gubernatorial authority. Unfortunately, most reforms fail to penetrate budget processes permanently and potential fades away. Voter anger leads to initiatives to curb institutional power, to mandate tax cuts, and to require spending for particular programs. Both institutions lose, but legislators lose more because term-limited governors are now joined by term-limited legislators.

Budget decisions are major policy decisions. Revenue shortfalls heighten gubernatorial legislative conflicts over budget outcomes. In the fish bowl of state government both governors and legislators utilize formal and informal powers to carry the day. As long as our political system maintains independent branches subject to short-term political influences, budget outcomes in the American states will remain a point of contention settled by persons who disagree on the best course of action.

# Index

# About the Contributors

**Robert L. (Bob) Bland** is Professor and Chair of the Department of Public Administration at the University of North Texas where he teaches graduate courses in public finance, governmental accounting, and budgeting. He has been on the faculty at UNT since 1982. He is the author of *A Revenue Guide for Local Government* (2nd ed., 2005) and coauthor with Irene Rubin of *Budgeting: A Guide for Local Governments* (1997) both published by the International City/County Management Association, and of several articles on the municipal bond market, property taxation, and municipal budgeting.

**Donald J. Boyd** is Director of the Fiscal Studies Program at the Rockefeller Institute of Government, the public policy research arm of the State University of New York. He has more than 20 years of experience analyzing state and local government fiscal issues in academia, private consulting, as well as the executive and legislative branches of state government. He holds a Ph.D. in Managerial Economics from Rensselaer Polytechnic Institute.

**Robert B. Bradley** is Professor and Associate Vice President for Academic Affairs at Florida State University. He has served as Director of the Florida Office of Planning and Budgeting and Director of the Florida Advisory Committee on Intergovernmental Relations. His research interests include state budgeting, intergovernmental relations, and public policy. In addition to other duties, he currently serves as Director of the Institute of Science and Public Affairs at Florida State University.

**Wes Clarke** is Associate Director of the Carl Vinson Institute of Government at the University of Georgia where he directs the Research and Policy Analysis

Division. His research interests include state and local budget processes, revenue policy, and debt management practices. He is developing a new research area concerning financial management in county government. Dr. Clarke's research has appeared in a variety of public administration and public finance journals.

**Edward J. Clynch** is Professor and Graduate Coordinator for the Department of Political Science and Public Administration at Mississippi State University. His research interests include public administration, education, and state budgeting. He has published numerous articles on these topics in professional journals. He is the coeditor of *Governors, Legislatures, and Budgets: Diversity Across the American States*.

**James K. Conant** is Professor of Government and Politics at George Mason University in Fairfax, VA. His research on budgeting and financial management, executive branch organization and management, and management education and training has been published in numerous books and journals. He is a coeditor of *Dollars and Sense: Policy Choices and the Wisconsin Budget*, Vol. II, and he is the author of *Wisconsin Politics and Government: America's Laboratory of Democracy*.

**Dall W. Forsythe** is a distinguished lecturer in the School of Public Affairs at Baruch College, City University of New York. Dr. Forsythe is the author of *Memos to the Governor: An Introduction to State Budgeting*, as well as a number of articles on state and local financial management. He also served as budget director for the State of New York under Governor Mario M. Cuomo.

**James J. Gosling** is Professor of Political Science at the University of Utah. His recent books include *Budgetary Politics in American Governments*, 4th ed., (Routledge, 2006); *Politics and Policy in American States and Communities* (with Dennis L. Dresang), 5th ed., (Pearson Longman, 2006); and *Explaining, Informing, and Appraising Public Policy* (Pearson Longman, 2004).

**Cole Blease Graham, Jr.,** is a professor in the Department of Political Science at the University of South Carolina. His research interests include administrative law, public management, and state constitutions. He has coauthored books on public organization management as well as South Carolina government and politics, and coedited a book on court management. His forthcoming book considers the development and features of the current South Carolina constitution.

**Merl M. Hackbart** is Professor of Finance and Public Administration at the University of Kentucky. He also serves as Associate Dean of the Gatton College of Business and Economics. He has served as State Budget Director for the state of Kentucky and serves on Kentucky's Consensus Revenue Forecasting Group. His research and publications have focused on state budgeting, debt management, and transportation finance issues.

**Thomas P. Lauth** is Dean of the School of Public and International Affairs at The University of Georgia. His articles on state budgeting have appeared in several academic journals. He is the coauthor of *Compromised Compliance: Implementation of the 1965 Voting Rights Act*, coauthor of *The Politics of State and City Administration*, and coeditor of *Governors, Legislatures, and Budgets: Diversity Across the American States*.

**Carol W. Lewis** is a professor of political science at the University of Connecticut. She is author of numerous journal articles and book chapters on her research interests in public budgeting and public sector ethics. She is coauthor of *The Ethics Challenge in Public Service: A Problem-Solving Guide*.

**Jerry L. McCaffrey** is Professor of Public Budgeting in the Graduate School of Business and Public Policy at the Naval Postgraduate School in Monterey California. His research interests include the defense policy-making and budget processes, defense financial management, and state and local budgeting. With Professor L. R. Jones, he is co-author of Budgeting and Financial Management for National Defense (2004).

**Barbara A. Patrick** is a Ph.D. student in the public policy and administration program in the Department of Political Science and Public Administration at Mississippi State University. She holds a doctoral fellowship awarded by the Southern Regional Education Board. She has coauthored a book chapter in *Politics in the New South: Representation of African Americans in Southern State Legislatures*. She received her MPPA from Mississippi State and B.A. in political science from Rust College in Holly Springs, MS.

**James R. Ramsey** is President and Professor of Economics and Public Policy at the University of Louisville. His research interests have included investment and cash management, debt management, state budgeting, and tax policies. He has published numerous articles on these topics in professional journals.

**Irene S. Rubin** is Professor Emerita from the Public Administration Division at Northern Illinois University. She is the former editor of *Public Budgeting and Finance and Public Administration Review* and the author of *The Politics of Public Budgeting; Balancing the Federal Budget: Trimming the Herds or Eating the Seed Corn; Class Tax and Power: Municipal Budgeting in the United States*; and many journal articles and chapters on budgeting at all levels of government in the United States. Her particular interests include causes and consequences of fiscal stress, contracting out and budgeting, and the relationship between budget processes and outcomes.

**Bill Simonsen** is a professor in the Department of Public Policy at the University of Connecticut and Director of its Master of Public Administration (MPA) program. His research and writing focuses on public sector financial management and policy.

**Douglas R. Snow** is Associate Professor and Chairperson of the Public Management Department at Suffolk University, Boston, MA. His primary research interest is budgeting and financial management in state and local governments. He has also published on the subject of on microfinance as an economic development tool.

**Paula D. Yeary** is a public service assistant for the Carl Vinson Institute of Government at the University of Georgia. Her research interests include public budgeting and taxation issues as well as annexation and form of government at the local level. In addition to her academic experience, Paula served the State of Nevada as a senior budget analyst and as an aide to Governor Bob Miller.